For Finn, Dan and Tiggy

FOREWORD

It is a curious feature of the development of modern Irish law that, for many years, constitutional law and company law were relatively close neighbours who barely spoke. Most early constitutional litigation was cast in the form of claims for declarations and was, thereby, automatically consigned to the chancery list, a long-time occupant of which was matters relating to companies, often, unhappily, of the liquidation variety. During all that time, as Ailbhe O'Neill demonstrates, there was little, if any, consideration addressed to the intersection between the subjects, or to the possibility that one might usefully illuminate the other. When the subject was addressed, the analysis was perfunctory.

That this should be so is attributable, I think, to the hidebound view that problems come already labelled like an undergraduate examination, as company law, or tort, or contract issues, and just as, if not more, importantly, to an absence of scholarly inquiry, which might alert the practitioner to the possibility of a useful line of argument. The development of the law in a common law system undoubtedly requires the unique propulsion that the urgent demands of the facts of an individual case can provide, and the acute insights that the partisanship of advocacy can bring, sometimes late at night, as deadlines approach. However, the law can also benefit from a more detached and measured examination of topics that cannot be addressed satisfactorily within the time-scale of a piece of litigation. As Ailbhe O'Neill shows in this book, it is important and fruitful to address the more abstract jurisprudential questions, such as "What is a company?" and "What does it mean to be the holder of a constitutional right, privilege or duty?"

If there was such a lacuna in Irish legal scholarship, it is comprehensively addressed in this book. It is an admirable and scholarly piece of work. Ailbhe O'Neill has, remarkably, turned to advantage the dearth of discussion in case law and text books by carrying out a meticulous comparative analysis and then applying the insights gained to the Irish constitutional context. She argues for a more sophisticated and nuanced response to the question of whether a company is entitled to benefit from a particular constitutional right. The conclusions she draws are, however, never forced upon the reader. Accordingly, even those who may differ on either the general proposition, or any particular conclusion, will find the text an invaluable source of ammunition for debate. The footnotes are themselves a storehouse of useful references. The book will be useful to the constitutional lawyer in casting new and fresh light upon constitutional topics; it may prompt the company lawyer to consider novel claims; and it may suggest to both that, in an increasingly specialised world, there is value to be gained from lateral thinking and from communication between office, court, and lecture theatre. It is a book which deserves, in the well-worn phrase, to be on every lawyer's bookshelf, but not to remain there. Instead, it will be taken down in puzzlement (and, sometimes, even desperation), consulted in admiration, and replaced with gratitude for the author's industry and application.

Donal O'Donnell S.C.
April 16, 2007

PREFACE

This book started life as a doctoral thesis researched at Trinity College Dublin under the supervision of Professor Gerry Whyte, for whose assistance I am most grateful. The idea for the project emerged in the course of the Company Law lectures given by Brian Murray S.C. at Trinity in 1999–2000 and the initial thesis proposal was developed following some helpful comments from Robert Heron of Matheson Ormsby Prentice Solicitors in August 2000.

For the most part, the research was completed using the facilities of the Trinity library and thanks are due to all of the staff there for their help over the years. Much of the research in Chapter One was completed in the Squire Library at the Faculty of Law in Cambridge and thanks are due to Dr Pippa Rogerson of Gonville and Cauis College for facilitating that arrangement in the summer of 2002.

I am indebted to Susan Rossney and Frieda Donohue of Thomson Round Hall for their patience and support over the last year. Thanks are also due to my family (who bore the burden of living with me and this project for what must have seemed like a very long year) as well as the various individuals who helped in a number of ways in the preparation of this book: Eoin Carolan, Anne O'Donovan. Paris O'Donnell, Robert Delany and Roderick Maguire B.L.

The law is as stated at the end of October 2006. Unless otherwise indicated the opinions expressed and any errors or omissions are the author's.

The preliminary work on this project was funded by a Government of Ireland Scholarship.

Ailbhe O'Neill,
Trinity College Dublin,
April 2007

THE CONSTITUTIONAL RIGHTS OF COMPANIES

AUSTRALIA
Law Book Co.
Sydney

CANADA and USA
Carswell
Toronto

HONG KONG
Sweet & Maxwell Asia

NEW ZEALAND
Brookers
Wellington

SINGAPORE and MALAYSIA
Sweet & Maxwell Asia
Singapore and Kuala Lumpur

THE CONSTITUTIONAL RIGHTS
OF COMPANIES

Ailbhe O'Neill

LL.B. (Dublin), LL.M. (Cantab.), Ph.D. (Dublin),
Lecturer, Faculty of Law, Trinity College, Dublin,
Barrister-at-Law

THOMSON ROUND HALL
2007

Published in 2007 by
Thomson Round Hall
43 Fitzwilliam Place
Dublin 2
Ireland

Typeset by
Gough Typesetting Services
Dublin

Printed by
MPG Books, Cornwall

ISBN 978-1-85800-459-4

A catalogue record for this book
is available from the British Library

TABLE OF CONTENTS

PART IV: GUARANTEES NOT APPLICABLE TO THE COMPANY UNDER BUNREACHT NA HÉIREANN

TABLE OF CASES

IRELAND

NORTHERN IRELAND

EUROPEAN COURT OF HUMAN RIGHTS

EUROPEAN COURT OF JUSTICE

ENGLAND AND WALES

AUSTRALIA

CANADA

TABLE OF LEGISLATION

CONSTITUTIONAL PROVISIONS

TABLE OF STATUTES

IRELAND

STATUTORY INSTRUMENTS

EUROPEAN UNION

EUROPEAN CONVENTIONS AND DECLARATIONS

INTERNATIONAL CONVENTIONS AND DECLARATIONS

UNITED KINGDOM

CANADA

NEW ZEALAND

UNITED STATES

INTRODUCTION

Since its promulgation in 1937, the Irish Constitution has generated a rich and varied jurisprudence and has been the subject of a number of studies, both thematic and systematic. One aspect of Irish constitutional law that has not been systematically explored, however, is the extent to which companies are within the scope of constitutional protection. The question is of more than mere academic interest. The extent to which corporate as well as individual rights and freedoms are protected is a matter of enormous practical significance and is becoming increasingly topical in the wake of the incorporation of the European Convention on Human Rights into Irish law.

The question of corporate constitutional protection has arisen in a number of Irish cases but the courts have generally failed to develop any consistent method of determining the application of constitutional guarantees to the company. The decisions vary from bare refusals[1] of protection to implicit acceptance[2] that the company is within the scope of the relevant constitutional provision. Up until relatively recently, however, no detailed analysis of the propriety of extending constitutional guarantees to the company appears in the Irish case law.

In 1995, the High Court decision of Keane J. in *Iarnród Éireann v Ireland*[3] disrupted this pattern and made some attempt to engage with the issue of corporate constitutional protection, relying on a number of interpretive methods to reach the conclusion that the corporate plaintiff in the case was entitled to rely on the right to private property. This judgment, which stands alone in its attempt to grapple with the issue of corporate constitutional protection, is explored in considerable detail in Chapter 8.

Apart from providing a description of the current status of companies under the Irish Constitution, this book also attempts to provide some principled basis upon which to assess corporate claims to constitutional protection. The existing

---

[1] *Private Motorists Protection Society v Att.-Gen. ("PMPS")* [1983] I.R. 339; *Chestvale Properties Ltd v Glackin* [1992] I.L.R.M. 221; *Abbey Films Ltd v Att.-Gen.* [1981] I.R. 158.

[2] *Pigs Marketing Board v Donnelly (Dublin) Ltd* [1939] I.R. 413; *Att.-Gen. v Southern Industrial Trust Ltd* (1957) 94 I.L.T.R. 161; *Pine Valley Developments Ltd v Minister for the Environment* [1987] I.R. 23, [1987] I.L.R.M. 747; *Educational Company of Ireland Ltd v Fitzpatrick* [1961] I.R. 345; *National Irish Bank Ltd, Re* [1999] 3 I.R. 145, [1999] 1 I.L.R.M. 312; *Dunnes Stores Ireland Co v Ryan* [2002] 2 I.R. 60; *Environmental Protection Agency v Swacliffe Ltd trading as Dublin Waste, Louis Moriarty and Eileen Moriarty*, unreported, High Court, Kearns J., May 21, 2004; *Att.-Gen. for England and Wales v Brandon Books Ltd* [1986] I.R. 597; *Ryanair v Labour Court* [2005] I.E.H.C. 330.

case law is criticised, not so much for protecting or refusing to protect companies, but rather for failing to provide any sound, consistent basis upon which to make such decisions.

The total exclusion of companies from constitutional protection, while possibly presenting some philosophical attractions, is contrary to the trend in the more recent case law and to developments elsewhere. What this book seeks to do is to place the existing legal position—which appears to be that companies are prima facie entitled to at least some constitutional protection—and place it on a sound theoretical basis. In particular, it is argued that it is possible and perhaps even desirable to find a space for corporate protection within the Constitution as long as the distinct basis for corporate, as opposed to individual, protection is understood.

The book is divided into four parts. Part I provides a theoretical framework for the discussion of the case law in the remainder of the book. Before exploring the extent to which companies can lay claim to the rights and protections guaranteed under Bunreacht na hÉireann, some analysis of the company as a legal subject is undertaken in this Part. The chapters in this Part are intended to provide some background for the remainder of the book as well as flagging some of the theoretical difficulties with accommodating the company within the Constitution. It is also in this Part that the methodology applied in the remainder of this book is set out.

Chapter 1 considers the historical development of the concept of legal personality and explains the theories of the corporation which will be referred to throughout this book and which have had a significant impact in the development of corporate constitutional rights under the United States Constitution. One of the central arguments of this book is that these theories are an inadequate basis upon which to determine the availability of constitutional protection to the company under the Irish Constitution.

Chapter 2 considers the description of the constitutional subject in the text of the Irish Constitution. The United States Constitution is also examined for comparative purposes. It uses similar languauge to the Irish Constitution and, like the Irish Constitution, it does not explicitly protect companies. The United States Supreme Court has, however, interpreted many of its provisions so as to include companies. The chapter goes on to consider a number of the methods of interpretation that have been applied to the Irish Constitution and assesses their possible impact on the question of corporate constitutional protection.

Chapter 3 turns to the question of the philosophical underpinnings of the Irish Constitution and the identification of the constitutional subject. It focuses in particular on the natural law influences on the Constitution and whether these influences might mean that the company is necessarily excluded from constitutional protection. The chapter concludes that they do not—in so doing it highlights the necessity of constructing the constitutional subject which, it is argued, is an inherently positivist project.

Parts II, III and IV comprise the main body of the work and these take an article by article approach to the position of companies under the Irish Constitution.

Part II examines the position of the company under Art.38. This Part concerns the extent to which the company may rely on Art.38 of the Irish

Constitution. The relevant parts[4] of that provision are arts 38.1 which guarantees a trial in due course of law and 38.5 which guarantees a trial by jury in relation to non-minor offences.[5] Article 38.1 has been held to include a number of specific guarantees and two of these—the right to silence and the rule against double jeopardy—receive detailed attention in separate chapters.

Chapter 4 introduces the concept of a trial in due course of law under Art.38.1 and explores the way in which the Irish courts have developed the content of that provision. It examines the extent to which the various protections identified under Art.38.1 ought to apply to the corporate criminal defendant.

Chapter 5 focuses on the right to silence. Examining the position of the company in relation to the right to silence in a number of jurisdictions, it explores two alternative ways of approaching the question of corporate constitutional protection. The first uses theories of the company to determine issues of corporate constitutional protection. The second focuses on the rationale for this due process protection. It is argued that the latter teleological approach is preferable.

Chapter 6 focuses on the rule against double jeopardy. Identifying both autonomy and utility values within this rule, it considers the possibility of applying a different version of the rule to the corporate defendant than that applying to the individual.

The application of Art.38.5 to the company is explored in Chapter 7.

Part III deals with a number of fundamental rights under Arts 40.3 and 40.6.

This Part considers the extent to which companies may claim protection under Arts 40.3[6] and 40.6[7] of the Constitution. Unlike Art.38.1, Art.40.3 refers

---

[3] [1996] 3 I.R. 321; [1995] 2 I.L.R.M. 161.

[4] Arts 38.3–4 and 38.6 concern special courts and military courts.

[5] Art.38.2, which provides for the summary trial of minor offences is also of relevance. See discussion below at paras 7–03 to 7–07.

[6] Chap. 13 explores those constitutional guarantees in Art.40 which are of no relevance to the company. A number of these guarantees also fall under Art.40.3.

[7] The full text of Art.40.6 is as follows:

"1   The State guarantees liberty for the exercise of the following rights, subject to public order and morality:

i.   The right of the citizens to express freely their convictions and opinions. The education of public opinion being, however, a matter of such grave import to the common good, the State shall endeavour to ensure that organs of public opinion, such as the radio, the press, the cinema, while preserving their rightful liberty of expression, including criticism of Government policy, shall not be used to undermine public order or morality or the authority of the State. The publication or utterance of blasphemous, seditious, or indecent matter is an offence which shall be punishable in accordance with law.

ii.   The right of the citizens to assemble peaceably and without arms. Provision may be made by law to prevent or control meetings which are determined in accordance with law to be calculated to cause a breach of the peace or to be a danger or nuisance to the general public and to prevent or control meetings in the vicinity of either House of the Oireachtas.

iii.   The right of the citizens to form associations and unions. Laws, however, may be enacted for the regulation and control in the public interest of the

to the "citizen" rather than the "person".[8] As is pointed out in Chapter 2, similar variations in terminology have not affected the availability of constitutional protection to the company under the United States Constitution and textual limitations have been disregarded in this jurisdiction also. It has been said of the Irish Constitution that:

> "It may be almost heretical to say so, but the experience of sixty years of constitutional jurisprudence suggests that in the case of what one may term the 'open-textured' provisions of Articles 40-44 of the Constitution, there is a sense in which the actual text and provenance of this text does not particularly matter. Instead, the accumulated sense of legal tradition and case-law, together with legal methodology and reasoning, make up a sort of *acquis constitutionnel* and it is this which really counts."[9]

Part III utilises the dichotomised analysis set out in Chapter 3 to assess the propriety of extending constitutional protection to the company under Art.40.3. arts 40.1 and 40.5[10] contain *additional* restrictive wording that may operate to limit the class of beneficiaries that may rely on them. These provisions are treated separately in Pt IV.

One of the most striking features of this aspect of constitutional rights jurisprudence is the lack of judicial attention it has received. There are a number of cases in which constitutional protection has been extended to the company *sub silentio*.[11] It has been pointed out that:

> "an obvious stratagem for avoiding any difficulties in this regard…is to

---

              exercise of the foregoing right.

    2   Laws regulating the manner in which the right of forming associations and unions and the right of free assembly may be exercised shall contain no political, religious or class discrimination."

[8] The full text of Art.40.3 is as follows:

    "1   The State guarantees in its laws to respect, and, as far as practicable, by its laws to defend and vindicate the personal rights of the citizen.

    2   The State shall, in particular, by its laws protect as best it may from unjust attack and, in the case of injustice done, vindicate the life, person, good name, and property rights of every citizen.

    3   The State acknowledges the right to life of the unborn and, with due regard to the equal right to life of the mother, guarantees in its laws to respect, and, as far as practicable, by its laws to defend and vindicate that right.

This subsection shall not limit freedom to travel between the State and another state.

This subsection shall not limit freedom to obtain or make available, in the State, subject to such conditions as may be laid down by law, information relating to services lawfully available in another state.

[9] Hogan, "The Constitution, Property Rights and Proportionality" (1997) 32 Irish Jurist 373 at 373–374.

[10] Art.40.1 guarantees equality and Art.40.5 guarantees inviolability of the dwelling. See Chaps 14 and 15 respectively.

[11] *Att.-Gen. for England and Wales v Brandon Book Publishers Ltd* [1961] I.R. 345; *Att.-Gen. v Hamilton (No.1)* [1992] 2 I.R. 542, [1992] I.L.R.M. 145; *Att.-Gen. v Hamilton (No.2)* [1993] I.L.R.M. 821; *Kerry Co-Operative Creameries Ltd v An Bord Bainne*

join an individual shareholder as a co-plaintiff for the purpose of invoking the fundamental rights provisions."[12]

Such an approach assumes that there is an identifiable individual whose interests coincide with those of the company. In *Iarnród Éireann v Ireland*,[13] for example, this was not a possibility and the company had to rely on the constitutional guarantee of property rights on its own behalf. The response in that case, which is considered in detail in Chapter 8, was to extend constitutional protection to the company on the basis of the interests of the shareholders.[14] The problems with this aggregate theory approach to corporate claims to constitutional protection are discussed in Chapter 8.

Chapter 8 examines the protection of corporate property under Arts 43 and 40.3 of the Constitution. Chapter 9 considers corporate freedom of expression under Art.40.6.1°(i). Chapter 10 considers whether companies are entitled to the right to a good name under Art.40.3. Chapter 11 focuses on the unenumerated right of access to the courts and Chapter 12 on the unenumerated right to justice and fair procedures.

Part IV covers those constitutional rights which appear to be unavailable to the company, with a particular focus on Arts 40.1 and 40.5 of the Constitution. This Part explores those constitutional guarantees that are unavailable to the company under Bunreacht na hÉireann. These can be divided into two broad categories. The first are those guarantees which, because of their very nature, are simply irrelevant to the company. These guarantees, which are dealt with briefly in Chapter 13, are inapplicable to the company because the company is not capable of enjoying them.

The second category is comprised of those guarantees which appear to be inapplicable to the company by virtue of the textual limitations of the Constitution but which could theoretically be applied to a company and have been so applied in other jurisdictions. These are dealt with in Chapters 14 and 15. Chapter 14 considers the extent to which the guarantee of equality before the law guaranteed by Art.40.1 could usefully be applied to a company. Chapter 15 considers the inviolability of the dwelling under Art.40.5 as well as considering whether there might be a corporate right to privacy.

As with Pt III, Pt IV focuses on the nature of the guarantees considered and whether they have a utilitarian function that would justify allowing the company to rely on them. It ultimately finds that neither Art.40.5 nor 40.1 have such a function. As with previous chapters, Chapters 14 and 15 highlight the way in which the utility/autonomy analysis sheds light on the philosophical inspiration underlying constitutional guarantees as a whole. This approach is contrasted in Chapter 14 with that taken by the United States Supreme Court in the context of the equal protection clause of the Fourteenth Amendment. It

---

[1990] I.L.R.M. 664.

[12] Hogan and Whyte, *Kelly: The Irish Constitution* (4th edn, Lexis-Nexis Butterworths, 2003), at p.1318.

[13] [1996] 3 I.R. 321, [1995] 2 I.L.R.M. 161.

[14] See also *Pine Valley Developments Ltd v Minister for the Environment* [1987] I.R. 23, [1987] I.L.R.M. 747, discussed below at para.8–16.

is shown how the reliance by that court on corporate theory and a failure to engage with the purpose of the equality guarantee arguably led to its distortion. The advantage of the approach outlined in this book is that it requires judges to justify the extension of constitutional protection to the company by relying on the Constitution itself. It thus ensures that each guarantee contained in Bunreacht na hÉireann is interpreted in a manner which best reflects its underlying values.

Ireland is not the only jurisdiction to face—or avoid—the issue of corporate constitutional protection. Companies have sought to rely on constitutional rights in the United States with a large degree of success and experience from across the Atlantic is considered in some detail in the following chapters. Also of interest is the extent of corporate protection under the European Convention on Human Rights. The incorporation of the Convention into Irish law means that this body of case law has acquired a more immediate significance and it is also referred to throughout this book.

PART I

THE COMPANY AND THE CONSTITUTIONAL SUBJECT

CHAPTER 1

THE DEVELOPMENT OF LEGAL PERSONALITY AND THEORIES OF THE CORPORATION

INTRODUCTION

1–01   This book is concerned with the extent to which companies have rights[1] under the Irish Constitution. Prior to examining the various constitutional provisions and their applicability to the company, some understanding of the concept of legal personality is necessary. This is because the recognition of a party as a "person" in law is an event which determines the extent to which that party is a "right and duty bearing unit".[2] As Colson has explained:

> "Person and personality are derived from the Latin '*persona*', a mask worn by an actor. Hence, a person is one capable of taking an active part in a drama. Thus legal personality is the attribute of any unit capable of playing a part in the legal drama."[3]

1–02   Indeed, this aspect of legal methodology is fundamental to any theory of rights, as further inquiry into the nature of law and legal rights cannot be engaged upon until we have a subject to work with. It is often stated that the essential feature of a right is that it must be attached to an entity. The reverse may also be stated—it is only with respect to its rights that something can be said to be a legal entity.[4] To avoid circularity, law must fix on a basic unit—the legal person. As one writer has put it:

> "Just as the concept 'one' in arithmetic is essential to the logical system developed and is yet not one something (*e.g.* apple or orange, etc.), so a

---

[1]   Throughout this book, the words "guarantee", "protection" and "right" are used to refer to the various claims a company might make under the Constitution. Whether what is at issue constitutes a privilege/liberty, a power, an immunity or a claim-right in Hohfeldian terms should be clear from the context.

[2]   *The Collected Papers of Frederic William Maitland* (Cambridge University Press, 1911), Vol.3, p.307.

[3]   Colson, "Corporate Personality" (1935) 24 Geo.L.J. 638 at 641–642.

[4]   Nekam, *Personality Conception of the Legal Entity: Harvard Studies in the Conflict of Laws, Volume III* (Harvard University Press, 1938).

legal system (or any system perhaps) must be provided with a basic unit before legal relationships can be devised ... The legal person is the unit or entity adopted. For the logic of the system it is just as much a pure 'concept' as 'one' in arithmetic. It is just as independent from a human being as one is from an 'apple'."[5]

1–03   Whether or not this positivist approach to legal rights can be usefully applied to *constitutional* rights will be considered in Chapter 3.[6] The function of this chapter is to explore the various conceptions of legal personality that have existed in law from Roman times—paras 1–05 to 1–08—and to explain theories of corporate personality in the context of the rise of the business company[7]—paras 1–09 to 1–42. The impact of these theories on the question of corporate constitutional protection will be referred to throughout the remainder of this book, particularly in connection with the United States Constitution. Their potential application in the context of the Irish Constitution is considered in paras 1–43 to 1–48 below.

1–04   The material discussed in this chapter illustrates the way in which the law identifies its subjects and how the company has been accommodated as a right and duty bearing unit. It is argued in paras 1–49 to 1–54 of this chapter that theories of the company, while they may shed some light on the nature of the company and justify the allocation or denial of rights to it, are too unstable a normative foundation upon which to build a theory of constitutional protection.

---

[5] Derham, "Theories of Legal Personality" in *Legal Personality and Political Pluralism* (Leicester and Webb eds, Melbourne, 1958) at p.5.
[6] Below at paras 3–01 to 3–37.
[7] The business company is the main subject of this book—wherever the word "company" is used, it can be assumed that it is a for-profit company, whether private or public, that is being discussed. There is an enormous amount written on theories of the corporation. A representative sample is as follows: Maitland, *Introduction to Gierke: Political Theories of the Middle Age* (Cambridge, 1900); Machen, "Corporate Personality" (1911) 24 Harv.L.Rev. 253; Laski, "The Personality of Associations" (1916) 19 Harv.L.Rev. 404; Vinogradoff, "Juridical Persons" (1924) 24 C.L.R. 594; Dewey, "The Historical Background of Corporate Legal Personality" (1926) 35 Yale L.J. 655; Radin, "The Endless Problem of Corporate Personality" (1932) 32 C.L.R. 643; Wolff, "On the Nature of Legal Persons" (1938) 54 L.Q.R. 494; Hart, "Definition and Theory in Jurisprudence" (1954) 70 L.Q.R. 37; Mitchell, "A Theory of Corporate Will" (1956) 56 Ethics 96; Derham, "Theories of Legal Personality" in *Legal Personality and Political Pluralism* (Webb ed., Melbourne University Press, 1958); Hessen, *In Defence of the Corporation* (Hoover Institution Press, 1979); Meir Dan-Cohen, *Rights, Persons, and Organizations: A Legal Theory for Bureaucratic Society* (University of California Press, 1986); Schane, "The Corporation is a Person: the Language of a Legal Fiction" (1987) 61 Tul.L.Rev. 563; Teubner, "Enterprise Corporatism: New Industrial Policy and the 'Essence' of the Legal Person" (1988) 36 Am.J.Comp.L. 130; Hallis, *Corporate Personality: A Study of Jurisprudence* (Oxford University Press, 1930).

A BRIEF OUTLINE OF THE HISTORY OF LEGAL PERSONALITY

Roman Law

1–05 The concept of legal personality can be traced to Roman Law. Writing at the end of the nineteenth century, Williston noted that the early English law of corporations was borrowed almost entirely from Roman Law[8] and it is from Roman Law that we can trace the idea of assigning legal personality to subjects.[9] Under Roman Law, the natural person alone was regarded as a *persona*—i.e. a party having full legal personality. Not all natural persons were *personae*, however, and slaves, for example, were not included within this concept.[10]

1–06 The Romans did not recognise the juristic person as such but they did grant the right to certain groups of persons to act as bearers of rights and duties, *e.g.* the state (*civitas*) or the treasury (*fiscus*).[11] In addition, two types of business association were recognised by Roman Law—the *societas* and the *universitas*. The *societas* was comprised of a contractual relation between its members—its assets were owned by them under the contract which bound them. The *universitas* was a separate legal entity which could hold property and had rights and obligations separate to those of its members. The *universitas* has been described as the "paradigm instance of corporate personality" because it cannot be reduced to contractual relations between its parts.[12] The *universitas* was not considered a *persona* because it was not a human being.[13] As for the notion that it was considered to have legal personality, there is marked dispute in the academic commentary whether the phrase *persona ficta* was ever actually used to describe the *universitas* in Roman times although there is agreement that some type of legal personality was attributed to it.[14]

The Middle Ages and canon law

1–07 The next period in which the concept of the legal person was extensively analysed is the Middle Ages. Maitland argued that it was probably scholars at this time that used the term *persona* to designate a legal entity as it does not

---

[8] Williston, "History of the Law of the Business Corporation Before 1800" (1888) 2 Harv.L.Rev. 149 at 164.

[9] See Wells, *Corporations and Criminal Responsibility* (2nd edn, Oxford University Press, 2001) at p.81.

[10] Duff, *Personality in Roman Private Law* (Cambridge University Press, 1938) at p.226.

[11] Von Zhyl, *History and Principles of Roman Law* (Butterworths, 1903).

[12] Scrutton, "Corporate Persons", Supp. Vol.LXIII, 1989, The Aristotelian Society, 239 at 242.

[13] Von Zhyl, *op.cit.*, p.80.

[14] Duff, op.cit.; Otto Von Gierke, *Community in Historical Perspective: A translation of selections from Das Deutsche Gennossenschaftsrecht* (Fischer trans., Black ed.,Cambridge University Press, 1990) and Otto von Gierke, *Das Wesen der menschlichen Verbande*, extracted in Mogi, *Otto von Gierke, his political teaching and jurisprudence* (P.S. King and Son Ltd, 1932); Maitland, *Introduction to Gierke: Political Theories of the Middle Ages* (Cambridge, 1900) at p.xviii.

appear in any Roman text.[15] He also wrote that the term "person" or "artificial person" was not used to describe an association. While such bodies were considered to be juristic persons capable of bearing rights, Maitland argued that the metaphor was probably introduced by the post glossators who were heavily influenced by Christian ethics which places the individual at the centre. According to Maitland, the first person to use the phrase *persona ficta* was Sinibald Fieschi who in 1243 became Pope Innocent IV. The description of the corporation as a *persona ficta* was directed at ecclesiastical bodies who were often the donees of property. Some way of enabling them to hold that property was required and thus, the idea of the *persona ficta* was born. The concept was adopted from canon law into the common law, where it was utilised in relation to corporations in the form of boroughs, hospitals and ecclesiastical foundations.[16]

1–08   It was during the Middle Ages that the concept of the modern state began to emerge.[17] Religious congregations and corporations of a feudal nature were seen as a threat to the sovereignty of the State.[18] A rule thus evolved whereby groups required a concession from the State before they could acquire legal personality.[19] The idea that it was the State that bestowed legal existence on associations was a strong weapon in the hand of a rising central government. One American author, writing at the beginning of the twentieth century, put it thus:

> "In its various forms of ecclesiastical bodies and foundations, gilds, municipalities, trading companies, or business organizations, the corporation has always presented the same problem of how to check the tendency of group action to undermine the liberty of the individual or to rival the political power of the state. The somewhat vague theory of the later Middle Ages that communal organization not sanctioned by prescription or royal license was illegal at least from the fifteenth century on supplemented by the technical doctrine, developed under canonist influences, that there was no capacity to act as a body corporate without positive authorization. To grant this authority has remained in England an attribute of the royal prerogative ... It is hardly possible to overestimate the theory that corporate existence depends on positive sanction as a factor in public and legislative policy."[20]

---

[15] *The Collected Papers of Frederic William Maitland* (Cambridge University Press, 1911), Vol.3.

[16] Foster, "Corporate Law Theory in Comparative Perspective" (2000) 48 Am.J.Comp.L. 573 at 581; Dewey, *op.cit.* at 666–669.

[17] Nekam, *op.cit.*

[18] Dewey, *op.cit.* at 666–669.

[19] Stokes, "Company Law and Legal Theory" in *Legal Theory and Common Law* (Twining, Blackwell, 1986).

[20] Freund, *Standards of American Legislation* (University of Chicago Press, 1917) at p.39, quoted in Dewey, *op.cit.* at 667.

THEORIES OF THE CORPORATION AND THE
HISTORY OF THE BUSINESS CORPORATION

Introduction

1–09 The theories of corporate personality discussed in this chapter reflect the problems faced by legal theory when presented with the corporation. One recurring theme is whether companies owe their existence to the State or to the individuals who decided to incorporate them. Another related theme is the extent to which a theory of the corporation justifies regulation of the corporation by the State. In later chapters, we will see that the theory of corporate personality chosen can impact on the question of constitutional protection.

1–10 The problem of corporate personality has been described as "endless".[21] Despite numerous attempts to end the debate over corporate personality, theoretical musings continue to abound in the academic literature.[22] While some of these are limited to highlighting the facile nature of the debate itself, the very continuation of its existence indicates that there are questions still in need of answers. One commentator has described the quest as follows:

> "At issue are two related questions concerning the social reality and legal status of the corporation. Is a corporation a real entity with its own will and purpose in society, or is it a mere association of real individuals forming a contract among themselves? Is its legal personality a truthful representation of the underlying social reality, or a fictitious or artificial being breathing only in the province of law?"[23]

1–11 What follows sets out the various theories of corporate personality. While these theories retain their vitality in modern times, the development of each of them was a product of its time[24] and the theories are placed in their historical context in the following account.

---

[21] Radin, *op.cit.*

[22] Marks, "The Personification of the Business Corporation in American Law" (1987) 54 U.Chi.L.Rev. 1441; Bratton, "The New Economic Theory of the Firm: Critical Perspectives From History" (1989) 41 Stan.L.Rev. 1471; Bratton, "The Nexus of Contracts Corporation: A Critical Appraisal" (1989) 74 Cornell L.Rev. 407; Millon, "Theories of the Corporation" [1990] Duke L.J. 201; Blumberg, "The Corporate Entity in and Era of Multinational Corporations" (1990) 15 Del.J.Corp.L. 283; Kraus, "Absolute Protection for Intracorporate Personnel Communications under Defamation Law: A Philosophical Reappraisal of the Nonpublication Doctrine" (1994) U.Mem.L.Rev. 155; Phillips, "Reappraising the Real Entity Theory of the Corporation" (1994) Fla.State Univ.L.Rev. 1061; Iwai, "Persons, Things and Corporations: The Corporate Personality Controversy and Corporate Governance" (1999) 47 Am.J.Comp.L. 583; Kim, "Characteristics of Souless Persons: The Applicability of the Character Evidence Rule to Corporations" [2000] U.Ill.L.Rev. 763; Note, "What We Mean When We Talk About Persons: The Language of a Legal Fiction" (2001) 114 Harv.L.Rev. 1745.

[23] Iwai, *op.cit.* at 583–584.

[24] See Watts, "Corporate Legal Theory under the First Amendment: *Bellotti* and *Austin*" (1991) 46 U.Miami L.Rev. 317 at 322–332.

1–12   It should be noted at the outset that the common law has not traditionally focused on the development of a coherent theory of corporate legal personality.[25] As Maitland pointed out:

> "The trust has given us a liberal substitute for a law about personified institutions. The trust has given us a liberal supplement for a necessarily meagre law of corporations."[26]

1–13   The prohibition in the Bubble Act of 1720 on companies trading as bodies corporate led to large numbers of deed of settlement companies.[27] The proliferation of these unincorporated trading associations meant that there was little need to grapple with the theoretical niceties of corporate personality during this time. It was, therefore, not until the nineteenth century that the rise of the modern incorporated company led to such theorising becoming commonplace among common law jurists.

The concession or fiction theory—the company as an artificial person

1–14   English law in the seventeenth century saw the corporation as an artificial legal construction.[28] The view was that the corporation was "invisible, immortal, and rests only in intendment and consideration of the law".[29] This was the prevalent view in the United States when its Constitution was drafted in 1787[30] and it was also reflected in the theorising in respect of the corporation in Continental jurisprudence. For example, writing in Germany in the first half of the nineteenth century, Savigny noted that corporations were said to own property. He took the view that to own property, the owner must have a will and that, as a corporation could not have such a will, it could only own property as a fictitious person.[31] This view was shared in French scholarship

---

[25] Duff, *op.cit.*

[26] *The Collected Papers of Frederic William Maitland* (Cambridge University Press, 1911), Vol.3.

[27] There was a boom in the flotation of companies at the beginning of the 18th century. Many company promoters did not bother with charters, which meant that even this minimal element of State regulation was not exercised. At one stage, The South Sea Company intended to acquire the National Debt. Parliament intervened in the form of the Bubble Act of 1720, which essentially prohibited trading by unincorporated undertakings unless they were partnerships. A huge lapse in public confidence ensued. The Act was very unclear in its effect and was perceived as only prohibiting the existence of freely transferable shares of unincorporated bodies. In any case, joint stock companies began to flourish by the middle of the 18th century without incorporation. These associations obtained the benefits of incorporation by using trusts. The company would be formed under a deed of settlement whereby the subscribers would agree to be associated in an enterprise with a prescribed joint stock divided into a specific number of shares.

[28] For a brief account of the development of the trading company, see Donaldson, *Corporations and Morality* (Prentice-Hall Inc, New Jersey, 1982), at pp.4–6.

[29] *Case of Sutton's Hospital* (1612) 10 Coke 23a, 30b–32b, (1612) 77 E.R. 960 at 970–973.

[30] Berle, "Constitutional Limitations on Corporate Activity—Protection of Personal Rights from Invasion through Economic Power" (1952) 100 U.Pa.L.Rev. 933 at 943–945.

[31] Machen, *op.cit.* at 255.

also.[32] According to the fiction theory, a corporation "has no existence apart from the law, and its personality is but a legal fiction".[33]

1–15   Corporations were, at this time, essentially a way to facilitate government projects. Akin to public authorities almost, in the seventeenth and eighteenth centuries the perception was that corporations were essentially agencies of the State. By the latter half of the nineteenth century, the corporation had become more widespread and was viewed less as a public authority and more as a private business organisation.[34] In the early days of the business corporation, however, its relationship with the State was emphasised. The practice of chartering corporations in the seventeenth to eighteenth centuries gave some degree of credence to the idea that the existence of corporations was at the sufferance of the State.[35] This gave rise to the growing influence of the concession theory of the corporation. This theory has its roots in the rise of the nation state during the Middle Ages.[36]

1–16   As has been pointed out,

> "The contraposition of state and individual citizen which characterized the theory of society that prevailed in Western political thought put all intermediary institutions in jeopardy. As such an institution, the corporation had to derive its powers from the state or else it would be perceived as a challenger to its authority."[37]

1–17   Allied to the fiction theory,[38] the concession theory of the corporation can be discerned in the writings of Blackstone[39] and Coke[40] and the approach is epitomised by the judgment of the United States Supreme Court in *Trustees of Dartmouth College v Woodward*,[41] where it was held that:

> "A corporation is an artificial being, invisible, intangible, and existing only in contemplation of law. Being the mere creature of law, it possesses

---

[32] *ibid.* at 255–256.

[33] Colson, *op.cit.* at 639.

[34] Berle, *op.cit.* He makes the point about the USA but it applies also to the UK.

[35] On the other hand, it has been argued that even at the earliest stages of the history of the corporation, the concession theory was misconceived. For example, until 1800, it was undecided whether debts owed to a dissolved corporation could be enforced on behalf of creditors or members of the corporation or for the benefit of the State. Williston, "History of the Law of the Business Corporation Before 1800" (1888) 2 Harv.L.Rev. 149 at 165. In the USA, the public dimension of corporations meant that they were required to respect the constitutional rights of individuals notwithstanding the consensus that the US Constitution and Bill of Rights is only vertically applicable. Berle, *op.cit.*

[36] Above at para.1–08; Dewey, *op.cit.* at 667.

[37] Marks, *op.cit.* at 1452.

[38] Colson, *op.cit.* at 645; Dewey, *op.cit.* at 666–669.

[39] Blackstone, *Commentaries on the Laws of England* (1st edn, Oxford, Clarendon Press, 1765), at pp.475–476.

[40] *Case of Sutton's Hospital, op.cit.*

[41] 17 U.S.(4 Wheat.) 518 (1819).

only those properties which the charter of its creation confers upon it, either expressly or as incidental to its very existence. These are such as are supposed best calculated to effect the object for which it was created."[42]

1–18   This quotation demonstrates that the fiction/artificial entity and concession theories of the corporation "fit together to form a coherent whole".[43] The fiction theory views the corporation as a:

"fictitious, artificial, legal person or entity with an existence distinct from the existences of the persons who form it. The concession theory, on the other hand, emphasizes the 'existing only in contemplation of law' portion of Marshall's definition. It does so by asserting that the corporation derives its being by concession from the State. For this reason, the concession theory appears to blend with fiction theory. If corporations are creatures of state law and nothing else, they almost certainly must be artificial, invisible, intangible, and fictional."[44]

1–19   In the remainder of this book, the phrase "concession theory" is used as a matter of convenience to describe this "coherent whole".[45]

1–20   In modern times, the concession theory can be said to have less to recommend it. The Joint Stock Companies Act 1844 introduced the concept of incorporation as of right in the United Kingdom and thus, undermined the idea that the existence of the company was at the pleasure of the State. In the United States, general incorporation became the norm in the 1870s, New York having enacted the first general incorporation statute as early as 1811.[46] It has been commented that:

"American incorporation practice had once helped to sustain belief in the artificiality of the corporation by suggesting that the privilege of incorporation was a considered grant by the state for a quasi-public purpose, often one defined as much by the desires of the legislature as by the incorporators. Free incorporation, however, suggested that the

---

[42] *ibid.* at 636. This theory was also prevalent in Continental jurisprudence at that time. See Machen, *op.cit.* at 255.

[43] Phillips, *op.cit.* at 1064.

[44] *ibid.* at 1065. See also Foster, *op.cit.* at 582: "In addition to being a useful doctrine for the increasingly centralizing governments of the post-feudal period, the concession theory had the advantage of fitting quite neatly with the fiction theory, as the fictitious person could be viewed as coming into existence through the concession." See also Marks, *op.cit.* at 1447–1448.

[45] Alternative names for this theory include the "artificial person theory" and the "weak entity theory". These alternative descriptions are abandoned for the sake of clarity and the title "concession theory" is used instead.

[46] New York Act of March 22, 1811, Chap.67. This was the first general incorporation statute in the world. Hurst, *The Legitimacy of the Business Corporation* (University Press of Virginia, 1970), at p.37.

corporate form was an individual's natural tool, as useful a device for independence and growth as a farmer's plow. Under free incorporation the process of chartering ceased to be a legislative matter and became an administrative and procedural one. While state incorporation statutes maintained structural control over the corporate form, the sovereign no longer considered the proposal of the corporators and then granted a charter."[47]

1–21   Indeed, the modern system of incorporation can scarcely be said to fit with the concession theory. This view is not, however, universal and the theory is still espoused by some:

"[T]he right to incorporate remains a privilege granted by the state, even if that privilege is now exercised through the companies legislation rather than through specific consents. Indeed, Maitland considered that the Companies Acts constituted 'an act of capitulation,' because rather than reducing the role of the state in controlling the existence of non-state groupings, it increased it, so reducing the amount of (traditionally English) freedom of association to a level more similar to that existing in continental countries."[48]

1–22   The concession theory can be identified in a number of judgments from the United States Supreme Court.[49] Its effect on the question of the availability of constitutional protection to the company reflects its origins. Generally speaking, a judgment which espouses the concession theory of the corporation will be in favour of corporate regulation and against extending constitutional protection to the company.[50]

The historical development of aggregate theories of the corporation

1–23   With the advent of modern incorporation legislation in England in the mid-nineteenth century,[51] private initiative played an increasingly significant role in the incorporation of companies:

"With equal access to the form assured, corporations no longer seemed a product of sovereign grace … widespread use of the corporate form directed attention … toward the social reality of the business and the creative energy of the individuals conducting it."[52]

---

[47] Marks, *op.cit.* at 1453–1454.

[48] Foster, *op.cit.* at 585 (references omitted).

[49] Below at paras 5–26 to 5–46, 9–53, 9–77 to 9–82 and 15–23 to 15–25.

[50] But see Dewey, *op.cit.* who said of the fiction and concession theories that "we cannot say, without qualification in respecting time and conditions, that either theory works out in the direction of limitation of corporate power", at 668. See also 667–668.

[51] The Joint Stock Companies Act 1844, discussed above at n.27. In the USA general incorporation laws were the norm by the 1870s. See Hurst, *op.cit.*

[52] Bratton, "The New Economic Theory of the Firm: Critical Perspectives From History", *op.cit.* at 1486.

1–24   During the second half of the nineteenth century, theorists began to analogise the company to the partnership, viewing the former as an aggregate constituted by the contractual relations of human beings. The aggregate theory[53] has been described as a variant of the principle of methodological individualism,[54] according to which:

> "[T]he ultimate constituents of the social world are individual people ... Every complex social situation, institution, or event is the result of a particular configuration of individuals ... [W]e shall not have arrived at rock-bottom explanations of such large-scale phenomena until we have deduced an account of them from statements about the dispositions, beliefs, resources, and inter-relations of individuals."[55]

1–25   The application of the aggregate theory of the corporation in the context of constitutional rights can be illustrated by a quotation from a judge of the United States Supreme Court,[56] who stated as follows:

> "Private corporations are, it is true, artificial persons, but ... they consist of aggregations of individuals united for some legitimate business ... It would be a most singular result if a constitutional provision intended for the protection of every person against partial and discriminating legislation by the states, should cease to exert such protection the moment the person becomes a member of a corporation ... On the contrary, we think that it is well established by numerous adjudications of the Supreme Court of the United States ... that whenever a provision of the constitution, or of a law, guarantees to persons the enjoyment of property ... the benefits of the provision extend to corporations, and that the court will always look beyond the name of the artificial being to the individuals whom it represents."[57]

1–26   It has been pointed out in respect of this theory that, logically speaking,

> "[i]f individuals are the ultimate sources of social explanation, and if groups such as corporations can be completely described through their human components, no distinct corporate entity should exist."[58]

---

[53] There are a number of variants of these theories, some of which are also referred to in the literature as "bracket", "collectivist" or "symbolist" theories of the corporation. Duff, *op.cit.* The collective term "associational theories" is also used. Blumberg, *op.cit.* at 294. In the interests of clarity, the term "aggregate" is used throughout this chapter to refer to these types of theory.

[54] Bratton, "The New Economic Theory of the Firm: Critical Perspectives From History", *op.cit.* at 1490–1491.

[55] Watkins, "Methodological Individualism and Social Tendencies" in *Readings in the Philosophy of the Social Sciences* (Brodbeck ed., Macmillan, 1968), quoted in Phillips, *op.cit.* at 1067.

[56] Field J., sitting on circuit, in *Railroad Tax Cases* 13 F 722 (1882).

[57] *ibid.* at 743–744, reproduced in Horowitz, *op.cit.* at 17.

[58] Phillips, *op.cit.* at 1067.

1–27 Furthermore, it might be thought that an aggregate theory of the corporation, which looks behind the legal entity to take account of the interests of the individuals concerned in it, might threaten the limited liability of the business company. As we shall see, however, the case law indicates that aggregate theories of the corporation are used to extend constitutional protection to the company while respecting its separate legal personality and limited liability.[59]

1–28 The most considered Irish High Court decision[60] extending constitutional protection to the company relies on an aggregate understanding of the company. This is not the first case to do so.[61] The problems with this approach will be considered in Chapter 8.[62]

The real entity theory

1–29 Towards the end of the nineteenth century, a new approach to corporations began to emerge as large corporations, dominated by management, became the norm.[63] The role of the shareholders, so prominent in the aggregate theory, had diminished as management became the controlling influence in business corporations. Thus, the actions of the company "had to be recognized as autonomous, the product of its organization and management".[64]

1–30 This conception of the corporation can be traced back as far as the Middle Ages. Otto von Gierke noted that in medieval times philosophers had grappled with the problem of legal recognition of the group:[65]

> "But wherever a community presents itself as a legally organised whole, there is presented to law the question whether and with what validity the social living unity is to be recognised as a union personality."[66]

1–31 Von Gierke wrote that the "organic theory" of the group was the prevalent theoretical explanation of the legal personality of the group at that time.[67] The organic theory describes the idea that a group is different to an individual because it has "a living existence in which the relationship of the unity of the whole to the plurality of the parts is subject to regulation by external

---

[59] Below, at paras 6–28, 8–55 to 8–56, 14–21 to 14–22 and 15–12 to 15–19. *Cf.* para.9–79.

[60] *Iarnród Éireann v Ireland* [1996] 3 I.R. 321; [1995] 2 I.L.R.M. 161.

[61] See also *Pine Valley Developments Ltd v Minister for the Environment* [1987] I.R. 23; [1987] I.L.R.M. 747, discussed below at para.8–16.

[62] Below at paras 8–51 to 8–59.

[63] Watts, *op.cit.*

[64] Marks, *op.cit.* at 1465.

[65] See *Community in Historical Perspective: A translation of selections from Das Deutsche Gennossenschaftsrecht, op.cit.* and *Das Wesen der menschlichen Verbande, op.cit.*

[66] *Das Wesen der menschlichen Verbande, op.cit.* at 25.

[67] The concept was Italian in origin but spread in the Middle Ages due to the revival of an interest in classical civilisation at that time. *Community in Historical Perspective: A translation of selections from Das Deutsche Gennossenschaftsrecht, op.cit.,* Vol.3.

norms of human will".[68] The writings of von Gierke were introduced into United States academic scholarship by Ernst Freund at the end of the nineteenth century,[69] around the same time that Maitland introduced the idea into English legal theory.[70]

1–32   Maitland's translation of von Gierke's description of the German fellowship is typical of a real entity theory description. It is:

> "No fiction, no symbol, no piece of the State's machinery, no collective name for individuals, but a living organism and a real person, with body and members and a will of its own. Itself can will, itself can act; it wills and acts by the men who are its organs as a man wills and acts by brain, mouth and hand. It is not a fictitious person ... it is a group-person, and its will is a group-will."[71]

1–33   In the 1920s, both Radin and Dewey were critical of this theory, stating that it "ignores that fact that certain entities cannot have a will".[72]

1–34   The theory can also be criticised for its tendency to anthropomorphise the company, leading to the use of crude metaphors. This has been particularly marked in the context of the criminal law, where references are made to the "hands" and "brain" of the company.[73]

1–35   The key difference between the organic theory and the concession theory of the corporation is that under the organic theory, the law does not create corporations. It recognises their existence, which existence is seen as being independent of that recognition. This theory is also known as the real entity, natural entity or strong entity theory—it will be referred to as the real entity theory for the remainder of this book.

> "Under this view, the corporation is a juridical unit with its own claims, much like those of a natural person, that extend beyond both the circumstances of its legal creation by the state and the claims or interests of its shareholders."[74]

---

[68] *Das Wesen der menschlichen Verbande, op.cit.* at 18.

[69] Freund, *The Legal Nature of Corporations* (University of Chicago Press, 1897). The realist theory of the corporation was endorsed in the USA by Laski, "The Personality of Associations" (1915) 29 Harv.L.Rev. 404.

[70] Maitland, *Introduction to Gierke, Political Theories of the Middle Ages* (Weimar, 1901).

[71] Otto von Gierke, *Political Theories of the Middle Ages* (Maitland trans., 1927), quoted in Phillips, *op.cit.* at 1069.

[72] Dewey, *op.cit.*; Radin, *op.cit.* Woolf has pointed out in this context that a co-resolution does not constitute a will, rather it is the result of the acts of will of various individuals. Woolf, "On the Nature of Legal Persons" (1938) 54 L.Q.R. 494 at 501–504.

[73] *Tesco Supermarkets Ltd v Natrass* [1972] A.C. 152. See also *Attorney General's Reference 2/1999*, unreported, CA (Criminal), February 15, 2000; *R(Rowley) v DPP*, unreported, English High Court, April 4, 2003. Cf. *Lennards Carrying Co. Ltd v Asiatic Petroleum Co. Ltd* [1915] A.C. 705; *H.L. Bolton (Engineering) Co. Ltd v T.J. Graham & Sons Ltd* [1957] 1 Q.B. 159.

[74] Blumberg, *op.cit.* at 295.

1–36 Unsurprisingly, the real entity theory of the corporation has led to the automatic extension of constitutional protection to the company.[75]

Modern incarnations of the aggregate perspective—the nexus of contracts theories

1–37 While the academic debate over the concession theory and the real entity theory of the corporation dwindled in the 1920s,[76] the 1980s saw a resurgence of interest in corporate theory and the development of modern aggregate theories of the firm which view it as a nexus of contracts.[77] This development in legal theory was preceded by two major insights into the modern business company. The first of these insights was provided in the work of Ronald Coase, who took the view that the firm could be seen as a number of enduring contractual arrangements between the factors of production designed to lower costs.[78] The second major insight into the nature of the company came from the work of Adolph Berle and Gardiner Means.[79] Their seminal work highlighted one of the most important features of the modern company— the separation of ownership and control.[80]

1–38 Both of these insights into the company have had an enormous impact on theorising about the company. In particular, the recognition of the separation of ownership and control gave rise to analysis of the company which transferred its focus from management to the protection of the interests of shareholders.[81]

---

[75] Below at paras 6–31 to 6–32, 9–53 to 9–55, 9–72 and 9–82.

[76] See Dewey, *op.cit.,* for an account of the facile nature of the debate.

[77] See Clarke, "Corporate Responsibility in Light of the Separation of Ownership and Control" (1997) D.U.L.J. 50 at 69–71.

[78] Writing in the 1930s, Coase had sought to explain the rise of the use of the firm as a means of conducting business. He conducted a comparative price analysis of organising production through the market and through the firm. He concluded that the firm was used where its costs were lower than the pricing mechanism of the market. From his perspective the owner of an input submitted to the hierarchy of the firm in order to achieve lower transaction costs. R.H. Coase, "The Nature of the Firm" *Economica*, New Series, Vol.4, No.16 (Nov. 1937), at 386–405.

[79] Berle and Means, *The Modern Corporation and Private Property* (rev. edn, Harcourt, Brace & World Inc, New York, 1967, first published in 1932).

[80] They pointed out the implications of this insight for the regulation of the company. Their main submission was that once control over property—what they call active property— has been relinquished, traditional theories of property rights no longer apply to the owners. Thus, shareholders should not necessarily be entitled to all the proceeds of the company. As the controllers of the property, management have no legitimate claim to the proceeds either; the book concludes that the wider community should stake a claim. Berle and Means, *op.cit.*, Book IV. This aspect of Berle and Means' work has a modern resonance to it and it laid the foundation for modern theories of corporate governance. However, the main influence of their work was to highlight the separation of ownership and control in the modern company. The more radical recommendations in relation to property rights were more or less ignored and the trend of modern law on companies—legislative and judicial—has been to protect shareholders from managers.

[81] Coase's work drew the attention of the law and economics movement in the 1960s. Scholars began to examine the corporation from a contractarian perspective and legal theorising about corporations took a manager centred view. In the 1960s and 1970s,

In the late 1970s, a new theoretical perspective began to gain support. Originating with the law and economics discourse, the nexus of contracts theories were the descendants of the aggregate theories of the nineteenth century. These new theories, which built on the work of Coase,[82] see the company as a nexus of contracts controlled by the market.[83] This displaces the managerial view of the corporation and sees it instead as a legal fiction which acts as a nexus for a set of contracting relations among various factors of production. From this perspective, management is not hierarchical; rather, it is a continuous process of negotiation and contracting.[84]

1–39 The nexus of contracts theories have been subject to criticism. Bratton has pointed out that if the company is no more than a nexus of contracts, surely all state control should have withered away, but this is not the case.[85] Furthermore, it has been argued that the theories fail to explain or describe how corporations act in the real world and that they fail to account for the undeniable individuality of the corporation.[86] There are some criticisms which make no claims to political neutrality. Faced with the rising power of corporations and the increasing public awareness of corporate human rights abuses, there has been a push towards increased corporate accountability, both to stakeholders and to the community at large.[87] The nexus of contracts corporation seems out of step with this modern trend.

---

criticism of the pro-managerial bias began to circulate. See Watts, *op.cit.* for an account of the development of these theories.

[82] Coase, *op.cit.*

[83] Alchian and Demsetz, "Production, Information Costs, and Economic Organization" (1972) 62 Am.Ec.Rev. 777; Jensen and Meckling, "Theory of the Firm: Managerial Behavior, Agency Costs and Ownership Structure", *Journal of Financial Economics*, Vol.3 (1976), at p.305.

[84] The nexus theory opens up the internal workings of the corporation to analysis under the tenets of neoclassical microeconomics. The nexus of contracts approach indicates that the separation of ownership and control is not key. As contracting is at arms length, there is no need to protect the interests of *e.g.* shareholders from managers. Contractual explanations of the firm can be seen as legitimising wealth transfers in favour of management and to the disadvantage of shareholders, particularly if it is accepted that shareholders may not always be able to bargain effectively with management.

[85] Bratton, "The Nexus of Contracts Corporation: A Critical Appraisal", *op.cit.* at 445. The adoption of a nexus on contracts theory renders outside regulation of the company illegitimate. As the market is the primary instrument of governance, there is no need for State intervention in the internal regulation of the corporation. Of course, it could be pointed out that the theories run the danger of over-estimating the efficacy of the market as a means of governance. Another criticism is that the theories stretch "unduly the notion of contracts"—Graver, "Personal Bodies: A Corporeal Theory of Corporate Personhood" (1999) 6 U.Chi.L.Sch.Roundtable 235 at 239.

[86] Graver, *op.cit.* at 239–240.

[87] Wymeersch, "Factors and Trends of Change in Company Law" (2000) 2 I.C.C.L.J. 481; Editorial, "The Accountability of Wealth" (2001) 3 I.C.C.L.J. iii; Sheikh, "Promoting Corporate Social Responsibilities within the European Union" (2002) 4 I.C.C.L.J. 143; Grossman, "Wresting Governing Authority from the Corporate Class: Driving People into the Constitution" in *Seattle Journal for Social Justice*, Vol.1 (2002), at p.147; Linzey, "Killing Goliath: Defending our Sovereignty and Environmental Sustainability through Corporate Charter Revocation in Pennsylvania and Delaware" (1997) 6 PSELR 31.

1–40   The key question about nexus of contracts theories for the purposes of this book, however, is in relation to its impact on corporate personality:

> "In the neoclassical picture, the corporate entity—a prominent figure in the managerialist picture—almost disappears. It dissolves into disaggregated but interrelated transactions among the participating human actors. Some transactions involve the fictive firm entity as a party, but only as a matter of convenience. The 'firm' has no precise boundaries; unlike legal academics, the neoclassicists have no interest in categorizing transactions as occurring inside or outside the firm."[88]

1–41   Thus, the same problem for corporate personality that arose in the context of the aggregate theory arises in this context also[89]—if we reduce the firm to nothing more than transactions, how can it have any legal personality of its own? Writing in 1989, Bratton provided a partial answer to this problem:

> "The nexus of contracts concept challenges many details of the generally accepted picture of the corporation, but it does not challenge that picture's fundamental outline. It does not assert that firm entities do not exist. Instead, it modifies the traditional juridical theme of the corporation as a combination of reified entity and aggregate parts, taking many directions already followed in twentieth century legal theory. It reinforces the proclivity to look through the entity to constitutive contractual relations, the proclivity to look at the entity reification as a means to the end of wealth creation, and the proclivity to resist the introduction of organicist thinking in business contexts."[90]

APPLYING CORPORATE THEORY TO THE IRISH CONSTITUTION

1–42   Theories of the corporation have been relied upon extensively in the United States Supreme Court to determine whether certain constitutional and Bill of Rights guarantees are applicable to the company.[91] Their influence can also be seen in other jurisdictions and is referred to at various points throughout the chapters of this book.[92] The Irish jurisprudence concerning the constitutional status of the company is limited. In general, the Irish cases in which companies have relied upon the Constitution have lacked analysis. In some cases, the courts have allowed the company to rely on constitutional guarantees *sub silentio*[93] and in other cases, constitutional protection has been

---

[88] Bratton, "The Nexus of Contracts Corporation: A Critical Appraisal", *op.cit.* at 420.
[89] Above, text accompanying n.58.
[90] Bratton, "The Nexus of Contracts Corporation: A Critical Appraisal", *op.cit.* at 427.
[91] *e.g.* see below at paras 5–26 to 5–46, 6–28, 6–31 to 6–32, 8–55 to 8–56, 9–53 to 9–55, 9–72, 9–77 to 9–82, 14–21 to 14–22, 15–12 to 15–19 and 15–23 to 15–25.
[92] See below at paras 5–47, 8–46 to 8–50, 8–52, 9–151 and 9–153 to 9–154.
[93] *Pigs Marketing Board v Donnelly (Dublin) Ltd* [1939] I.R. 413; *Att-Gen v Southern Industrial Trust Ltd* (1957) 94 I.L.T.R. 161; *Educational Co. of Ireland Ltd v Fitzpatrick*

denied without explanation.[94] More recent cases indicate that judges are apt to rely on a theory of the company in this context and the most significant High Court authority[95] relies on an aggregate conception of the company to justify the vindication of corporate property rights under Art.40.3.[96] Conversely, the concession theory has been relied upon to deny a company protection[97] and hints of a real entity theory of the company appear in another case.[98]

1–43 This section considers the potential impact each theory could have on the Irish Constitution. The next section will then consider the deficiencies of relying on corporate theory alone as a methodology for determining constitutional protection.

The concession theory and the Irish Constitution

1–44 Espousing the concession theory of the corporation would resolve the matter of constitutional protection against the company. If the company is seen as the creation of statute alone, then it could hardly be said to have rights superior to legislative interference. On the other hand, as has already been discussed, this approach is undermined somewhat by the general availability of incorporation within the State. Furthermore, as mentioned above, the right to freedom of association in Art.40.6.1(iii) adds some constitutional underpinning to the existence of companies insofar as they are considered associations. In any case, while the Oireachtas might be able to repeal the Companies Acts without being in breach of this provision, the wholesale dissolution of all companies within the State would affect the *existing* property rights of shareholders as they could no longer participate in the company as per the terms of their shareholding. Thus, the constitutional status of the system

---

[1961] I.R. 345; *Att-Gen for England and Wales v Brandon Book Publishers Ltd* [1986] I.R. 597; [1987] I.L.R.M. 135; *Att-Gen v Hamilton (No.1)* [1993] 2 I.R. 250; [1993] I.L.R.M. 81; *Att-Gen v Hamilton (No.2)* [1993] 3 I.R. 227; [1993] I.L.R.M. 821; *An Blascaod Mór Teoranta v Commissioners of Public Works* [2000] 1 I.R. 6; [2000] 1 I.L.R.M. 401; *Kerry Co-Operative Creameries Ltd v An Bord Bainne* [1990] I.L.R.M. 664; *National Irish Bank Ltd, Re* [1999] 1 I.R. 145; [1999] 1 I.L.R.M. 321; *Zoe Developments Ltd v DPP*, unreported, High Court, Geoghegan J., March 3, 1999; *Environmental Protection Agency v Swacliffe Ltd trading as Dublin Waste, Louis Moriarty and Eileen Moriarty*, unreported, High Court, May 21, 2004.

[94] *Chestvale Properties Ltd v Glackin* [1992] I.L.R.M. 221; *P.M.P.S. Ltd v Att-Gen* [1983] I.R. 339; [1984] I.L.R.M. 88. See also *Att-Gen v Paperlink Ltd* [1984] I.L.R.M. 373, where the parties agreed that the company did not enjoy the rights guaranteed under Art.40.3.

[95] *Iarnród Éireann v Ireland* [1996] 3 I.R. 321; [1995] 2 I.L.R.M. 161.

[96] See also *Pine Valley Developments Ltd v Minister for the Environment* [1987] I.R. 23; [1987] I.L.R.M. 747, "when the lands were then purchased, the shareholders in Pine Valley had in the eyes of the law as then understood acquired through their company valuable property rights in the land" Henchy J., [1987] I.R. 23 at 42; [1987] I.L.R.M. 747 at 763.

[97] *Dunnes Stores Ireland Co. v Ryan* [2002] 2 I.R. 60 at 100, Herbert J., discussed below, Chap.5.

[98] Barrington J. in *Irish Times Ltd v Ireland* [1998] 1 I.R. 359 at 404–405; [1998] 2 I.L.R.M. 161 at 192, discussed below at para.9–07.

of incorporation under the Companies Acts is protected, albeit indirectly, by Art.43 of the Constitution.[99] As was noted above, there have been a number of Irish cases in which companies have successfully relied on the Constitution so that the concession theory, while it may make occasional appearances in judicial rhetoric,[100] seems unlikely to enjoy widespread support among the judiciary.

The real entity theory and the Irish Constitution

1–45   One way of justifying the extension of constitutional protection to the company is to adopt the real entity approach. By treating the company as a real entity with a will comparable to that of the individual, its entitlement to constitutional protection can be based on its similarities with the individual. This approach to the company is often taken in the context of allocating civil or criminal liability to it.[101] The problem with the real entity approach is that it is little more than a metaphor which obscures more than it exposes. In particular, it ignores the fact that companies are not comparable to individuals in relation to their moral status. While it might be appropriate to respect the rights of individuals simply because of the fact that they are individuals, the same argument does not apply in the case of the company. The company is an entity whose very existence is predicated on its being a means to an end. The individual, on the other hand, is an entity that is properly considered an end in itself. This Kantian insight informs many of the guarantees under the Irish Constitution. These matters are explored in further detail in Chapter 3.[102]

The aggregate theory and the Irish Constitution

1–46   The aggregate theory[103] is also problematic. As it has been relied on in the most important Irish case in this area, its deficiencies are given detailed attention in Chapter 8.[104] The basic result of applying an aggregate theory of the company to the question of constitutional protection is a finding that companies have rights because of the interests of the individuals concerned in them:

> "[G]iven that the interests of each association of people are partly dependant on the interests of its members individually, and given that

---

[99]   Of course, if the State was willing to compensate shareholders, the situation would be different. *Article 26 and the Planning and Development Bill, 1999, Re* [2000] 2 I.R. 321; [2001] 1 I.L.R.M. 81.

[100]   See the extract from the judgment of Herbert J. in *Dunnes Stores Ireland Co. v Ryan* [2002] 2 I.R. 60 at 100. Reproduced below at para.5–36.

[101]   See cases cited above, n.73.

[102]   See discussion of autonomy-based rights below at paras 3–24 to 3–35.

[103]   The nexus of contracts theory to the company entails a similar approach to this issue. See Butler and Ribstein, *The Corporation and the Constitution* (The AEI Press, Washington DC, 1995).

[104]   Below, at paras 8–51 to 8–59.

the interests of each association are always the interests of its members qua collectivity, the central function of corporate rights is tied essentially to the interests of individual human agents (insofar as they are individuals and—even more—insofar as they are constitutive of a group.) ... associations of people have interests that necessarily involve and incorporate certain interests of human individuals ... One's classification of corporate bodies as potential right-holders is not only conceptually impeccable but also morally fitting."[105]

1–47   For present purposes, it is sufficient to note that the extension of constitutional protection to the company on the basis of the interests of individuals concerned in it—usually the shareholders—begs the question of the nature of those interests. While the Irish courts have accepted the not uncontroversial proposition that shares constitute property,[106] the nature of that property is that it confers only a contractual right of participation in the company on the terms set out in the articles of association. Thus, any act which damages the company's property can only violate the constitutional rights of the company.[107]

1–48   In any case, the central argument of this book is that it is not appropriate only to take account of the interests of the individuals concerned in the company to explain its constitutional protection. Instead, the focus should also be on the broader impact of allocating constitutional protection to companies. Essentially, the argument canvassed in Chapter 3 is that companies should be entitled to constitutional protection where that entitlement would serve some purpose that furthers the values of the Irish Constitution. That purpose might be the promotion of an institutional value, such as the preservation of the integrity of the criminal justice system. Or it might be some other general good, such as contributing to the marketplace of ideas. This utilitarian approach to constitutional guarantees will not apply in every case and thus, not every constitutional guarantee is applicable to the company. Those rights which are based on autonomy values, such as equality, are not appropriate for application to the company. By taking an approach which focuses on the values underlying the Constitution instead of adopting one or other theory of the corporation, a more flexible approach can be taken to this constitutional issue, one which better respects the values underlying constitutional guarantees.

---

[105] Kramer, "Getting Rights Right" in *Rights, Wrongs and Responsibilities* (Kramer ed., Palgrave, 2001) at pp.46–47.
[106] *Kerry Co-Operative Creameries Ltd v An Bord Bainne* [1990] I.L.R.M. 664, discussed below at paras 8–28 to 8–29. McConvill, "Do shares constitute property? Reconsidering a fundamental, yet unresolved, question" (2005) 79 ALJ 251.
[107] See discussion below at paras 8–28 to 8–29 and 8–55 to 8–59.

THE LIMITATIONS OF THEORIES OF CORPORATE PERSONALITY AS A
METHODOLOGY FOR DETERMINING CONSTITUTIONAL PROTECTION

1–49   It has been argued convincingly that theories of the corporation are of
limited use as a normative tool. They nevertheless remain tempting to the
judge faced with a corporate claim to constitutional protection because they
have infiltrated legal discourse and present themselves as neutral. As Hart
pointed out in his article, "Definition and Theory in Jurisprudence",[108]

> "It is, of course, clear that the assertion that corporate bodies are real
> persons and the counter-assertion that they are fictions of the law were
> often not the battle cries of analytical jurists. They were ways of asserting
> or denying the claims of organised groups to recognition by the State.
> But such claims have always been confused with the baffling analytical
> question 'What is a corporate body?' so that the classification of such
> theories as Fiction or Realist or Concessionist is a criss-cross between
> logical and political criteria."[109]

1–50   Legal Realists commented on this as early as 1926, and in a seminal
article on the manipulability of corporate theory, John Dewey wrote that:

> "The fact of the case is that there is no clear-cut line, logical or practical,
> through the different theories which have been advanced, and which are
> still advanced in behalf of the 'real' personality of either 'natural' or
> associated persons. Each theory has been used to serve the same ends,
> and each has been used to serve opposing ends ... Corporate groups ...
> have had real personality ascribed to them, both in order to make them
> more amenable to liability...and to exalt their dignity and vital power, as
> against external control. Their personality has been denied for like
> reasons ...".[110]

1–51   Dewey's article, which can be seen as part of the Legal Realist tradition
of attacking conceptualism,[111] has been cited as ending the debate over
corporate personality[112] but, as noted above,[113] theories of corporate personality
have yet to disappear from academic discourse.

1–52   While there has been a resurgence of interest in corporate theory in the
form of the nexus of contracts theories, the descriptive nature of theories of
the corporation makes them an unsound normative basis upon which to build
a theory of corporate constitutional rights. Essentially, the theories described
in this chapter are little more than metaphors. While each has some insight to

---

[108] (1954) 70 L.Q.R. 37.
[109] *ibid.* at 40.
[110] Dewey, *op.cit.* at 669–670.
[111] Marks, *op.cit.* at 1480.
[112] Mayer, "Personalizing the Impersonal: Corporations and the Bill of Rights" (1990) 41
Hastings L.J. 577 at 639–640.
[113] See the recent literature cited above at n.22.

offer into the metaphysics of the company, no one theory fully captures the complex social, legal and economic reality of the company. It is, therefore, submitted that the accommodation of the company within Irish constitutional jurisprudence requires a more solid foundation. This is a matter of importance. As has been pointed out:

> "The deployment of legal metaphors can perform a distinctly ideological role by not only reifying and abstracting the meaning of social phenomena from their underlying contexts but also covertly reproducing a series of potentially controversial assumptions."[114]

1–53 This has certainly been the case in the United States Supreme Court where companies have been able to take advantage of a vast number of constitutional guarantees without any reasoned justification.

1–54 The corporate theories described above are not in and of themselves a sufficient basis for determining the question of corporate constitutional protection. They are useful insofar as they each present a description of the company which captures, at least partially, some of its essential features. Each of them can be seen as a lens through which the company may be viewed. In rejecting the use of these lenses in the context of the interpretation of the Irish Constitution, this book is not denying their descriptive usefulness. It is not possible to discuss "the company" without implicitly adopting *some* notion of the subject. Indeed, in its tendency to reify the company, the discussion in this book arguably espouses a shorthand description of the company which closely resembles the "real entity" theory. That some metaphysical notion of the company is adopted is unavoidable. It is also unobjectionable provided that it remains distinct from issues of constitutional interpretation. This book, in highlighting the tendency of corporate theories to present themselves as neutral guides to the issue of corporate constitutional protection, firmly rejects the role of corporate theory in this important normative task.

1–55 Some method of approaching claims to constitutional protection must be developed in this jurisdiction so that judges justify the extension—and denial—of the guarantees contained within Bunreacht na hÉireann to companies in a manner which fits in with the values of the Constitution and ensures that the rights of individuals are adequately protected also.[115]

1–56 It will be argued in Chapter 3 that the best approach to this issue is to recognise the differing basis for corporate, as opposed to individual, constitutional protection. The key to this, as mentioned above, lies in the adoption of a utilitarian approach to rights where the company is concerned.

1–57 First, however, Chapter 2 turns to consider the text of the Irish Constitution and whether it is possible, as a matter of interpretation, to envisage the company as a "constitutional person" as well as a legal person.

---

[114] Culley and Salter, "Why Study Metaphors?" (2004) 15 K.C.L.J. 347 at 366.
[115] See discussion below at paras 3–24 to 3–35.

CHAPTER 2

CONSTRUCTING THE CONSTITUTIONAL SUBJECT I: TEXT AND INTERPRETATION

INTRODUCTION

2–01 The last chapter set out the various theories of legal and corporate personality that have evolved from Roman times up to current legal scholarship. As was stated at the beginning of that chapter,[1] rights and duties do not exist in a vacuum; their subject must be identified. This is no less true of constitutional rights than rights of any other pedigree. This chapter explores the idea of the constitutional subject and, in particular, whether companies are *a priori* excluded from the protection of the Irish Constitution.

2–02 It was mentioned in the preface to this book that the company is not specifically referred to anywhere in the text of the Constitution. The framers of Bunreacht na hÉireann were obviously aware of the existence of these entities[2] and it might be thought that their omission from the text indicates an intention to exclude them from constitutional protection.

2–03 While it is true to say that there are no specific references to the company in the provisions of the Constitution, those guarantees which refer to the "person"[3] may be interpreted so as to include the company. Indeed, the Interpretation Act 1937, enacted in the same year as the promulgation of the Constitution, indicates that this was the commonly understood meaning of the word in its legislative usage.[4] Of course, that does not settle the question of the guarantees expressed to be for the benefit of "citizens", which are considered below.[5] In the specific context of freedom of expression, Art.40.6.1(i) specifically refers to the rights of organs of public opinion, a reference which has been held to include legal persons.[6] Of course, this part of the guarantee seems to be aimed at the media which arguably constitutes a separate category

---

[1] Above at paras 1–01 to 1–02.
[2] See quotation from the judgment of Keane J. in *Iarnród Éireann v Ireland* [1996] 3 I.R. 321 at 345; [1995] 2 I.L.R.M. 161 at 183, reproduced below at para.8–22.
[3] Arts 38.1 and 38.5, both discussed below at paras 2–09 to 2–12.
[4] s.11(c) of the Interpretation Act 1937 provides that: "The word 'person' shall, unless the contrary intention appears, be construed as importing a body corporate ... as well as an individual." See also s.1(1)(c) of the Interpretion Act 1923.
[5] At paras 2–08 and 2–10 to 2–14.
[6] Barrington J., *Irish Times Ltd v Ireland* [1998] 1 I.R. 359 at 406; [1998] 2 I.L.R.M. 161 at 194. The quotation is reproduced below at para.9–07.

of company in this context.[7] More general recognition of the company can be found in Art.40.6.1(iii), which guarantees freedom of association. This perhaps can be interpreted as a constitutional mandate for the incorporation of companies.[8]

2–04   This chapter addresses the question of corporate constitutional protection by focusing on the text and interpretation of Bunreacht na hÉireann.

2–05   Paragraphs 2–07 to 2–22 examine the wording of various provisions of the Irish Constitution and whether they necessarily exclude companies from their ambit. Reference is made to the United States Constitution for comparative purposes. It will be noted that the text of the United States Constitution has not been interpreted uniformly in this context.

2–06   Paragraphs 2–23 to 2–34 consider various methods of interpretation that have been applied to the Irish Constitution and whether they might have an impact on corporate constitutional protection. The Constitution itself does not define its subjects[9] and uses a number of different words to identify the parties envisaged in different provisions. This section explores whether this difference in phraseology is of any significance for the company. There are five methods of constitutional interpretation[10] that may bear on this: the literal approach, the historical approach, the broad approach, the doctrine of harmonious interpretation and the natural law approach. The first four are discussed in paras 2–23 to 2–34, below. The last is discussed in Chapter 3 at paras 3–03 to 3–15.

TEXTUAL REFERENCES TO THE RIGHT AND DUTY BEARING UNIT IN THE IRISH AND UNITED STATES CONSTITUTIONS

The Irish Constitution

2–07   Bunreacht na hÉireann uses a variety of epithets to describe its subjects. Some provisions clearly apply only to specific human beneficiaries. Thus, Art.40.3.3 acknowledges the "right to life of the unborn" as well as the "equal right to life of the mother". The mother also gets a specific mention in Art.41, as does the family. Parents and children are guaranteed protection under Art.42 and the latter are mentioned again in Art.44.2.4.[11]

---

[7] See below at paras 9–01 to 9–17.

[8] Forde, *Company Law in Ireland* (3rd edn, Round Hall, 1999), at p.62. Most of the cases concerning this guarantee have been concerned with trade unions and the internal relations between such bodies and their individual members. Hogan and Whyte, *Kelly: The Irish Constitution* (4th edn, Lexis-Nexis Butterworths, 2003), at p.1793.

[9] Although there is some guidance to the definition of "citizenship" in Art.9. The term "subjects" is meant to refer to the beneficiaries of constitutional guarantees. For possible alternative meanings of the word in the context of a Constitution, see Rosenfeld, "The Identity of the Constitutional Subject" (1995) 16 Cardozo L.Rev. 1049.

[10] Hogan and Whyte, *op.cit.* at pp.3–32.

[11] The "natural and imprescriptible rights of the child" are recognised in Art.42.5. Article 44.2.4 guarantees "the right of any child to attend a school receiving public money

2–08   Apart from these specific provisions which clearly cannot be interpreted to apply to the company, there are references throughout the Constitution to both the "person" and the "citizen". The question arises whether this textual difference is of any significance to the company attempting to avail of constitutional guarantees.

2–09   The guarantees stated to apply to persons both arise in the context of due process protections in criminal proceedings. Thus, Art.38.1[12] states that "No person shall be tried on any criminal charge save in due course of law" and Art.38.5[13] guarantees a trial by jury for any "person" charged with a non-minor offence.

2–10   On the other hand, the personal rights guaranteed under Art.40.3[14] are described as the "rights of the citizen". The "citizen" is also the beneficiary of guarantees in relation to personal liberty under Art.40.4.1 and freedom of expression under Art.40.6.1(i),[15] freedom of assembly under Art.40.6.1(ii), freedom of association under Art.40.6.1(iii),[16] and freedom of conscience and the free profession and practice of religion under Art.44.2.1.

2–11   In addition to the above guarantees which appear to be limited to the "citizen", there are provisions which contain additional indicia that they are intended to apply to the individual alone. Thus, Art.40.1 guarantees that "All citizens shall, as human persons, be held equal before the law." The inviolability of "the dwelling" is a guarantee in relation to the "citizen" under Art.40.4.5.[17] Finally, in Art.43, there is a reference to the property rights of "man", who enjoys rights of property "in virtue of his rational being".[18]

2–12   There is no definition of the term "person" in the Constitution although, as mentioned above, the Interpretation Act 1937 suggests that it was understood to include the company.[19] The meaning of "citizen" in this context is given some exposition in Art.9. This provides that former citizens of Saorstát Éireann are citizens.[20] Article 9.1.2 states that: "The future acquisition and loss of Irish nationality and citizenship shall be determined in accordance with law", subject to the provision, in Art.9.1.3, that: "No person may be excluded from Irish nationality and citizenship by reason of the sex of such person." Article

---

without attending religious instruction at that school". Children also enjoy rights under Art.40.3: *PW v AW*, unreported, High Court, April 21, 1980; *Article 26 and the Adoption (No.2) Bill 1987, Re* [1989] I.R. 656; [1989] I.L.R.M. 266.

[12] Below, Chaps 4, 5 and 6.
[13] Below, Chap.7.
[14] Below, Chaps 8, 10, and 13.
[15] Below, Chap.9.
[16] Above, n.8.
[17] See below, Chap.15.
[18] Art.43.
[19] See n.4 above. Section 18(c) of the Interpretation Act 2005 makes similar provision.
[20] Art.9.1.1.

9.3[21] states that: "Fidelity to the nation and loyalty to the State are fundamental political duties of all citizens."

2–13   The reference to citizenship appears to contemplate only natural persons. It is difficult—although perhaps not impossible—to imagine that a company could have fundamental political duties such as those described in Art.9.2. Furthermore, the wording of Art.9.1.3 suggests that the "person" is a natural person who has a sex. On the other hand, read closely, the provision could be intended to mean simply that where a "person" is of a sex, that feature shall not exclude him or her from the benefits—and duties—of citizenship.

2–14   Article 9 delegates further definition to the law. The Nineteenth Amendment of the Constitution Act 1998 amended Art.2 of the Constitution so that all persons born on the island of Ireland were entitled to citizenship.[22] Again, the reference to birth could logically refer only to those putative citizens capable of being born. The Twenty-seventh Amendment of the Constitution added a section to Art.9[23] which provides that persons born in Ireland who do not have at least one parent who is, or is entitled to be, an Irish citizen are not constitutionally entitled to Irish citizenship or nationality.[24] Again, in relation to the notion of place of birth, it is possible as a matter of logic that that requirement refers only to those citizens who are born—it does not necessarily exclude those who are not capable of being born.[25]

The United States Constitution and the relegation of the text

2–15   Like the Irish Constitution, the United States Constitution describes its subjects using both the word "person" and the word "citizen". The experience under the United States Constitution has been that neither of these words

---

[21] This was formerly Art.9.2 but was renumbered by virtue of the Twenty-Seventh Amendment of the Constitution Act 2004.

[22] Post-1998, the relevant part of Art.2 read as follows:
   "It is the entitlement and birthright of every person born in the island of Ireland, which includes its islands and seas, to be part of the Irish nation. That is also the entitlement of all persons otherwise qualified in accordance with law to be citizens of Ireland."
   See also s.6(1) of the Irish Nationality and Citizenship Act 1956 as substituted by s.3 of the Irish Nationality and Citizenship Act 2001. See Hogan and Whyte, *op.cit.* at p.162.

[23] The section is numbered Art.9.2 and the former Art.9.2 is now Art.9.3.

[24] The new section reads as follows:
   "Notwithstanding any other provision of this Constitution, a person born in the island of Ireland, which includes its islands and seas, who does not have, at the time of the birth of that person, at least one parent who is an Irish citizen or entitled to be an Irish citizen is not entitled to Irish citizenship or nationality, unless provided for by law. This section shall not apply to persons born before the date of the enactment of this section."

[25] While it might be possible to construct some crude metaphor for the "birth" of a company, the anthropomorphising of the company is something this book seeks to avoid. See quotation from Cully and Salter, "Why Study Metaphors?" (2004) 15 K.C.L.J. 347 at 366, reproduced above at para.1–52.

necessarily excludes the company[26] from constitutional protection. In addition, there are some guarantees which are phrased as general prohibitions on government and companies have been able to benefit from these.

2–16   The federal guarantee of indictment by a grand jury, the rule against double jeopardy, the privilege against self-incrimination and the right not to be deprived of life, liberty or property without due process of law are all guaranteed to the "person" by the Fifth Amendment.[27] Despite the uniform reference to the "person" in the Fifth Amendment, it has not been uniformly applied to the company claiming constitutional protection.[28] While a company can rely on the double jeopardy clause[29] and the due process clause,[30] it cannot rely on the privilege against self-incrimination.[31]

2–17   The Fourth Amendment refers to "the right of the people to be secure in their persons, houses, papers, and effects, against unreasonable searches and seizures" and requires that any warrants granted must conform to certain requirements.[32] The company is entitled to rely on both of these guarantees.[33]

---

[26] US case law generally refers to the "corporation" rather than the "company". As Sealy has pointed out, the tendancy of the English lawyer is to use the word "company". Sealy, "Perception and Policy in Company Law" in *Corporate and Commercial Law: Modern Developments* (Feldman and Miesel eds, Lloyd's of London Press Ltd, 1996). The words are used interchangeably throughout this book, depending on the language employed by the relevant court.

[27] The Fifth Amendment reads:
"No person shall be held to answer for a capital, or otherwise infamous crime, unless on a presentment or indictment of a Grand Jury, except in cases arising in the land or naval forces, or in the Militia, when in actual service in time of War or public danger; nor shall any person be subject for the same offence to be twice put in jeopardy of life or limb; nor shall be compelled in any criminal case to be a witness against himself, nor be deprived of life, liberty, or property without due process of law; nor shall private property be taken for public use, without just compensation."

[28] The takings clause is expressed negatively without reference to any constitutional subject. It has been applied to the corporate property owner in *Pennsylvania Coal Co. v Mahon* 260 U.S. 393 (1922).

[29] *United States v Martin Linen Supply Co.* 430 U.S. 564 (1977).

[30] *Noble v Union River Logging R. Co.* 147 U.S. 165 (1893).

[31] *Hale v Henkel* 201 U.S. 43 (1906).

[32] The full text of the Fourth Amendment, which was added in 1791, is as follows:
"The right of the people to be secure in their persons, houses, papers, and effects, against unreasonable searches and seizures shall not be violated, and no Warrants shall issue, but upon probable cause, supported by Oath or affirmation, and particularly describing the place to be searched, and the persons or things to be seized."

[33] *Hale v Henkel* 201 U.S. 43 (1906)—unreasonable searches and seizures. But see *United States v Morton Salt Co.* 338 U.S. 632 (1950). *Marshall v Barlow's Inc* 436 U.S. 307 (1978)—warrant requirements. There are exceptions in relation to industries traditionally subject to close regulation: *Colonnade Catering Corp v United States* 397 U.S. 72 (1970)—exception for the liquor industry; *United States v Biswell* 406 U.S. 311 (1977)—exception for firearms industry; *Donovan v Dewey* 452 U.S. 594 (1981)—exception for mining industry.

2–18   The Fourteenth Amendment[34] requires that the states refrain from depriving any "person" of life, liberty or property without due process of law and requires that each State extend the equal protection of the laws to any person within its jurisdiction. Both the due process clause[35] and equal protection clause[36] have been held to apply to the company, but the privileges and immunities clause has been held not to apply.[37] As for the liberty clause, it was initially held to be inapplicable to the company,[38] but a later case suggests that it may now apply.[39]

2–19   It was held early on that companies were not "citizens" for all purposes under Art.III of the United States Constitution.[40] They were, however, held to be citizens for diversity jurisdiction.[41] This finding was based on the citizenship of their members.[42] Companies are not, however, "citizens" for the purposes of the privileges and immunities clause of Art.IV.[43]

2–20   The Sixth Amendment provides that the right to a trial by jury is enjoyed by "the accused ... in all criminal prosecutions" and it is thus unsurprising

---

[34] The Fourteenth Amendment provides in s.1 that:
> "All persons born or naturalized in the United States, and subject to the jurisdiction thereof, are citizens of the United States and of the State wherein they reside. No State shall make or enforce any Law which abridges the privileges or immunities of citizens of the United States; nor shall any State deprive any person of life, liberty, or property, without due process of law; nor deny to any person within its jurisdiction the equal protection of the laws."

[35] *Minneapolis & St. Louis Ry v Beckwith* 129 U.S. 26 (1889).

[36] *Santa Clara County v Southern Pacific Ry* 118 U.S. 394 (1886).

[37] *Pembina Mining Co. v Pennsylvania* 125 U.S. 181 (1888).

[38] *Northwestern National Life Insurance Co. v Riggs* 203 U.S. 243 (1906).

[39] *First National Bank v Bellotti* 435 U.S. 765 at 778–779 (1978).

[40] *Bank of United States v Deveraux* 9 U.S. (5 Cranch.) 61 (1809). Section 2(1) of Art.III provides as follows:
> "The judicial Power shall extend to ... Controversies ... between a State and Citizens of another State;—between Citizens of different States;—between Citizens of the same State claiming Lands under the Grants of different States, and between a State, or the Citizens thereof, and foreign States, Citizens or Subjects."

[41] *Bank of the United States v Devereaux*, *op.cit.* Diversity jurisdiction refers to the jurisdiction of federal courts where the parties on either side of a dispute are citizens of different states. If any plaintiff shares a common citizenship with any defendant, then diversity is destroyed and along with it federal jurisdiction. *Strawbridge v Curtis* 7 U.S. (3 Cranch.) 267, 2 L Ed 435 (1806).

[42] In *Louisville, Cincinatti & Charleston Railroad Co. v Leston* 43 U.S. (2 How.) 314 (1853) relying on the real entity theory, the court held that, for purposes of *Strawbridge v Curtis*, *op.cit.* diversity, the corporation is considered a person and a citizen of the state of incorporation. In *Marshall v Baltimore & Ohio Railroad Co.* 57 U.S. (6 How.) 314 (1853) it was held that all shareholders are presumed to be citizens of the state of incorporation.

[43] In *Bank of Augusta v Earle* 38 U.S. (13 Pet.) 519 (1839), the US Supreme Court held that corporations could not claim the rights of a person under the privileges and immunities clause. Art.IV.2.1 contains this clause which reads as follows:
> "The Citizens of each State shall be entitled all the Privileges and Immunities of Citizens in the several States."

that it has been held to apply to the corporate defendant[44] notwithstanding the use of the masculine pronoun later in the text of the Amendment.[45]

2–21 The takings clause of the Fifth Amendment[46] is stated as a general prohibition on the federal government and companies have relied on it successfully.[47] The contracts clause in Art.I is another example of a general prohibition upon which companies may rely.[48] Furthermore, the First Amendment's statement that Congress shall make no law abridging freedom of expression has been held to protect the corporate speaker.[49]

2–22 The position under the United States Constitution raises a number of interesting points of comparison when exploring the position of the company under the Irish Constitution. The fact that the definition of the "citizen" in the United States Constitution refers to the citizen being "born or naturalized in the United States, and subject to the jurisdiction thereof"[50] has not precluded companies from relying on some provisions which apply to the "citizen" only. Also, the use of the word "citizen" or "person" is not always dispositive when considering the matter of corporate constitutional protection. A company may be considered a "person" or "citizen" for some purposes but not for others. This is so even in relation to different clauses of the same provision. As will be shown later in this book, the application or non-application of a given constitutional guarantee is often determined—or justified—by reliance on one or other theory of the corporation.[51]

METHODS OF INTERPRETING THE IRISH CONSTITUTION

2–23 A number of methods of, or approaches to, interpretation have been developed by judges in relation to the Irish Constitution. This section explores the potential impact of these methods of interpretation on the subject matter of this book. It should be noted that judges may rely on more than one interpretive approach within the same judgment. For example, the account below demonstrates how the judgment of Keane J. in *Iarnród Éireann v Ireland*[52]

---

[44] *Armour Packing Co. v United States* 209 U.S. 56 (1908).
[45] The full text of the Sixth Amendment reads as follows:
   "In all criminal prosecutions, the accused shall enjoy the right to a speedy and public trial, by an impartial jury of the State and district wherein the crime shall have been committed, which district shall have been previously ascertained by law, and to be informed of the nature and cause of the accusation; to be confronted with the witnesses against him; to have compulsory process for obtaining witnesses in his favor; and to have the Assistance of Counsel for his defence."
[46] "… nor shall private property be taken for public use, without just compensation".
[47] *Pennsylvania Coal Co. v Mahon* 260 U.S. 393 (1922).
[48] *Trustees of Dartmouth College v Woodward* 17 U.S. (4 Wheat.) 518 (1819).
[49] *First National Bank v Bellotti* 435 U.S. 765 at 778–779 (1978).
[50] Fourteenth Amendment. See full text of first paragraph, reproduced above at n.34.
[51] Below, see references at para.1–42, n.91–92.
[52] [1996] 3 I.R. 321; [1995] 2 I.L.R.M. 161. Note that the Supreme Court did not address the matter of whether the company enjoys constitutional rights.

incorporates a number of methods of interpretation in order to come to the conclusion that:

> "[T]he expression 'every citizen' is not confined in Article 40, s 3, sub-s 2, to citizens in their individual capacity as human persons and that artificial legal entities must also be protected by the laws of the State against unjust attacks on their property rights."[53]

2–24   In the following account of approaches to constitutional interpretation, it will be noted that three different approaches were utilised by Keane J. in reaching the above conclusion.

The literal approach

2–25   The Constitution contains a number of guarantees which refer to the "citizen",[54] as well as some[55] which contain additional indicia[56] that they are intended for the benefit of the individual rather than the company. As far as the distinction between the "citizen" and the "person" is concerned, it might be possible to construe the latter as including the legal person[57] and thus the company, but the former would surely be excluded. It may, however, be possible for individual citizens to assert their constitutional rights through the corporate form. Such an outcome would be based on an aggregate conception of the company and the potential consequences of this are considered in a later chapter.[58] For the moment, however, we shall confine ourselves to the question of the company itself directly claiming constitutional protection. Does the use of the term "citizen" exclude this possibility? It has been noted that a literal approach to constitutional interpretation,[59] while appropriate in the context of some of the more technical aspects of the document, is not suited to interpreting fundamental rights provisions.[60] In the latter context, a broader approach is to be preferred.

The historical approach

2–26   Another approach which has been utilised to interpret the Irish Constitution is the historical approach.[61] This approach has been used in

---

[53] [1996] 3 I.R. 321 at 346; [1995] 2 I.L.R.M. 161 at 184.
[54] See comments of Keane J. in *Iarnród Éireann v Ireland* [1996] 3 I.R. 321 at 346; [1995] 2 I.L.R.M. 161 at 184.
[55] Arts 40.1 and 40.5, considered below in Chaps 14 and 15 respectively.
[56] Namely the words "as human persons" in Art.40.1 and the reference to the "dwelling" in Art.40.5.
[57] See s.11(c) of the Interpretation Act 1937, reproduced above at n.19.
[58] Below, Chap.8.
[59] *The State (Browne) v Feran* [1967] I.R. 147; *DPP v O'Shea* [1982] I.R. 384.
[60] Hogan and Whyte, *op.cit.* at pp.4–5; see also Casey, *Constitutional Law in Ireland* (3rd edn, Round Hall, Sweet & Maxwell, 2000), at pp.377–378.
[61] *Article 26 and the Offences Against the State (Amendment) Bill, 1940, Re* [1940] I.R. 470, (1940) 74 I.L.T.R. 161; *O'Donovan v Att.-Gen.* [1961] I.R. 114, (1962) 96 I.L.T.R. 121; *Melling v Ó Mathghamhna* [1962] I.R. 1, (1962) 97 I.L.T.R. 60; *Conroy v Att.-*

relation to such "fundamental concepts" as the guarantee of free primary education in Art.42.4[62] and the definition of a minor offence under Art.38.2.[63] The historical approach supported a claim by a company to constitutional protection in *Iarnród Éireann v Ireland*,[64] where Keane J., in reaching the conclusion that a company was entitled to the protection of its property rights under Art.40.3.2, referred to the fact that:

> "The 'property' referred to clearly includes shares in companies formed under the relevant companies' legislation which was already a settled feature of the legal and commercial life of this country at the time of the enactment of the Constitution."[65]

2–27 As far as the rights of the "person" are concerned, the historical approach could lend support to a corporate claim to constitutional protection given that the Interpretation Act 1937, promlugated the same year as the Constitution itself, included companies within the definition of "person".[66]

2–28 It has been convincingly argued that the historical approach is better suited to interpreting those parts of the Constitution that are concerned with the institutions and procedures of government and that a present tense approach ought to be taken in relation to constitutional rights.[67] It has thus been stated that:

> "[M]any fundamental concepts—trial in due course of law, equality before the law, personal liberty, property rights—were left deliberately vague and imprecise. One can only assume that the drafters intended that the ambit of these clauses would become clearer in the light of experience as they were applied to novel and ever-changing facts and circumstances."[68]

The harmonious approach

2–29 The doctrine of harmonious interpretation reflects the idea that:

Gen. [1965] I.R. 411; *McMahon v Att.-Gen.* [1972] I.R. 69; *Att.-Gen. v Hamilton (No.1)* [1993] 2 I.R. 250, [1993] I.L.R.M. 81; *Att.-Gen. v Hamilton (No.2)* [1993] 3 I.R. 227, [1993] I.L.R.M. 821; *Campaign to Separate Church and State Ltd v Minister for Education* [1998] 3 I.R. 321; *Sinnott v Minister for Education* [2001] 2 I.R. 505; *Maguire v Ardagh* [2002] 1 I.R. 385.

[62] See the judgment of Murphy J. in the Supreme Court in *Sinnott v Minister for Education* [2001] 2 I.R. 505.

[63] *Melling v Ó Mathghammhna* [1962] I.R. 1, (1962) 96 I.L.T.R. 29.

[64] [1996] 3 I.R. 321, [1995] 2 I.L.R.M. 161.

[65] [1996] 3 I.R. 321 at 345, [1995] 2 I.L.R.M. 161 at 183.

[66] See s.11(c) of the Interpretation Act 1937, reproduced above at n.19.

[67] Kelly, "The Constitution: Law and Manifesto" in *The Constitution of Ireland 1937–1987* (Litton ed., Institute of Public Administration, 1988), at p.215.

[68] Hogan and Whyte, *op.cit.* at p.24.

"[C]onstitutional provisions should not be construed in isolation from all the other parts of the Constitution among which they are embedded, but should be so construed as to harmonise with the other parts. This doctrine is no more than a presumption that the people who enacted the Constitution had a single scale of values, and wished those values to permeate their charter evenly and without internal discordance."[69]

2–30   One possible application of this doctrine to the question of corporate constitutional rights would be to contrast the textual differences outlined above. This might result in the conclusion that those provisions which refer to the "person" are applicable to the company, while references to the "citizen" are intended to exclude it. Such an approach would come close, however, to the literalism that has been criticised in the context of fundamental rights.[70]

2–31   In any case, the use of the harmonious approach in *Iarnród Éireann v Ireland* assisted a company claiming constitutional protection. Here, Keane J. contrasted the wording of Art.40.1 with that of Art.40.3:

"Article 43 undoubtedly treats the general right of private property, the abolition of which in its entirety is expressly prohibited, as one inhering in 'man in virtue of his rational being' and, in that sense, as being 'antecedent to positive law', including the Constitution itself. But it does not necessarily follow that the property rights of the individual citizens which are protected against 'unjust attack' by Article 40.3 are confined to rights enjoyed by human persons. Had the framers of the Constitution wished to confine the comprehensive guarantee in Article 40.3 in that manner, there was nothing to prevent them including a similar qualification to that contained in Article 40.1."[71]

The broad approach

2–32   Avoiding "excessive literalism",[72] this approach avoids the application of rules of statutory interpretation, such as *expressio unius exclusio alterius*, which could restrict its scope considerably. It has been phrased as follows:

"The Constitution is a political instrument as well as a legal document and in its interpretation the courts should not place the same significance on differences of language used in two succeeding sub-paragraphs as would, for example, be placed on differently drafted subsections of a Finance Act. A purposive, rather than a strictly literal approach to the interpretation of the sub-paragraphs is appropriate."[73]

---

[69] Hogan and Whyte, *op.cit.* at p.8.
[70] Above, n.60 and accompanying text.
[71] [1996] 3 I.R. 321 at 345, [1995] 2 I.L.R.M. 161 at 183.
[72] Hogan and Whyte, *op.cit.* at p.5.
[73] Costello J. in *Att.-Gen. v Paperlink Ltd* [1984] I.L.R.M. 373 at 385. In that particular case, it was held, *obiter*, that an unenumerated right to communicate did not apply to the

2–33 The broad approach to constitutional interpretation has been taken in a number of cases[74] and its application in the context of this book might mean that the references to the "citizen" would not necessarily exclude the company from relevant constitutional guarantees.

2–34 Using this approach, the availability of constitutional guarantees to a company would depend on whether that would marry well with the Constitution's "purpose and objective in protecting human rights".[75] That analysis would look to the purpose of any constitutional provision before determining its scope and would eschew formalistic parsing of the text.[76] Again, traces of this approach can be identified in the judgment of Keane J. in *Iarnród Éireann v Ireland* where he held that there would be:

> "[A] spectacular deficiency in the guarantee to every citizen that his or her property rights will be protected against 'unjust attack' if such bodies were incapable in law of being regarded as 'citizens', at least for the purposes of [Art.40.3]."[77]

CONCLUSION

2–35 This chapter has considered whether the text of the Irish Constitution indicates that companies are intended to benefit from its provisions. It appears that no definite answer can be given to this question. It has been noted that under the United States Constitution, the wording of guarantees has not been dispositive of corporate constitutional protection. As far as methods of interpretation are concerned, it has been noted that the historical, harmonious and broad methods of interpretation have all been relied upon to extend constitutional protection to the company. The literal approach is arguably unsuited to constitutional interpretation but if used, would presumably result in a denial of constitutional protection to the company, at least in relation to those guarantees expressed to be for the benefit of citizens. The remaining interpretive method is the natural law approach. This method, which is considered in detail in the next chapter, might be thought to exclude companies from the ambit of the Irish Constitution. The next chapter argues that this is not necessarily the case.

---

company. See Chap.9, nn 152 and 153 and accompanying text. The passage quoted has been subsequently approved in *Riordan v An Tánaiste* [1995] 3 I.R. 62 at 82, [1996] 2 I.L.R.M. 107 at 125; *Sinnott v Minister for Education* [2001] 2 I.R. 505 at 688.

[74] *NUR v Sullivan* [1947] I.R. 77, (1947) 81 I.L.T.R. 55; *Sullivan v Robinson* [1954] I.R. 151, (1954) 88 I.L.T.R. 169; *Melling v Ó Mathghamhna* [1962] I.R. 1, (1962) 97 I.L.T.R. 60; *Murray v Ireland* [1985] I.R. 532, [1985] I.L.R.M. 542; *Riordan v An Tánaiste* [1995] 3 I.R. 62, [1996] 2 I.L.R.M. 107; *Sinnott v Minister for Education* [2001] 2 I.R. 505.

[75] *Murray v Ireland* [1985] I.R. 532 at 539; [1985] I.L.R.M. 542 at 548.

[76] *Att.-Gen. v Paperlink Ltd* [1984] I.L.R.M. 348.

[77] [1996] 3 I.R. 321 at 345; [1995] 2 I.L.R.M. 161 at 183.

2–36   This chapter has engaged with the text of the Constitution in order to assess the position of companies thereunder. This is not, of course, a mere act of neutral interpretation. The text being ambivalent, the inclusion of a company within the definition of "person" or "citizen" implies a view that such entities are appropriate rights bearers under the Constitution. The determination of who "counts" as a constitutional subject reveals much about the values underlying the Constitution[78] and we shall see in later chapters that the question "Can the company invoke guarantee X under the Constitution?" is, in fact, another way of asking "What values underlie guarantee X?" The correlation of these two questions will be explained further in the next chapter.

---

[78] *e.g.* see some of the literature relating to the abortion controversy under the US Constitution: McHugh, "What is the Difference Between a 'Person' and a 'Human Being' within the Law" (1992) Rev.Pol. 445; Aljalian, "Fourteenth Amendment Personhood: Fact or Fiction?" (1999) 73 St John's L.Rev. 495. For interesting post-modern analysis of the problematic nature of constitutional personhood, see Rosenfeld, "The Identity of the Constitutional Subject" (1995) 16 Cardozo L.Rev. 1049 and Ohlin, "Is the Concept of the Person Necessary for Human Rights?" (2005) 105 Colum.L.Rev. 209 at 226–228.

CHAPTER 3

CONSTRUCTING THE CONSTITUTIONAL SUBJECT II: PHILOSOPHICAL ANALYSIS

INTRODUCTION

3–01   This chapter considers whether the extension of constitutional protection to companies is compatible with the philosophical underpinnings of the Irish Constitution as a whole and proposes a methodology for resolving cases where companies claim constitutional protection. Paragraphs 3–03 to 3–14 explain briefly what is meant by the natural law method of constitutional interpretation. It might be thought that the natural law basis of some constitutional guarantees presents an obstacle to the company attempting to rely on the Constitution. Paragraphs 3–15 to 3–23 will argue that this is not the case for two reasons. It is noted that the identification of the legal subject is an event which highlights the clash between the natural law influences on the Irish Constitution—and modern human rights scholarship in general—and the positivism inherent in constructing legal personality in general—and the constitutional subject in particular. As all constitutional subjects are constructed, the allocation of constitutional protection to a company is not inconsistent with the Constitution *per se*. This is simply a problem within legal theory which cannot be circumvented even in the case of human beings.

3–02   Paragraphs 3–24 to 3–35 will argue that it is possible that at least some constitutional rights have a dual rationale. To the extent that they are concerned with the protection of certain interests that inhere only in human beings, they will be described as being based on autonomy. Such rights are stronger than those whose basis lies in their instrumentality—these rights will be described as being based on utility. While rights based on autonomy are not absolute, they are nonetheless stronger than utility rights, so that the strength of a company's protection may be weaker than that of an individual relying on the same constitutional guarantee. The former type of right can be usefully described as a "natural right"—one which "advanc[es] values which are good in themselves, rather than being justified by reference to consequentialist arguments".[1] This is not to say that such rights are "trumps" of the kind envisaged by Dworkin.[2] The Irish Constitution makes it clear that rights are

---

[1]   Feldman, *Civil Liberties and Human Rights in England and Wales* (2nd edn, Oxford University Press, 2002), at p.24.

[2]   Dworkin, *Taking Rights Seriously* (Duckworth, 1978), at p.ix.

qualified by some communitarian values, it being left to the Oireachtas and ultimately the Supreme Court to fully work out the appropriate balance in specific cases.[3]

NATURAL LAW AND THE INTERPRETATION OF THE IRISH CONSTITUTION

3–03 The influence of natural law on both the drafting and the early interpretation of the Irish Constitution has been well documented.[4] The natural law approach to constitutional interpretation describes two related features of the jurisprudence. Generally, it describes the approach taken by some judges which relies on sources external to the Constitution to assist in its interpretation. One matter of controversy has been the extent to which such sources may be superior to the Constitution.[5] It appears that this matter is now settled and the Supreme Court has indicated that the Constitution itself is the highest source of law in the State.[6]

---

[3] To the extent that it recognises this balancing act as an appropriate one in the context of rights, Finnis's theory of natural law and natural rights seems more appropriate to the Irish constitutional context. See Finnis, *Natural Law and Natural Rights* (Oxford: Clarendon Press, 1980), at p.218. Note that he expressly avoids the question of corporate personality, p.153. For an application of Finnis's theory of rights to the Irish Constitution, see de Blacam, "Justice and Natural Law" (1997) 32 Ir. Jur. (New Series) 335 at 329–330.

[4] See Hogan and Whyte, *Kelly: The Irish Constitution* (4th edn, Lexis-Nexis Butterworths, 2003), at pp.374–376.

[5] Prior to the 1937 Constitution, the Irish Supreme Court had held that natural law played no role under the 1922 Constitution in *The State (Ryan) v Lennon* [1935] I.R. 170, (1935) 69 I.L.T.R. 125. Kennedy C.J. had dissented, stating that legislation "repugnant to the Natural Law ... would be necessarily unconstitutional and invalid, and it would be, therefore, absolutely null and void and inoperative". Writing prior to his judicial appointment, Henchy J. noted in 1962 that:

> "From the point of view of jurisprudence, the most striking change effected by the present Constitution is the break with the positivist character of the common law which had been developed in comparatively modern times ... The Irish Constitution rejects such a basis for law. Its Preamble makes clear that the Constitution and the laws which owe their force to the Constitution derive, under God, from the people and are directed to the promotion of the common good. If a judicial decision rejects the divine law or has not as its object the common good, it has not the character of law. This idea is no strange addition to the common law; it is as old as Coke Henchy,
> 'Precedent in the Irish Supreme Court' (1962) 25 Modern Law Review 544, at 577."

Following a number of constitutional amendments concerning the right to life of the unborn, a potential constitutional crisis was identified in the academic literature. A High Court judge, writing extra-curially, argued that the power to amend the Constitution, under Art.46 thereof, was limited to those amendments compatible with natural law, O'Hanlon, "Natural Rights and the Irish Constitution" (1993) 11 I.L.T. 8. That argument provoked a debate: Murphy, "Democracy, Natural Law and the Irish Constitution" (1993) I.L.T. 81; O'Hanlon, "The Judiciary and the Moral Law" (1993) I.L.T. 129; Clarke, "The Constitution and Natural Law: A Reply to Mr. Justice O'Hanlon" (1993) I.L.T. 177. See also Duncan, "Emergency Legislation, Fundamental Rights and Article 28.3.3 of the Irish Constitution" (1977) Ir. Jur. (New Series) 217.

[6] *Article 26 and the Regulation of Information (Services Outside the State for the Termination of Pregnancies) Bill 1995, Re* [1995] 1 I.R. 1; [1995] 2 I.L.R.M. 81. In that case, it was argued that the Fourteenth Amendment to the Constitution was itself invalid

3–04   The other related way in which natural law has featured, and the one most relevant to this book, is in the enumeration of personal rights under Art.40.3.1. It has been noted that the 1937 Constitution:

> "not only recognized God as the source of all lawful authority, but stated several fundamental personal rights in terms which clearly acknowledged their source in the law of nature".[7]

3–05   It was in the seminal unenumerated rights case, *Ryan v Att.-Gen.*,[8] that the natural law basis of the 1937 Constitution was confirmed. In this case,[9] the plaintiff challenged legislation which provided for the fluoridation of water. In so doing, she relied on a putative "right of bodily integrity". Kenny J. held that that right, while not specifically mentioned in the Constitution, was contemplated by Art.40.3.1. He held that:

> "There are many personal rights of the citizen which follow from the Christian and democratic nature of the State which are not mentioned in Article 40 at all—the right to free movement within the State and the right to marry are examples of this … The conclusion, that there is a right of bodily integrity, gets support from the passage in the Encyclical Letter 'Peace on Earth': 'Beginning our discussion of the rights of man, we see that every man has the right to life, to bodily integrity and to the means which are necessary and suitable for the proper development of life; these are primarily food, clothing, shelter, rest, medical care, and finally the necessary social services'."[10]

3–06   In *The State (Nicalaou) v An Bord Uchtála*,[11] the Supreme Court hinted that natural rights would be enforced under the Constitution[12] and in *McGee v*

---

for being contrary to natural law. The Supreme Court rejected this argument. First, Hamilton C.J. emphasised that the State and all its organs were subject to the Constitution and the law. As has been pointed out in Hogan and Whyte, *op.cit.* at p.1257, it appears that the reference to the Constitution was intended as a reference to positive law alone, an interpretation which appears to clash somewhat with the natural law influence which can be discerned in a number of constitutional provisions.

[7] Hogan and Whyte, *op.cit.* Examples include the reference to the family in Art.41, which states that it constitutes "the natural primary and fundamental unit group of Society, and a moral institution possessing inalienable and imprescriptable rights, antecedent and superior to all positive law". The family is also referred to in Art.42 where it is described as the "primary and natural educator of the child" and respect for the "inalienable right and duty of parents" to educate their children is guaranteed. Art.43 states that "man, in virtue of his rational being, has the natural right, antecedent to positive law, to the private ownership of external goods".

[8] [1965] I.R. 294.

[9] *ibid.* See Hogan, "Unenumerated Personal Rights: Ryan's Case Re-Evaluated" (1990–1992) 25–27 Ir. Jur. (New Series) 95.

[10] [1965] I.R. 294 at 312. See discussion of this case in Hogan and Whyte, *op.cit.* at pp.1251–1252.

[11] [1966] I.R. 567; (1968) 102 I.L.T.R. 1.

[12] The applicant in that case relied on the "natural right" of the father of an illegitimate child to have a say in the child's upbringing. Walsh J. held that he was not convinced that such a right existed under natural law, thereby hinting that had he been so convinced,

Att.-Gen.,[13] Walsh J. confirmed that was the case. *McGee* concerned a challenge to legislation which penalised the importation of contraceptives. The plaintiff argued that this infringed her personal right of privacy within her marriage. The court held in her favour, Walsh J. stating that:

> "Articles 41, 42 and 43 emphatically reject the theory that there are no rights without laws, no rights contrary to the law and no rights anterior to the law. They indicate that justice is placed above the law and acknowledge that natural rights, or human rights, are not created by law but that the Constitution confirms their existence and gives them protection ...
>
> In this country it falls finally upon the judges to interpret the Constitution and in so doing to determine, where necessary, the rights which are superior or antecedent to positive law ... The very structure and content of the Articles dealing with fundamental rights clearly indicates that justice is not subordinate to the law. In particular, the terms of Article 40.3 expressly subordinate the law to justice."[14]

3–07   Natural rights arose again in the case of *Healy v Donoghue*,[15] where the meaning of a "trial in due course of law" guaranteed by Art.38.1 was at issue. Gannon J. referred to the "natural rights" of an accused person and stated that:

> "The sense of justice is so fundamental in human nature and from it derive essential rights which do not require any positive law for their enunciation".[16]

3–08   He referred to a list of rights which came under the concept of a trial in due course of law and stated that: "In my view, they are rights which are anterior to and do not merely derive from the Constitution."[17]

3–09   In *Article 26 and the Regulation of Information (Services Outside the State for the Termination of Pregnancies) Bill 1995, Re*,[18] the Supreme Court rejected the argument that the Constitution could not be amended in a way contrary to natural law and thus affirmed the superior status of the document.[19] It went on to consider the cases in which unenumerated rights had been identified and insisted that:

---

such a right would have been guaranteed under Art.40.3.1. See Hogan and Whyte, *op.cit.* at p.1252.

[13] [1974] I.R. 284; (1975) 109 I.L.T.R. 29.

[14] [1974] I.R. 284 at 318; (1975) 109 I.L.T.R. 29 at 41. See Walsh, "Existence and Meaning of Fundamental Rights in Ireland" (1980) 1 HRLJ 171.

[15] [1976] I.R. 325; (1976) 110 I.L.T.R. 9.

[16] [1976] I.R. 325 at 335; (1976) 110 I.L.T.R. 9 at 13.

[17] *ibid.* See also *O'Flynn v Clifford* [1988] I.R. 740 and *Murray v Ireland* [1991] I.L.R.M. 465; *Murphy v PMPA Insurance Co.* [1978] I.L.R.M. 25; *Northants Co. Council v ABF* [1982] I.L.R.M. 164.

[18] [1995] 1 I.R. 1; [1995] 2 I.L.R.M. 81.

[19] See n.6 above.

"It is manifest that the Court in each case had satisfied itself that such personal right was one which could reasonably be implied from and was guaranteed by the provisions of the Constitution, interpreted in accordance with the ideas of prudence, justice and charity.

The courts, as they were and are bound to do, recognised the Constitution as the fundamental law of the State to which the organs of the State were subject and at no stage recognised the provision of natural law as superior to the Constitution."[20]

3–10 The court went on to hold that the Constitution was properly amended by the use of Art.46 and that, as amended, it constituted "the fundamental and supreme law of the State representing as it does the will of the people".[21]

3–11 While the decision establishes that natural law cannot be relied upon to challenge the validity of any amendment to the Irish Constitution, it seems that some role for natural law was envisaged. In relation to the identification of unenumerated rights, the court held that:

"In determining, where necessary, the rights which are superior or antecedent to positive law or which are imprescriptible or inalienable, [the courts] must act in accordance with the aforesaid guidelines as laid down in the Constitution and must interpret them in accordance with their ideas of prudence, justice and charity."[22]

3–12 This quote indicates that some role for natural rights remains. Its precise nature, however, is unclear. In *WO'R v EH*,[23] a case was stated to the Supreme Court concerning, *inter alia*, the nature of the rights of the natural father in respect of his children. The majority took the view that such rights were not constitutional in nature. Barrington J., however, took a different view. He held that the natural father had rights and duties which could be referred to as natural or constitutional rights and duties and further, that in the context of Arts 41 and 42, these two descriptions were interchangeable. Murphy J., on the other hand, held that natural fathers had no constitutional rights in respect of their children and went on to state:

"What are described as 'natural rights' whether arising from the circumstances of mankind in a primitive but idyllic society postulated by some philosophers but unidentified by any archaeologist, or inferred by moral philosophers as the rules by which human beings may achieve the destiny for which they were created, are not recognised or enforced as such by the courts set up under the Constitution. The natural rights aforesaid may be invoked only insofar as they are expressly or implicitly

---

[20] [1995] 1 I.R. 1 at 43, [1995] 2 I.L.R.M. 81 at 107. See Whyte, "Natural Law and the Constitution" (1996) 14 I.L.T. 8.
[21] [1995] 1 I.R. 1 at 43, [1995] 2 I.L.R.M. 81 at 107.
[22] *ibid*. See de Blacam, *op.cit.* at 335–352.
[23] [1996] 2 I.R. 248.

recognised by the Constitution; comprised in the common law; superimposed onto common law principles by the moral intervention of the successive Lord Chancellors creating the equity jurisdiction of the courts, or expressly conferred by any Act of the Oireachtas, or other positive human law made under or taken over by, and not inconsistent with, the Constitution."[24]

3–13   The complete relegation of natural law in the context of the fundamental rights provisions of the Constitution seems unlikely to be universally endorsed by the judiciary. In *W v Ireland (No.2)*,[25] Costello J. referred to "fundamental rights which the Constitution recognises that man has by virtue of his rational being antecedent to positive law"[26] and references to natural law are still made in this context.[27] In any case, there appear to be indications in the text itself that envisage some role for natural law, whether that be of a secular or Catholic social flavour.[28]

3–014   Where natural law does play a role, it might be thought that only human beings are entitled to the benefit of constitutional guarantees. Thus, in *Iarnród Éireann v Ireland*,[29] Keane J. parsed the constitutional provisions relating to property as follows:

> "Article 43 undoubtedly treats the general right of private property, the abolition of which in its entirety is expressly prohibited, as one inhering in 'man in virtue of his rational being' and, in that sense, as being 'antecedent to positive law', including the Constitution itself. But it does not necessarily follow that the property rights of the individual citizens which are protected against 'unjust attack' by Article 40.3 are confined to rights enjoyed by human persons. Had the framers of the Constitution wished to confine the comprehensive guarantee in Article 40.3 in that manner, there was nothing to prevent them including a similar qualification to that contained in Article 40.1."[30]

3–15   This part of his judgment can be read as dividing the constitutional provisions relating to property into those with a natural law basis—Arts 43 and 40.1—and those without that basis—Art.40.3—so that the latter, but not the former, are applicable to the company.[31] Paragraphs 3–24 to 3–35 of this chapter will propose an alternative approach to constitutional interpretation in

---

[24] *ibid.* at 294.

[25] [1997] 2 I.R. 141.

[26] *ibid.* at 164.

[27] *DPP v Best* [2000] 2 I.R. 17, [2000] 2 I.L.R.M. 1; *In the Matter of Article 26 of The Constitution & In the Matter of the Health (Amendment) (No.2) Bill 2004* [2005] I.E.S.C. 7.

[28] See Arts 41, 42 and 43. See Whyte, *op.cit.* at 11.

[29] [1996] 3 I.R. 321, [1995] 2 I.L.R.M. 161.

[30] [1996] 3 I.R. 321 at 345, [1995] 2 I.L.R.M. 161 at 183.

[31] On the current approach to the interaction between the property guarantees in Arts 43 and 40.3, see Chap.8 below.

this context, one which explores the possibility of a dual rationale for at least some constitutional guarantees.

LEGAL PERSONALITY AND POSITIVISM—THE CONTINGENCY OF CONSTITUTIONAL PERSONHOOD

3–16 It has been stated that "[t]he human being is the paradigmatic subject of rights."[32] The identification of any human being as a beneficiary of a right can be seen as a contingent, rather than an automatic, choice. From a positivist perspective, anything can become a legal person:

> "Everything, therefore, that the community chooses to regard as such can become a subject—a potential center—of rights, whether a plant or an animal, a human being or an imagined spirit; and nothing, if the community does not choose to regard it so, will become a subject of rights, whether human being or anything else. There is nothing in the notion of the subject of rights which in itself would, necessarily, connect it with human personality, or even with anything experimentally existing. The only circumstance which makes a subject of rights of something is the fact that it is looked upon by the community as a unit having interests which need and deserve social protection; and it is entirely immaterial whether such an entity really exists as an objective reality or not, whether it has a will or not—or still less, whether or not it possesses a personality, natural or artificial, imagined or proved ... Those theories, therefore, which assert that the human being or the human personality is in some way a natural substratum of rights cannot be substantiated by empirical evidence. If none the less they are accepted and believed in, this acceptance can be based only on emotional conviction."[33]

3–17 It has thus been noted that:

> "From a positivist perspective, the designation of any party as a 'person' in law is not indicative of the moral or other capacity of that party. The crucial question for law is not which metaphysical properties are required to count as a person but rather whether certain rights and duties should be ascribed within a given set of legal relations."[34]

3–18 Under ancient law, the family was considered the holder of rights and in the Middle Ages, it was often the collectivity.[35] While methodological

---

[32] Ducor, "The Legal Status of Human Materials" (1996) Drake L.Rev. 195 at 200.

[33] Nekam, *Personality Conception of the Legal Entity: Harvard Studies in the Conflict of Laws III*, (Harvard University Press, 1938), at 26-27.

[34] Naffine, "Who are law's persons? From Cheshire cats to responsible subjects" (2003) 65 M.L.R. 346 at 354. See also Colson, "Corporate Personality" (1935) 24 Geo.L.J. 638, at 641–642.

[35] Nekam, *op.cit.* at 22–23; Donaldson, *Corporations and Morality* (Prentice-Hall Inc, New Jersey, 1982), at pp.3–4.

individualism[36] has held sway ever since, even after the Middle Ages, only certain individuals were legal persons. For example, slaves were not legal persons.[37] Married women in this jurisdiction did not enjoy full legal personality up until relatively recently.[38] Convicts[39] and infants[40] and the insane[41] are not accorded full legal personality and the dead and the unborn are traditionally not considered legal persons.[42] From a positivist perspective, the designation of human beings as legal persons depends only on their social importance and may vary as perceptions of this vary:

> "It is only an episode in history, one would almost say a coincidence, that the legal importance of every individual should in our society so generally be acknowledged and so uniformly be ensured. It has been different in the past and with changes in the social evaluation it may be different again."[43]

3–19   Of course, the natural law influences on the Constitution, it might be argued, mean that only natural persons should be able to rely on its guarantees. A corollary of this seems to be that the rights enshrined in the Constitution should be available to all natural persons. Thus, in *Finn v Att.-Gen.*,[44] Barrington J. considered whether the provisions of Arts 40–44 could protect persons other than citizens. He held that:

> "It is arguable that these rights derive not from a man's citizenship but from his nature as a human being. The State does not create these rights, it recognises them and promises to protect them. The French Declaration of Rights, 1789, is entitled 'Declaration of the Rights of Man and the Citizen'. Sometimes the citizen is referred to in the text, but Article 1 opens with the statement 'Men are born and remain free and equal …' A similar switching of gear can be seen in Articles 40–44 of the Constitution. Articles 41, 42 and 43 recognise that man has certain rights which are antecedent and superior to positive law. By doing so, the Constitution accepts that these rights derive not from the law but from the nature of man and society, and guarantees to protect them accordingly … The fact that the wording of Article 40.3 commits the State to protect and vindicate

---

[36] See para.1–24.
[37] Note "What we mean when we talk about persons: The language of a legal fiction" (2001) 114 Harv.L.Rev. 1745 at 1747–1750.
[38] Compare the Married Women's Property Act 1882 with the Married Women's Status Act 1957.
[39] The Forfeiture Act 1870 imposes a number of restrictions on convicts, particularly in relation to their property rights.
[40] A person does not enjoy full legal capacity until he or she reaches the age of majority— Age of Majority Act 1985.
[41] Lunacy Regulation (Ireland) Act 1871.
[42] Thus, it was felt that it was necessary to add Art.40.3.3 to the Constitution to safeguard the right to life of the unborn.
[43] Nekam, *op.cit.* at 116–117.
[44] [1983] I.R. 154.

the life of 'every citizen' does not justify the inference that it relieves the State of the obligation to defend and vindicate the lives of persons who are not citizens. This is because the whole scheme of moral and political values which are clearly accepted by the Constitution indicates otherwise."[45]

3–20   Interestingly, in *Shirley v O'Gorman & Co Ltd*,[46] the availability of rights to non-citizens—which in *Finn* appears to be based on the common humanity of man—was relied upon to justify extending constitutional protection to a non-resident corporation.[47]

3–21   The idea that all human beings are constitutional subjects has an attractive simplicity to it. Proponents of a natural law approach to rights often invoke unpalatable results as the potential pitfall of legal postivism.[48] However, the claim that basing rights in natural law is preferable is one which often seems based in consequentialism.[49]

3–22   Whatever the resolution of the positivist/natural law debate, it cannot be denied that at the point where a constitution is interpreted, positivism is unavoidable. This is because whatever its philosophical rationale, a putative constitutional right is recognised in law only at the point at which it is positively adjudicated on. Take, for example, the abortion controversy. In *Roe v Wade*,[50] the United States Supreme Court held that the foetus was not a "person" under the Fourteenth Amendment. If the court had decided that question the other way around, the right to life of the unborn, while perhaps ultimately emanating from some natural law concept of personhood, would be recognised in that legal system by virtue of the positive declaration of law. Concern that the Irish Constitution might be interpreted in a similar manner in relation to the unborn[51] led to the amendment of the Constitution by the addition of Art.40.3.3, which specifically acknowledges the right to life of the unborn.

---

[45] *ibid.* at 159.

[46] [2006] I.E.H.C. 27.

[47] Peart J. relied on the decision in *Article 26 and ss 5 and 10 of the Illegal Immigrants (Trafficking) Bill 1999, Re* [2002] 2 I.R. 360.

[48] *e.g.* Finnis refers to *Scott v Sandford* 60 U.S. 398 (1856) to support an argument in favour of natural rights for human beings. Finnis, "The Priority of Persons", in *Oxford Essays in Jurisprudence* (Horder ed., 4th Series, Oxford University Press, 1999), at pp.7–8.

[49] Is Finnis anti-positivist because he is anti *Roe v Wade* 410 U.S. 113 (1973)? The Irish experience with natural law has indicated a degree of unpredictability in relation to natural law which suggests that its use to further a conservative social agenda may not be successful. For example, in *McGee v Att.-Gen.* [1974] I.R. 284, (1975) 109 I.L.T.R. 29, a papal encyclical was relied upon in support of a right to marital privacy including the use of contraception.

[50] 410 U.S. 113 (1973). For an interesting comparison between the status of the foetus with that of the company under the US Constitution, see Aljalian, "Fourteenth Amendment Personhood: Fact or Fiction?" (1999) 73 St John's L.Rev. 495.

[51] See Hogan and Whyte, *op.cit.* at pp.1496–1498.

3–23 In a similar vein, the recent constitutional amendment in relation to citizenship[52] indicates that positive law in the form of the constitutional text cannot be discounted. What is morally or philosophically undesirable may be nevertheless politically and legally possible.[53] The point of this excursus is simply to highlight the fact that, even where natural law is used as a guide to constitutional interpretation, it is impossible to avoid the task of constructing the constitutional subject. This is inevitably an exercise in positive law and claims to the contrary overestimate the possibilities of natural law within the legal system. In any case, if natural law is seen as the basis for human beings' status as constitutional subjects, that does not necessarily mean that no non-human beings can claim constitutional protection. It might be the case, however, that the protection of the former is based on different considerations than that of the latter. This possibility is explored further in the next section.

THE PHILOSOPHICAL UNDERPINNINGS OF MODERN RIGHTS THEORY—THE CO-EXISTENCE OF UTILITY AND AUTONOMY

3–24 The reliance by the Irish judiciary on natural law is in tune with the general trend of Western jurisprudence in the latter half of the twentieth century.[54] While the specific references to Catholic social teaching give the Irish jurisprudence a particular theological flavour, the emphasis on the dignity and autonomy of the human person in rights jurisprudence is not peculiar to Ireland. The eschewing of positivism and utilitarianism and the development of a human rights culture in the wake of the Second World War occurred in a variety of Western legal systems:

> "In the post-World War II period, the various streams of ideas about rights that had been agitating Western minds for over 200 years coalesced into a universal language of rights … The United States Supreme Court, which had retrenched from its strong defense of economic liberties in the 1930s, began in the 1950s to expand the constitutional protection of a broad range of personal rights—freedom of expression, equal protection of the laws, and various rights of criminal defendants. Meanwhile, all Europe was reexamining fundamental legal ideas in the light of the experience with National Socialism. Legal positivism, the notion that one's rights are no more or no less than what the law says they are, now seemed untenable … The idea of prepolitical 'human' rights thus came to have wide appeal, although there was no consensus on any secular foundation for such rights or on their precise content."[55]

---

[52] The amendment is explained above at para.2–14.

[53] *e.g.* consider the position of slavery under the US Constitution.

[54] Glendon, *Rights Talk: The Impoverishment of Political Discourse* (The Free Press, 1991), at pp.38–40; Kelly, *A Short History of Western Legal Theory* (Clarendon Press, 1992), at pp.395–399 and 418–430.

[55] Glendon, *op.cit.* at p.38. See also Kelly, *op.cit.* at p.395. This trend is reflected also in international law. The opening statement of the Universal Declaration of Human Rights reflects this in its:

3–25   Together with this development came the tendency to entrench such rights by listing them and providing for tribunals with powers of review[56] to examine the compatibility of executive and legislative activity with them.[57] As Hart pointed out:

> "The new faith is that the truth must lie not with a doctrine that takes the maximization of aggregate or average general welfare for its goals, but with a doctrine of basic human rights, protecting specific basic liberties and interests of individuals, if only we could find some sufficiently firm foundation for such rights to meet some long familiar objections."[58]

3–26   Such an approach is in direct contradiction to positivist analytical jurisprudence which sees legal personality as something created by positive law alone:

> "That man and person are two entirely different concepts may be regarded as a generally accepted result of analytical jurisprudence ... The physical (moral) person is the personification of a set of legal norms which by constituting duties and rights containing the conduct of one and the same human being regulate the conduct of this being. The relation between the so-called physical (natural) person and the human being with whom the former is often erroneously identified consists in the fact that those duties and rights which are comprehended in the concept of the person all refer to the behaviour of that human being."[59]

3–27   The idea that certain rights are fundamental to, and enjoyed by, human beings simply by virtue of their human personality is one which has prevailed in twentieth and twenty-first century jurisprudence.[60] Theorising about justice and equality and the role of rights in that context thus focuses on the individual and the tendency in modern jurisprudence is to ignore the group.[61]

"recognition of the inherent dignity and of the equal and inalienable rights of all members of the human family in the foundation of freedom, justice and peace" and Art.1 of the Declaration states: "All humans beings are born free and equal and in dignity."

[56] The idea of judicial review is itself an ancient concept. It can be traced back as far as the writings of the Physiocrats in the 1760s and was first exercised in the US Supreme Court case of *Marbury v Madison* (1803) 1 Cranch 137. Kelly, *op.cit.* at pp.277–278.

[57] Glendon, *op.cit.* at p.38.

[58] Hart, "Between Utility and Rights" (1979) 79 Colum.L.Rev. 828; reprinted in Hart, *Essays in Jurisprudence and Philosophy* (Clarendon Press, 1983), at p.198.

[59] Kelsen, *General Theory of Law and State* (Harvard University Press, 1949).

[60] *e.g.* see Rawls, "A Theory of Justice" (Clarendon Press, 1972; rev. edn, Oxford University Press, 1999); Dworkin, *op.cit.*

[61] Rawls, for example, refers to human beings and "nations, provinces, business firms, churches, teams, and so on" but goes on to state:
> "There is, perhaps, a certain logical priority to the case of human individuals: it may be possible to analyze the actions of so-called artificial persons as logical constructions of the actions of human persons ..."
Rawls, "Justice as Reciprocity" in *John Stuart Mill, Utilitarianism* (Gorovitz, ed., Indianapolis: Bobbs-Merrill, 1971), at pp.244–245, discussed in French, "The Corporation

3–28   From this perspective, which can be conveniently referred to as Kantian, human beings are ends in themselves and must thus be treated with respect. Rights are protected to the extent that their vindication is bound up with the autonomy of the rights holder.[62] As companies are "unfit objects of the moral concern"[63] underlying an autonomy-based explanation of rights, they are excluded from protection if this approach is taken.

3–29   The approach just described can be contrasted with a utilitarian theory of rights. From this perspective, rights are protected only insofar as their protection contributes to the general welfare. Such an approach is unconcerned with the metaphysical and moral status of the rights-bearer. As Hart has put it:

> "In the perspective of classical maximizing utilitarianism separate individuals are of no intrinsic importance but only important as the points at which fragments of what *is* important, *i.e.*, the total aggregate of pleasure or happiness, are located. Individual persons for it are therefore merely the channels or locations where what is of value is to be found."[64]

3–30   Applying such an approach to the company does not raise the same objections encountered in respect of individuals. To the extent that recognising and upholding a company's constitutional rights furthered the common good, there would be no philosophical objection to doing just that *on that basis.*

3–31   When constructing an overarching theory of rights, the main criticism levelled at autonomy/rights based theories of justice is that they fail to adequately account for the existence of rights.[65] Utilitarianism, on the other hand, is unpalatable to many modern theorists because it ignores the Kantian insight that human beings should be valued as ends in themselves and not instrumentalities toward some goal.[66] The utility/autonomy dialogue is not necessarily a zero sum game, however. When exploring the various rights and

---

as a Moral Person" (1979) 16 Am.Phil.Q. 207 at 207–209. In *A Theory of Justice, op.cit.*, Rawls' consideration of the parties in his thought experiment include "associations"— states, churches, or other corporate bodies—but he makes no further reference to these bodies. See also Raz, *The Morality of Freedom* (Clarendon Press, 1986) where he states at 176:

> "There is little that needs to be said here of the capacity of corporations and other 'artificial' persons to have rights. Whatever explains and accounts for the existence of such persons, who can act, be subject to duties, etc. also accounts for their capacity to have rights."

See also Finnis, "The Priority of Persons", *Oxford Essays in Jurisprudence* (Horder ed., 4th series, Oxford University Press, 1999), at pp.7–8.

[62]   Dan-Cohen, *Rights, Persons and Organizations: A Legal Theory for Bureaucratic Society* (University of California Press, 1986), at p.61.

[63]   *ibid.* For the view that the company is a "moral person", see French, *Collective and Corporate Responsibility* (Colombia University Press, 1984).

[64]   Hart, "Between Utility and Rights" (1979) 79 Colum.L.Rev. 828 at 829.

[65]   See MacCormick, "Dworkin as pre-Benthamite" in *Ronald Dworkin and Contemporary Jurisprudence* (Cohen ed., 1983), at p.193—criticising the circularity in Dworkin, *op.cit.*

[66]   Nozick, *Anarchy, State and Utopia* (Blackwell, 1975); Dworkin, *op.cit.*

guarantees under the Irish Constitution, it is possible that some are grounded in utility and others in autonomy or that some are grounded in both, with one or other value being realised depending on the circumstances.[67]

3–32   This philosophical parsing of constitutional guarantees may not be to every theorist's taste.[68] Much time and energy has been expended in attempts to construct a self-contained deontological or teleological theory of rights.[69] Such an undertaking is not, however, the subject matter of this book. Its project is more modest in scope—namely, to provide a guide to the position of the company under the provisions of the Irish Constitution through the use of a methodology that respects the values underpinning its guarantees and ensures an appropriate level of protection for individuals as well as companies.

3–33   The operation of this autonomy/utility methodology in the context of the Irish Constitution can be illustrated by considering the right to freedom of expression under Art.40.6.1(i). Where a company invokes this substantive right, it may be entitled to constitutional protection because its exercise contributes to some common good—perhaps the functioning of the market or the furtherance of political debate.[70] Where an individual exercised that same right, the justification for its vindication might be based on that same utility interest and/or on the autonomy of individuals which underlies their interest in self-expression. Furthermore, the exercise of a right such as freedom of expression serves the autonomy interests of the audience, regardless of whether speakers themselves have autonomy interests deserving of protection. Where the exercise of a right furthers the constitutionally protected autonomy interests of a third party, it can be seen as a utility based right from the point of view of the rights bearer. The extent to which the autonomy/utility analysis applies to freedom of expression is considered in further detail in Chapter 9.

3–34   Where procedural rights are concerned, individuals who invoke them may do so because they have an underlying autonomy based interest which is also constitutionally protected. For example, in the context of the right to a trial in due course of law, the individual's personal liberty might be at stake. It might also be the case that individuals are entitled to a fair trial simply because they are individuals—they are deserving of this protection because the

---

[67] See Dan-Cohen, *op.cit.* at pp.55–118.

[68] For the arguments that some rights may be based on utilitarian considerations, see Raz, "Hart on Moral Rights and Legal Duties" (1984) 4 O.J.L.S. 123; Gray, "Indirect Utility and Fundamental Human Rights" in *Human Rights* (Paul, Miller and Paul eds, Oxford University Press, 1984).

[69] Whether such an enterprise is doomed to failure is not the concern of this book. See Feldman, *op.cit.* at p.6. See also Freeman, *Lloyd's Introduction to Jurisprudence* (7th edn, Sweet & Maxwell, London, 2001), at pp.547–548. For classic statements of the argument that utilitarianism and rights are inconsistent, see Hart, *Essays on Bentham* (Oxford University Press, 1984), at Chap.4; Lyons, "Utility and Rights" in *Theories of Rights* (Waldron ed., Oxford University Press, 1985).

[70] On the extent to which companies may rely on the guarantee of freedom of expression, see Chap.9 below.

Constitution recognises that this is the appropriate way to deal with autonomous human beings. Such an analysis does not necessarily mean that the company should be excluded. One utility value that arguably underlies the right to a fair trial is the maintenance of institutional integrity. This value is implicated whenever a criminal trial takes place, regardless of whether the defendant is an individual or a company. These and related matters are considered in detail in Part II.

3–35 Recognising that corporate constitutional protection may only be based on utility may mean that companies enjoy a lower level of protection than individuals making the same claim. This is because "the special weight claimed for autonomy rights by their proponents is their most important and distinctive feature."[71] If a dual analysis is undertaken in relation to Irish constitutional guarantees, then this "special weight" will be taken into account in cases involving individual claims to constitutional protection but not in cases involving claims by a company.[72] This approach has the advantage of alleviating the danger that, in extending constitutional protection to the company, the constitutional rights of individuals are in some way degraded. This is because, by recognising the differing rationales for individual, as opposed to corporate, constitutional protection, the restriction in some cases of the latter should not undermine the scope of the former. This will also be of relevance when we come to consider the horizontal application of constitutional rights and duties later in this book.[73]

CONCLUSION

3–36 This Part, in particular Chapter 1, has been concerned with setting out some of the background relevant to the remainder of this book. It has also explored some preliminary questions which need to be addressed when exploring the application of provisions of the Irish Constitution to the company. In particular, in Chapter 2, it has examined whether the text of the Constitution assists and has analysed the potential impact of methods of interpretation in this context.

3–37 It has been noted that the wording used in the United States Constitution has not been a reliable guide to the question of corporate constitutional protection. In the case law from the United States Supreme Court discussed in Parts II and III of this book, we will see that that court has relied heavily on the theories of the company explained in Chapter 1. The deficiencies of these theories highlighted in that chapter will become more apparent as examples from the case law are discussed in Parts II and III.

---

[71] Dan-Cohen, *op.cit.* at p.93. *Cf.* n.2 above.
[72] See Chap.5 below.
[73] See discussion below at paras 12–22 to 12–27.

3–38 Chapter 3 has considered whether the natural law influence on the Irish Constitution means that companies are excluded from its ambit. This chapter introduced the idea of a dual rationale for constitutional protection. This idea is referred to throughout the remainder of this book in order to ascertain whether each constitutional protection considered ought to be available to the company.

PART II

THE COMPANY UNDER ARTICLE 38

CHAPTER 4

INTRODUCING ARTICLE 38.1

INTRODUCTION

4–01   Chapters 5 and 6 explore two specific due process protections which arise in the course of criminal trials—the right to silence and the rule against double jeopardy. The guarantee of a trial in due course of law under Art.38.1 has, however, been held to encompass a number of general principles and the purpose of this chapter is to assess the extent to which these may apply to the company.[1]

4–02   Paragraphs 4–03 to 4–05 introduce Art.38.1 and the equivalent provisions of the United States Constitution and the European Convention on Human Rights. Paragraphs 4–06 to 4–30 flesh out the content of Art.38.1 and consider its development by the courts and the extent to which its protections

---

[1] There has been much discussion of the philosophical and practical implications of prosecuting companies. This material is not within the ambit of this book, which takes as its starting point the premise that companies in this jurisdiction may be prosecuted. See s.18(c) of the Interpretation Act 2005, which clearly envisages that the statutory criminal law is generally applicable to companies. The position at common law is also long established—*DPP v Kent and Sussex Contractors Ltd* [1944] K.B. 146; *R. v ICR Haulage Ltd* [1944] K.B. 551; *Moore v Bressler* [1944] 2 All E.R 515; *HL Bolton (Engineering) Co. Ltd v TJ Graham & Sons Ltd* [1957] 1 Q.B. 159; *Tesco Supermarkets Ltd v Nattrass*, [1972] A.C. 153; *Attorney General's References 2/1999 under Section 36 of the Criminal Justice Act 1972*, unreported, Court of Criminal Appeal, Rose L.J., Potts and Curtis JJ., February 15, 2000 and *R (Rowley) v DPP*, unreported, High Court, Kennedy L.J. and Hooper J., April 4, 2003 *Cf. Canadian Dredge & Dock Company Ltd v R..* [1985] 1 S.C.R. 662. For a sample of the academic literature on the topic, see Wolf, "The Legal and Moral Responsibility of Organizations" in *Criminal Justice* (Chapman and Pennock eds, New York University Press, 1985); Stone, "A Comment on Criminal Responsibility in Government" in *Criminal Justice, op.cit.*; Leigh, *The Criminal Liability of Corporations in English Law* (LSE Research Monographs 2, 1969); McCann, "Companies and Conspiracy" (1990) 8 I.L.T. 197; Wells, *Corporations and Criminal Responsibility* (2nd edn, Oxford University Press, 2001); Wells, "Corporations: Culture, Risk and Criminal Liability" [1993] Crim. L.R. 551; Fisse and Braithwaite, *Corporations, Crime and Acountability* (Cambridge University Press, 1993); Clarkson, "Kicking Corporate Bodies and Damning Their Souls" (1996) 59 M.L.R. 557; Stessens, "Corporate Criminal Liability: A Comparative Perspective" (1994) 43 I.C.L.Q. 493; Gobert, "Corporate Criminality: New Crimes for the Times" [1994] Crim. L.R. 722; Sullivan, "Expressing Corporate Guilt" (1995) 15 O.J.L.S. 281; Burles, "The Criminal Liability of Corporations" [1991] N.L.J. 609; Gobert "Corporate Criminality: Four Models of Fault" (1994) 14 L.S. 393; Coffee, "'No Soul to Damn: No Body to Kick': An Unscandalized Inquiry into the Problem of Corporate Punishment" [1981] 79 Mich.L.Rev. 386.

have been applied to the corporate defendant in this jurisdiction. Paragraphs 4–31 to 4–33 consider the nature of the protections guaranteed under Art.38.1 and whether they are appropriate for application to the company.

WHAT IS MEANT BY A TRIAL "IN DUE COURSE OF LAW"?

4–03   Article 38.1 of the Constitution provides: "No person shall be tried on any criminal charge save in due course of law." The origins of this constitutional guarantee were discussed by Kenny J. in *Conroy v Att.-Gen.*,[2] where he stated:

> "I think that s 1 of the Article is an echo of the Great Charter of Ireland granted in 1216 ... [The] phrase 'due process of law' was adopted by those who drafted the Fifth Amendment to the Constitution of the United States of America which prevents any person being deprived of life, liberty or property without due process of law. I think that s 1 of the Article gives a constitutional right to every person to be tried in accordance with due course or due process of law."[3]

4–04   The comparison with the United States Constitution has been made in other cases as well.[4] The United States Supreme Court has held that the Fourteenth Amendment's due process clause[5] protects a defendant from conviction under vague and imprecise laws,[6] excludes illegally obtained evidence,[7] guarantees a speedy trial,[8] and the right to legal representation.[9] The amendment also incorporates the Fifth Amendment double jeopardy clause[10] and the privilege against self-incrimination[11] and requires that the states observe these due process guarantees.

4–05   Due process protections are also guaranteed under Art.6 of the European Convention on Human Rights, which safeguards the presumption of innocence—Art.6.2—and guarantees "a fair and public hearing within a reasonable time by an independent and impartial tribunal established by law"— Art.6.1. Specific minimum rights are guaranteed to the criminal defendant by Art.6.3.[12]

---

[2]   [1965] I.R. 411.

[3]   *ibid.* at 415.

[4]   *Goodman International v Hamilton (No.1)* [1992] 2 I.R. 542 at 609, [1992] I.L.R.M. 145 at 185; *National Irish Bank Ltd, Re* [1999] 1 I.R. 145 at 180, [1999] 1 I.L.R.M. 321 at 353.

[5]   Reproduced above in Chap.2, n.27.

[6]   *Papachrisitou v City of Jacksonville* 405 U.S. 156 (1971).

[7]   *Mapp v Ohio* 367 U.S. 543 (1961).

[8]   *Klopfer v North Carolina* 386 U.S. 213 (1967).

[9]   *Gideon v Wainwright* 372 U.S. 335 (1963).

[10]   *Benton v Maryland* 395 U.S. 784 (1969).

[11]   *Murphy v Waterfront Comm'n of NY Harbor* 378 U.S. 52 (1964).

[12]   Art.6 in its entirety reads as follows:
    "(1) In the determination of his civil rights and obligations or of any criminal charge against him, everyone is entitled to a fair and public hearing within a reasonable

4–06 Article 38.1 has been interpreted generously and it has been thus described by Costello J. in *Heaney v Ireland*:[13]

> "It is an Article couched in peremptory language and has been construed as a constitutional guarantee that criminal trials will be conducted in accordance with basic concepts of justice. Those basic principles may be of ancient origin and part of the long established principles of the common law, or they may be of more recent origin and widely accepted in other jurisdictions and recognised in international conventions as a basic requirement of a fair trial. Thus, the principle that an accused is entitled to the presumption of innocence, that an accused cannot be tried for an offence not known to the law, or charged a second time with the same offence, the principle that an accused must know the case he has to meet and that evidence illegally obtained will generally speaking be inadmissible at his trial, are all principles which are so basic to the concept of a fair trial that they obtain constitutional protection from this Article. Furthermore, the Irish courts have developed a concept that there are basic rules of procedure which must be followed in order to ensure that an accused is accorded a fair trial and these basic rules must be followed if constitutional invalidity is to be avoided."[14]

4–07 This extract sets out a number of the specific principles which have been identified as part of the constitutional requirement of a trial in due course of law. It should be noted that the list of guarantees identified in Art.38.1 is one that may expand over time. The phrases "due course of law" and "due process of law" have been said to embody "dynamic constitutional concepts into which lawyers have obtained deeper insights as society has evolved".[15]

4–08 For example, Hogan and Whyte have pointed out that:

---

time by an independent and impartial tribunal established by law. Judgment shall be pronounced publicly but the press and public may be excluded from all or part of the trial in the interests of morals, public order or national security in a democratic society, where the interests of juveniles or the protection of the private life of the parties so require, or to the extent strictly necessary in the opinion of the court in special circumstances where publicity would prejudice the interests of justice. (2) Everyone charged with a criminal offence shall be presumed innocent until proven guilty according to law. (3) Everyone charged with a criminal offence has the following minimum rights: (a) to be informed promptly, in a language which he understands and in detail, of the nature and cause of the accusation against him; (b) to have adequate time and facilities for the preparation of his defence; (c) to defend himself in person or through legal assistance of his own choosing or, if he has not sufficient means to pay for legal assistance, to be given it free when the interests of justice so require; (d) to examine or have examined witnesses against him and to obtain the attendance and examination of witnesses on his behalf on the same conditions as witnesses against him; (e) to have the free assistance of an interpreter if he cannot understand or speak the language used in court."

[13] [1994] 3 I.R. 593, [1994] 2 I.L.R.M. 240.

[14] [1994] 3 I.R. 593 at 605, [1994] 2 I.L.R.M. 420 at 430.

[15] *National Irish Bank Ltd, Re*, Barrington J., [1999] 1 I.R. 145 at 180, [1999] 1 I.L.R.M. 321 at 353.

"[T]here has developed since the late 1970s, and with great rapidity, the more general notion of 'fair procedures' ... it is perhaps best to look at it as a sort of fine-mesh catch-all notion, intended to fill with the general instinct of fair play whatever interstices may be left between more traditional rules and principles of criminal justice ...".[16]

4–09   In relation to this "catch-all" principle, it appears that the right to fair procedures is a personal right under Art.40.3 when it arises in the context of civil proceedings,[17] but is implicated by Arts 34 and 38.1 in the context of criminal proceedings.[18] It has also been stated that it is "[a]mong the natural rights of an individual whose conduct is impugned and whose freedom is put in jeopardy".[19]

THE CONTENT OF ARTICLE 38.1

Offence must be known to law

4–10   Taking first the rule that "an accused cannot be tried for an offence not known to the law", it has been described as "a fundamental feature of our system of government by law (and not by decree or diktat)".[20] The rule is closely allied to the principle that penal statutes should be interpreted restrictively.[21] It is further buttressed by Art.15.5.1, which forbids the Oireachtas to "declare acts to be infringements of the law which were not so at the time of their commission". Furthermore, retroactive penal sanctions appear to be prohibited under Art.38.1.[22]

4–11   Insofar as this rule is a corollary of Art.15.5.1, it is clearly an aspect of the institutional competences regulated under the Constitution and thus binds the legislature in all cases.[23] As far as common law offences are concerned, however, the company must seek refuge under Art.38.1. As indicated in the quotation above, the rule is an aspect of the rule of law. As such, it implicates institutional values and should apply in the case of corporate, as well as individual, defendants.

---

[16] Hogan and Whyte, *Kelly: The Irish Constitution* (4th edn, Lexis-Nexis Butterworths, 2003), at p.1121.

[17] *Haughey, Re* [1971] I.R. 217. See below, Chap.12.

[18] *Healy v Donoghue* [1976] I.R. 325, (1976) 110 I.L.T.R. 9.

[19] *Healy v Donoghue* [1976] I.R. 325 at 329, (1976) 110 I.L.T.R. 9 at 13.

[20] *King v Att.-Gen.* [1981] I.R. 223 at 263.

[21] *de Gortari v Smithwick (No.2)* [2001] 1 I.L.R.M. 354 at 369.

[22] *Enright v Ireland* [2003] 2 I.R. 321. See also Art.7(1) of the European Convention on Human Rights which provides that: "Nor shall a heavier penalty be imposed than the one that was applicable at the time the criminal offence was committed."

[23] It must, therefore, apply for the benefit of companies as well as individuals.

Sentencing and Art.38.1

4–12   It is a fundamental rule that a sentence must be pronounced in court.[24] This is as much an aspect of Art.34.1 as it is related to Art.38.1.[25] That being the case, the rule is thus clearly an aspect of the administration of justice dealt with in Art.34 and should apply in all cases, whether the conviction is of an individual or company.

4–13   There is also a general principle that penalties for conviction should be neither arbitrary nor disproportionate in their operation.[26] In *DPP v WC*,[27] Flood J. held that the Constitution required the courts to "impose a sentence which is appropriate to the level of guilt, taking into account all relevant circumstances as they arise in that case".[28] He found that there was a constitutional principle of proportionality which required in this context that:

> "the imposition of a particular sentence must strike a balance between the particular circumstances of the commission of a relevant offence and the relevant circumstances of the person sentenced".[29]

4–14   This is an interesting conundrum in the case of the corporate criminal defendant. As such defendants may have large resources at their disposal, presumably greater financial penalties are proportionate when sentencing the company than would be acceptable in the case of the individual.[30]

4–15   The Irish courts have never considered the application of this rule to the corporate defendant, nor has the United States Supreme Court determined whether the prohibition on "excessive fines" contained in the Eighth Amendment so applies.[31] In the early twentieth century, before the extension

---

[24] *Kieran v de Búrca* [1963] I.R. 348; *Molloy v Sheehan* [1978] I.R. 438. There is also a requirement, not relevant to the company, that the duration of any custodial sentence must be certain. *Keating v Ó hUadhaigh*, unreported, High Court, Finlay P., May 11, 1984; *Gleeson v Martin* [1985] I.L.R.M. 577; *Dixon v Martin* [1985] I.L.R.M. 240; *Cox v Ireland* [1992] 2 I.R. 503. See O'Malley, *Sentencing Law and Practice* (Round Hall Sweet & Maxwell, 2000), at pp.355–356.

[25] *Kieran v de Búrca* [1963] I.R. 348 at 366; *DPP v Heeney* [2001] 1 I.R. 736.

[26] *Cox v Ireland* [1992] 2 I.R. 503.

[27] [1994] 1 I.L.R.M. 321.

[28] *ibid.* at 325.

[29] *ibid.*

[30] It has been pointed out that imposing fines on companies is an ineffective method of punishing them, assuming that the purpose of such punishment is deterrence. This is premised on the notion that a company, being a rational actor will only be deterred if the expected punishment cost of an action exceeds the expected gain. This is not calculated simply with reference to the likely amount of any penalty. The likelihood of apprehension and conviction are also factored in. As well as this, the maximum fine that can be levied against a company is limited by its wealth. Because corporate crime often has diffuse effects, it usually carries a low chance of apprehension and conviction, so that a "deterrence trap" is created. See Coffee, *op.cit.* at 389–390.

[31] The full text of the Eighth Amendment reads as follows: "Excessive bail shall not be required, nor excessive fines imposed, nor cruel and unusual punishments inflicted."

of the excessive fines clause to the states,[32] the Supreme Court held that fines imposed on companies could be reviewed under the due process clause of the Fourteenth Amendment on the basis that, in some circumstances, such fines could constitute a "taking" under that clause.[33] It has been argued that the prohibition on excessive fines should apply to corporate defendants because its purpose is to limit "the arbitrary use of the government's prosecutorial power".[34] If a similar purpose underlies the equivalent Irish constitutional rule, then that argument seems sound. Once again, the key question is whether the predominant purpose of the rule is to protect autonomy or utility based vales. To the extent that the requirement of proportionality might be concerned with the liberty of the individual, it could be that it is an autonomy promoting rule unsuited to application to the company.

The burden of proof and the presumption of innocence

4–16 Article 38.1 requires that all criminal trials be conducted in accordance with the presumption of innocence.[35] Unlike the aspects of Art.38.1 considered above, which are clearly concerned with the rule of law and the integrity of the criminal justice system as a whole, the presumption of innocence is less clearly concerned with such institutional values. It has been described in the Supreme Court as:

> "personal to the dignity and status of every citizen. It means that he or she is entitled to the status of a person innocent of criminal charges until such has been proven in a court conducted in accordance with law."[36]

4–17 It has yet to be determined by the Irish courts whether the presumption of innocence applies to the company faced with a criminal trial. Given the traditional place of that presumption at the heart of the accusatorial criminal justice system at common law, it seems that it is likely to be viewed as so inherent to that system as to be indispensable.[37] Again, the application of the presumption to the company would be based on the utility value of preserving the integrity of the accusatorial criminal justice system.

Aspects of fair procedures

4–18 There are a number of general principles which have been recognised

---

[32] *Browning–Ferris Industries of Vermont Inc v Kelco Disposal Inc* 492 U.S. 257 (1989).

[33] *Waters-Pierce Oil Co v Texas* 212 U.S. 86 (1909); *St Louis Iron Mountain & Southern Ry v Williams* 251 U.S. 63 (1919). For a discussion of the takings clause of the Fourteenth Amendment, see below, Chap.8, paras 8–32 and 8–38 to 8–45.

[34] Salisbury Warren, "The Case for Applying the Eighth Amendment to Corporations" (1996) 49 Vand.L.Rev. 1313 at 1345.

[35] *O'Leary v Att.-Gen.* [1993] 1 I.R. 102; [1991] I.L.R.M. 454; [1995] 1 I.R. 254.

[36] *POC v DPP* [2000] 3 I.R. 87 at 103, Murray C.J.

[37] It should of course be noted that the presumption is not immutable even in the case of the individual defendant and alterations of the burden of proof have been tolerated by the courts Hogan and Whyte, *op.cit.* at pp.1068–1072.

as falling under Art.38.1 and which can conveniently be described as aspects of fair procedures. Among these are the right to be informed of the charge[38] and the opportunity to mount a defence.[39] The latter includes the right to test the evidence against the defendant by cross-examination,[40] a right which cannot be unreasonably postponed.[41] It also includes the right to adequate time in which to prepare a defence.[42] The accused must have an opportunity to meet the case.[43] All of these requirements under Art.38.1 are aspects of the common law maxim *audi alteram partem*.

4–19 Another common law maxim which has been imported into Irish constitutional law[44] is *nemo iudex in causa sua*—nobody shall be a judge in his own cause.

4–20 Both of these maxims reflect the view that the accusatorial system of justice requires safeguards in order to guarantee the correct outcome of criminal trials. As they are thus concerned with the integrity of the criminal trial process as a whole, the identity of the defendant should have no bearing on their application as a matter of principle.

Exclusion of evidence

4–21 There[45] is a general rule that evidence of previous convictions ought not to be introduced[46] and that evidence whose prejudicial effect outweighs its probative value should be excluded.[47] These rules are concerned with the safety of verdicts, and thus the integrity of the criminal justice system as a whole. This utility based value is furthered by the application of these rules to all defendants, corporate or individual.

4–22 There is also a rule that evidence obtained as a result of a deliberate breach of the constitutional rights of the accused ought to be excluded unless there are extraordinary excusing circumstances which justify its admission.[48]

---

[38] *Howard v Donnelly* [1966] I.R. 51.

[39] *Haughey, Re* [1971] I.R. 217; *Leonard v Garavan*, unreported, High Court, McKechnie J., April 30, 2002.

[40] *Haughey, Re* [1971] I.R. 217; *Gill v Connellan* [1987] I.R. 541; *Ó Broin v Ruane* [1989] I.R. 214; *Dineen v Delap* [1994] 2 I.R. 228; *McNally v Martin* [1995] 1 I.L.R.M. 350.

[41] *Maguire v Ardagh* [1998] 1 I.R. 385.

[42] *Curran v Att.-Gen.*, unreported, High Court, Gavan Duffy J., February 27, 1941; *O'Callaghan v Clifford* [1993] 3 I.R. 603.

[43] *Walshe v Murphy* [1981] I.R. 275.

[44] *Att.-Gen. v Singer* [1975] I.R. 408; *DPP v Tobin* [2001] 3 I.R. 469, [2002] 1 I.L.R.M. 428.

[45] See McGrath, "The Exclusionary Rule in Respect of Unconstitutionally Obtained Evidence" (2004) D.U.L.J. 108; McGrath, *Evidence* (Thomson Round Hall, 2005), at pp.335–356.

[46] *King v DPP* [1981] I.R. 233; *DPP v Keogh* [1998] 4 I.R. 416, [1998] 1 I.L.R.M. 72.

[47] *DPP v Marley* [1985] I.L.R.M. 17; *DPP v Conroy* [1986] I.R. 460; [1988] I.L.R.M. 4; *DPP v McGrail* [1990] 1 I.R. 38.

[48] Hogan and Whyte, *op.cit.* at p.1101.

The rationale for this principle was set out by Finlay C.J. in *Trimbole v Governor of Mountjoy Prison*:[49]

> "The courts not only have an inherent jurisdiction but a positive duty: (i) to protect persons against invasion of their constitutional rights, (ii) if such invasion has occurred, to restore as far as possible the person damaged to the position in which he would be if his rights had not been so invaded; and (iii) to ensure as far as possible that persons acting on behalf of the executive who consciously and deliberately invade the constitutional rights of citizens do not for themselves or their superiors obtain the planned results of the invasion."[50]

4–23 It appears that there is a dual purpose to the exclusionary rule.[51] First, there is the concern to restore persons whose rights have been invaded to their pre-invasion position. Where a company is the accused, it may be that the constitutional rights of either the company or an individual officer of the company are breached in the gathering of evidence. Where an individual's rights have been invaded, the company should not be able to rely on this aspect of the rule in its own defence, as this would offend against the *jus tertii* rule.[52] Where some constitutional right of the company, such as property,[53] has been invaded this restorative aspect of the exclusionary rule is still inapplicable as it is concerned with respecting the autonomy of individuals rather than any utilitarian purpose.

4–24 The second rationale for the rule, however, seems to be to deter the Gardaí from invading constitutional rights in the gathering of evidence by depriving them of the fruits of that invasion. In that respect, it is not as significant that the party whose rights are infringed is not the party against whom criminal proceedings are being brought. The deterrence aspect of the rule is concerned with the institutional value of ensuring correct police procedures and there is no reason why a company should not be able to rely on it whether its own or an individual's rights have been infringed.

4–25 The deterrence principle can be seen as a reflection of an overarching principle that unconstitutionally obtained evidence must be excluded so as to preserve the integrity of the criminal justice system as a whole. This is the

---

[49] [1985] I.R. 550, [1985] I.L.R.M. 465.

[50] [1985] I.R. 550 at 573, [1985] I.L.R.M. 465 at 484.

[51] McGrath argues that there are three purposes to the rule: deterrence and vindication as described here and a third purpose—the preservation of the integrity and reputation of the criminal justice system. McGrath, *Evidence*, (Thomson Round Hall, 2005) at 335–338. The deterrence rule is really just an aspect of this larger principle. See below at para.4–25.

[52] *Cahill v Sutton* [1980] I.R. 269; *TD v Minister for Education* [2001] 4 I.R. 259.

[53] See Chap.8.

explicit basis of the rule in Canada[54] and has been alluded to in a number of decisions of the United States Supreme Court[55] also.

Pre-trial publicity

4–26   The courts have evolved a rule that a trial cannot proceed where there is a real risk that it will be an unfair trial due to pre-trial publicity prejudicial to the accused.[56] This aspect of a fair trial arose in the context of a criminal prosecution of a company in *Zoe Developments Ltd v DPP*.[57] The applicant company sought judicial review to prevent a criminal prosecution against it by the first respondent. As against the second respondent—the National Authority for Occupational Safety and Health—an order was sought preventing the publication or circulation of information which could prejudice a jury. Geoghegan J. considered the authorities on pre-trial publicity and referred, in particular, to *Z v DPP*,[58] where Finlay C.J. referred in his decision to the "fundamental nature of the constitutional right involved". Referring to the fact that previous convictions had been mentioned in a press release, the judge found that in the circumstances of this case there was no serious risk of an unfair trial, but directed that it be postponed for six months to allow the fade factor to operate.[59] Again, insofar as this protection seeks to ensure jury impartiality and the consequent safety of verdicts, there is no reason why it should not apply to the company.

Delay

4–27   The right to a trial "within a reasonable time"[60] is specifically protected under Art.6 of the European Convention on Human Rights[61] and the Sixth Amendment guarantees a "speedy ... trial".[62] The Supreme Court has repeatedly confirmed that Art.38.1 protects the right to an early trial.[63]

---

[54] s.24(2) of the Canadian Charter of Rights and Freedoms provides that where:
"a court concludes that evidence was obtained in a manner that infringed or denied any rights or freedoms guaranteed by this Charter, the evidence shall be excluded if it is established that, having regard to all the circumstances, the admission of it in the proceedings would bring the administration of justice into disrepute".

[55] *Olmstead v United States* 277 U.S. 438 (1977); *Terry v Ohio* 392 U.S. 1 (1968); *Calandra v United States* 414 U.S. 338 (1974).

[56] *D v DPP* [1994] 2 I.R. 465, [1994] 1 I.L.R.M. 435; *Z v DPP* [1994] 2 I.R. 476; *Magee v O'Dea* [1994] 1 I.R. 500.

[57] Unreported, High Court, Geoghegan J., March 3, 1999.

[58] [1994] 2 I.R. 476.

[59] On the fade factor in this context, see Hogan and Whyte, *op.cit.* at pp.1126–1127.

[60] For a general discussion of the way in which the Irish courts have dealt with the matter of delay in criminal trials, see Hogan and Whyte, *op.cit.* at pp.1144–1170.

[61] The Irish jurisprudence on delay in the context of criminal trials rarely refers to Art.6. Instead, the preferred rationale for the Irish approach to this issue is that taken in *Barker v Wingo* 407 U.S. 514 (1972)—see quotation cited below at n.64. For cases approving this and failing to refer to the European Convention on Human Rights, see *B v DPP* [1997] 3 I.R. 140; *Blood v DPP*, unreported, Supreme Court, March 2, 2005; *PM v DPP*, unreported, Supreme Court, April 5, 2006.

[62] The full text of the Sixth Amendment is reproduced below at para.7–10.

[63] *O'Connell v Fawsitt* [1986] I.R. 362; *DPP v Byrne* [1994] 2 I.R. 236 at 244, [1994] 2

4–28 The United States Supreme Court has held that the purpose of the guarantee of a "speedy ... trial" is to protect the interests of the defendant and that the rule was there to:

"(i)   prevent oppressive pretrial incarceration;
(ii)   minimise anxiety and concern of the accused; and
(iii) limit the possibility that the defence will be impaired."[64]

4–29 This rationale for the rule has been endorsed by the Irish Supreme Court in a number of cases.[65] Such aims seem inappropriate in the case of a corporate criminal defendant although (iii) above might be thought to contribute to the safety of verdicts, which is an institutional value. Concern for the individual is not, however, the only purpose of the right to an early trial and in *PM v Malone*,[66] Keane C.J. stated that, in upholding this aspect of Art.38.1, a court is not only:

"vindicating and protecting the rights of all persons coming before the courts to the dispatch of criminal proceedings to a trial within reasonable expedition. It is also upholding the general public interest in the speedy prosecution of crime."[67]

4–30 Again, this "general public interest" aspect means that undue delays in the prosecution of companies might be constitutionally impermissible. On the other hand, the fact that corporate prosecutions may require complex evidence gathering may mean that delays in such cases are more excusable. Provided that such delays do not cause undue prejudice of the kind that might render a verdict unsafe, the approach of Walsh J. in *O'Flynn v Clifford*[68] seems appropriate. In that case, a delay of some 18 months was excused on the basis that there was "no evidence that the prosecuting authorities were in a position to institute their prosecution before they did so".[69] In such a case, the public interest in the speedy meting out of justice is not implicated.

The nature of the due process protections and their application to the company

4–31 As can be seen from the foregoing, Art.38.1 has been interpreted generously to encompass a number of discrete protections. Whether or not each protection ought to be available to the company should be determined by analysing the purpose of that protection. It has been noted that:

I.L.R.M. 91 at 95; *DOR v DPP* [1997] 2 I.R. 273; *Knowles v Malone*, unreported, High Court, April 6, 2002.
[64] *Barker v Wingo* 407 U.S. 514 (1972) at 532.
[65] *DPP v Byrne* [1994] 2 I.R. 236 at 246; *PC v DPP* [1999] 2 I.R. 25 at 65; *SF v DPP* [1999] 3 I.R. 235 at 240–253, cited in Hogan and Whyte, *op.cit.* at p.1145.
[66] [2002] 2 I.R. 560.
[67] *ibid.* at 579, reproduced in Hogan and Whyte, *op.cit.* at p.1145.
[68] [1989] I.R. 524.
[69] *ibid.* at 529.

"Companies can benefit in an incidental way ... from rights that were aimed at individual persons; indeed they can benefit from rights whose justifying force (say, in terms of privacy for and dignity of the accused individual in the sphere of criminal procedure rights) evaporates when applied to business entities."[70]

4–32 It has been argued above that many of the protections developed under Art.38.1 are concerned with the integrity of the criminal justice system as a whole. To deny a corporate defendant the right to meet the case against it by calling witnesses, for example, would be damaging to the accusatorial system of criminal justice. Not all of the protections under Art.38.1, however, are necessarily concerned with such institutional values and each protection should be analysed before assuming it applies to the corporate criminal defendant.[71] Thus, the presumption of innocence might be seen as respecting the dignity of the individual defendant and, consequently, may be less appropriate for application to the corporate defendant. On the other hand, the presumption could be viewed as an inherent aspect of the accusatorial system of justice. Its denial to any criminal defendant might thus be seen as detrimental to the integrity of the criminal justice system. These two possible interpretations of the presumption highlight the way in which a determination of corporate constitutional protection can illuminate the values underlying constitutional guarantees in general.[72] Thus, the question: Can the company rely on the right to X? may be rephrased as: With what values is the right to X concerned?

4–33 The next two chapters of this Part explore the right to silence and the rule against double jeopardy respectively. Chapter 5 engages in a comparative analysis of the application of the right to silence to the company in other jurisdictions. It examines two different approaches to corporate constitutional protection. The first relies on theories of the company and the second explores the values underlying the right to silence. The chapter concludes that the latter is the best approach to apply when analysing the Irish Constitution. Chapter 6 examines the rule against double jeopardy and proposes that a different version of the rule might be required in relation to the company in order to reflect the values underlying this rule when applied to the company.

---

[70] Allan, "Why Business Learns to Love Bills of Rights" [2001] J.Civ.Lib. 214 at 229.

[71] The more usual approach is for the court to simply assume that a corporate criminal defendant is to be protected in the same way as an individual as in *Zoe Developments Ltd v DPP*, unreported, High Court, Geoghegan J., March 3, 1999 *Cf.* the decision of the High Court of Australia in *Chief Executive Officer of Customs v Labrador Liquor Wholesale Pty* 201 ALR 1 (2003). For an indication that the position might be different under the Canadian Charter of Fundamental Rights and Freedoms, see *R. v Wholesale Travel Group Inc* [1991] 3 S.C.R. 154.

[72] See below, Chap.9, where the discussion of corporate freedom of expression has a similar result.

CHAPTER 5

THE RIGHT TO SILENCE

INTRODUCTION

5–01   This chapter considers the extent to which companies may rely on the Irish Constitution to provide them with a number of protections, described collectively as "the right to silence", of which the privilege against self-incrimination is one example.[1] It will be shown that, while the Irish courts have, perhaps unwittingly, allowed companies to invoke the right to silence, the Oireachtas has indicated that the company is not entitled to this constitutional protection.

5–02   This chapter also looks at the treatment of this matter in other jurisdictions and considers two approaches to the question of corporate rights. First, there are those jurisdictions where theories of the corporation have been invoked to determine whether the company can rely on the right to silence. This case law is examined in paras 5–26 to 5–47. Second, there are other jurisdictions which have explored the rationale for the guarantee in detail in order to determine its application to the company. This case law is explored in paras 5–48 to 5–54. This approach is one which facilitates the utility/autonomy analysis set out in Chapter 3. This chapter concludes that the latter approach is the preferable one to use in relation to the Irish Constitution. It also notes, however, that the right to silence can perhaps be seen as a special case, so that the utility/autonomy analysis may not, in fact, be necessary to determine its application to the company.

WHAT IS THE "RIGHT TO SILENCE"?

5–03   Before considering the extent to which companies can rely on the right to silence, some further definition of the term will improve the clarity of the rest of this chapter.[2] As mentioned above, the "right to silence" is essentially an umbrella term for a number of protections. In *R. v Director of the Serious*

---

[1]   See below, paras 5–03 to 5–05.
[2]   The High Court of Australia has noted the potential for confusion in this context, *Mule v R.* 221 ALR 85 (2005) at [22]:
    "The expression 'right to silence' is used to refer to a number of distinct legal rules. It is a useful shorthand expression but it is a general description which does not always provide a safe basis for reasoning to a conclusion."

Fraud Office, Ex p. Smith,[3] Lord Mustill described the right to silence as follows:

> "In truth it does not denote a single right, but rather refers to a disparate group of immunities, which differ in nature, origin, incidence and importance, and also as to the extent to which they have already been encroached upon by statute. Amongst these may be identified: (1) a general immunity, possessed by all persons and bodies, from being compelled on pain of punishment to answer questions posed by other persons or bodies; (2) a general immunity, possessed by all persons and bodies, from being compelled on pain of punishment to answer questions the answers to which may incriminate them; (3) a specific immunity, possessed by all persons under suspicion of criminal responsibility, whilst being interviewed by police officers or others in similar positions of authority, from being compelled on pain of punishment to answer questions of any kind; (4) a specific immunity, possessed by accused persons undergoing trial, from being compelled to answer questions put to them in the dock; (5) a specific immunity, possessed by persons who have been charged with a criminal offence, from having questions material to the offence addressed to them by police officers; (6) a specific immunity (at least in certain circumstances)…possessed by accused persons undergoing trial, from having adverse comment made on any failure (a) to answer questions before the trial, or (b) to give evidence at the trial."[4]

5–04   These protections originated at common law and applied under English law as far back as 1637.[5] They are sometimes divided by the Irish courts into two main categories.[6] The right of suspects in criminal investigations to refuse to answer questions which could tend to incriminate them is commonly referred to as "the right to silence". The "privilege against self-incrimination" proper,[7] on the other hand, applies to the right of accused persons not to testify in the course of their criminal trial. This latter immunity is specifically protected under the Fifth Amendment to the United States Constitution[8] and the European Court of Human Rights (ECHR) has stated that:

---

[3]   [1993] A.C. 1.
[4]   *ibid.* at 30. This analysis was approved of by Costello J. in *Heaney v Ireland*, [1994] 3 I.R. 593 at 602, and by Kearns J. in *Dunnes Stores Ireland Co v Ryan* [2002] 2 I.R. 60 at 155–156. There is also a specific immunity from answering questions or providing evidence in the course of an action which might expose the party to contempt proceedings, *Memory Corporation v Sidhu* [2002] 2 W.L.R. 1106.
[5]   Robertson, *Freedom, the Individual and the Law* (7th edn, Penguin, 1993), at p.32, discussing the heresy trial of John Lilburn, a.k.a. "the Leveller", who challenged his interrogation by the Star Chamber.
[6]   See the judgment of Costello J. in *Heaney v Ireland* [1994] 3 I.R. 593, discussed below, para.5–06.
[7]   Expressed in the Latin maxim *nemo tenetur se ipsum accusare.*
[8]   The Double Jeopardy Clause of the Fifth Amendment provides that no person shall "be subject for the same offense to be twice put in jeopardy of life or limb".

"The right to remain silent under police questioning and the privilege against self-incrimination are generally recognised international standards which lie at the heart of the notion of a fair procedure under Article 6."[9]

5–05 As well as considering the position under the United States Constitution and the European Convention on Human Rights, this chapter will also examine case law from New Zealand, Canada, Australia and England and Wales.[10]

THE RIGHT TO SILENCE UNDER THE IRISH CONSTITUTION

5–06 Whether the right to silence was protected under the Irish Constitution remained unclear until 1996. The Supreme Court expressly reserved the question as late as 1992 in *DPP v Quilligan (No.3)*.[11] In *Heaney v Ireland*,[12] it held that the privilege was enshrined in the Constitution. *Heaney* concerned the constitutionality of s.52 of the Offences Against the State Act 1939, which provided that persons could be imprisoned for, *inter alia*, failure to give an account of their movements. In the High Court, Costello J. had held that the privilege against self-incrimination was part of the guarantee of a trial in due course of law in Art.38.1. He noted that the common law recognises two immunities, that of the suspect and that of an accused person under trial. The function of the suspect's immunity is to obviate the risk of untrue confessions. The evolution of the accused's immunity from testifying was a reaction to the abuses perpetrated by the judges of the Star Chamber in the misuse of interrogation under oath.[13] The Supreme Court did not opine whether Art.38.1 included the privilege or not, O'Flaherty J. stating that the right to silence was a corollary of the right to freedom of expression, which is subject to public order and morality.[14] Both the High Court and the Supreme Court mentioned the relevance of the concept of proportionality and O'Flaherty J. found that

---

[9] *Murray v UK* (1996) 22 E.H.R.R. 29 at [45].

[10] Below, paras 5–26 to 5–54.

[11] Unreported, Supreme Court, July 14, 1992. See Hogan and Whyte, *Kelly: The Irish Constitution* (4th edn, Lexis-Nexis Butterworths, 2003), at pp.1083–1085. In *McCarthy v Lennon* [1936] I.R. 485, the Supreme Court appeared to reject the notion that the privilege was a constitutional norm, but recognised that it was part of Irish law as a continuation from the common law position under Art.73 of the 1922 Constitution. In the circumstances, it would have made no difference to the outcome of the case whether the privilege was constitutionally protected or not. See Barrington J. in *National Irish Bank Ltd, Re* [1999] 3 I.R. 145 at 182–187; [1999] 1 I.L.R.M. 321 at 347–350.

[12] [1994] 3 I.R. 593 (High Court), [1996] 1 I.R. 580 (Supreme Court).

[13] This is also pointed out by Shanley J. in *National Irish Bank Ltd, Re* [1999] 1 I.R. 145, [1999] I.L.R.M. 321.

[14] Art.40.6.1 of the Constitution provides as follows:
"The State guarantees liberty for the exercise of the following rights, subject to public order and morality:
    i. The right of the citizens to express freely their convictions and opinions.

    The education of public opinion being, however, a matter of such grave import to the common good, the State shall endeavour to ensure that organs of public opinion, such as the radio, the press, the cinema, while preserving their rightful liberty of expression, including criticism of

s.52, when viewed in the context of the state's need to maintain public order, did not constitute a disproportionate interference with the "constitutional right".[15]

5–07 The right to silence and the privilege against self-incrimination were considered in the context of the Companies Act 1990 in *National Irish Bank Ltd, Re*[16] and in *Dunnes Stores Ireland Co. v Ryan*.[17] In *National Irish Bank Ltd, Re*,[18] inspectors appointed to investigate the National Irish Bank under Pt II of the Companies Act 1990 sought from the High Court, *inter alia*:

> "A determination that persons (whether natural or legal) from whom information, documents or evidence are sought by the Inspectors in the course of their investigation under the Companies Acts, 1990 are not entitled to refuse to answer questions put by the Inspectors on the grounds that the answers or documents tend to incriminate him, her or it."[19]

5–08 The background to the case was the initiation of the investigation procedure provided for in Pt II of the Companies Act 1990.[20] This provided that the High Court, on the application of the Minister for Enterprise and Employment[21] or a number of other persons specified in the Act,[22] could appoint one or more inspectors to investigate the affairs of a company in certain circumstances. Various powers were bestowed on inspectors to assist them in this task. In the investigation at issue in *National Irish Bank, Re*,[23] ss.10 and 18 of the 1990 Act arose for consideration. Section 10, in the relevant part,[24] provided that:

Government policy, shall not be used to undermine public order or morality or the authority of the State.

The publication or utterance of blasphemous, seditious, or indecent matter is an offence which shall be punishable in accordance with law."

[15] [1996] 1 I.R. 580 at 589–590, [1997] 1 I.L.R.M. 117 at 127. See Hogan and Whyte, *op.cit.* at pp.1085–1086 for criticism of the Supreme Court decision in *Heaney*, which is described at p.1085 as "one of the least impressive Supreme Court judgments of recent times".

[16] [1999] 1 I.R. 145, [1999] 1 I.L.R.M. 321.

[17] [2002] 2 I.R. 60.

[18] [1999] 3 I.R. 145, [1999] 1 I.L.R.M. 321.

[19] [1999] 3 I.R. 145 at 150, [1999] 1 I.L.R.M. 321 at 325.

[20] This *schema* was described by Shanley J. in *National Irish Bank, Re* [1999] 3 I.R. 145 at 165, as follows:

> "Part II of the 1990 Act as stated provides a mechanism for the investigation of companies by inspectors. The scheme of the Act of 1990 allows the appointment of inspectors by the court on the application of the Minister where there are circumstances which suggest to the court that the company has been operated in an unlawful or fraudulent manner. The inspectors are given investigative powers including a power to compel answers from officers and other persons. It is clearly envisaged by the Act of 1990 that prosecutions can follow."

[21] s.8(1), Companies Act 1990.

[22] s.7, Companies Act 1990.

[23] [1999] 3 I.R. 145, [1999] 1 I.L.R.M. 312.

[24] Subs.(2) makes similar provision for persons other than officers or agents of the company. Subs.(3) was struck down for unconstitutionality in *Desmond v Glackin* [1993] 3 I.R. 67.

"(1) It shall be the duty of all officers and agents of the company ... to produce to the inspectors all books and documents of or relating to the company ... which are in their custody or power, to attend before the inspectors when required to do so and otherwise to give to the inspectors all assistance in connection with the investigation which they are reasonably able to give ...

(4) An Inspector may examine on oath, either by word of mouth or on written interrogatories, the officers and agents of the company ... in relation to its affairs and may—

   a. administer an oath accordingly

   b. reduce the answers of such person to writing and require him to sign them

(5) If any officer or agent of the company ... refuses to produce to the inspectors any book or document which it is his duty under this section so to produce, refuses to attend before the inspectors when required to do so or refuses to answer any question which is put to him by the inspectors with respect to the affairs of the company ... the inspectors may certify the refusal under their hand to the court, and the court may thereupon enquire into the case and, after hearing any witnesses who may be produced against or on behalf of the alleged offender and any statement which may be offered in defence the court may

(6) ... make any order or direction it thinks fit, including a direction to the person concerned to attend or re-attend before the inspector or produce particular books or documents or answer any particular question put to him by the inspector, or a direction that the person concerned need not produce a particular book or document or answer a particular question put to him by the inspector."[25]

5–09 The relevant part of s.18 provided as follows:

"An answer given by a person to a question put to him in exercise of powers conferred by

   (a) section 10 ...

may be used in evidence against him, and a statement required by section 224 of the Principal Act may be used in evidence against any person making or concurring in making it."

5–10 The respondents argued that ss.10 and 18, read together, constituted a breach of the privilege against self-incrimination. Shanley J. considered the common law origins of the privilege against self-incrimination and found that there were certain values which underpinned it—it respects the will of an accused person to stay silent and it recognises the right to privacy. It is also a reflection of the common law's sense of "fair play".[26] As with the High Court

---

[25] This represents the content of s.10(5) and (6) minus those portions of the provisions found unconstitutional in *Desmond v Glackin* [1993] 3 I.R. 67.

[26] See below, paras 5–55 to 5–64 on the rationale for the privilege.

and Supreme Court in *Heaney*, he found that a proportionality test ought to be applied when considering restrictions placed on the right by the Oireachtas. The respondents in the case had argued that there was a right under Art.38.1 not to have compelled testimony used against an accused at trial. Shanley J. stated that was a matter for the trial judge to decide once a party had been arraigned. On its own, the statutory obligation to answer self-incriminatory questions was not inconsistent with a trial in due course of law. He thus determined the matter in favour of the inspectors, his decision referring to legal persons as well as natural persons without distinction.

5–11   When the case was appealed to the Supreme Court, the appellants stated in their written submissions that they were concerned only with the rights of natural persons and were not making the case for legal persons.[27] The Supreme Court upheld the decision of Shanley J., adding the *caveat* that incriminating answers would not be admissible in subsequent criminal proceedings unless the trial judge was satisfied that the inculpatory statements were made voluntarily.[28] Barrington J. noted that the Supreme Court had already held that the right to silence was protected under the rubric of Art.40.6.1(i). However, he considered the principle that involuntary statements against interest were inadmissible to be an aspect of the right to a trial in due course of law under Art.38.1 and pointed out that proportionality was not an appropriate concept to apply in the context of the right to such a trial.[29]

5–12   The Company Law Enforcement Act 2001 made a number of amendments to Pt II of the Companies Act 1990. One of these was to amend s.18(1) by substituting the word "individual" for the word "person". The relevant part of the section now reads as follows:

> "An answer given by an individual to a question put to him in exercise of the powers conferred by:
> (a) section 10 …
> may be used in evidence against him in any proceedings whatsoever (save proceedings for an offence (other than perjury in respect of such an answer))."

5–13   This amendment was enacted to reflect the approach of the Supreme Court and the ECHR.[30] The amendment, which safeguards the privilege against self-incrimination of the individual, indicates that the legislature is not willing

---

[27] [1999] 3 I.R. 145 at 170, [1999] 1 I.L.R.M. 321 at 344. Indeed, the company was not represented at the appeal stage.

[28] [1999] 3 I.R. 145 at 188–189, [1999] 1 I.L.R.M. 312 at 359.

[29] The proportionality test appears, however, to have survived in this context. See *Dunnes Stores Ireland Co. v Ryan* [2002] 2 I.R. 60. For criticism of the application of such a test in the context of the right to a fair trial, see Hogan and Whyte, *op.cit.* at pp.1047–1048.

[30] Seanad Éireann, Vol.167, June 26, 2001, Company Law Enforcement Bill 2000: Second Stage. *Cf.* the prescient remarks in Murray, "The Right to Silence and Corporate Crime" in *Law and Liberty in Ireland* (Whelan ed., Oak Tree Press, 1993) at p.67.

to extend that right to the corporate defendant.[31] As we shall see below, that approach is in line with the approach taken by the Supreme Court of the United States.[32]

5–14 In *Dunnes Stores Ireland Co. v Ryan*,[33] the High Court considered the constitutionality of s.19(5) and (6) of the Companies Act 1990. These provisions concern the powers and functions of "authorised officers" appointed by the Minister for Enterprise, Trade and Employment under Pt II of the 1990 Act. The purpose of the appointment of, and investigation by, such an authorised officer is essentially to determine whether there are circumstances existing which would justify the appointment of an inspector by the High Court. Section 19(2) provided, broadly, that the minister may give directions to a company to produce books or documents, or may authorise an officer to do so. Under s.19(4), a body or other person can be required to provide an explanation of any books or documents produced. The challenged provisions were as follows:

> "19(5) If a requirement to produce books or documents or provide an explanation or make a statement which is imposed by virtue of this section is not complied with, the body or other person on whom the requirement was so imposed shall be guilty of an offence; but where a person is charged with an offence under this subsection in respect of a requirement to produce any books or documents, it shall be a defence to prove that they were not in his possession or under his control and that it was not reasonably practicable for him to comply with the requirement.
>
> 19(6) A statement made by a person in compliance with a requirement imposed by virtue of this section may be used in evidence against him."

5–15 The applicants, two companies and an individual,[34] sought declarations that s.19(5) and 19(6) breached their fundamental rights and were contrary to Arts 38.1 and 40.1 of the Constitution.[35] They relied on their rights to confidentiality and/or privacy, the privilege against self-incrimination, their right to fair procedures, natural and constitutional justice, equality before the law, and their property rights.[36]

---

[31] s.11(c) of the Interpretation Act 1937 provides that the use of the word "person" in a statute indicates that it is to apply to bodies corporate, as well as individuals. Somewhat surprisingly, no mention of this shift is made in the *Dáil Debates* relating to the Corporate Law Enforcement Bill 2000.

[32] See below, paras 5–26 to 5–46.

[33] [2002] 2 I.R. 60. Hereafter referred to as *Dunnes Stores*.

[34] Dunnes Stores Ireland Co., Dunnes Stores (Ilac Centre) Ltd and Margaret Heffernan.

[35] *Dunnes Stores Ireland Co. v Ryan* [2002] 2 I.R. 60 at 102. They also sought a declaration that s.19(6) did not permit the use of statements made by a person in evidence in any criminal prosecution or that s.19(4) did not abrogate any privilege that person would otherwise possess. *ibid.*

[36] Kearns J. ignored most of these grounds, although he does make brief reference to the arguments based on property rights, [2002] 2 I.R. 60 at 123–124. See discussion of the company's right to property below, Chap.7. He decided the case on the basis of Art.40 in

5–16 Kearns J., in the High Court, contrasted the provisions of s.19 with those of s.10, pointing out that authorised officers were in a different position to inspectors under the Companies Act 1990. The latter are appointed by the court to carry out an investigation. Authorised officers are appointed for the more limited purpose of determining whether an inspector ought to be appointed to conduct such an investigation.[37] Furthermore, where an inspector is appointed, officers and agents of the company are not merely required to produce books and documents, they may also be required to attend before the inspector and give all assistance in connection with the inspection that they are reasonably able to give. Inspectors can examine persons under oath, reduce their answers to writing and require them to sign them.[38]

5–17 After carrying out this analysis of the legislation, he turned to consider the right to silence. He referred to the decision of Lord Mustill in *R. v Director of the Serious Fraud Office, Ex p. Smith*[39] and noted that "the list of immunities recorded by Lord Mustill indicates a hierarchy of different situations in which the requirement not to infringe the right has a greater or lesser degree of importance".[40] In his view, the case at hand was "at the lower hand of the spectrum or hierarchy identified by Lord Mustill".[41] The rationale for this was that there was no imminent criminal trial, neither was any suspect detained. Also, the incriminating material had an objective reality. Kearns J. referred to the decision of the South African Constitutional Court in *Ferreira v Levin NO*[42] and the decision of the ECHR in *Quinn v Ireland*.[43] Both of these cases indicate that the right is concerned with respecting the will of an accused person to remain silent. The more objective the existence of the incriminating material, the less the need for the protection. Kearns J. emphasised strongly the public interest in company investigations.[44] He accepted the point made by the respondents that, "[t]hose who enjoy the benefits of incorporation must also ... accept the concomitant duties and obligations of incorporation."[45]

5–18 Taking all of these factors into account, he found that s.19(5) passed the proportionality test set out by Costello J. in *Heaney v Ireland*[46] and was thus not contrary to Art.40 of the Constitution. He stated:

---

relation to s.19(5) and Art.38.1 together with Art.40 in relation to s.19(6), at 123. While he never states which aspects of Art.40 are being relied upon, as he refers only to the right to silence, it is presumably Art.40.6.1(i) he is referring to. The applicants specifically relied on Art.40.6.1(i) in their submissions relating to s.19(5). See discussion of the Supreme Court decision in *Heaney v Ireland* [1996] 1 I.R. 580, above at para.5–06.

[37] [2002] 2 I.R. 60 at 116.
[38] *ibid.* at 106–108.
[39] [1993] A.C. 1.
[40] [2002] 2 I.R. 60 at 116.
[41] *ibid.*
[42] (1996) 1 B.C.L.R. 1.
[43] (2001) 33 E.H.R.R. 334.
[44] [2002] 2 I.R. 60 at 117–119.
[45] *ibid.* at 118.
[46] [1994] 3 I.R. 593 at 607 (High Court), Costello J.:

"There is, at the end of the day, a world of difference between the position of a vulnerable suspect, held in police custody, say for example, for the investigation of a domestic homicide and that of a large corporation which may engage in all sorts of stratagems and then call on vast financial resources and expertise to protect and defend its position to the ultimate."[47]

5–19   The judge then went on to consider the constitutionality of s.19(6). Again, he compared this provision to the legislation applicable to inspectors under s.10. He noted that s.10 leaves open the possibility that responses to questions could be voluntary in nature[48] and this was the basis for the decision in *National Irish Bank, Re*[49] so that the cases were not analogous.[50] In any event, Kearns J. found the two-step analysis[51] in that case unconvincing in this case. As there was no room for suggesting that answers under s.19(5) could be voluntary in nature, there was no point in leaving that issue for determination at trial.[52] Referring to two decisions of the ECHR,[53] Kearns J. justified a dichotomised approach to the right to silence and privilege against self-incrimination. There was, on this view, no incongruity in extracting information on pain of penalty, provided that the information so obtained was not admissible in subsequent criminal proceedings.[54] Section 19(6) implicated both Arts 40 and 38.1. In its failure to immunise answers given under s.19(5) from use in criminal proceedings, the provision failed the *Heaney* test in the sense that it did not constitute the minimum invasion of rights necessary to reach the object of the legislation.[55]

5–20   Section 19 of the Companies Act 1990 was repealed and substituted by s.29 of the Company Law Enforcement Act 2001 so that s.19(7) now reads:

"A statement made or an explanation provided by an individual in compliance with a requirement imposed by virtue of this section may be used in evidence against him in any proceedings whatsoever (save

---

"The objective of the impugned provision must be of sufficient importance to warrant overriding an important constitutionally protected right. It must relate to concerns pressing and substantial in a free and democratic society. The means chosen must pass a proportionality test. They must—
    a)   be rationally connected to the objective, and not be arbitrary, unfair or based on irrational considerations;
    b)   impair the right as little as possible; and
    c)   be such that their effects on rights are proportional to the objective."

[47] [2002] 2 I.R. 60 at 119.
[48] This is because the effect of s.10(1) and (6) is essentially that a person who refuses to cooperate has a defence.
[49] [1999] 3 I.R. 145, [1999] 1 I.L.R.M. 312.
[50] [2002] 2 I.R. 60 at 122.
[51] See discussion of Shanley J.'s judgment above at paras 5–07 to 5–10.
[52] [2002] I.R. 60 at 123.
[53] *Quinn v Ireland* (2001) 33 E.H.R.R. 334; *Saunders v UK* (1997) 23 E.H.R.R. 313.
[54] [2002] I.R. 60 at 123.
[55] *ibid.*

proceedings for an offence (other than an offence under subsection (6) or (8)))."

5–21   As was pointed out by Kearns J. in *Dunnes Stores*,[56] s.19(6) of the 1990 Act has been replaced in s.29(6) and (8) of the Company Law Enforcement Act 2001, so that answers given to an authorised officer are immunised from use in subsequent criminal proceedings, except where these are with regard to a refusal to answer or the giving of a false or misleading answer.[57]

5–22   Kearns J. had an opportunity to consider this area again in *Environmental Protection Agency v Swacliffe Ltd trading as Dublin Waste, Louis Moriarty and Eileen Moriarty.*[58] This was a case stated from a trial in the District Court involving one corporate and two individual defendants, accused of a number of criminal offences relating to breaches of a waste licence under the Waste Management Act 1996.[59] Under the terms of that legislation, persons operating under a waste licence could be required, under pain of penalty, to maintain records.[60] The applicants had objected at trial to the admissibility of written and oral evidence based on these records. In the course of the case stated, an attempt was made by the applicants to draw an analogy between the case at hand and *Dunnes Stores* on the basis that the evidence based on the records could not be said to be voluntarily provided by the applicants. This argument was rejected by the High Court, which found that the privilege against self-incrimination was not involved in this case because, in applying for a waste licence, the applicants freely accepted any conditions which were envisaged under the statutory scheme. As with the cases on company investigations discussed above, the judgment emphasises the context in which the case arose. Stressing the societal interest in an effective waste management system, Kearns J. found that none of the purposes underlying the privilege were really at stake in this case. He noted that there was no real coercion by the State in obtaining the information and that the accused and the State were not in an adversarial relationship at the time the evidence was obtained. He went on to state that he foresaw no increased risk of untrue confessions or risk of abuses of power by the State as a result of his findings.

5–23   The prosecution had relied on a Canadian case, *R. v Fitzpatrick*,[61] and Kearns J. accepted the submission that the case at hand was "on all fours" with it. This is somewhat surprising, as that case had concerned only an individual defendant and the Canadian Supreme Court has held that

---

[56] [2002] 2 I.R. 60.
[57] This legislative amendment brings the Act into accordance with the decision of the ECHR in *Quinn v Ireland* (2001) 33 E.H.R.R. 334.
[58] Unreported, High Court, May 21, 2004. Hereafter referred to as *Swacliffe*.
[59] This statute was enacted, *inter alia*, to comply with the requirements of Directive 75/442/EEC—the "Waste Framework Directive".
[60] s.41(2)(a)(viii).
[61] [1995] 4 S.C.R. 154.

corporations cannot avail of the privilege against self-incrimination.[62] Earlier in his judgment, Kearns J. had stated that the right to silence and the privilege protected both "societal and individual" interests and that the protections "are linked to the value placed by society upon individual privacy, personal autonomy and dignity", a view which one would imagine to weigh against applying the privilege to the corporate defendant.

5–24 As can be seen from the above, it has not yet been definitively determined whether the right to silence and privilege against self-incrimination are applicable to corporate defendants. The judgment of Shanley J. in *National Irish Bank, Re*[63] made no distinction between legal and natural persons.[64] The appellants explicitly stated that they were not concerned to argue that the privilege was applicable to legal persons when the case came before the Supreme Court and the decision of that court expressed no view on the matter.[65] The decision of Kearns J. in *Dunnes Stores*[66] makes no reference to the corporate status of two of the applicants in determining whether the impugned provisions were unconstitutional. He did make reference to the public interest in corporate governance,[67] and his remarks in this regard are reminiscent of the concession theory of the corporation discussed above in Chapter 1.[68] As will be shown from the analysis of the jurisprudence of the United States Supreme Court below, the espousal of the concession theory of the corporation may easily lead to a denial of corporate constitutional rights.[69] His observations on the purpose of the legislation were, however, equally applicable to the position of the individual applicant and there was no attempt to distinguish between her rights under the Constitution and those of the companies. On the other hand, the quotation reproduced above, together with the comments of Herbert J. in the Supreme Court,[70] suggest that the Irish courts are unlikely to take an expansive view of the rights of companies in this context. The legislature's amendments to the Companies Act 1990, which protect only the individual defendant in subsequent criminal proceedings, indicate that the Oireachtas has taken the view that the privilege against self-incrimination is unavailable to companies. While the nature of the right to silence and the privilege against self-incrimination may support such a view,[71] it is to be regretted that neither the High Court nor the Supreme Court has seen fit to explicitly address the matter and explain why this is so.

5–25 Given the lack of explicit judicial consideration of this issue in this jurisdiction, a comparative survey of jurisprudence from elsewhere may be of

---

[62] *R. v Amway Corp* (1989) 56 D.L.R. (4th) 309. Discussed below at para.5–51.
[63] [1999] 3 I.R. 145, [1999] 1 I.L.R.M. 312.
[64] Above at paras 5–07 to 5–10.
[65] *ibid.*
[66] [2002] 2 I.R. 60.
[67] *ibid.* at 118.
[68] Above at paras 1–14 to 1–22.
[69] Below, paras 5–26 to 5–46.
[70] This quotation is reproduced below at para.5–36.
[71] See discussion below, paras 5–55 to 5–68.

use. The case law from other common law jurisdictions exhibits a marked divergence of judicial views on the propriety of allowing companies to rely on the privilege against self-incrimination. What follows explores this case law in order to establish a general picture of the state of the law in the United States and New Zealand, England and Wales, Canada and Australia. One interesting feature that emerges from this survey is the extent to which corporate theory has influenced the courts' perspective in the United States and New Zealand. Having identified this feature, an attempt to relate it to the Irish case law will be made before going on to consider the approach taken in the latter mentioned jurisdictions in paras 5–48 to 5–54.

THE IMPACT OF CORPORATE THEORY—THE UNITED STATES AND NEW ZEALAND

The United States

5–26 The privilege against self-incrimination is protected under the Fifth Amendment of the United States Constitution,[72] the relevant portion of which states that no person "shall be compelled in any criminal case to be a witness against himself".[73] The case from the United States Supreme Court discussed below demonstrates the potential impact of theories of the corporation on decisions relating to corporate constitutional protection. Essentially, there are two predominant theoretical perspectives that feature in the approach taken by the United States Supreme Court. The concession theory of the corporation, described in Chapter 1,[74] emphasises the fact that companies owe their existence to the State. Unsurprisingly, this viewpoint results in a restrictive approach to corporate constitutional protection. The aggregate approach, also described in Chapter 1,[75] is where judges look behind the company and recognise the individuals whose interests are at stake where the company is concerned. Again, somewhat unsurprisingly, this approach generally leads to a more generous application of constitutional rules to the company.

5–27 In 1906, in *Hale v Henkel*,[76] the United States Supreme Court rejected the contention of a secretary and treasurer of a company that he could rely on the privilege against self-incrimination in relation to criminal proceedings under the Sherman Act which named the company as respondent.[77] The case concerned a subpoena issued to the petitioner requiring him to appear before a

---

[72] It is binding on the states through incorporation into the Due Process Clause of the Fourteenth Amendment, *Murphy v Waterfront Comm'n of NY Harbor* 378 U.S. 52 (1964).

[73] The full text of the Fifth Amendment is reproduced above, Chap.2, n.27.

[74] Above at paras 1–14 to 1–22.

[75] Above at paras 1–23 to 1–28 and 1–37 to 1–41.

[76] 201 U.S. 43 (1906).

[77] The court accepted that the Fourth Amendment applied to the corporation. See discussion below at paras 5–29 to 5–30. See also paras 15–12 to 15–33. See Henning, "The Conundrum of Corporate Criminal Liability: Seeking a Consistent Approach to the Constitutional Rights of Corporations in Criminal Prosecutions" 63 Tenn.L.Rev. 793 for an analysis of this case.

grand jury, to produce various books and documents relating to the company and to answer questions relating to them. There was an immunity statute[78] in place which effectively prevented such testimony being used against the witness in subsequent criminal proceedings. It was argued that this was insufficient as the statute did not extend to protect the corporation. Brown J. delivered the judgment of the court. He stated that the purpose of the privilege was not to protect the corporation:

> "The right of a person to refuse to incriminate himself is purely a personal privilege of the witness. It was never intended to permit him to plead the fact that some third person may be incriminated by his testimony, even though he were the agent of such person ... The question whether a corporation is a 'person' within the meaning of this amendment really does not arise ...".[79]

5–28   The judge went on to state that to hold otherwise would defeat the Sherman Act altogether.[80] Dealing with the challenge to the subpoena itself, he emphasised this point again[81] and reiterated the non-application of the privilege to corporations. In so doing, he appeared to espouse the concession theory of the corporation, contrasting the position of the individual, who "may stand on his rights as a citizen"[82] with that of the corporation, "a creature of the state". This "creature":

> "is presumed to be incorporated for the benefit of the public. It receives certain special privileges and franchises, and holds them subject to the laws of the state and the limitations of its charter. Its powers are limited by law. It can make no contract not authorised by its charter. Its rights to act as a corporation are only preserved to it so long as it obeys the laws of its creation. There is a reserved right in the legislature to investigate its contracts and find out whether it has exceeded its powers."[83]

5–29   In the course of his decision, Brown J. examined the relationship between the Fifth Amendment's privilege against self-incrimination and the Fourth Amendment's prohibition on unreasonable searches and seizures.[84] He found that this prohibition applied to corporations as well as individuals and could apply in the context of an overly broad subpoena.[85] Interestingly, in

---

[78] 32 Stat. 894–904, Chap.755, U.S. Comp. Stat. Supp. 1905, p.602.
[79] 201 U.S. 43 at 69–70.
[80] Sherman Antitrust Act, July 2, 1980, ch.647, 26 Stat.209, 15 U.S.C. §1.
[81] *ibid.* at 74.
[82] *ibid.*
[83] *ibid.* at 74–75.
[84] *ibid.* at 70–78. The Fourth Amendment provides as follows:
   "The right of the people to be secure in their persons, houses, papers, and effects, against unreasonable searches and seizures, shall not be violated, and no Warrants shall issue, but upon probable cause, supported by oath or affirmation, and particularly describing the place to be searched, and the persons or things to be seized."
[85] 201 U.S. 43 at 76–78.

this part of his judgment, he appears to endorse an aggregate theory of the corporation:

> "[W]e do not wish to be understood as holding that a corporation is not entitled to immunity, under the 4th Amendment, against unreasonable searches and seizures. A corporation is, after all, but an association of individuals under an assumed name and with a distinct legal entity. In organising itself as a collective body it waives no constitutional immunities appropriate to such body. Its property cannot be taken without compensation. It can only be proceeded against by due process of law, and is protected, under the 14th Amendment, against unlawful discrimination ... Corporations are a necessary feature of modern business activity, and their aggregated capital has become the source of nearly all great enterprises."[86]

5–30 Harlan J.[87] commented on the inconsistency of allowing the corporation to rely on the Fourth Amendment while denying it the protection of the Fifth. Quoting from the *Dartmouth College Case*,[88] he applied a fiction theory approach,[89] referring to the corporation as "an artificial being, invisible, intangible, and existing only in contemplation of law".[90] He stated that corporations were thus not included in the references to "people" and "persons" in the Fourth Amendment.[91]

5–31 Brewer J. dissented.[92] He stated that the protections contained in the Fourteenth, Fifth and Fourth Amendments:

> "are available to a corporation so far as, in the nature of things, they are applicable. Its property may not be taken for public use without just compensation. It cannot be deprived of life[93] or property without due process of law."[94]

5–32 He then went on to undertake a textual analysis of the three

---

[86] *ibid*. at 76 (references omitted).

[87] He concurred in the result of the decision, and agreed with the majority in relation to the Fifth Amendment.

[88] 17 U.S. (4 Wheat.) 518 (1819). The quotation, which Harlan J. does not actually attribute, is reproduced above at para.1–17.

[89] See Chap.1 on the fiction theory of the corporation.

[90] *Hale v Henkel* 201 U.S. 43 at 79.

[91] 201 U.S. 43 at 79. For the text of the Fourth Amendment, see n.83 above. McKenna J. also found fault with the majority analysis, which granted corporations the protection of one amendment and not the other. This was mainly because he felt that the two provisions complemented each other and it was illogical to exclude one and then allow the other. His view was that neither ought to apply to corporations. 201 U.S. 43 at 82–83.

[92] He was joined in his dissent by the Chief Justice.

[93] Brewer J. did not explain what he meant by the reference to a company being deprived of "life".

[94] 201 U.S. 43 at 83–84. See Chap.8 below, on corporate property rights.

amendments.[95] He referred to the decision in *Santa Clara County v Southern Pacific Railroad Co*,[96] where the Chief Justice held that the equal protection clause of the Fourteenth Amendment applied to corporations.[97] As the Fourteenth Amendment referred to "persons", Brewer J. reasoned that "if the word 'person' in that amendment includes corporations, it also includes corporations when used in the 4th and 5th Amendments".[98] He pointed out that the corporation is a citizen for the purposes of jurisdiction of federal courts. His judgment reflects an aggregate theory of the corporation, stating that the corporation is:

> "essentially but an association of individuals, to which is given certain rights and privileges, and in which is vested the legal title. The beneficial ownership is in the individuals, the corporation being simply an instrumentality by which the powers granted to these associated individuals may be exercised."[99]

5–33 He agreed, however, with the majority that the protection under the Fifth Amendment:

> "is personal to the individual, and does not extend to an agent of an individual, or justify such agent in refusing to give testimony incriminating his principal".[100]

5–34 As can be seen from above, the application of a given theory of the corporation impacts on the extent of constitutional protection guaranteed. Where a judge espouses a variant of the concession theory, constitutional protection is denied. Where an aggregate theory influences the judge, constitutional protection is granted. The majority opinion illustrates the significance of corporate theory in this context. Within the same opinion, a concession theory approach denied the corporation the protection of the Fifth Amendment, whereas the aggregate view taken in the latter part of the decision justified granting to the corporation the protection of the Fourth Amendment. Read in this way, the decision is confusing and sets no standard for predicting the outcome of subsequent cases. As is evident from the dissent by Brewer J.,

---

[95] The Fourteenth Amendment provides as follows:
   "Nor shall any state deprive any person of life, liberty, or property without due process of law; nor deny to any person within its jurisdiction the equal protection of its laws."
   The Fourth Amendment is reproduced above at n.84. The Fifth Amendment is reproduced above, Chap.2 at n.27.

[96] 118 U.S. 394.

[97] Waite C.J.'s decision on the point was terse:
   "The court does not wish to hear argument on the question whether the provision in the 14th Amendment to the Constitution, which forbids a state to deny to any person within its jurisdiction the equal protection of the laws, applies to these corporations. We are all of the opinion that it does." 118 U.S. 394 at 396.

[98] 201 U.S. 43 at 85.

[99] *ibid.*

[100] *ibid.* at 83.

the answer does not lie within the text of the provisions. Indeed, in subsequent decisions, the Supreme Court accepted that the double jeopardy clause of the Fifth Amendment applied to corporations,[101] while maintaining consistently that the self-incrimination clause was inapplicable.[102] As both clauses apply to "persons", it is clear that the textual description alone is an unreliable method of identifying the constitutional subject.

5–35 The case just discussed[103] demonstrates the potential impact of corporate theory in cases where constitutional protection is at issue. What is of more immediate interest is the extent to which corporate theory could have an impact on Irish constitutional law.

5–36 While it has been suggested that early Irish case law appeared to espouse a concession theory of the corporation,[104] the case law is conflicting.[105] So far, there is little indication of a current judicial trend in any direction. In *Swacliffe*, Kearns J. quoted from the judgment of Herbert J. in the Supreme Court, where he stated:

> "Incorporation under the Companies Acts involves accepting the overseeing power of the second respondent. Persons who bind themselves together to constitute the legal entity known as the 'company' cannot choose to enjoy the manifold privileges and benefits of incorporation while rejecting the less convenient aspects, such as the supervisory role of the second respondent."[106]

5–37 This approach, which appears to take a concession theory stance on the company, echoes that of Brown J. in *Hale v Henkel*[107] and would, it is submitted, be against the extension of constitutional rights to the company. On the other hand, the decision of Keane J. in *Iarnród Éireann v Ireland*[108] is suggestive of an aggregate perspective on the company, one which lends itself to a sympathetic view of the corporate litigant seeking to claim constitutional protection. In his judgment, he stated:

---

[101] See *Puerto Rico v Shell Co (PR)* 302 U.S. 253 (1937); *Fong Foo v United States* 369 U.S. 142 (1962); *United States v Martin Linen Supply Co.* 430 U.S. 564 (1977). See Chap.6.

[102] See *United States v White* 322 U.S. 694 (1944); *Fisher v United States* 425 U.S. 391 (1976); *Bellis v United States* 417 U.S. 85 (1984); *Braswell v United States* 487 U.S. 99 (1988).

[103] See also *Wilson v United States* 221 U.S. 361 (1911); *United States v White* 322 U.S. 694 (1944); *Bellis v United States* 417 U.S. 85 (1974).

[104] Ussher, *Company Law in Ireland* (Sweet and Maxwell, 1986), Introduction.

[105] *Iarnród Éireann v Ireland* [1996] 3 I.R. 321, [1995] 2 I.L.R.M. 161; *Att-Gen for England and Wales v Brandon Book Publishers Ltd* [1986] I.R. 597, [1987] I.L.R.M. 135; *PMPS Ltd v Att.-Gen.* [1983] I.R. 339, [1984] I.L.R.M. 88; *Chestvale Properties Ltd v Glackin* [1992] I.L.R.M. 221.

[106] [2002] 2 I.R. 60, Herbert J. at 100, Kearns J. at 118.

[107] See above, text accompanying n.78.

[108] [1996] 3 I.R. 321, [1995] 2 I.L.R.M. 161.

"There would ... be a spectacular deficiency in the guarantee to every citizen that his or her property rights will be protected against 'unjust attack', if such bodies (companies) were incapable in law of being regarded as 'citizens', at least for the purposes of this article, and if it was essential for the shareholders to abandon the protection of limited liability to which they are entitled by law in order to be protected, not only in their own rights as shareholders, but also the property rights of the corporate entity itself, which are in law distinct from the rights of its members."[109]

5–38   Of course, that case concerned the property rights of the company and it is fair to say that of all the claims to constitutional protection a company might make, a claim relating to property rights is intuitively one of the most appealing.[110] Nonetheless, it is interesting to note that in this case, the explicit extension of constitutional protection to a company is accompanied by an endorsement of an aggregate view of the company which is similar to that contained in the judgment of Brewer J. in *Hale v Henkel*.[111]

5–39   It has been argued that the differing application of the Fourth and Fifth Amendments in *Hale v Henkel*[112] represents a coherent approach by the United States Supreme Court to corporate constitutional rights which balances crime control interests with the prevention of government oppression. A corporate right to assert the privilege could frustrate prosecutions for corporate crimes utterly but applying the protections of the Fourth Amendment has the advantage that only unreasonable government intrusions are prohibited.[113]

5–40   That corporate crime control was the rationale for the decision in *Hale v Henkel*,[114] is supported by subsequent decisions of the United States Supreme Court.[115] In *Wilson v United States*,[116] a corporation president was subpoenaed to produce corporate documents before a grand jury which was investigating mail fraud in the issuing of the corporation's securities. Unlike the treasurer in *Hale*, Wilson was arguing the privilege on his own behalf, as he had no immunity. He tried to argue that the documents prepared and signed by him should attract the privilege. The court found that all of the documents belonged to the corporation and rejected the arguments based on the privilege. This decision was in accordance with the rationale in *Hale v Henkel*.[117] Corporations can only respond to subpoenas through their agents and frequently the documents requested will tend to incriminate those individuals. If they could

---

[109] [1996] 3 I.R. 321 at 345, [1995] 2 I.L.R.M. 161 at 183.
[110] See Chap.8.
[111] Reproduced above, text accompanying n.98.
[112] 201 U.S. 43.
[113] Henning, *op.cit.* at 796–797.
[114] 201 U.S. 43.
[115] These are discussed in Henning, *op.cit.* at 826–841.
[116] 221 U.S. 361 (1911).
[117] 201 U.S. 43 (1906).

claim the privilege in this context then corporate law enforcement would be severely restricted.[118]

5–41   In *United States v White*,[119] the United States Supreme Court considered the claim of a union official who relied on the privilege in response to a subpoena to produce union records issued in the course of a grand jury investigation. The respondent stated that he was refusing to produce the documents because they might tend to incriminate the union or himself as an officer thereof, or individually. In considering whether the respondent had properly been placed in contempt of court, Murphy J. emphasised the personal nature of the privilege and delivered an exposition of its rationale which is worth reading in full:

> "It grows out of the high sentiment and regard of our jurisprudence for conducting criminal trials and investigatory proceedings upon a plane of dignity, humanity and impartiality. It is designed to prevent the use of legal process to force from the lips of the accused individual the evidence necessary to convict him or to force him to produce and authenticate any personal documents or effects that might incriminate him. Physical torture and other less violent but equally reprehensible modes of compelling the production of incriminating evidence are thereby avoided. The prosecutors are forced to search for independent evidence instead of relying upon proof extracted from individuals by force of law. The immediate and potential evils of compulsory self-disclosure transcend any difficulties that the exercise of the privilege may impose on society in the detection and prosecution of crime. While the privilege is subject to abuse and misuse, it is firmly embedded in our constitutional and legal framework as a bulwark against iniquitous methods of prosecution. It protects the individual from any disclosure, in the form or oral testimony, documents or chattels, sought by legal process against him as a witness."[120]

5–42   He referred to *Hale v Henkel*[121] and pointed out that, due to the personal nature of the privilege, it cannot be used by, or on behalf of, an organisation such as a corporation. He stated that when individuals act in their official capacity they cannot claim their personal privileges. "Rather they assume the rights, duties and privileges of the artificial entity or association of which they are agents or officers ...".[122] They have no privilege against self- incrimination as regards the records and papers of the organisation as these do not embody any element of personal privacy. This is so even if the documents could incriminate the individuals personally.[123] The reason behind restricting the

---

[118]   See Fiebach, "The Constitutional Right of Associations to Assert the Privilege Against Incrimination" (1964) 112 U.Pa.L.Rev. 394 (1964) at 403.

[119]   322 U.S. 694. See also *Bellis v United States* 417 U.S. 85 (1974).

[120]   322 U.S. 694 at 698–699.

[121]   201 U.S. 43 (1906).

[122]   322 U.S. 694 at 699.

[123]   *ibid*. at 699–670.

privilege to natural persons acting in their private capacities was to ensure effective government control over the economic activities of organisations.[124] Later in the judgment, echoing what was said in *Hale v Henkel*,[125] the judge noted that the union itself did not possess the privilege and that in any case, the privilege is personal to the witness called so that he cannot set up the privilege of a third person as an excuse for refusal to answer or produce documents.[126]

5–43   The majority opinion in *Hale v Henkel*[127] in relation to the privilege had been based on the concession theory of the corporation.[128] The Supreme Court in this case abandoned this former rationale for the decision in *Hale* and held that the representatives of any collective group act as agents and cannot, therefore, claim Fifth Amendment protection.[129] The court later made it clear that this would apply to even the smallest corporations.[130]

5–44   The application of the privilege in a corporate context arose again in *Braswell v United States*.[131] Rehnquist C.J., delivering the majority judgment of the court,[132] again emphasised that the custodian of corporate records acts as an agent when producing them:

> "Any claim of Fifth Amendment privilege asserted by the agent would be tantamount to a claim of privilege by the corporation—which of course possess no such privilege."[133]

5–45   Again, the Supreme Court, referring back to *White*, emphasised the potential detrimental effect of the Fifth Amendment on the control of white collar crime.[134] In a strong dissent, Kennedy J., along with three of his

---

[124] *ibid.*

[125] 201 U.S. 43 (1906).

[126] Note that there were cases which assumed that the custodian of corporate documents waived the privilege, *e.g. Fisher v United States* 425 U.S. 391 (1976). See discussion of these in *United States v Braswell* 487 U.S. 99 (1988).

[127] 201 U.S. 43 (1906).

[128] Above at paras 5–27 to 5–35. The decision relied on the "visitorial powers" of the State over corporations owing their existence to the State. This is the principle that corporations under state law are subject to the State's visitorial power to inspect corporate records to prevent violations of corporate charters. See Fiebach, *op.cit.* at 396.

[129] See *United States v White*, 322 U.S. 694, at 699. The court held, at p.701, that the test for a collective group for these purposes is as follows:
"The test ... is whether one can fairly say under all the circumstances that a particular type of organisation has a character so impersonal in the scope of its membership and activities that it cannot be said to embody or represent the purely private or personal interests of its constituents, but rather to embody their common or group interests only. If so, the privilege cannot be invoked on behalf of the organisation or its representatives in their official capacity."

[130] *Braswell v United States* 487 U.S. 99 (1988).

[131] *ibid.*

[132] He was joined by White, Blackmun, Stevens and O'Connor JJ.

[133] 487 U.S. 99 at 110.

[134] *ibid.* at 115–116. The court went on to state that the act of production in these cases is

colleagues, condemned the denial of the Fifth Amendment on crime control grounds.[135]

5–46   In *Braswell*, the United States Supreme Court's decision appears to take a similar view of the privilege to that taken by the Oireachtas under s.29 of the Company Law Enforcement Act 2001[136] in that it seeks to protect the individual at the trial stage without providing immunity for the corporate suspect.

New Zealand

5–47   The position in New Zealand is that the privilege is available to corporations at common law. In *Pear and Apple Marketing Board v Master & Sons Ltd*,[137] the New Zealand Court of Appeal held that there was no policy reason against granting the privilege to corporations and that, as corporations could be convicted through the out-of-court statements and acts of their officers, they should be entitled to claim the privilege when they speak through them. The court also noted that many small family businesses incorporate and this mode of carrying on a business should not deprive the individuals concerned of the privilege. The decision provides another example of how an aggregate view of the company results in the extension of protections to it.[138] This is of

---

deemed the act of the corporation and in later proceedings against the individual, the Government cannot introduce into evidence the fact that the subpoena was served on and the documents delivered by the particular individual. The Government may, however, use the corporation's act of production against such an individual and could offer testimony to demonstrate that the corporation had produced the subpoenaed records. 487 U.S. 99 at 115–119.

[135]   487 U.S. 99 at 119–131. He was joined by Brennan, Marshall and Scalia JJ. He stated, at 129:

> "The majority's abiding concern is that if a corporate officer who is the target of a subpoena is allowed to assert the privilege, it will impede the Government's power to investigate corporations, unions, and partnerships, to uncover and prosecute white-collar crimes, and otherwise to enforce its visitorial powers. There are at least two answers to this. The first, and most fundamental, is that the text of the Fifth Amendment does not authorise exceptions premised on such rationales. Second, even if it were proper to invent such exceptions, the dangers prophesied by the majority are overstated."

He also disagreed with the Chief Justice on the basis that the case at hand was one where the very production of the documents would be incriminating, not the contents thereof. In such circumstances, the authorities were, he opined, in favour of granting Fifth Amendment protection to the petitioner. He rejected the idea that Braswell was a mere agent and pointed out that the precise reason the subpoena was addressed to him was because the Government saw him as more than a mere custodian of corporate records. "The majority gives the corporate agent fiction a weight it simply cannot bear." 487 U.S. 99 at 128.

[136]   See discussion above at paras 5–12 to 5–21.

[137]   [1986] 1 N.Z.L.R. 191.

[138]   It should be noted that the NZ Bill of Rights applies to corporations by virtue of s.29 of the New Zealand Bill of Rights Act:

> "Except where the provisions of this Bill of Rights otherwise provides, the provisions of this Bill of Rights apply, so far as is practicable, for the benefit of all legal persons as well as for the benefit of all natural persons."

particular relevance when considering the possible direction the Irish case law might take as, like New Zealand, Ireland is a jurisdiction in which the majority of companies are small, private companies. In cases involving such entities, there may be a strong temptation to look behind the corporate veil and grant constitutional protection.

CONSIDERING THE NATURE OF THE RIGHT—ENGLAND AND WALES, CANADA, AUSTRALIA

5–48   The case law considered in paras 5–26 to 5–47 demonstrates the impact of corporate theory in this context. It also demonstrates the inherent manipulability of such theories of corporate personality. In particular, the judgment of Brown J. in *Hale v Henkel* utilises one perspective to deny constitutional protection under the Fifth Amendment and another to extend it under the Fourth Amendment. As the opinions of Harlan and Brewer JJ. demonstrate, there is no textual basis within the amendments for this distinction and the majority opinion makes no attempt to grapple with the nature of the constitutional guarantees. This approach, also evident in the New Zealand *Pear and Apple Marketing Board* case, can be contrasted with that taken in England and Wales, Canada and Australia considered in this section.

England and Wales

5–49   The English courts have generally assumed that the common law privilege against self-incrimination is applicable to companies. In *Westinghouse Uranium Contract, Re*,[139] the House of Lords followed an earlier Court of Appeal decision, *Triplex Safety Glass Co. v Lancegaye Safety Glass Ltd*,[140] and held, without any discussion, that a corporation can claim the privilege. In the *Triplex* case, du Parcq L.J. had referred to a Canadian decision[141] and stated:

> "[I]t is true that a company cannot suffer all the pains to which a real person is subject. It can, however, in certain cases be convicted and punished, with grave consequences to its reputation and to its members, and we can see no ground for depriving a juristic person of those safeguards which the law of England accords even to the least deserving of natural persons. It would not be in accordance with principle that any person capable of committing, and incurring the penalties of, a crime should be compelled by process of law to admit a criminal offence."[142]

---

[139] [1978] A.C. 547.
[140] [1939] 2 K.B. 395.
[141] *Webster v Solloway Mills and Co.* (1931) 1 D.L.R. 831.
[142] [1939] 2 K.B. 395 at 409. See also *R. v Hertfordshire County Council, Ex p. Green Environmental Industries Ltd* [2000] 2 A.C. 412, [2000] 1 All E.R. 773, [2000] 2 W.L.R. 373, where the House of Lords considered the argument that the privilege against self-incrimination applied in respect of records maintained under the United Kingdom

5–50   The Court of Appeal's approach emphasises the importance of the privilege in preserving "fair play". While it recognises that a distinction may be drawn between the position of the corporate and the individual defendant, it finds that it would be contrary to "principle" to try and punish corporate defendants without applying the appropriate safeguards. This emphasis on the institutional values[143] served by the privilege can be contrasted with the approach of both the Canadian Supreme Court and the Australian High Court.

Canada

5–51   In *Webster v Solloway Mills & Co.*,[144] the Supreme Court of Alberta held that the privilege could be invoked by a company but gave no reason for this part of its decision.[145] Section 11(c) of the Canadian Charter of Rights and Freedoms provides that only a witness can claim the privilege against self-incrimination[146] and in *R. v Amway Corp*,[147] the Canadian Supreme Court, reflecting the decision of its United States counterpart in *Hale v Henkel*,[148] held that a corporation could not be a witness. Sopinka J. considered the rationale of the privilege, stating that s.11(c) of the Charter is:

> "intended to protect the individual against the affront to dignity and privacy inherent in a practice which enables the prosecution to force the person charged to supply the evidence out of his or her own mouth. Although disagreement exists as to the basis of the principle against self-incrimination, in my view, this factor plays a dominant role."[149]

Australia

5–52   In *Environmental Protection Authority v Caltex Refining Co. Pty Ltd*,[150] the Australian High Court was faced with this issue. After finding that the historical justifications for the privilege could not be said to apply,[151] the court

---

Environmental Protection Act 1990. The defendants were an individual and a company and Lord Hoffman did not challenge the assumption that the privilege against self-incrimination was available to both, although he found that the privilege was not applicable to the defendants on the facts of the case.

[143]   See discussion of the values underpinning the privilege below at paras 5–55 to 5–64.

[144]   (1931) 1 D.L.R. 831 (Supreme Court of Alberta).

[145]   *ibid*. at 833–834. Harvey C.J.A. stated briefly:
"The last objection was that this claim of privilege should be limited to natural persons and that it could not be taken advantage of by a corporation. On principle one cannot see any reasonable ground for the support of such view."

[146]   s.11(c) of the Charter provides as follows:
"Any person charged with an offence has the right: ...
   (c)   not to be compelled to be a witness in proceedings against that person in respect of the offence."

[147]   [1989] 1 S.C.R. 21.

[148]   201 U.S. 43 (1906).

[149]   [1989] 1 S.C.R. 21 at 31.

[150]   (1993) 178 CLR 477.

[151]   See para.32 of the judgment. See also the judgment of Costello J. in *Heaney v Ireland* [1994] 3 I.R. 593.

went on to consider the modern rationale for its retention and found that it was bound up with the concept of human rights, and a desire to protect the dignity of the individual.[152] This rationale for the guarantee would not justify its extension to corporate persons. The court then examined the argument that the privilege was there to maintain a fair state–individual balance and that it served to maintain the integrity of the common law accusatorial system of criminal justice. The first point was rejected on the basis of the vast resources of companies as opposed to individuals. The second argument was also rejected as the court found that the privilege, which was already heavily eroded by statute, was not fundamental to an accusatorial system of justice.[153] The court also emphasised the difficult nature of corporate crime control as part of its reasoning. The denial of the privilege to corporations has continued.[154]

5–53   The highest courts in Canada and Australia have thus eschewed the temptations of corporate theory in favour of an approach that assesses carefully the rationale behind the privilege against self-incrimination and whether it would be consistent with that rationale to extend protection to the corporate person. It is submitted that this approach is superior to that taken in the United States and New Zealand. The majority opinion in *Hale v Henkel* demonstrates that Dewey's criticisms of the manipulability of corporate theory were well founded.[155]

5–54   Interestingly, while using the same approach, the courts in Canada and Australia have taken a different stance on this matter to the Court of Appeal in England and Wales. This is because the former have emphasised the autonomy based values which justify the protection, whereas the latter has focused instead on the institutional values it serves. As was noted earlier,[156] exploring the question of corporate constitutional protection by focusing on the nature of the guarantee has the useful side effect of exposing the values underlying the provisions of the Irish Constitution. The next section considers the nature of the right to silence in some detail before going on to consider the appropriate solution under the Irish Constitution.

The Nature of the Right to Silence and Companies

5–55   The origins of the privilege against self-incrimination and the right to

---

[152] Paras 33 and 34 of the judgment.

[153] In a more recent case, involving an individual, the High Court of Australia described the right to silence as one of the "principles that are designed, among other things, to achieve an equilibrium between the state and accused persons". *R. v Lavender* [2005] HCA 37, 43 MVR 1 at [89].

[154] *e.g. Louis James Carter v the Managing Partner, Northmore, Hale, Davy and Leake* [1995] HCA 33, (1995) 129 ALR 593, (1995) 183 CLR 121, where it was noted by Tuohy J. that: "The privilege against incrimination is a basic tenet of our law, at least in the case of individuals."

[155] See Dewey, above at para.1–50.

[156] Above at para.2–36.

silence were explored by Costello J. in *Heaney*.[157] Essentially, these protections evolved as part and parcel of the common law adversarial system of criminal justice. They were developed to prevent abuses of state power and to maintain the integrity of that system.[158] The rationale for these protections has, however, been stated differently in modern times. The following quote from *Murphy v Waterfront Comm'n of NY Harbor*[159] contains a comprehensive description by the United States Supreme Court of the modern rationale for the privilege against self-incrimination:

> "It reflects many of our fundamental values and most noble aspirations: our unwillingness to subject those suspected of crime to the cruel trilemma of selfaccusation, perjury or contempt; our preference for an accusatorial rather an inquisitorial system of criminal justice; our fear that incriminating statements will be elicited by inhumane treatment and abuses; our sense of fair play which dictates a fair state-individual balance by requiring the government to leave the individual alone until good cause is shown for disturbing him and by requiring the government in its contest with individuals to shoulder the entire load; our respect for the inviolability of the human personality and the right of every individual to a private enclave where he may lead a private life, our distrust of deprecatory statements; and our realisation that the privilege, while sometimes a shelter to the guilty, is often a protection to the innocent."[160]

5–56 It is submitted that this extract describes accurately the modern basis for the privilege, which can be seen as reflecting both autonomy and institutional values.[161] Modern Irish case law supports the idea that there is now a dual rationale underlying the right to silence generally and the privilege against self-incrimination in particular. An examination of the judgment of Shanley J. in *National Irish Bank, Re* reveals that the privilege is concerned with the common law's sense of fair play, as well as the free will and privacy interests of the defendant.[162] This dual rationale for the privilege is also reflected in the

---

[157] Above at para.5–06.

[158] Furthermore, at the time of their development, the corporate criminal was simply not envisaged and as late as the 18th century, Holt C.J. held that a corporation could not be indicted but that its members could. *Anonymous Case* (1701) 12 Mod. 559, cited in Leigh, *The Criminal Liability of Corporations in English Law* (LSE Research Monographs 2, 1969), at p.15. See also *R. v Great North of England Ry* (1846) 9 Q.B. 315. See also O'Neill, "The Rule Against Double Jeopardy and the Company and Some Thoughts on Interpretive Seepage" (2005) 15(3) I.C.L.J. 16.

[159] 378 U.S. 52 (1964).

[160] *ibid.* at 55.

[161] Dennis states that there are four values which are commonly assumed to underlie the privilege: the presumption of innocence, preventing wrongful convictions, protecting privacy and protecting the accused from the cruel trilemma—"Instrumental Protection, Human Right or Functional Neccessity? Reassessing the Privilege Against Incrimination" [1995] C.L.J. 342. On the values underpinning the right to silence, see McGrath, *Evidence* (Thomson Round Hall, 2005), at 623–630.

[162] See also *United States v Balsys* 524 U.S. 666, 118 S.Ct. 2218, 141 L Ed 2d 575 (1998),

judgments of Kearns J. in both *Dunnes Stores* and *Swacliffe*. In the former case, he emphasised the significance of the fact that the incriminating material in that case had an objective reality.[163] As he took the view that the right to silence was concerned with the free will of the suspect,[164] this was an important factor in his determination that the interference complained of was proportionate. Of course, the fact that material exists objectively also indicates that its use is unlikely to lead to a false conviction. Thus, Kearns J.'s judgment can also be read as recognising the institutional values underlying the right to silence. Similarly, in *Swacliffe*, while he did make reference to the autonomy interests which justify the privilege against self-incrimination, he also pointed out that this was not a case where, in his opinion, there was an increased risk of untrue confessions or abuses of power by the State.[165]

5–57   More recently, in *Curtin v Dáil Éireann*,[166] the Supreme Court, referring to the decision of the ECHR in *Saunders v UK*,[167] held that the privilege does not apply to real evidence and endorsed the view that it is concerned rather with respecting the will of the individual. Interestingly, the ECHR held more recently, in *Jalloh v Germany*,[168] that the privilege can be invoked where real evidence is concerned. That case concerned the administration of emetics to an individual to obtain evidence, a procedure which was found by the court to violate Art.3 of the Convention—inhuman and degrading treatment.

5–58   Insofar as a right is guaranteed to ensure the integrity of the criminal justice process, there is no reason why it should be applicable to individuals alone.[169] It has been noted that:

> "Much of the emotional appeal of maintaining an accusatorial system vaporizes when an artificial entity claims the privilege against incrimination, particularly if that entity has great economic power."[170]

5–59   While some of the dicta above advert to the vast resources of companies as a justification for denying them protections such as the privilege against

---

where Breyer J., joined by Ginsberg J., dissenting stated that the privilege respects human dignity and privacy, prevents governmental overreaching and helps to preserve an accusatorial system of criminal justice.

[163] *ibid.*

[164] This concern to protect the free will of the individual influenced the Canadian Supreme Court in taking a narrow view of the circumstances in which the protection can be said to have been waived by an individual—*R. v Turcotte* [2005] 2 S.C.R. 519.

[165] *ibid.*

[166] [2006] I.E.S.C. 14.

[167] (1997) 23 E.H.R.R. 313.

[168] Application No. 54810/00, [2006] 20 B.H.R.C. 575. See also *Funke v France* Application No. 10828/84 (1993) and *JB v Switzerland* Application No. 31827/96 (2001).

[169] See Feldman, "Corporate Rights and the Privilege Against Self-Incrimination" in *Corporate and Commercial Law: Modern Developments* (Feldman and Miesel eds, Lloyd's of London Press Ltd, 1996) for a similar classification of the types of values underlying the privilege.

[170] Fiebach, *op.cit.* at 395.

self-incrimination, this is only an intuitive argument which does not bear scrutiny. Surely nobody would suggest that the burden of proof be reversed in criminal trials of wealthy individuals. On the other hand, it seems counter-intuitive to protect undercapitalised companies, but not those with extensive resources. To justify the denial of constitutional protection to companies, the better approach is to steer clear of mere intuition and examine the values which underlie that protection and whether these would be best served by providing or denying constitutional protection to the company.

5–60   One institutional value reflected in the extract from *Murphy* reproduced above is the preference for an accusatorial criminal justice system. This was certainly the traditionally understood basis of the privilege at common law.[171] It has been said of the privilege against self-incrimination that its "general affinity with the traditional burden of proof in criminal proceedings and the presumption of innocence is self-evident".[172] In this respect, it can be seen as part of the common law tradition of fair play. An important aspect of this tradition is that it is up to the State to obtain the necessary evidence to prove its case. The right to silence and the privilege against self-incrimination can be seen as integral to this system.[173] This appears to have influenced the Court of Appeal's decision in *Triplex Safety Glass Co. v Lancegaye Safety Glass Ltd.*[174] This connection with fair procedures as an institutional value is also reflected in the case law of the European Court of Justice, which has held that the right to silence is applicable to corporate entities in the context of competition law.[175]

5–61   Another aspect of the constitutional guarantee of the right to silence is the concern to protect the innocent from conviction.[176] This serves both the liberty of the innocent individual—an autonomy value—and the integrity of the criminal justice system—an institutional value. Insofar as the safety of verdicts is concerned, there may be no good reason for distinguishing between the individual and the corporate person. False convictions in either case damage the legitimacy of the criminal justice system as a whole. It has been noted that that rationale is most logically applicable to the right to silence of those in police custody, as it is these suspects who may break down under the pressure of interrogation and incriminate themselves, despite being innocent.[177] It could also usefully be applied to persons being questioned under the procedure set out in Pt II of the Companies Act 1990—as amended.[178] The corporate

---

[171] See the discussion of Costello J.'s judgment in *Heaney v Ireland* [1994] 3 I.R. 593, above at para.5–06.

[172] Murray, *op.cit.* at p.71.

[173] Although numerous statutory encroachments may suggest otherwise.

[174] [1939] 2 K.B. 395. Above at paras 5–49 to 5–50. This argument did not convince the Australian High Court. Above at para.5–52.

[175] *EC v SGL Carbon AG* [2006] All E.R. (D) 357 (Jun). See *Case T-112/98 Mannesmannrohren-Werke v Commission* [2001] E.C.R. II-729 at [66] and [67].

[176] *Report of the Royal Commission on Criminal Justice*, Cm.2263, 1993, Chap.4.

[177] Dennis, *op.cit.* at 348–353.

[178] See n.19 above, for a summary of the scheme under Pt II of the Act. In this context, it has been noted that:

defendant can only give oral evidence through its individual officers. It is possible that a company could be falsely convicted if a corporate officer broke down during questioning and made a false confession which also implicated the company. While individuals are now immune from the subsequent use of such information in criminal proceedings against them, the company is not immune.[179]

5–62   It should be noted, however, that even in the case of the right to silence of a person in custody, where institutional values are arguably at stake, the modern trend is to emphasise the free will of the individual as the protected interest—an autonomy value—as opposed to the possibility of a wrongful conviction—which implicates institutional as well as autonomy values. For example, the Canadian Supreme Court has held that fairness, rather than the potential for unreliable confessions, is the crucial factor where this protection is concerned.[180] Similarly, the Australian High Court has emphasised that the right to silence in this context is concerned with the matter of an individual's right to choose to speak, as opposed to any concerns about the veracity of admissions.[181]

5–63   If the autonomy values underlying the protection are emphasised, their application to the corporate accused is difficult to justify. *Murphy* refers to the "cruel trilemma of selfaccusation, perjury or contempt" and the theory that the privilege against self-incrimination protects against cruel choices appears in the Irish case law also.[182] This theory is difficult to apply to companies, as it is premised on the ability of the party claiming the protection to experience "cruelty". While an individual company officer might suffer such cruelty, we are concerned here with the position of the company as a suspect or accused person. If we take as an example a situation where a company officer is

---

"[P]ersons accused of criminal offences of this nature [corporate crime] tend to be inherently less sympathetic than others who might seek with greater apparent moral justification to rely upon a right to silence. Persons involved in complex corporate fraud are more likely to be adequately educated, well advised and in a better position to avail tactically of the liberties conferred by a right of this nature, than other criminals. As such there is a common perception that such persons are less likely genuinely to require the protection of the privilege."
Murray, *op.cit.* at p.82.

[179] See s.29 of the Companies Enforcement Act 2001, discussed above at paras 5–12 to 5–21.

[180] *R. v Herbert* [1990] 2 S.C.R. 151; *R. v Broyles* [1991] 3 S.C.R. 595.

[181] *R. v Swaffield* (1998) 192 CLR 159; *Pavic v The Queen* [1998] HCA 1. See also *C Plc v P (Secretary of State for the Home Department intervening)* [2006] Chap. 549, where Evans-Lombe J., in the High Court of England and Wales, expressed the view that the privilege, as encompassed by Art.6 of the European Convention on Human Rights, was concerned primarily with respecting the will of the individual. The Irish Court of Criminal Appeal has held that this respect for the will of the individual in custody does not require the cessation of questioning where that individual indicates that he does not wish to answer questions—*The People (at the Suit of the DPP) v Jie*, unreported, Court of Criminal Appeal, July 25, 2005.

[182] For more on the prevention of cruel choices, see Greenawalt, "Silence as a Moral and Constitutional Right" (1981) 23 Wm.& Mary L.Rev. 15.

questioned in respect of an investigation into the company in which the company, and not the officer, is under suspicion, then it becomes apparent that the company cannot rely on the right to silence on the basis of the cruel trilemma theory, as the officer is faced with no such dilemma. The cruel trilemma rationale has been subject to heavy criticism, ever since Bentham attacked it for protecting only the guilty on the basis that the innocent are faced with no trilemma.[183] Whatever its merit,[184] the rationale highlights the unusual position of the company in relation to the privilege which arises also with respect to the right to silence. As a company can act only through individuals, it cannot claim the privilege directly, and the question is whether it can claim it through them.[185]

5–64   Privacy has also been mooted as the modern rationale for the privilege against self-incrimination[186] and the applicants in *Dunnes Stores* specifically relied on the "right to privacy" in the context of their submissions in relation to s.19(5) and the right to silence.[187] Privacy is an immunity that is inherently connected to the liberty of the individual and is categorically an autonomy based interest. As noted above, the United States Supreme Court has held that companies are entitled to protection against searches of business premises and seizure of corporate property under the Fourth Amendment.[188] That aspect of the case arguably conflates property rights with the right to privacy.[189] While the two are connected where the individual is concerned, that is because they both serve to protect the liberty of the individual. To take a similar approach to the company is misguided. In any case, in the context of the privilege, it appears that it is a very specific aspect of privacy that is at stake. For example, in relation to individuals, the privilege does not apply in relation to the gathering of bodily samples.[190] This suggests that if privacy is the rationale, it is privacy in a narrower sense, such as mental privacy.[191] In any event, the same difficulty

---

[183] Bentham, *Rationale of Judicial Evidence* (J. Bowring ed., Edinburgh, 1843), vol.VII, B.IX, 452–454, where he described this as the "foxhunter's reason" or the "old woman's reason" for the privilege. There is a variant of this theory which argues that the instinct for preservation is such that a suspect in custody may lie and that silence is better than misleading the police. Westen and Mandell, "To Talk, to Balk, or to Lie: The Emerging Fifth Amendment Doctrine of the 'Preferred Response'" (1982) 19 Am.Crim.L.Rev. 521.

[184] One advantage of this theory is that it fits well with the scope of the privilege in that it covers decisions to make disclosure and not other evidence. Dennis, *op.cit.* at 358–359.

[185] Below, Conclusion.

[186] See *Hammond v Commonwealth* (1982) 152 CLR 188 at 210; Murray, *op.cit.* It should be noted that this is a modern reinterpretation insofar as privacy in this context is recognised as a constitutional norm. The common law recognised no free-standing right to privacy in the sense that it is used in modern rights discourse. For criticism of the notion of privacy as the rationale for the privilege, see Dennis, *op.cit.* at 356–358. He argues that if privacy was the rationale, then the prohibition on the use of compelled testimony in later criminal proceedings would not satisfy the privilege.

[187] [2002] 2 I.R. 60 at 108.

[188] *Hale v Henkel* 201 U.S. 43.

[189] *cf. Hoecsht AG v Commission* (Joined cases 46/87 and 227/88) [1989] E.C.R. 02859.

[190] *McGonnell v AG*, unreported, High Court, McKechnie J., September 16, 2004.

[191] Dennis, *op.cit.* at 359.

as arose in the context of the "cruel trilemma" rationale arises in relation to privacy—the individual claiming the privilege is doing so on behalf of another.

CONCLUSION

5–65 The United States Supreme Court, the Canadian Supreme Court and the Australian High Court have made it clear that the corporate defendant cannot benefit from the privilege against self-incrimination.[192] It is submitted that this is the better conclusion. Of these three courts, the first reached this conclusion by applying a particular perspective on corporate personality. While there is some support in the Irish cases for a concession theory of the company, the case law is not clear on this[193] and there is some support for an aggregate approach to the company also.[194] The problematic implications of the latter approach will be addressed in Chapter 8. The important point of this chapter is to highlight Dewey's point that theories of the corporation are too manipulable to provide a sound basis for constitutional protection. Indeed, writing in the context of the English courts, it has been pointed out that:

> "Rather than being a coherent body of carefully elaborated principles, the … 'theories' constitute a collection of ideas acquired or formulated at various times in various circumstances to serve various purposes … In this landscape, a search for logic, clarity or coherence is a wild goose chase. Moreover, in one sense, any criticism of the theories as lacking these qualities is missing the point. They are not intended to be subjected to this sort of examination, but rather to be available for use if necessary … It is rather unfortunate that such dicta are expressed in general, theoretical terms because they are used more on a case-by-case basis: if it seems to lead to a reasonable result (the analysis of what is a 'reasonable result' probably being reached on a pragmatic, partly instinctive, basis) idea X will be used rather than idea Y."[195]

5–66 Indeed, as can be seen from the decision in *Hale v Henkel*,[196] the adoption of theoretical positions in relation to the company can lead to inconsistency in this context. The better approach is to evaluate the purpose of the constitutional protection and take that as the starting point when determining

---

[192] It has been argued that companies should be able to claim at least two of the elements mentioned in *Murphy v Waterfront Comm'n NY Harbor* 378 U.S. 52 (1964). See Zornow and Krakaur, "On the Brink of a Brave New World: The Death of Privilege in Corporate Criminal Investigations" (2000) 37 Am.Crim.L.Rev. 147 at 151.

[193] Ussher, *op.cit. Iarnród Éireann v Ireland* [1996] 3 I.R. 321, [1995] 2 I.L.R.M. 161; *Att.-Gen. for England and Wales v Brandon Book Publishers Ltd* [1986] I.R. 597, [1987] I.L.R.M. 135; *PMPS Ltd v Att.-Gen.* [1983] I.R. 339, [1984] I.L.R.M. 88; *Chestvale Properties Ltd v Glackin* [1992] I.L.R.M. 221.

[194] *Iarnród Éireann v Ireland* [1996] 3 I.R. 321.

[195] Foster, "Company Law Theory in Comparative Perspective: England and France" (2000) 48 Am.J.Comp.L. 573 at 590–591.

[196] 201 U.S. 43 (1906).

its beneficiaries. Of course, such an analysis may lead to different conclusions, as evidenced by the contrasting conclusions reached by the Court of Appeal of England and Wales compared with the outcome in Australian High Court and Canadian Supreme Court.[197] Nevertheless, it is submitted that an explicit consideration of the purposes served by constitutional protection is the most appropriate way to approach the question under the Irish Constitution. To the extent that different courts may come to different conclusions, this reflects their different understanding of these due process protections. Thus, to ask whether the Irish Constitution protects the company in this context is to seek an explanation of the basis of these due process protections and how they fit into the Irish Constitution.[198]

5–67 As has been noted above, the Irish courts have taken the approach that the right to silence prior to trial and the privilege against self-incrimination are protected under different provisions of the Constitution.[199] It may prove instructive to explore this nomenclature and its implications, if any, for the corporate defendant. Locating the pre-trial aspects of the right to silence within Art.40.6.1(i) may be justified on a literal reading of Art.38.1, as the latter refers only to the trial stage of criminal proceedings. On the other hand, it could be argued that this particular immunity is more akin to the constitutional right to privacy[200] than the right to freedom of expression. Such an analysis would place the right under the rubric of Art.40.3.1.[201] The fact that this provision refers to the rights of the "citizen" is unlikely to be fatal to the application of the rights thereunder to companies.[202] As we have seen from the discussion above, however, the type of privacy at issue here is not applicable to a company.[203] Relocating the right to silence under Art.40.3.1, therefore, might resolve the issue of its application to companies. As far as the privilege against self-incrimination at trial is concerned, it appears that the most appropriate locus for it is under Art.38.1. The values which underlie it, insofar as they are based on individual autonomy, may serve to exclude the privilege in this context also. As suggested above,[204] the application or otherwise of these protections to the company under the Irish Constitution should depend

---

[197] The discrepancy between the outcome in the Australian High Court and the Court of Appeal of England and Wales is all the more remarkable due to the common law basis of the protection in both jurisdictions.

[198] *cf.* para.2–36.

[199] Above at paras 5–06 and 5–11. That the right to silence comes under Art.40.6.1(i) has been confirmed by the Supreme Court in *Rock v Ireland* [1998] 2 I.L.R.M. 3; *Gilligan v Criminal Assets Bureau* [1998] 3 I.R. 185; *DPP v Finnerty* [1999] 4 I.R. 364, [2000] 1 I.L.R.M. 191.

[200] *Kennedy v Ireland* [1987] I.R. 587, [1988] I.L.R.M. 472; *X. v Flynn*, unreported, High Court, May 19, 1994; *Hanahoe v Hussey* [1998] 3 I.R. 69.

[201] *ibid.* This reads as follows: "The State guarantees in its laws to respect, and, as far as practicable, by its laws to defend and vindicate the personal rights of the citizen." See Part III.

[202] *Iarnród Éireann v Ireland* [1996] 3 I.R. 321, [1995] 2 I.L.R.M. 161. See also *Hale v Henkel* 201 U.S. 43.

[203] Above at paras 3–27 to 3–35.

[204] Above at paras 3–24 to 3–38.

on the extent to which the Irish courts emphasise their function in protecting institutional or autonomy interests in a given case.

5–68   In the final analysis, the most convincing pragmatic argument against extending the right to silence and the privilege to companies is that made by the United States Supreme Court in *Hale v Henkel*[205] —as a company can only give evidence through third parties, and the privilege applies only to the person testifying, the corporate defendant can never be in a position to assert the privilege. The same considerations apply in relation to the right to silence generally. The denial of these constitutional protections to the corporate defendant, together with the exclusion of involuntarily obtained inculpatory material from later proceedings against the person who disclosed it, allows for the protection of the individual agent of the company without bringing corporate law enforcement to a standstill.

---

[205] 201 U.S. 43 (1906). See also the Canadian Supreme Court in *R. v Amway Corp* [1989] 1 S.C.R. 21.

CHAPTER 6

THE RULE AGAINST DOUBLE JEOPARDY AND THE COMPANY

INTRODUCTION

6–01   This chapter continues to explore the extent to which due process guarantees are available to the company under the Irish Constitution. Its focus is on the rule against double jeopardy. Like the right to silence, the rule against double jeopardy was protected at common law before being imported into the Irish Constitution, albeit with some uncertainty as to its correct location thereunder.[1] In *Registrar of Companies v Judge David Anderson and System Partners Ltd*,[2] a company relied on the rule against double jeopardy and its claim was rejected on the merits without any comment about the propriety of allowing a company to rely on the rule. Paragraphs 6–02 to 6–08 introduce the rule and explain its origins. Paragraphs 6–09 to 6–24 examine the way in which the Irish courts have referred to the rule as a constitutional guarantee to the criminal defendant. This section also considers the recent Irish Supreme Court decision mentioned above. Paragraphs 6–25 to 6–32 explore the position of the rule under the Fifth Amendment of the United States Constitution and consider the case law in which companies have successfully relied on the rule in the United States. Paragraphs 6–33 to 6–38, applying the preferred approach mentioned in Chapter 3, analyse the nature of the rule as protected under the Irish Constitution and whether companies should be permitted to rely on it. They conclude that the rule is underpinned by both autonomy and institutional values and find that this may mean that a different version of the rule applies to the company than that which applies to the individual.

WHAT IS THE RULE AGAINST DOUBLE JEOPARDY?

6–02   The prohibition on double jeopardy has its roots as far back as Ancient Greece.[3] The rule was established early on at common law that "no man is to be brought into jeopardy of his life more than once for the same offence."[4] It

---

[1]   See discussion below, paras 6–11 to 6–13.
[2]   Unreported, Supreme Court, December 16, 2004; [2004] I.E.S.C. 103.
[3]   See Rehnquist J. (dissenting) in *Whalen v United States* 445 U.S. 684 at 699 (1980) where he quotes *1 Demosthenes 589* (J. Vincent trans., 4th edn, 1970). See also, McDermott, *Res Judicata and Double Jeopardy* (Butterworths, 1999), at p.200.
[4]   Blackstone, 4 *Commentaries* 335 (1809).

was reflected in four pleas a defendant could make to bar subsequent prosecutions: *autrefoit acquit, autrefoit convict, autrefoit attaint* and former pardon.[5] The modern doctrine comprises the first of these two pleas.

6–03   At common law, the doctrine *autrefoit acquit* operated so that:

> "When a man is once fairly found not guilty upon any indictment, or other prosecution, before any court having competent jurisdiction of the offence he may plead such acquittal in bar of any subsequent accusation for the same crime."[6]

6–04   This common law rule applied to erroneous acquittals and the general rule was that:

> "an acquittal made by a court of competent jurisdiction and made within its jurisdiction, although erroneous in point of fact, cannot as a rule be questioned and brought before any other court."[7]

6–05   This principle could be overridden by statute only where this was clearly stated to be the intent of the legislature.[8]

6–06   The plea of *autrefoit convict* precluded subsequent trials for an offence of which the defendant had already been found guilty. Where a conviction within jurisdiction is quashed, the defendant may raise a plea in bar to prevent a further trial.[9]

6–07   The rule, as it applies in the United States, has been described as follows:

> "The modern rule against double jeopardy operates so as to prevent more than one prosecution for the same offence where the defendant has already been convicted or acquitted and precludes the application of multiple punishments in respect of the same offence."[10]

---

[5]   *United States v Wilson*, 420 U.S. 332 (1975) at 341–342.
[6]   O'Higgins C.J. citing Blackstone in *DPP v O'Shea* [1982] I.R. 384 at 406.
[7]   Palles C.B. in *R.(Kane) v Tyrone Justices* (1906) 40 I.L.T.R. 181 at 182.
[8]   *ibid.*
[9]   *Tynan v Keane* [1968] I.R. 348.
[10] Henning, "The Conundrum of Corporate Criminal Liability: Seeking a Consistent Approach to the Constitutional Rights of Corporations in Criminal Prosecutions" 63 Tenn.L.Rev. 793. The US Supreme Court has held that multiple punishments may be allowed where this is clearly the intention of the legislature. *Garrett v United States* 471 U.S. 773 (1985). While the rule has no express constitutional protection in Australia, the High Court of Australia has recognised its application to the Commonwealth of Australia—*Rogers v R* (1994) 181 CLR 251. While it applies as a principle of common law, the High Court of Australia has also made reference to its international obligation to recognise the rule against double jeopardy. See *Fardon v Att.-Gen.* 210 ALR 50 (2004) at [181].

6–08   The Irish law in relation to the rule is not so absolute.[11] It has been stated to apply only where there has been a trial on the merits before a court of competent jurisdiction[12] and a directed acquittal will not bar a retrial.[13]

IRELAND

6–09   The Irish courts have not yet addressed the issue of whether companies can rely on the rule against double jeopardy. In *The Registrar of Companies v Judge David Anderson and System Partners Ltd*,[14] a company had been prosecuted for failing to file annual returns after having paid the higher fee due with the late filing. During the prosecution in the District Court, the company had argued that such proceedings offended against the rule against double jeopardy. The District Court judge struck the summonses out and the Registrar of Companies sought judicial review of that decision. The application failed in the High Court and he appealed to the Supreme Court. Murray J. referred to the rule as one of common law. He found that it was not offended in this case because the first penalty had been merely administrative in nature. Geoghegan J. stated that the rule was "well known throughout the common law world"[15] and that it had constitutional protection under the United States Constitution. He made no mention, however, of the rule having constitutional status in this jurisdiction. Neither judge made any reference to the corporate status of the defendant in the case.

6–10   The implications of this decision for the constitutional status of the rule against double jeopardy in general, as well as for the corporate criminal defendant, will be considered later in this section. First, however, some exposition of the treatment of the rule under the Irish Constitution will be undertaken.

6–11   As with the privilege against self-incrimination, there is no specific reference to the rule against double jeopardy in the Irish Constitution.[16] It was vigorously defended in the Kings Bench Dublin by Lord Earlsfort in *R. v James Foy*[17] and was undoubtedly protected at common law in this jurisdiction prior to the enactment of the Constitution. Its current basis is less clear. In 1980, in *O'Leary v Cunningham*,[18] the rule was described as being based on the common law.

---

[11] See below at paras 6–09 to 6–17.

[12] O'Dálaigh J. in *Att.-Gen. v O'Brien* [1963] I.R. 92 at 100, (1964) 98 I.L.T.R. 107 at 111.

[13] *Att.-Gen. v Judge Binchy* [1964] I.R. 395. This is because the accused cannot be said to have been put in jeopardy; *DPP v O'Shea*, [1982] I.R. 384.

[14] Unreported, Supreme Court, December 16, 2004.

[15] *ibid.*

[16] The rule is specifically protected in the constitutions of South Africa, India, Canada and the United States, McDermott, *op.cit.* at p.201.

[17] (1788) Vern.& Scr. 540 at 594. Cited in McDermott, *op.cit.* at p.208. See also Palles C.B. in *R.(Kane) v Tyrone Justices* (1906) 40 I.L.T.R. 181.

[18] [1980] I.R. 367 at 378.

6–12 It appears that the rule now has constitutional status although there is some confusion as to which provision of the Constitution encompasses it. In *DPP v O'Shea*,[19] it was argued that the rule applied by virtue of Arts 38.1[20] and 38.5.[21] O'Higgins C.J. rejected the attempt to locate the rule within Art.38.1, stating:

> "I do not see that trial in due course of law has any relevance to the question whether the decision arrived at as a result of the trial may or may not be appealed. The phrase 'in due course of law' denotes fair and just procedures in the conduct of the trial and the due application of the relevant law; it denotes no more."[22]

6–13 Finlay P. found that the rule was "one of the essential ingredients of trial with a jury" guaranteed under Art.38.5.[23] Henchy J. also agreed that the rule was a "quintessential feature of the jury trial".[24] Walsh J., on the other hand, took the view that the plea of *autrefoit acquit* was "equally applicable to convictions in non-jury trials as it is to convictions arising from jury trials" although he was unclear whether this was "to be regarded as a tradition or as a rule of law".[25] He took the view that jury trials where verdicts are wrong in law or secured by improper means are not trials in accordance with law and *must* thus be liable to appeal in order to satisfy the requirements of Art.38.1.[26]

6–14 Whatever constitutional umbrella it falls under, the rule is limited in this jurisdiction by specific constitutional provisions which make reference to appeals. For example, Art.34.4.3 provides that all High Court decisions may be appealed to the Supreme Court and leaves it to the Oireachtas to restrict this appellate jurisdiction.[27] It was held in *DPP v O'Shea*[28] that, in the absence of legislation to the contrary, the jurisdiction of the Supreme Court encompassed acquittals by the Central Criminal Court.[29] Similarly, there is no constitutional

---

[19] [1982] I.R. 384.

[20] The text of Art.38.1 is reproduced above at para.4–03.

[21] [1982] I.R. 384 at 394. Walsh J. appears to be of the view that only Art.38.5 was relied upon, *ibid.* at 419. The text of Art.38.5 is reproduced below, at para.7–04.

[22] [1982] I.R. 384 at 403.

[23] *ibid.* at 411. See also 411–414. The High Court of Australia has taken the view that the rule applies outside of the context of jury verdicts. See *Island Maritime Ltd v Filipowski* 228 ALR 1 (2006).

[24] [1982] I.R. 384 at 431.

[25] *ibid.* at 416.

[26] *ibid.* at 420.

[27] Art.34.4.3 provides that:
"The Supreme Court shall, with such exceptions and subject to such regulations as may be proscribed by law, have appellate jurisdiction from all decisions of the High Court, and shall also have appellate jurisdiction from such decisions of other courts as may be prescribed by law."

[28] [1982] I.R. 384. This was a majority decision of the Supreme Court and two strong dissents were delivered by Finlay P. and Henchy J.

[29] The Central Criminal Court is the High Court exercising its criminal jurisdiction, s.11 Courts (Supplemental Provisions) Act 1961.

bar to the legislature providing for appeals from the District Court to the Circuit Court.[30] *O'Shea* has been recently approved in the Supreme Court[31] and it appears that the Irish Constitution thus provides only a limited version of the protection against double jeopardy. Of course, the mere allowing of an appeal itself, without the power to retry a criminal offence, would mean that the rights of an acquitted person would be *de facto* protected to a certain extent. It is not entirely clear what the position is in relation to this under Art.38.1.

6–15 In *DPP v Quilligan*,[32] the Supreme Court allowed an appeal from a directed acquittal in the Central Criminal Court and the matter of a retrial arose. A majority of three indicated that the case was one in which no retrial would be appropriate. Two of that majority also emphasised that the Supreme Court had no power to order a retrial, Henchy J. stating that:

> "This rule … which is sometimes referred to as the rule against double jeopardy, is but an aspect of the canon of fundamental fairness of legal procedures inherent in our Constitution, which is expressed in the maxim *nemo debet bis vexari pro eadem causa*."[33]

6–16 Earlier in his judgment, Henchy J. posited the view that a hypothetical statute which provided generally for retrials from acquittals on indictment might be unconstitutional:

> "on grounds such as that it would not accord with fundamental fairness or that it would not be compatible with what is inherent in the constitutional guarantee of trial by jury".[34]

6–17 Section 11 of the Criminal Procedure Act 1993 abolished appeals from the Central Criminal Court to the Supreme Court, except insofar as such appeals related to the constitutionality of any law. Appeals under s.34 of the Criminal Procedure Act 1967 are also retained.[35] These occur where the Attorney-

---

[30] *Considine v Shannon Regional Fisheries Board* [1997] 2 I.R. 404, [1998] 1 I.L.R.M. 11. This case concerned s.310 of the Fisheries (Consolidation) Act 1959, which permitted the prosecution to appeal an acquittal in a fisheries prosecution from District Court to the Circuit Court. It was held by the Supreme Court that this was not a violation of Art.34.3.4, which provides that "the Courts of First Instance shall also include courts of local and limited jurisdiction with a right of appeal as determined by law."

[31] *Fitzgerald v DPP*, unreported, Supreme Court, July 25, 2003. This case concerned s.4 of the Summary Jurisdiction Act 1857, which permits an appeal by way of case stated from an acquittal.

[32] [1986] I.R. 495 (*Quilligan No.1*); [1989] I.R. 45 (*Quilligan No.2*).

[33] [1989] I.R. 45 at 90. He was joined by Griffin J.

[34] *Quilligan No.2* [1989] I.R. 45 at 56.

[35] s.11 of the Criminal Procedure Act 1993 reads as follows:
"(1) The right of appeal to the Supreme Court, other than an appeal under section 34 of the Criminal Procedure Act, 1967, from a decision of the Central Criminal Court is hereby abolished.
(2) This section shall not apply to a decision of the Central Criminal Court in so

General refers to the Supreme Court a question of law arising from a directed acquittal, without prejudice to the acquittal itself.[36]

6–18   As can be seen from the dicta cited above, the view has been expressed in the Supreme Court judgments that the rule against double jeopardy is an aspect of the right to trial by jury under Art.38.5. As this provision does not apply to minor offences,[37] the position in relation to summary trials arises.

6–19   Under s.2 of the Summary Jurisdiction Act 1857, as amended by s.51 of the Courts (Supplemental Provisions) Act 1961—which provides for appeals by way of case stated to the High Court—a person acquitted on summary trial may be tried again on the same charge. Yet the rule against double jeopardy has been applied in the context of summary offences.[38] For example, the *Quilligan* approach has been followed by the Supreme Court to prevent the prosecution from initiating a retrial of a summary offence where the original trial has collapsed due to the absence of an essential proof.[39]

6–20   Perhaps the correct interpretation is that the rule has constitutional status in relation to indictable offences, but in the context of a summary offence, it is rule at common law without constitutional force. The United States takes this dual approach in relation to those cases which fall outside the Fifth Amendment.[40]

6–21   Alternatively, the rule could be located under Art.38.1—it could be categorised as an aspect of a trial in due course of law in the sense that a

---

far as it relates to the validity of any law having regard to the provisions of the Constitution."
See also s.3, 1st Sch., Pt II of the Courts and Court Officers Act 1995 and s.44 thereof.
[36] s.34 of the Criminal Procedure Act 1967 provides as follows:
  "(1) Where, on a question of law, a verdict in favour of an accused person is found by direction of the trial judge, the Attorney General may, without prejudice to the verdict in favour of the accused, refer the question of law to the Supreme Court for determination.
    (2) The statement of the question to be referred to the Supreme Court shall be settled by the Attorney General after consultation with the judge by whom the direction was given and shall include any observations which the judge may wish to add.
    (3) The Supreme Court shall assign counsel to argue in support of the decision."
  Also, where accused persons succeed in applications to dismiss the charges against them under s.1A of the Criminal Procedure Act 1967—as inserted by s.9 of the Criminal Procedure Act 1999—the prosecution may appeal against that dismissal to the Court of Criminal Appeal under s.4E(7) of the Criminal Procedure Act 1967. Where such an appeal succeeds, s.4E(8)(b) provides that the trial will continue as if the charges had never been dismissed.
[37] Art.38.2.
[38] *Ó Maonaigh v Fitzgerald* [1964] I.R. 458; *O'Leary v Cunningham* [1980] I.R. 367.
[39] *Mulligan v Judges of the Dublin Circuit Criminal Court*, unreported, Supreme Court, May 19, 1999.
[40] See Fisher, "Double Jeopardy, Two Sovereignties and the Intruding Constitution" (1961) 28 U.Chi.L.Rev. 591.

second trial on the same charge following an acquittal or a conviction would not constitute such a trial. This would mean that the rule had a constitutional basis in relation to all trials—summary or on indictment.

6–22 A further possibility, evident in the judgment of Henchy J. in *Quilligan*, was reiterated in *Feeney v District Justice Clifford*,[41] a case which concerned a summary trial, where Barr J. indicated that double jeopardy deprived an accused of her "constitutional right to fair procedures".[42] Perhaps the rule could thus be seen as an aspect of that unenumerated constitutional right under Art.40.3.[43]

6–23 Yet two other possible solutions are that the rule is an aspect of trial by jury in the case of non-minor offences, but is protected under Arts 38.1 or 40.3 in the context of summary offences.

6–24 Before exploring the implications, if any, of this taxonomy for the corporate defendant, it is proposed to examine the position of the corporate defendant under the double jeopardy clause of the Fifth Amendment to the United States Constitution.

UNITED STATES

6–25 The Fifth Amendment to the United States Constitution prohibits placing a person twice in jeopardy for the same offence. The relevant clause reads as follows: "nor shall any person be subject for the same offence to be twice put in jeopardy of life or limb".[44] The double jeopardy clause was extended to state courts under the Fourteenth Amendment's due process clause in *Benton v Maryland*.[45]

6–26 The United States Supreme Court has held that the rule protects against a second prosecution for the same offence after an acquittal or a conviction and it protects against multiple punishments for the same offence.[46] As is the case in the Irish courts, the rule has been subject to a number of exceptions in the United States.[47] A retrial may be ordered where there is "manifest necessity" for one or where "the end of public justice would be defeated" without one.[48] In practice, this has resulted in retrials where there is some problem with the

---

[41] [1989] I.R. 668.

[42] *ibid.* at 673.

[43] For a consideration of the extent to which companies may rely on this unenumerated constitutional right, see below, Chap.12.

[44] The full text of the Fifth Amendment is reproduced in Chap.2 at n.27.

[45] 395 U.S. 784 (1969).

[46] *North Carolina v Pearce* 395 U.S. 711 (1969).

[47] "[T]he finality guaranteed by the Double Jeopardy Clause is not absolute, but instead must accommodate the societal interest in prosecuting and convicting those who violate the law." O'Connor J. in *Garrett v United States* 471 U.S. 773 at 790 (1985).

[48] *United States v Perez* 22 U.S. (9 Wheat.) 579 at 580 (1824).

jury[49] and where the dismissal of an indictment is unrelated to the guilt or innocence of the accused.[50] A defendant whose appeal against conviction is successful cannot prevent a retrial.[51]

6–27 Unlike the Irish courts, the United States Supreme Court has been presented with a number of opportunities to consider whether the rule against double jeopardy applies to companies. In *Puerto Rico v Shell Co. (PR)*,[52] the court stated *obiter* that the rule applied in that case to preclude a second prosecution. In *Rex Trailer Co. v United States*,[53] the court rejected a corporation's argument based on the double jeopardy clause on the merits, without considering the prior question whether the clause protected such a body. The matter arose in relation to corporate defendants again in *Fong Foo v United States*,[54] where the directed acquittals of three defendants, a corporation and two of its employees, had been set aside by the Court of Appeals. The Supreme Court did not distinguish between defendants in holding that the double jeopardy clause had been violated when the appeal had succeeded and retrials had been ordered.[55]

6–28 Lower courts in the United States have taken a similar approach to that of the Supreme Court in *Fong Foo v United States*.[56] In *United States v Armco Steel Corp*,[57] the government sought to retry corporations on a charge that had been dismissed in a previous prosecution. The federal district court prohibited the retrial on the basis of the Fifth Amendment, stating that it seemed "beyond doubt … that the constitutional jeopardy extended to 'persons' includes corporations". While the court pointed out that there was no authority on the matter, it found that "either directly or indirectly persons own all corporations and thus 'persons' must ultimately suffer whatever penalties are imposed upon the corporation."[58]

6–29 Other district court decisions have simply assumed the clause applies to corporations to prevent subsequent prosecutions and applied it without reflection.[59] Lower courts have precluded the government from challenging errors made at trial which have resulted in the acquittal of a corporate defendant.

---

[49] *Richardson v United States* 468 U.S. 317 (1984)—retrial after mistrial due to deadlocked jury; *Arizona v Washington* 434 U.S. 497 (1978)—manifest necessity where defence opening statement may have biased jurors. See Henning, *op.cit.* at 843–844.

[50] *United States v Scott* 437 U.S. 82 (1978).

[51] *United States v Ball* 163 U.S. 662 (1876).

[52] 302 U.S. 253 (1937).

[53] 350 U.S. 148 (1956).

[54] 369 U.S. 142 (1962).

[55] *cf.* the decision of the High Court of Australia in *Island Maritime Ltd v Filipowski* 228 ALR 1 (2006).

[56] 369 U.S. 142 (1962).

[57] 252 F.Supp. 364 (C.D.Cal. 1996).

[58] *ibid.* at 368.

[59] *United States v American Honda Motor Co.* 273 F.Supp. 810; *United States v American Honda Co.* 271 F.Supp. 979 (N.D.Cal.1967); *United States v Unites States Gypsum Co.* 404 F.Supp. 619 (D.D.C. 1975).

In *United States v Southern Ry*,[60] the district court had dismissed an indictment against a corporation for alleged violations of the Elkins Act on the ground that the evidence presented did not disclose criminal conduct. The government appealed and the United States Court of Appeals for the Fourth Circuit found that the dismissal was an acquittal and that no further proceedings could be taken. The court cited *Fong Foo v United States*[61] and *United States v Armco Steel Corp*[62] as authority that "the double jeopardy clause of the Fifth Amendment has been applied to corporations as well as to natural persons."[63]

In *United States v National Security Bank*,[64] the United States Court of Appeals for the Second Circuit precluded the government from challenging jury instructions following the acquittal of a corporate criminal defendant. The court noted that the petitioner in *Fong Foo v United States*[65] had set forth arguments in favour of applying the double jeopardy clause to corporations. While conceding that the Supreme Court had not explicitly accepted these, it went on to set out reasons why the clause should apply. It stated that many corporations have one or few shareholders and "the small entrepreneur is not spared the embarrassment, expense, anxiety and insecurity resulting from repeated trials on criminal charges, simply because he has incorporated his modest business."[66] The judgment goes on to state that: "In this unequal contest, 'fundamental fairness' requires that the Government, having had a full try at establishing criminal wrongdoing, shall not have another."[67] This seems inconsistent with the Supreme Court's stance on the Fifth Amendment insofar as it protects the privilege against self-incrimination.[68] *Braswell v United States*[69] held that the privilege does not apply to closely held corporations, regardless of the size of the corporation or any effect the incriminating material may have on any individual shareholder.

6–30   The application of the double jeopardy clause to corporations arose before the Supreme Court again in *United States v Martin Linen Supply Co.*[70] Again, the court neglected to consider the implications of applying the protection to corporate defendants. The district court in this case entered judgments of acquittal for two corporate defendants where the jury had been deadlocked and, thus, discharged. The prosecution appealed this order. The power of the government to appeal in criminal cases was set out in a statute[71] which allowed such appeals unless "the double jeopardy clause of the United States Constitution prohibits further prosecution". The Supreme Court referred

---

[60] 485 F.2d 309 (4th Cir. 1973).
[61] 369 U.S. 142 (1962).
[62] 252 F.Supp. 364 (C.D.Cal. 1996).
[63] *ibid.* at 312.
[64] 546 F.2d 492 (2nd Cir. 1976), cert. denied, 430 U.S. 950 (1977).
[65] 369 U.S. 142 (1962).
[66] 546 F.2d 492 at 494.
[67] *ibid.* at 495.
[68] Henning, *op.cit.* at 848–849.
[69] 487 U.S. 99 (1988).
[70] 430 U.S. 564 (1977).
[71] 18 U.S.C. §3741 1988.

back to *Fong Foo v United States*[72] and held that any verdict of acquittal disposes of the issue. It thus held that any consideration of the merits of the appeal would violate the Fifth Amendment.

6–31 The United States Court of Appeals for the First Circuit considered the application of the clause to corporations in *United States v Hospital Monteflores, Inc.*[73] Here, a hospital and its director were indicted for submission of false Medicare reimbursement forms. The district court entered judgments of acquittal in relation to both defendants. The government appealed against the order in relation to the corporate defendant only, arguing that the double jeopardy clause did not protect corporations. The Court of Appeals rejected this submission and held that both corporations and individuals are similarly protected under the clause. The court noted that:

> "[C]orporations do not have human emotions, but that does not mean that they do not 'suffer' during criminal trials in the sense of experiencing harm to a legitimate, protectible interest."[74]

6–32 It went on to note that:

> "corporate well-being is heavily dependent on that elusive quality known as 'good will' ... [and] corporations can be made very insecure by prolonged periods of bad publicity."[75]

THE NATURE OF THE RULE AGAINST DOUBLE JEOPARDY AND COMPANIES

6–33 The Irish case law discussed in paras 6–11 to 6–23 above demonstrates that the constitutional basis of the rule against double jeopardy is unclear. If it is considered an aspect of Art.38.5, it has been suggested that jury trial in Ireland is a "constitutional imperative" as opposed to a "personal right" and that, as such, there is no reason why the protections of Art.38.5 should be inapplicable to the legal person.[76] If the rule was constitutionally protected by virtue of Art.40.3, different considerations might apply.[77] While the constitutional locus of the rule is an interesting question, it is really only significant to the extent that it tells us something about the purpose of the rule.

---

[72] 369 U.S. 142 (1962).

[73] 575 F.2d 332 (1st Cir. 1978).

[74] *ibid.* at 335.

[75] *ibid.*

[76] Hogan and Whyte, *Kelly: The Irish Constitution* (4th edn, Lexis-Nexis Butterworths, 2003), at p.1221. The authors are of the opinion that the classification of trial by jury as a personal right would make little difference in the light of the decision of Keane J. in *Iarnród Éireann v Ireland* [1996] 3 I.R. 321, [1995] 2 I.L.R.M. 161. This case is discussed below in Chap.8, at paras 8–19 to 8–27. For a discussion of the application of the jury trial envisaged by Art.38.5 to the company, see Chap.7.

[77] For a general discussion of the company and the unenumerated right to fair procedures under Art.40.3, see below, Chap.12.

As the matter is unresolved, we must look elsewhere to understand the rationale of the rule and the propriety of applying it to the corporate defendant.

6–34 Like the privilege against self-incrimination, the rule against double jeopardy has a dual rationale in that it serves both institutional and autonomy interests.[78] The rule has been described by the United States Supreme Court as follows:

> "The underlying idea, one that is deeply ingrained in at least the Anglo-American system of jurisprudence, is that the State with all its resources and power should not be allowed to make repeated attempts to convict an individual for an alleged offense, thereby subjecting him to embarrassment, expense and ordeal and compelling him to live in a state of anxiety and insecurity, as well as enhancing the possibility that even though innocent he may be found guilty."[79]

6–35 In considering whether the rule against double jeopardy ought to be applied to the company, the dual rationale for the rule should be examined. The rule can be said to perform five specific functions.[80] It prevents prosecutorial harassment of defendants through multiple trials for the same conduct. It protects the acquitted and convicted defendant by ensuring that the ordeal of the trial itself is over. It obviates the risk that the innocent will be convicted by preventing the prosecution from securing an unfair advantage through multiple trials. It prevents jury nullification and allows the jury to perform its function within the criminal justice system. It also ensures proportionate punishment by prohibiting multiple sentences and penalties for the same conduct.[81]

---

[78] Henning, *op.cit.* He uses the term "personal interests" but it is submitted that the adjective "autonomy" accurately describes the interests at stake. The related doctrine of issue estoppel has been held not to form part of the criminal law in Ireland—*Lynch v Moran* [2006] I.E.S.C. 31; *cf. Kenny v Doyle* [2006] I.E.H.C. 155.

[79] *Green v United States* 355 U.S. 184 (1957) at 187–188.

[80] King, "Portioning Punishment: Constitutional Limits on Successive and Excessive Penalties" (1995) 144 U.Pa.L.Rev. 101. See also *Double Jeopardy and Prosecution Appeals*, UK Law Commission, 2001, Pt IV. See also the minority concurring opinion of Gummow and Hayne JJ. of the High Court of Australia in *Island Maritime Ltd v Filipowski* 228 ALR 1 (2006), where they noted at [41]:
> "'Double jeopardy' is an expression that is not always used with a single meaning. It is an expression used in relation to several different stages of the process of criminal justice: prosecution, conviction and punishment. It describes values which underpin a number of aspects of the criminal law, rather than a rule that can be stated as the premise for deductive reasoning. The essence of these values is most often seen as captured in three maxims: interest reipublicae ut sit finis litium (it is in society's interest that there be an end to litigation), res judicata pro veritate accipitur (what is adjudicated is taken as the truth), and nemo debet bis vexari pro una et eadem causa (no one should twice be vexed for one and the same cause)."

[81] Arguably, some of these interests are already protected outside of the Fifth Amendment to the US Constitution. It has been argued that the due process clause of the Fourteenth Amendment and the bar on excessive fines under the Eighth Amendment can adequately guarantee most of the interests identified as falling within the ambit of the rule against

6–36   The rule can thus be seen as one which promotes institutional values.[82] It constrains prosecutorial power and prevents its misuse. Where defendants are acquitted, the state cannot keep trying them until the "right" result is achieved.[83] Similarly, where defendants are convicted, they cannot be retried to inflict further penalties in respect of the same violation. These effects of the rule guard against excessive use of prosecutorial powers. It precludes successive prosecutions where trials collapse due to, *inter alia*, mistakes by the prosecution, and in this way, serves to encourage more efficient trial preparation. In this regard, the rule can be seen as one which is of relevance to the integrity of the criminal justice system as a whole, regardless of the identity of the defendant. Such an analysis indicates that its application to corporate defendants is justified.

6–37   As well as these institutional values, however, the rule is there to protect the criminal defendant from the hardship of further trials as well as further punishments. The dicta which reflect this value suggest that the rule against double jeopardy is caught up with the autonomy and dignity of natural persons. Anthropomorphising the corporation to fit within this paradigm is unconvincing. While a corporation may suffer "embarrassment" in the sense of loss of goodwill,[84] such loss is really pecuniary. The question is really whether the rule against double jeopardy protects property as well as dignity and autonomy. While it might be stated that the protection of individual defendants from multiple punishments could have the effect of protecting their property rights, it is submitted that this is only one aspect of the rule, an aspect that is subsidiary to the primary purposes of preventing hardship of a type that can only be experienced by human beings. The question thus arises whether the aspects of the rule against double jeopardy can be parsed into those which respect the first rationale and those which respect the latter.

6–38   One solution is to apply the rule to companies to prohibit a second prosecution for the same offence after conviction and to prevent the infliction of multiple punishments on the corporation where such additional punishment is not authorised by the legislature. Such an approach answers the concerns voiced in *United States v Armco Steel Corp*[85] in relation to protecting shareholders. The corporate defendant should not, however, be protected from

---

double jeopardy. The High Court of Australia has held that the rule against double jeopardy applies to the quantification of punishment—see *Pearce v R* (1998) 194 CLR 610.

[82]   See the judgment of Gaudron and Gummow JJ. of the High Court of Australia in *R. v Carroll* (2002) 213 CLR 635, where they refer to the rule as one which touches "upon matters fundamental to the structure and operation of the legal system and to the nature of judicial power". 213 CLR 635 at 661.

[83]   See the reference to the "enormous prosecutorial power of the Government to subject an individual to embarrassment, expense and ordeal … compelling him to live in a continuing state of anxiety". Souter J. in *Will v Hallock* 126 S.Ct. 952 (2006), referring to *Abney v United States,* 431 U.S. 651 (1977).

[84]   See quote above at para.6–34.

[85]   252 F.Supp. 364 (C.D.Cal. 1996).

further trials following an acquittal.[86] To the extent that this may involve hardship for the small entrepreneur mentioned in *United States v National Security Bank*,[87] the individuals concerned in the company still enjoy constitutional immunity from repeated prosecution for indictable offences in their personal capacities. The argument for this application of a limited version of the rule to the company is that the first two situations concern the acceptable limits of the power of the State to prosecute and punish criminal defendants. Where there has been an erroneous acquittal, the corporate defendant should not benefit from that windfall which is a social harm. That harm is acceptable where defendants are individuals because they merit protection against insecurity and anxiety.

CONCLUSION

6–39 The Supreme Court's decision in *System Partners Ltd* contains dicta which suggest that the rule against double jeopardy can now be viewed as one which pertains at a constitutional level only in the context of indictable offences. This is the only interpretation of the case which is consistent with the preceding case law.[88] While this deprives the individual and the corporate defendant of the benefit of the rule at a constitutional level in the context of a summary trial, the pleas remain open to the defendant at common law, subject to any statutory provision to the contrary. Where an indictable offence is involved, the individual defendant should enjoy the protection of the rule at a constitutional level. The corporate defendant, whether charged with a minor or serious offence, should only enjoy the protection of the rule to the extent outlined above,[89] whether the rule is protected at common law or under the Constitution. The idea that a constitutional protection might apply in a different way to the corporate than to the individual defendant is consistent with the dual rationale underlying many constitutional provisions.

---

[86] Henning, *op.cit.* at 852. He also argues that:
> "attempts to inflict multiple punishments on the corporation, to the extent the additional punishment is not authorised by the legislature, should not be sanctioned by the Court. Any punishment greater than that adopted by the legislature is an obvious misuse of judicial authority to the detriment of the defendant." *ibid.*

[87] 546 F.2d 492 (2nd Cir. 1976), cert. denied, 430 U.S. 950 (1977).

[88] If the rule is protected under Art.38.1, then the judgments would imply that the constitutional basis for the rule has been removed. It is unlikely that such a major departure would be made without a more extensive analysis.

[89] The desirability of this distinction between minor and serious offences is not under discussion here. If the rule was protected under Art.38.1, then the decision in *System Partners Ltd* would be of far more dramatic effect.

CHAPTER 7

TRIAL BY JURY

INTRODUCTION

7–01 This chapter considers whether the company is entitled to rely on Art.38.5 of the Irish Constitution, which provides for the trial by jury of certain criminal offences.[1] In 1957, a company attempted to rely on its putative right to a trial by jury under Art.38.5 in relation to a customs offence. Both the High Court and the Supreme Court rejected the argument on the basis that the offence concerned was not criminal in nature and, therefore, fell outside the ambit of the constitutional guarantee. Neither court took objection to the fact that the defendant in the case was a company[2] and the matter has not arisen for judicial consideration since. Paragraphs 7–02 to 7–03 of this chapter introduce the concept of the jury trial and explain its origins. Paragraphs 7–04 to 7–09 describe its treatment under Bunreacht na hÉireann. Paragraphs 7–10 to 7–17 explore the case law under the United States Constitution, which has been interpreted so as to allow companies to claim a right to trial by jury. Paragraphs 7–18 to 7–27 consider the nature of the Irish constitutional guarantee of trial by jury and whether the values it serves would be furthered by allowing companies to rely on it.

TRIAL BY JURY

7–02 The criminal jury trial originated at common law. It is an institution of considerable vintage:

> "To the Englishman of the fourteenth century … it had become an 'ancient prerogative' to have twelve laymen stand between him and the vengeance of the king in a criminal prosecution of any kind, whether the charge were tippling at the inn or murder."[3]

7–03 From the mid-seventeenth century, however, in both England and America, legislatures made exceptions to the requirement of trial by jury due

---

[1] See below at paras 7–04 to 7–09 for an explanation of the position under the Irish Constitution. The text of Art.38.5 is reproduced below at para.7–04.

[2] *Att.-Gen. v Southern Industrial Trust Ltd* (1957) 94 I.L.T.R. 161, discussed below at para.8–13.

[3] Frankfurter and Corcoran, "Petty Federal Offenses and the Constitutional Guaranty of Trial by Jury" (1926) 39 Harv.L.Rev. 917 at 971.

to its cost and inefficiency. By the time of the adoption of the United States Constitution, summary offence legislation was commonplace in England and in the American colonies. It has thus been assumed by the United States Supreme Court that the United States Constitution and the Sixth Amendment were not intended to preclude the federal legislature from excluding "petty" offences from jury trial.[4]

IRELAND

7–04 This arrangement is explicit in the Irish Constitution. Jury trials are provided for in Art.38.5 which states as follows:

> "Save in the case of the trial of offences under section 2,[5] section 3[6] or section 4[7] of this Article no person shall be tried on any criminal charge without a jury."

7–05 Article 38.2 states that: "Minor offences may be tried by courts of summary jurisdiction." The only court of summary jurisdiction is the District Court.[8] There is no constitutional definition of what constitutes a minor offence. The Supreme Court, in *Melling v Ó Mathghamhna*,[9] set out a number of criteria by reference to which an offence could be designated minor. The most important of these indicia is the severity of the punishment.[10] The moral quality of the act will also be taken into account. In *Melling*, Lavery J. pointed out that:

> "Opinions based on moral considerations as to the seriousness of offences against the Customs Acts vary greatly but I think it cannot be doubted that an element of moral blame should be imputed to those who, on a commercial scale, violate the Revenue Acts."[11]

7–06 Kingsmill Moore J. stated that:

---

[4] *ibid.* See also Adlestein, "A Corporation's Right to a Jury Trial under the Sixth Amendment" (1994) 27 U.C.Davis L.Rev. 375, 390–393. There is no recognition of the right to jury trial under Art.6 of the European Convention on Human Rights. *X and Y v Ireland*, No. 8299/78 3 D.R. 10 (1980); *Callaghan v UK*, No. 14739/89, 60 D.R. 296 (1989). *Cf.* Blom-Cooper, "Article 6 and Modes of Criminal Trial" [2001] E.H.R.L.R. 1.

[5] This refers to minor offences. See discussion below at paras 7–05 to 7–07.

[6] Article 38.3.1° provides for the establishment of special courts "for the trial of offences where ... the ordinary courts are inadequate to secure the effective administration of justice, and the preservation of public peace and order".

[7] Article 38.4 concerns military tribunals and trials of members of the Defence Forces.

[8] The criminal jurisdiction of the District Court is prescribed by s.33(1) of the Courts (Supplemental Provisions) Act 1961.

[9] [1965] I.R. 1, (1963) 97 I.L.T.R. 60.

[10] *Conroy v Att.-Gen.* [1965] I.R. 411; *Cullen v Att.-Gen.* [1979] I.R. 394; *Kostan v Ireland* [1978] I.L.R.M. 12; *Clancy v Wine* [1980] I.R. 228; and *L'Henryenat v Ireland* [1983] I.R. 193. See discussion of these cases in Hogan and Whyte, *Kelly: The Irish Constitution* (4th edn, Lexis-Nexis Butterworths, 2003), at pp.1176–1179.

[11] *Melling v Ó Mathghamhna* [1965] I.R. 1 at 15, (1963) 97 I.L.T.R. 60 at 67.

"From a moral point of view the offence of smuggling varies enormously. The importation of a pair of silk stockings for personal use would not be too sternly reprobated by even strict moralists; but large-scale smuggling of valuable articles, organised and conducted as a profitable business has not only been reprobated in severe terms by judges but would be regarded by most as involving moral delinquency."[12]

7–07   The above dicta suggest strongly that commercial scale tax evasion and smuggling offences will be less likely to be considered minor offences than one-off, individual violations. As the former are arguably more likely to be committed by companies, the question arises whether Art.38.5 applies to legal persons who have committed non-minor offences.

7–08   In *Att.-Gen. v Southern Industrial Trust Ltd*,[13] both the High Court and Supreme Court considered arguments that proceedings for forfeiture under the Customs Consolidation Act 1876 constituted criminal proceedings requiring trial by jury. In rejecting this argument on the basis that the proceedings were civil in nature, neither court referred to the fact that the defendant to the proceedings was a company.

7–09   Thus ends the case law on the matter. The United States Supreme Court has considered this issue in some depth and it is proposed to examine how that court has dealt with the matter before exploring the position of companies under Art.38.5.[14]

The United States

7–10   Article 38.2 and Art.38.5 are mirrored in the United States Constitution. Article III thereof provides: "the trial of all Crimes … shall be by Jury",[15] and the Sixth Amendment states:

"In all criminal prosecutions, the accused shall enjoy the right to a speedy and public trial, by an impartial jury of the State and district wherein the crime shall have been committed."[16]

7–11   While, at first blush, the above seems to indicate that the United States Constitution requires a jury trial for every crime, the United States Supreme

---

[12] *Melling v Ó Mathghamhna* [1965] I.R. 1 at 34, (1963) 97 I.L.T.R. 60 at 77. See also *O'Sullivan v Hartnett* [1983] I.L.R.M. 79, where McWilliam J. drew a distinction between the offence of catching a single salmon unlawfully and being in possession of an illegal haul of over 900 salmon.
[13] (1957) 94 I.L.T.R. 161.
[14] Below at paras 7–18 to 7–27.
[15] US Constitution, Art.III, §2, clause 3.
[16] US Constitution, Amendment VI. In 1968, in *Duncan v Louisiana* 391 U.S. 145 (1968), the Supreme Court held that the due process clause of the Fourteenth Amendment guarantees a right of jury trial in state as well as federal criminal cases.

Court has interpreted the protection as meaning that the right to a jury trial attaches to all offences which are "serious", but not those which are "petty". Thus, as early as 1888, the Supreme Court asserted that the United States Constitution imported the common law distinction between serious and petty offences, stating that "there are certain minor or petty offences that may be proceeded against summarily, and without a jury."[17] As is the case in the Irish courts, the designation of an offence as minor or serious in nature will depend largely on the severity of any penalty attaching to it, with a six-month sentence being the demarcation line.[18]

7–12   The issue of whether there could ever be a right to a jury trial where the defendant was not susceptible to imprisonment first arose for consideration in the United States Supreme Court in *Muniz v Hoffman*.[19] An injunction had been issued during an industrial relations dispute and the district court found the relevant labour union in contempt for a number of violations and fined it $10,000. The court did not consider whether a union could assert the right to jury trial in a criminal contempt proceeding. It also omitted to decide whether a fine alone can render an offence "serious" enough to require a jury trial. Instead, the court delivered a rhetorical judgment, stating that the union "was not deprived of whatever right to jury trial it might have under the Sixth Amendment".[20] In the circumstances, the fine was not "of such magnitude that a jury should have been interposed to guard against bias or mistake".[21]

7–13   In the subsequent case of *United Mine Workers v Bagwell*,[22] the Supreme Court removed one obstacle to jury trials for corporate entities by deciding that a heavy fine alone can place an offence in the "serious" category and trigger the right to a jury trial.[23] The matter is dealt with tersely in a footnote to Blackmun J.'s opinion,[24] which referred to *Muniz* and went on to state as follows:

---

[17]   *Callan v Wilson* 127 U.S. 540 at 552 (1888).

[18]   Henning, "The Conundrum of Corporate Criminal Liability: Seeking a Consistent Approach to the Constitutional Rights of Corporations in Criminal Prosecutions" 63 Tenn.L.Rev.793 at 864–866. In *Callan*, the Supreme Court focused on the nature of the offence of conspiracy. It found that it was "grave in character, affecting the public at large". 127 U.S. 540 at 555. It was thus found to require a jury trial despite the fact that the maximum period of imprisonment was 30 days. It was not until *United Mine Workers v Bagwell* 114 S.Ct. 2552 (1994) that the court developed its policy of looking at the penalty alone.

[19]   422 U.S. 454 (1975).

[20]   *ibid.* at 477. A similarly rhetorical approach was taken by Judge Greene in the District Court for the District of Colombia in *United States v NYNEX Corp*, 781 F.Supp. 19 (D.D.C. 1990) at 27 where he felt able to assume "without deciding, that corporations have a jury trial right at all where only a fine is imposed".

[21]   422 U.S. 454 at 476.

[22]   114 S.Ct. 2552 (1994).

[23]   The Supreme Court focused most of its attention on determining whether the case concerned constituted civil or criminal contempt.

[24]   In which the majority joined him in relation to this particular point.

"We need not answer today the difficult question where the line between petty and serious contempt fines should be drawn, since a $52,000,000 fine unquestionably is a serious contempt sanction."[25]

7–14   After *Bagwell* and *Muniz*, it could be stated that an organisation not susceptible to imprisonment could nonetheless invoke the right to jury trial in proceedings for criminal contempt. It is noteworthy that both of the organisations claiming the right to jury trial were unincorporated trade unions. They were, thus, arguably more susceptible to an aggregate theory analysis. Indeed, the trade union is a classic subject for such an approach.[26]

7–15   One author[27] has argued on the basis of *Bagwell* and *Muniz* that the right of a corporation to jury trial under the United States Constitution is limited to criminal contempt proceedings. This is because such proceedings present a "structural danger"[28] that government power could be misused by a judge who prosecutes, adjudicates and sentences such offences. In criminal contempt proceedings, the judge is vindicating its power and dignity over the accused and, thus, its neutrality is more likely to be compromised than in ordinary criminal proceedings.[29]

7–16   In this jurisdiction, criminal contempt is not an offence which attracts a jury trial even where it is a serious offence. It is, thus, an unusual exception to Art.38.5.[30] The reason for this is considered by Henchy J. in *DPP v Walsh*,[31] where he stated that a perverse but irreversible jury verdict could "set at nought the constitutional guarantee that basic fairness of procedures will be observed" and could also "undermine the independence of the judiciary".[32] This approach is very different to that taken by the United States Supreme Court. That court has found that "convictions for criminal contempt are indistinguishable from ordinary criminal convictions, for their impact on the individual defendant is the same."[33]

---

[25]   See n.5 of Blackmun J.'s opinion.

[26]   On the aggregate theory of the corporation see Chap.1.

[27]   Henning, *op.cit.* at 872–876.

[28]   *ibid.* at 872. But see Adlestein, *op.cit.* at 381:

> "As the Supreme Court has repeatedly declared that there is no difference between criminal contempt and any other criminal offense regarding the constitutional right to jury trial, those contempt cases involving organisations, together with the Supreme Court decisions involving an individual's right to a criminal jury in traditional criminal prosecutions, provide important material for the consideration of a corporation's right to a jury trial."

[29]   Henning, *op.cit.*

[30]   *DPP v Walsh* [1981] I.R. 412. The Supreme Court indicated in that case that a person accused of criminal contempt is entitled to a jury trial on a matter of factual dispute. For an analysis suggesting that approach might be unconstitutional, see Hogan and Whyte, *op.cit.* at p.1236.

[31]   [1981] I.R. 412.

[32]   *ibid.* at 440. See also O'Higgins C.J. at 429, where he indicates that criminal contempt is not an offence dealt with under Art.38.5 of the Constitution. Indeed, he suggests that Art.38 in its entirety may be inapplicable to such offences, a proposition which is surely of doubtful constitutionality.

[33]   *Bloom v Illinois* 391 U.S. 194 at 201 (1968). See also *Frank v United States* 395 U.S.

7–17 In any case, the Irish courts are unlikely to develop a body of law specifically referable to the right of companies to jury trials when charged with criminal contempt. What, then, of the proposition that Art.38.5 applies to companies generally?

The Nature of the Right to Trial by Jury and Companies

7–18 As has been mentioned above, there has been no Irish case which specifically considers the propriety of jury trials for corporate defendants. There are a number of English cases where companies have been tried by jury, but no reference is made to the propriety or otherwise of the mode of trial in the judgments.[34] It has been suggested that jury trial in Ireland is a "constitutional imperative", as opposed to a personal right.[35] Indeed, the wording of this Article,[36] together with the fact that it does not appear under the heading "Fundamental Rights", but rather, under the heading "Trial of Offences"[37] lends credence to such a classification.

7–19 Referring to the mandatory language of Art.38.2, the authors of *Kelly: The Irish Constitution* have opined that:

> "Article 38.2 and Article 38.5 are more clearly bound up with the fabric and structure of the proper administration of criminal justice and what the Constitution deems to be the allocation of cases to their proper level (District Court or trial on indictment) within the criminal justice system than with a purely 'personal' constitutional right. On this basis, therefore, the provisions of Article 38.2 and Article 38.5 apply, irrespective of whether the accused is a natural or a legal person."[38]

7–20 This analysis is supported by the judgment of Walsh J. in *de Búrca v Att.-Gen.*,[39] where he stated:

> "[T]he Constitution has enshrined and entrenched the principle of trial with a jury and, quite clearly, the law of the State must make provision for trial with a jury and also for the manner in which the jurors will be selected. The wording of this constitutional provision relating to the trial of criminal cases with a jury is in mandatory terms. Trial with a jury is

---

147 (1969). At 148: "For the purposes of the right to trial by jury, criminal contempt is treated just like all other criminal offenses."

[34] *R. v ICR Haulage Ltd* [1944] K.B. 551; *R. v Great North of England Ry* 115 E.R. 1294; (1846) 9 Q.B. 315.

[35] Hogan and Whyte, *op.cit.* at p.1221.

[36] Compare with the wording of the Sixth Amendment to the US Constitution, reproduced above at para.7–10.

[37] The only other provision which appears under this heading is Art.39, which delineates the criminal offence of treason.

[38] Hogan and Whyte, *op.cit.* at pp.1193–1194.

[39] [1976] I.R. 38.

thus not simply an option open to the accused but is a system imposed by the Constitution, subject only to exceptions mentioned."[40]

7–21 The judiciary, however, frequently refer to Art.38.5 as establishing a "right" to a jury trial and the language of rights has infiltrated the case law.[41] The authors of *Kelly* state that even if Art.38.5 does create purely personal rights, there is no reason why a legal person could not invoke the right to jury trial.[42] In so stating, they refer to the decision of Keane J. in *Iarnród Éireann v Ireland*.[43] That case, which concerns the constitutional right to property, is considered in detail in another chapter.[44] As it is a mainstay of this book that each constitutional provision must be carefully examined in order to assess its applicability to companies,[45] the *Iarnród Éireann* analogy alone will not suffice. Instead, we have to look at the purpose of Art.38.5 in more detail.

7–22 It is submitted that this constitutional provision serves a number of purposes which were summarised by Henchy J. in *de Búrca v Att.-Gen.*[46] as follows:

> "[T]o ensure that every person charged with an offence will be assured of a trial in due course of law by a group of laymen who, chosen at random from a reasonably diverse panel of jurors drawn from the community, will produce a verdict of guilty or not guilty free from the risks inherent in a trial conducted by a judge or judges only, and which will therefore carry with it the assurance of both correctness and public acceptability that may be expected from the group verdict of a such a cross-section of the community."[47]

7–23 The *de Búrca* case concerned the constitutionality of the system of jury selection under the Juries Act 1927 which allowed only owners of property over a certain rateable valuation to serve as jurors, and excluded women unless they specifically requested otherwise. The two defendants in the case were women who were accused of offences involving damage to property, and the case considered their argument that the list from which juries were selected must be representative of the community as a whole. Thus, the Supreme Court emphasised that juries should, at least potentially, be comprised of the peers of the accused.[48] This is one aspect of the right to trial by jury which a company cannot enjoy.

---

[40] *de Búrca v Att.-Gen.* [1976] I.R. 38, Walsh J. at 66.
[41] *e.g.* Finlay C.J. refers to "the constitutional right to a trial with a jury contained in Article 38.5", *People v Davis* [1993] 2 I.R. 1 at 13, [1992] I.L.R.M. 407 at 414. See also *de Búrca v Att.-Gen.* [1976] I.R. 38, O'Higgins C.J. at 61, Walsh J. at 66, Henchy J. at 74; *Gilligan v Special Criminal Court* [2005] I.E.S.C. 86.
[42] Hogan and Whyte, *op.cit.*
[43] [1996] 3 I.R. 321, [1995] 2 I.L.R.M. 161.
[44] Below at paras 8–19 to 8–27.
[45] See discussion above at paras 1–49 to 1–56 and 3–24 to 3–38 and Chap.5.
[46] [1976] I.R. 38.
[47] *ibid.* at 74.
[48] See, *e.g.* the decision of Griffin J. [1976] I.R. 38 at 82.

7–24 As pointed out in the quote from Henchy J. set out above, another purpose of jury trials is to avoid "risks inherent in a trial conducted by a judge or judges only". In *DPP v Walsh*,[49] he referred to this again where he noted that trial by jury was constitutionally preferred to a trial which was based on:

> "factual findings made by a single judge who might be thought biased, legalistic, remote or, at best, to be carrying the risk of error that is inherent in a professional dispenser of justice sitting without a jury."[50]

7–25 Insofar as the purpose of Art.38.5 is to avoid error in the criminal justice system, it must surely be equally applicable to companies. The "correctness and public acceptability" of verdicts is a crucial aspect of the legitimacy of the criminal justice system as a whole and, therefore, it is important to preserve these values in all criminal trials, regardless of the nature of the defendant. It is thus submitted that companies should be held to have a prima facie right to trial by jury.

7–26 One practical difficulty with applying Art.38.5 to the corporate defendant concerns the interpretation of Art.38.2 in this context. The difficulty was highlighted in the judgment of White J. in *Muniz*,[51] where he stated:

> "It is one thing to hold that the deprivation of an individual's liberty beyond a six-month term should not be imposed without the protections of a jury trial, but it is quite another to suggest that, regardless of the circumstances, a jury is required where any fine greater than $500 is contemplated. From the standpoint of determining the seriousness of the risk and the extent of possible deprivation faced by a contemnor, imprisonment and fines are intrinsically different. It is not difficult to grasp the proposition that six months in jail is a serious matter for any individual, but it is not tenable to argue that the possibility of a $501 fine would be considered a serious risk to a large corporation or labor union."[52]

7–27 As noted above, the court went on to state that a fine of $10,000 in this case would not take the offence out of the petty category. Such an approach highlights a viewpoint that trial by jury is most necessary in cases involving deprivation of individual liberty. It also indicates a willingness on the part of the United States Supreme Court to examine the impact of fines with reference to the financial position of the defendant. This approach has been adhered to by some lower courts in the United States also.[53] Such an approach could

---

[49] [1981] I.R. 412.

[50] *ibid.* at 439.

[51] He delivered the opinion of the court, joined by Burger C.J. and Brennan, Blackmun and Rehnquist JJ.

[52] *Muniz v Hoffman* 422 U.S. 454 at 477 (1975).

[53] *Musidor, BV v Great American Screen* 658 F.2d 60 (2d Cir. 1981), cert. denied, 455 U.S. 944 (1982); *United States v NYNEX Corp* 781 F.Supp. 19 (D.D.C. 1990). But see *United States v Twentieth Century Fox Film Corp* 882 F.2d 656 (2d Cir. 1989), cert. denied, 493 U.S. 1021 (1990).

usefully be employed in this jurisdiction and would be a helpful gloss on the *Melling* criteria discussed above.[54]

CONCLUSION

7–28 It appears from the foregoing that the requirement of a trial by jury is as applicable to the corporate as to the individual defendant. Jury trials perform an important function in that they involve the public in the criminal justice process. There is no reason in principle why they ought not to apply to the company. Perhaps, however, the application of Art.38.2 may be different in relation to the company than it is in relation to the individual. A fine which might render an offence serious when committed by an individual might not have the same impact in relation to a company.

7–29 A number of points can be made on the basis of the material discussed in Chapters 4, 5, 6 and 7. First, we can see that an approach which examines the purpose of each constitutional protection before determining its applicability to companies reveals that not all of the protections implicated under Art.38 can be treated in the same way in this context. Thus, the right to jury trial is arguably applicable to the corporate defendant, but the privilege against self-incrimination is not. Similarly, we can see from the above that an analysis of the function of each protection may result in a finding that, when applied to corporate defendants, may differ in scope to that applicable to individual defendants. For example, the rule against double jeopardy is susceptible to such analysis.

7–30 The comparative case law considered in Chapter 5 illustrates the potential effect of theories of the corporation in this context. It is the contention of this book that the mere espousal of one or other corporate theory is an unhelpful way to approach the issue of corporate constitutional rights. While theories of the corporation are useful as descriptive devices, the better approach is to rely on a theory of the Constitution—to examine the nature of the constitutional right at issue and then to determine its applicability or otherwise to the corporate person.

7–31 Applying the methodology set out in Chapter 3, it was found that where the purpose of a due process right is to protect the autonomy and dignity of the individual, it should be inapplicable to a company. Where, on the other hand the protection has some utilitarian basis, such as a concern to uphold institutional

---

[54] Adlestein has pointed out that:

"[I]n a practical sense, it seems highly unlikely … that a maximum fine as low as $10,001 would be pragmatically suitable as a constitutional marker of 'seriousness' for every organizational defendant. That sum is obviously not a very high figure, even for the small businesses that make up the large majority of corporate enterprises, and to analogize $10,001 to more than six months in prison as a constitutional requirement for jury trial seems intuitively inappropriate."

Adlestein, *op.cit.* at 424.

or structural values which are crucial to the integrity of the criminal justice system, it should be available to all defendants, whether they are natural or legal persons. As we have seen from the above examples, often both values will be implicated and the question will be one of balance and perhaps altering the scope of the right when applied to companies.

7–32 Due process protections render the administration of criminal justice more costly, both in terms of time and expense, as well as in the risk that the guilty may go free. While these costs are accepted as the price society pays to ensure the liberty of the innocent individual, the same balance may not apply in the context of the corporate person. On the other hand, an unsophisticated "crime control" approach may undermine the integrity of the criminal justice system as a whole. It is submitted that the preferable approach is to protect companies only to the extent necessary to preserve the legitimacy of the system. Control of corporate crime itself is an important part of this and should be factored into the balance. As one commentator has put it:

> "The test of whether a corporation can assert a criminal constitutional right should involve weighing the extent to which the exercise of the right will undermine the government's enforcement program with whether the right will protect a corporation against a significant misuse of the government's power."[55]

7–33 Protecting a company against such "misuse" furthers the utilitarian aspect of many due process protections. By restraining state excesses, the integrity of the criminal justice system as a whole is served. Whether allowing the company to rely on substantive constitutional guarantees is similarly appropriate requires a case-by-case analysis and analogies between constitutional provisions without such analysis are to be avoided. This is the case even in respect of rights guaranteed under the same Article. The experience in the United States has been that unsubstantiated analogies led to a proliferation of corporate constitutional rights with undesirable effects.[56]

---

[55] Henning, *op.cit.* at 872–873. He concludes that the right of a corporation to a jury trial should be limited to criminal contempt proceedings as to do otherwise would unduly hinder law enforcement.

[56] Mayer, "Personalizing the Impersonal: Corporations and the Bill of Rights" (1990) 41 Hastings L.J. 577.

Part III

The Company and Fundamental Rights Under Articles 40.3 and 40.6

CHAPTER 8

PROPERTY

INTRODUCTION

8–01 Of all the claims to constitutional protection that a company might make, those relating to private property are intuitively the most appealing. In general, the Irish courts have failed to consider in any depth the propriety of making constitutional guarantees available to the company, but in the area of property rights, such protection has been explicitly extended on the basis of some considered analysis in the case of *Iarnród Éireann v Ireland*.[1] This case, which was discussed in Chapter 2 in the context of methods of constitutional interpretation, is thus analysed in some detail in this chapter.[2]

8–02 Paragraphs 8–03 to 8–30 assess the extent to which companies have been able to rely on the Irish Constitution to protect their property rights and explore the contradictory Irish case law on this issue. Paragraphs 8–31 to 8–45 examine the position of corporate property rights under the United States Constitution and paras 8–46 to 8–50 look to the European Convention on Human Rights. As it explicitly grants the protections of property in Art.1 of Protocol 1 to legal persons as well as individuals, the European Court of Human Rights ("ECHR") has had no need to consider the desirability of extending such protection to companies. However, it has considered the extent to which the interests of the shareholders may be identified with those of the company so as to grant the former victim status[3] and this case law is of relevance to the matters discussed in this chapter. Paragraphs 8–51 to 8–68 explore the judgment of Keane J. in *Iarnród Éireann* in some detail and consider the nature of the constitutional provisions relating to property and the extent to which they are appropriate for application to the company.

IRELAND

8–03 The Irish case law on this issue has been conflicting,[4] although the more recent case law[5] suggests strongly that companies do enjoy constitutional

---

[1] [1996] 3 I.R. 321, [1995] 2 I.L.R.M. 161. Hereafter referred to as *Iarnród Éireann*.
[2] For an analysis of the methods of constitutional interpretation used in that case, see Chap.2, paras 2–23 to 2–34.
[3] See below at paras 8–46 to 8–50.
[4] *cf. MMDS Television Ltd And Suir Nore Relays Ltd v South East Community Deflector Assoc Ltd And Kirwan*, unreported, High Court, Carroll J., April 8, 1997.

protection for their property rights. Before considering the cases in detail, however, some explanation of the relevant constitutional arrangements for the protection of property rights is required.

8–04   There are two provisions concerning property in the Irish Constitution, which led to a certain amount of confusion in the case law. Article 43 provides:

> "1 (1) The State acknowledges that man, in virtue of his rational being, has the natural right, antecedent to positive law, to the private ownership of external goods.
>   (2) The State accordingly guarantees to pass no law attempting to abolish the right of private ownership or the general right to transfer, bequeath, and inherit property.
> 2 (1) The State recognises, however, that the exercise of the rights mentioned in the foregoing provisions of this Article ought, in civil society, to be regulated by the principles of social justice.
>   (2) The State, accordingly, may as occasion requires, delimit by law the exercise of the said rights with a view to reconciling their exercise with the exigencies of the common good."

8–05   Property is also specifically referred to in Art.40.3 which states that:

> "(1) The State guarantees in its laws to respect, and, as far as practicable, by its laws to defend and vindicate the personal rights of the citizen.
>   (2) The State shall, in particular, by its laws protect as best it may from unjust attack and, in the case of injustice done, vindicate the life, person, good name, and property rights of every citizen."

8–06   The view taken of the interaction between these two provisions oscillated in the case law and the various approaches taken over the years have been explored exhaustively in the academic literature.[6] The current position is exemplified by the decision in *Dreher v Irish Land Commission*,[7] where Walsh J. stated as follows:

> "The State in exercising its powers under Article 43 must act in accordance with the requirements of social justice but clearly what is social justice must depend on the circumstances of the case. In Article 40.3.2° 'the State undertakes by its laws to protect as best it may from unjust attack, and in the case of injustice done, vindicate ... (the) property rights of every citizen.' I think it is clear that any State action that is

---

[5] *Iarnród Éireann v Ireland* [1996] 3 I.R. 321, [1995] 2 I.L.R.M. 161. *Cf. BUPA Ireland Ltd v Health Insurance Authority* [2005] I.E.S.C. 80; *Caldwell v Mahon* [2006] I.E.H.C. 86.

[6] For a comprehensive summary, see *Report of the Constitution Review Group* (Stationery Office, Dublin, 1996, Pn 2632), at pp.359–360; Casey, *Constitutional Law in Ireland* (3rd edn, Round Hall, 2000), at pp.662–680; Hogan and Whyte, *Kelly: The Irish Constitution* (4th edn, Lexis-Nexis Butterworths, 2003), at pp.1983–1993.

[7] [1984] I.L.R.M. 94.

authorised by Article 43 of the Constitution and conforms to that Article cannot by definition be unjust for the purpose of Article 40.3.2°. It may well be that in some particular cases social justice may not require the payment of any compensation upon an acquisition that can be justified by the State as being required by the common good."[8]

8–07   The Supreme Court authoritatively explained its approach to the two provisions in *Article 26 and the Planning and Development Bill 1999, Re*,[9] where Keane C.J. approved the approach taken in *Dreher*. Referring to some of the earlier case law on property rights,[10] he stated that:

"It is no doubt the case that the individual citizen who challenges the constitutional validity of legislation which purports to delimit or regulate the property rights undertakes the burden of establishing that the legislation in question constitutes an unjust attack on those rights within the meaning of Article 40."[11]

8–08   He went on to point out that, in most cases, a constitutional challenge arises:

"in circumstances where the State contends that the legislation is required by the exigencies of the common good. In such cases, it is inevitable that there will be an enquiry as to whether, objectively viewed, it could be regarded as so required and as to whether the restrictions or delimitations effected of the property rights of individual citizens (including the plaintiff in cases other than references under Article 26) are reasonably proportionate[12] to the ends sought to be achieved."[13]

---

[8]   [1984] I.L.R.M. 94 at 96. Approved by the Supreme Court in *Article 26 and the Planning and Development Bill, 1999, Re* [2000] 2 I.R. 321, [2001] 1 I.L.R.M. 81 and *Article 26 of The Constitution and the Health (Amendment) (No.2) Bill 2004, Re* [2005] I.E.S.C. 7. See also *PMPS Ltd and Moore v Att.-Gen.* [1983] I.R. 339 and *O'Callaghan v Commissioners of Public Works* [1985] I.L.R.M. 364.

[9]   [2000] 2 I.R. 321, [2001] 1 I.L.R.M. 81.

[10]   *Buckley v Att.-Gen.* [1950] I.R. 67; *Att.-Gen. v Southern Industrial Trust* (1960) 94 I.L.T.R. 161; *Central Dublin Development Association v Att.-Gen.* (1975) 109 I.L.T.R. 69; *Blake v Att.-Gen.* [1982] I.R. 117 and *Dreher v Irish Land Commission and Att.-Gen.* [1984] I.L.R.M. 94.

[11]   [2000] 2 I.R. 321 at 348.

[12]   The relevant proportionality test is that set out by Costello J. in *Heaney v Ireland* [1994] 3 I.R. 593 at 607:
"The objective of the impugned provision must be of sufficient importance to warrant overriding an important constitutionally protected right. It must relate to concerns pressing and substantial in a free and democratic society. The means chosen must pass a proportionality test. They must—
  a)   be rationally connected to the objective, and not be arbitrary, unfair or based on irrational considerations;
  b)   impair the right as little as possible; and
be such that their effects on rights are proportional to the objective."
This test was applied in the context of property rights in *Daly v Revenue Commissioners* [1995] 3 I.R. 1 and *Iarnród Éireann v Ireland* [1996] 3 I.R. 321, [1995] 2 I.L.R.M. 161.

[13]   [2000] 2 I.R. 321 at 348. While the judgment refers to "individual citizens" as the potential

8–09   The actual application of the proportionality test is not of relevance to the matters at issue in this chapter. Of more concern is the current tendency to interpret the Constitution so that Art.43 and Art.40.3.2 mutually inform each other. What are the implications of this for the corporate plaintiff?

8–10   At first reading, the language used in Arts 43 and 40.3 of the Irish Constitution does not bode well for the corporate owner. Article 43 posits a natural law basis for the protection of the institution of private property, referring specifically to the rationality of man as the basis for this natural right.[14] Article 40.3.2 is no more promising, as it applies only to guarantee the rights of "citizens". As was discussed in Chapter 2, however, the words of the text are not necessarily dispositive when it comes to constitutional protection. Indeed, it has been commented—in the context of the development of the proportionality doctrine—that "it might not be too much to say that the courts have now jettisoned all but the most superficial reliance on the actual text".[15]

8–11   The nature of the rights protected under Arts 40.3.2 and 43 will be considered in greater detail in paras 8–60 to 8–67 of this chapter. The remainder of this section concerns those Irish cases in which a company has invoked them.

8–12   In an early case, *Pigs Marketing Board v Donnelly (Dublin) Ltd*,[16] Hanna J. considered a constitutional challenge to the system of price fixing established by the Pigs and Bacon Acts 1935 and 1937. The company based its challenge on Art.43 of the Constitution. Hanna J. rejected the challenge on the merits, making no mention of the fact that the defendant in the case was a company.[17]

8–13   In *Att.-Gen. v Southern Industrial Trust Ltd*,[18] the defendant company challenged the constitutionality of s.5(1) of the Customs (Temporary Provisions) Act 1945. A car owned by the defendant company and let on hire-purchase to a third party was alleged to have been illegally exported from the jurisdiction by him without the defendant's knowledge. It was seized by the customs authority and the Attorney-General requested that it be forfeited. Davitt P. found against the company, but what is interesting for the current inquiry is

---

plaintiffs in constitutional challenges based on property rights, the case arose from an Art.26 reference so that there was no plaintiff making the challenge in the case. The *Dreher* approach was also approved by Murray C.J. in *Article 26 of The Constitution and the Health (Amendment) (No.2) Bill 2004, Re* [2005] I.E.S.C. 7.

[14] This does not mean that there is no alternative rationale for the constitutional protection of property. See below, para.8–65.

[15] Hogan, "The Constitution, Property Rights and Proportionality" (1997) 32 Ir. Jur. (New Series) 373 at 396.

[16] [1939] I.R. 413.

[17] While some aspects of the High Court's interpretation of Art.43 in that case have been superceded by subsequent case law on property rights, none of the later cases referring back to Hanna J.'s decision refer to this point.

[18] (1957) 94 I.L.T.R. 161.

that he referred to the "exercise by the Southern Industrial Trust of their rights of property".[19] Similarly, the Supreme Court, while finding the impugned provision to be constitutional, also assumed that the company was entitled to rely on the property rights guaranteed by the Constitution.[20]

8–14 In *East Donegal Co-Operative Livestock Mart Ltd v Att.-Gen.*,[21] a private company sought to challenge the licensing regime set up under the Livestock Marts Act 1967. It was argued that the discretionary powers ceded to the Minister for Agriculture under the scheme were contrary to Arts 40.1, 40.3 and 43 of the Constitution. The Attorney-General argued that the action was premature and based on hypothetical violations of the plaintiff's rights. O'Keeffe P. responded to that submission by stating:

> "Artificial persons may possibly not be entitled to rely on constitutional guarantees (although they have been held to be so entitled in the United States) but in my opinion a citizen of Ireland, who may possibly be prejudicially affected by the operation of a statute which is unconstitutional, need not wait until what he apprehends may happen has in fact happened before bringing proceedings to have the statute declared repugnant to the Constitution. If the societies which are plaintiffs in this case are not entitled to maintain this action, I am satisfied that each of the individuals who are plaintiffs has a right to question in the present proceedings the constitutionality of the legislation."[22]

8–15 In *Private Motorists Protection Society v PMPS*,[23] Carroll J. expressed the view that legal persons could not invoke the protections of Arts 43 or 40.3.2. The Supreme Court reserved its position on the issue, holding that the shareholders in the company were considered to have property rights which were constitutionally protected.

8–16 In *Pine Valley Developments Ltd v Minister for the Environment*,[24] both the High Court and the Supreme Court appeared to take the view that the plaintiff company had constitutionally protected property rights. In this case, an individual had applied for, and received, planning permission from the defendant. Pine Valley Developments Ltd had then bought the property to which the permission attached. It transpired that the planning permission was invalid. Legislation passed to retrospectively validate such permissions provided that it was not to apply where such validation would interfere with the constitutional rights of any person. This meant that the plaintiff company, which had exercised its right to challenge the permission in the courts, could not benefit from the legislation. Both courts considered—and ultimately

---

[19] *ibid.* at 171.
[20] *ibid.* at 175–178.
[21] [1970] I.R. 317.
[22] *ibid.* at 333.
[23] [1983] I.R. 339.
[24] [1987] I.R. 23, [1987] I.L.R.M. 747.

dismissed—arguments based on Art.40.3.1 and 40.3.2 of the Constitution on their merits and no mention of the corporate nature of the plaintiff was made.[25]

8–17   The matter arose again in *Chestvale Properties Ltd v Glackin,*[26] where it was argued that Pt II of the Companies Act 1990, which provided for company investigations,[27] would be unconstitutional if it was interpreted as applying retrospectively. The company relied on the guarantee by the State in Art.40.3.2 to protect and vindicate property rights. The Attorney-General, relying on the *PMPS* case, argued that this guarantee was not applicable to corporate applicants. In the High Court, Murphy J. noted that this difficulty was often overcome by joining a shareholder as a party to the proceedings. He pointed out that counsel in this case had deliberately chosen not to take this step and stated:

> "While I accept that the court should be astute to protect the rights of citizens even when they are attacked only indirectly through corporate structures it does seem to me that in the particular circumstances of this case the absence of an individual Irish citizen asserting his own constitutional rights is fatal to the argument based on the constitutionality of the 1990 litigation."[28]

8–18   His judgment went on to find, however, that the arguments put forward in this case would fail on the merits in any case.

8–19   The matter arose again in *Iarnród Éireann v Ireland,*[29] where Keane J. gave it its first detailed analysis. The case arose out of a railway accident for which the company had been found 30 per cent liable, the other 70 per cent being attributed to a third party. Section 12(1) of the Civil Liability Act 1961 provided that concurrent wrongdoers were each liable for the whole of any damage caused. As the third party in this case was unable to make any significant contribution, virtually the entire sum fell on the company. The company and a shareholder with a £1 share in the company argued that s.12(1) constituted an unconstitutional interference with its property rights.

8–20   Counsel for the State submitted that, even if corporate bodies could rely on Art.40.3, Iarnród Éireann was in a different position because it was incorporated by statute. The state also referred to *PMPS* and *Chestvale Properties* and argued that companies could not rely on Arts 40.3 and 43.

---

[25] The ECHR took the view that the circumstances were such that there had been a breach of Art.14 of the European Convention on Human Rights when read together with Art.1 of Protocol 1 thereof as the plaintiff was being discriminated against in the peaceful enjoyment of its possessions. *Pine Valley Developments Ltd v Ireland* (1992) 14 E.H.R.R. 319.

[26] [1992] I.L.R.M. 221.

[27] For a description of Pt II of the Companies Act 1990, see above Chap.5, n.19.

[28] [1992] I.L.R.M. 221 at 229.

[29] [1995] 2 I.L.R.M. 161, [1996] 3 I.R. 321.

According to the State, this could not be circumvented by joining the shareholder in this case as his shareholding was nominal and, unlike the shareholders in *PMPS*, his proprietary rights were unaffected.

8–21 Counsel for the plaintiffs argued that there was no rational reason to deprive corporate bodies of the benefit of such constitutional guarantees as were of their nature capable of benefiting such bodies.[30] It was argued that *Att.-Gen. v Southern Industrial Trust* implicitly recognised the constitutional right of corporate bodies to private property. It was also urged on the court that the Supreme Court in *PMPS* had expressly declined to comment on that aspect of Carroll J.'s judgment. It was further argued that where any group of citizens organised as a company in good faith invoked the jurisdiction of the court to investigate the constitutionality of laws passed by the Oireachtas, in circumstances where they could demonstrate that their interests could be seriously damaged, it would not be in the public interest if the court was obliged to decline jurisdiction on the grounds that the Article extended protection only to citizens as individuals.[31]

8–22 Keane J., in the High Court, noted that the ability of companies to rely on Art.40.3 had not been questioned in decisions prior to 1969 when such bodies challenged the constitutionality of legislation in cases such as *Southern Industrial Trust* and *Educational Company of Ireland Ltd v Fitzpatrick*.[32] He noted that the Supreme Court had ignored O'Keefe P.'s comments on the matter in *East Donegal Co-Operative*. He made reference to *Chestvale Properties*, *PMPS*, and the decision of Walsh J. in *Quinn's Supermarket Ltd v Att.-Gen.*[33] but refused to follow the approach taken by Carroll J. in *PMPS*, as he found that this was based on an incorrect interpretation of Arts 40.3 and 43. He noted that Carroll J. in that case had expressly stated that the property rights at issue in the case derived from Art.43 and that such an approach, with its premise that property rights inhere in "man, by virtue of his rational being", might no longer be good law following the decision in *Blake v Att.-Gen.*[34]

> "In contrast to Article 40.1 and Article 43, Article 40.3.2° in enumerating the rights which are thereby guaranteed, refers simply to 'the property rights of every citizen'. If the decision in *PMPS* is to be supported, it must be on the ground that the 'property rights of every citizen' thereby guaranteed are confined to rights enjoyed by the citizens as human persons.
>
> Undoubtedly, some at least of the rights enumerated in Article 40, s.3. sub-s.2—the rights to life and liberty—are of no relevance to

---

[30] *cf.* the decision of the Supreme Judicial Court of Massachusetts in *First National Bank v Att.-Gen.* 371 Mass. 773, 359 N.E.2d 1262 (1976), discussed below at para.9–38.

[31] It was also pointed out that s.11(c) of the Interpretation Act 1937 states that the word "person" includes a company.

[32] [1961] I.R. 345. This case concerned freedom of association.

[33] [1970] I.R. 317. This case is discussed in the context of equality in Chap.14 at paras 14–44 to 14–46.

[34] [1982] I.R. 117.

corporate bodies and other legal entities. Property rights are, however, in a different category. Not only are corporate bodies themselves capable in law of owning property, whether moveable or immoveable, tangible or intangible. The 'property' referred to clearly includes shares in companies formed under the relevant companies' legislation which was already a settled feature of the legal and commercial life of this country at the time of the enactment of the Constitution. There would accordingly be a spectacular deficiency in the guarantee to every citizen that his or her property rights will be protected against 'unjust attack', if such bodies were incapable in law of being regarded as 'citizens', at least for the purposes of this article, and if it was essential for the shareholders to abandon the protection of limited liability to which they are entitled by law in order to be protected, not only in their own rights as shareholders, but also the property rights of the corporate entity itself, which are in law distinct from the rights of its members.

Article 43 undoubtedly treats the general right of private property, the abolition of which in its entirety is expressly prohibited, as one inhering in 'man in virtue of his rational being' and, in that sense, as being 'antecedent to positive law', including the Constitution itself. But it does not necessarily follow that the property rights of the individual citizens which are protected against 'unjust attack' by Article 40.3 are confined to rights enjoyed by human persons. Had the framers of the Constitution wished to confine the comprehensive guarantee in Article 40.3 in that manner, there was nothing to prevent them including a similar qualification to that contained in Article 40.1.

I am satisfied that the expression 'every citizen' is not confined in Article 40, s.3. sub-s.2, to citizens in their individual capacity as human persons and that artificial legal entities must also be protected by the laws of the State against unjust attacks on their property rights. In the case of injustice done, it is peculiarly the role of the courts to vindicate the property rights of such entities in accordance with Article 40, s.3, subs.2 ...".[35]

8–23 As for the argument that the statutory basis of the company distinguished it from other companies, Keane J. found that there was no reason to assume that the Oireachtas intended that, unlike other companies, it could not invoke the protection of the Constitution.[36]

8–24 He also made the point that if bodies corporate could not invoke constitutional rights, then the challenge at issue might never have been taken:

"The law could hardly be said to be in a satisfactory state if, in an area

---

[35] [1996] 3 I.R. 321 at 345–346, [1995] 2 I.L.R.M. 161 at 183–184.
[36] [1996] 3 I.R. 321 at 347–348, [1995] 2 I.L.R.M. 161 at 186. The decision in *Iarnród Éireann* led Peart J. to conclude, in *Shirley v O'Gorman & Co. Ltd* [2006] I.E.H.C. 27, that, as far as the constitutional property rights of the company are concerned, "[t]he position is beyond any real argument."

where the interests of a large number of corporate bodies were unquestionably affected, a challenge to the validity of the legislation would be entirely dependant on the willingness of the shareholders of a particular category to abandon the protection of limited liability."[37]

8–25 A number of criticisms can be made of this decision. In it, Keane J. indicates some support for extending whatever personal rights and guarantees a company is capable of enjoying to the company.[38] Thus, his starting point is the fact that companies are capable in law of holding property. Of course, the mere fact that a person—artificial or human—has a statutory or common law right to something does not mean that that right is automatically deserving of constitutional protection—capacity in law does not translate into constitutional protection in every case. Keane J. makes this point in order to highlight the fact that constitutional protection of this type of right is possible. Its justification, however, lies in the fact that shares are protected property. From this, he extrapolates that it is necessary for the Constitution to protect the property rights of the company. In the case before him, of course, there was no shareholder whose rights were infringed so that his basing of the company's rights on those of a hypothetical individual shareholder is somewhat unconvincing.

8–26 He does make some attempt to ground his conclusion that the company can rely on the Constitution in the actual text, drawing a distinction between the wording in Art.40.1 and Art.40.3.2.[39] It scarcely needs pointing out that the fact that Art.40.1 guarantees that "All citizens shall, as human persons, be held equal before the law …" does not alter the fact that Art.40.3.2 refers to "citizens" and gives no indication that this includes artificial persons.

8–27 Keane J.'s judgment may be seen as espousing an aggregate theory of the company[40] in that he bases the constitutional protection of the company on the interests of the shareholders. The difficulties with relying on that approach in this context are discussed below in paras 8–51 to 8–59.

8–28 The High Court decision in *Iarnród Éireann*[41] appears to contradict earlier authorities in relation to the nature of the share. In *Kerry Co-Operative Creameries Ltd v An Bord Bainne*,[42] for example, Costello J. considered the extent to which a shareholding in an industrial and provident society was protected under the Constitution. He took the view that principles of company

---

[37] [1996] 3 I.R. 321 at 352, [1995] 2 I.L.R.M. 161 at 190.
[38] *cf.* Brewer J. dissenting in *Hale v Henkel* 201 U.S. 43 at 83–84. Reproduced above at para.5–31.
[39] This part of his decision is discussed in Chap.2.
[40] The methods of constitutional interpretation used in his judgment have been discussed above, in Chap.2.
[41] The Supreme Court declined to explore this aspect of the case.
[42] [1990] I.L.R.M. 664.

law were applicable.[43] The plaintiff's arguments in this case amounted to a claim that, as well as the usually recognised contractual rights attendant to shareholding, *i.e.* the right to be repaid the amount subscribed and to share in the distribution of any surplus assets in the event of a winding-up, a shareholder was entitled to a share in the value of the board's underlying assets and those of its subsidiaries. Costello J. pointed out that the company legally owns any assets it acquires and that no shareholder enjoys a legal right to any particular portion of those assets. He found that, while a shareholding was a property right, its nature and extent was determined by the relevant contractual arrangements.[44]

8–29 This approach to shareholders' property rights appears to be in conformity with the general position at common law as highlighted by the Supreme Court decision in *O'Neill v Ryan*.[45] In this case, the court rejected the argument that shareholders might bring personal actions in relation to the reduction in value of their shareholding resulting from damage to the company against the party who caused that damage. The court, referring to an English authority,[46] held that shares constitute a mere right of participation in the company on the terms set out in the articles of association and that, while the value of shares might be reduced by virtue of losses suffered by the company, the right of participation would not be affected.

8–30 The implications of these cases for the constitutional protection of corporate property will be returned to in paras 8–58 to 8–59.

UNITED STATES

8–31 The United States Constitution, as originally enacted, contained no general statement in relation to the protection of the right to private property.[47] Some protection was provided indirectly by Art.I(10) of the Constitution which provides that: "No State shall … pass any … Law impairing the Obligation of Contracts."[48] It was not until the addition of the Fifth Amendment in 1791 that such general protection was introduced. It protects property rights from the reach of the federal government in the due process clause: "No person shall be … deprived of life, liberty, or property, without due process of law;"

---

[43] *ibid.* at 713. In the Supreme Court, McCarthy J. agreed with this view. O'Flaherty J. on the other hand indicated that perhaps the arguments put forward by the plaintiff would have been more appropriate if the case had involved a limited liability company. [1991] I.L.R.M. 851.

[44] [1990] I.L.R.M. 664 at 709–717.

[45] [1993] I.L.R.M. 557.

[46] *Prudential Assurance Co. Ltd v Newman Industries Ltd* [1982] 1 Chap. 204.

[47] See also the Canadian Charter of Fundamental Rights and Freedoms which does not include a right to private property. *Cf. Irwin Toy Ltd v Quebec* [1989] 1 S.C.R. 927.

[48] For the view that contract and property rights are concerned with distinct matters, see Penner, *The Idea of Property in Law* (Oxford University Press, 2000).

and under the takings clause: "nor shall private property be taken for public use, without just compensation".

8–32   The States were later generally restricted from interfering with property rights under the due process clause of the Fourteenth Amendment, enacted in 1868: "nor shall any State deprive any person of life, liberty, or property, without due process of law".

8–33   Thus, there are four key constitutional provisions which protect property rights. As the case law developed, these provisions were often treated similarly. As one commentator has put it:

> "[A]ny quest for doctrinal precision in the analysis of property and economic rights is bound to fail. Rules devised for interpreting one clause of the Constitution frequently spill over to another. There has been a large degree of overlap, for example, between legal arguments based on the takings clause and the due process clause of the Fourteenth Amendment."[49]

8–34   Such problems of nomenclature notwithstanding, it is proposed to take the provisions set out above separately and to examine their application to the company.

The contracts clause

8–35   This was the first restriction on the states' regulation of property rights and its interpretation was thus an important aspect of establishing the federal supervisory jurisdiction in the early years of the Union. In *Dartmouth College v Woodward*,[50] the Supreme Court considered a constitutional challenge to New Hampshire legislation which sought to alter a college's royal charter and place it under state control. The court found that a corporate charter was a "contract for the security and disposition of property", so that any legislative amendment of its terms was void under the contracts clause.[51] Story J. pointed out that states were free to place clauses in such charters reserving the right to amend them in the future. This practice grew so that the contracts clause did not become as effective a protection for corporate property rights as it might have.[52] Furthermore, later cases[53] indicated that the court would interpret the charter contract restrictively, thus increasing the potential for State regulation. In 1848, the Supreme Court held that the contracts clause did not affect the states' power of eminent domain.[54] These developments, together with the

---

[49] Ely, *The Guardian of Every Other Right: A Constitutional History of Property Rights* (2nd edn, Oxford University Press, 1998), at p.8.
[50] 17 U.S. 518 (1819).
[51] *ibid.* at 644.
[52] Ely, *op.cit.* at pp.65–66.
[53] *e.g. Charles River Bridge v Warren Bridge* 36 U.S. 420 (1837).
[54] *West River Bridge Company v Dix* 47 U.S. 507 (1848).

rise of substantive economic due process under the Fourteenth Amendment,[55] meant that companies sought protection for their property rights elsewhere. This does not mean, however, that the contracts clause is necessarily a dead letter.[56] While it does not explicitly protect property rights, companies have successfully invoked it to that effect. For example, in *Allied Structural Steel Co. v Spannaus*,[57] a company successfully challenged a Minnesota law that retroactively altered the obligations of a company under its pension plan. Stewart J. held that the legislature was not entitled to impose additional obligations on the company in violation of the contracts clause.[58] As the contracts clause is stated as a general prohibition on the legislature rather than a positive right, its application to the company is relatively unproblematic.[59]

The Fifth Amendment—due process

8–36   In *Sinking Fund Cases*,[60] the court explicitly declared that the United States "equally with the States ... are prohibited from depriving persons or corporations of property without due process of law".[61] *Noble v Union River Logging Railroad*[62] concerned a company which had applied for, and been granted, a right of way under a statute. This right of way was later revoked on the basis that the statute was intended to benefit public railroad companies, whereas the company in question was primarily a private logging company. The Supreme Court held that the grant of a right of way caused a property right to vest in the company and the revocation was an attempt to deprive it of its property without due process of law.[63]

The Fifth Amendment—eminent domain

8–37   The takings clause of the Fifth Amendment reads as a general prohibition on the federal government to restrain it from taking private property without just compensation. The text itself does not refer to persons or citizens and its application in cases where there is a taking of corporate property is, thus, relatively unproblematic.[64]

---

[55] See *Lochner v New York* 198 U.S. 45 (1905), discussed below at para.8–42.

[56] *United States Trust Co. v New Jersey* 431 U.S. 1 (1977); *Allied Structural Steel Co. v Spannaus* 438 U.S. 234 (1978); but see *Energy Reserves Group v Kansas Power & Light Co.* 459 U.S. 400 (1983); *Keystone Bituminous Coal Association v DeBenedictis* 480 U.S. 470 (1987); *General Motors Corp v Romein* 503 U.S. 181 (1992).

[57] 438 U.S. 234 (1978).

[58] The contracts clause does not apply to the federal government but similar principles have been developed in that context also—see *United States v Winstar Corporation* 116 S.Ct. 2432 (1996).

[59] See also the First Amendment, discussed below, Chap.9.

[60] 99 U.S. 700 (1879).

[61] *ibid*. at 718–719.

[62] 147 U.S. 165 (1893).

[63] *ibid*. at 176.

[64] *Pennsylvania Coal Co. v Mahon* 260 U.S. 393 (1922).

The Fourteenth Amendment—due process

8–38 In *Munn v Illinois*,[65] the Supreme Court considered a constitutional challenge to an Illinois statute which set maximum charges for the storage of grain. The argument, based on the due process clause of the Fourteenth Amendment, failed on the merits, although the court was fully willing to entertain such submissions from a company without comment. In *Smyth v Ames*,[66] the court considered the constitutionality of legislation setting the rates railroad companies could charge. The court referred to a number of cases decided under the equal protection clause of the Fourteenth Amendment[67] and noted: "That corporations are persons within the meaning of this amendment is now settled."[68]

8–39 The court also referred to a number of cases under the due process clause which established that companies enjoyed protection of their property rights thereunder[69] before going on to state that:

> "It cannot be assumed that any railroad corporation, accepting franchises, rights, and privileges at the hands of the public, ever supposed that it acquired, or that it was intended to grant to it, the power to construct and maintain a public highway simply for its benefit, without regard to the rights of the public. But it is equally true that the corporation performing such public services, and the people financially interested in its business and affairs, have rights that may not be invaded by legislative enactment in disregard of the fundamental guaranties for the protection of property. The corporation may not be required to use its property for the benefit of the public without receiving just compensation for the services rendered by it."[70]

8–40 The passage above reflects the function of the company in that case, which was to "perform public services" as well as to make a profit. The approach taken in *Smyth v Ames* was not, however, particular to transport corporations. In *Liggett Co. v Baldridge*,[71] the court considered a constitutional challenge to a Pennsylvania statute which provided, *inter alia*, that a permit was required to carry on the business of a pharmacy and that for a corporation to get such a permit, its stockholders must all be registered pharmacists. The

---

[65] 94 U.S. 113 (1877).

[66] 169 U.S. 466 (1898).

[67] *Santa Clara Co. v Southern Pacific Ry* 118 U.S. 394; *Railroad v Gibbes* 142 U.S. 386; and *Ry v Ellis* 165 U.S. 150. The application of the equal protection clause to companies is considered in Chap.13 below.

[68] 169 U.S. 466 (1898) at 522.

[69] *Railroad Commission Cases* 116 U.S. 307; *Dow v Beidelman* 125 U.S. 680; *Banking Co. v Smith* 128 U.S. 174; *Chicago, M. & St. P. Ry v Minnesota* 134 U.S. 418; *Ry v Wellman* 143 U.S. 339; *Budd v New York* 143 U.S. 517; *Reagan v Trust Co* 154 U.S. 362; *Ry v Gill* 156 U.S. 649; *Road Co. v Sandford* 164 U.S. 578; *Chicago, B. & Q. R. Co. v City of Chicago* 166 U.S. 226.

[70] 169 U.S. 466 (1898) at 546.

[71] 278 U.S. 105 (1928).

court held that such a requirement was a deprivation of the corporation's property rights contrary to the due process clause.[72]

Compensation under the Fourteenth Amendment

8–41   As noted above,[73] the court took a similar approach to the Fourteenth and Fifth Amendments insofar as they related to property rights. The court interpreted the Fourteenth Amendment as requiring compensation where property was taken for a public use. For example, in *City of Monterey v Del Monte Dunes at Monterey Ltd*,[74] the Supreme Court confirmed that a company had to be compensated for a regulatory taking.[75] Essentially, this means that companies are entitled to compensation for takings whether by state or federal action.

Economic due process and its decline

8–42   *Liggett* can be viewed as part of the Supreme Court's economic due process jurisprudence. The *locus classicus* of this anti-regulation approach is *Lochner v New York*.[76] That case concerned a challenge by an individual to a legislative provision which limited the legal working hours in bakeries. Peckham J. delivered the majority opinion of the court which held that the limitations constituted a violation of liberty of contract, which the court found to be protected under the due process clause of the Fourteenth Amendment.[77] As corporations had already been held to enjoy the protection of this clause,[78] they were able to invoke the doctrine to prevent legislative initiatives which would have impacted on their property rights. In this way, the Supreme Court's economic due process case law provided a "powerful wedge" for corporations.[79]

---

[72] Holmes J., joined by Brandeis J., dissented. For a similar case—one concerning the requirement of a licence to produce ice, see *New State Ice Co. v Liebman* 285 U.S. 262 (1932).

[73] At para.8–33.

[74] 526 U.S. 687 (1999).

[75] Regulatory takings refer to the situation that arises where property is devalued under a regulatory scheme. This is considered a taking under the Fifth Amendment. *Pennsylvania Coal Co. v Mahon* 260 U.S. 393 (1922).

[76] 198 U.S. 45 (1905).

[77] The dissents included the celebrated opinion of Holmes J., in which he advocated judicial restraint.

[78] *Santa Clara Co. v Southern Pacific Ry* 118 U.S. 394. Discussed below at paras 14–19 to 14–22.

[79] Mayer, "Personalizing the Impersonal: Business Corporations and the Bill of Rights" (1990) 41 Hastings L.J. 577 at 588:

> "From the 1905 Lochner decision until the middle of the 1930s, the Court invalidated approximately two hundred economic regulations, usually under the due process clause of the fourteenth amendment; many of the challenges were brought by corporate plaintiffs. Most decisions centered on labor legislation, the regulation of prices, and restrictions on entry into businesses. Cases involving corporations often concerned state restrictions on entries into a new business."

Mayer, *op.cit.* at 589, references omitted.

8–43 The New Deal and Roosevelt's "court-packing" proposal threatened a constitutional crisis, which the Supreme Court avoided by departing from the doctrine of economic due process in *West Coast Hotel Co. v Parrish*.[80] Shortly after that case, the court signified a sea change in its approach to the protection of property rights in *United States v Carolene Products Co.*,[81] where it considered the constitutionality of federal legislation which prohibited the sale of filled milk in interstate commerce. Upholding its constitutionality, the court adopted a low level of scrutiny for economic regulation. As long as such provisions rested on some rational basis, they would not be interfered with. Further, such a rational basis would be presumed. Stone J.'s judgment contained a footnote,[82] in which he stated that this presumption would not have the same application in cases where legislation infringed specific provisions of the Bill of Rights.

> "By separating property rights from individual freedom, the Carolene Products analysis instituted a double standard of constitutional review under which the Supreme Court afforded a higher level of protection to the preferred category of personal rights. Economic rights were implicitly assigned a secondary constitutional status."[83]

8–44 This approach meant that companies could no longer rely on due process to protect their property interests and turned instead to the Bill of Rights.[84]

8–45 The approach of the United States Supreme Court to corporate property rights post-*Lochner* can be seen as having been largely dictated by its holding in an earlier case[85] that the company was a "person" within the context of the Equal Protection Clause of the Fourteenth Amendment. On the other hand, it could be pointed out that similar uniformity of interpretation has not been evident in relation to the clauses of the Fifth Amendment.[86] While some of the decisions referred to above can be read as assuming a "real entity" theory of the company, with *Smyth v Aymes* perhaps combining this with an aggregate approach, there is little theorising in the opinions which appear to almost automatically extend protection to the company. Perhaps this is partially due to the intuitive association of property rights with companies mentioned at the beginning of this chapter.

---

[80] 300 U.S. 379 (1937).
[81] 304 U.S. 144 (1938).
[82] *ibid.*, n.4. Reproduced below at para.14–36.
[83] Ely, *op.cit.* at p.133. For the view that this lower level of scrutiny is misguided, see Smith, "Life Liberty and Whose Property?: An Essay on Property Rights" (1996) 30 U.Rich.L.Rev. 1055.
[84] Mayer, *op.cit.* at 606–620.
[85] *Santa Clara Co. v Southern Pacific Ry*, discussed below at paras 14–19 to 14–22.
[86] Above at paras 5–26 to 5–46.

THE EUROPEAN CONVENTION ON HUMAN RIGHTS

8–46   Initially, the failure to agree on a form of words meant that no property rights guarantee was contained in the European Convention on Human Rights.[87] One was added two years later in the form of Art.1, Protocol 1, which reads as follows:

> "Every natural or legal person is entitled to the peaceful enjoyment of his possessions. No one shall be deprived of his possessions except in the public interest and subject to the conditions provided for by law and by the general principles of international law.
>
>   The preceding provisions shall not, however, in any way impair the right of a State to enforce such laws as it deems necessary to control the use of property in accordance with the general interest or to secure the payment of taxes or other contributions or penalties."

8–47   The Article has been interpreted as containing three basic rules, all of which are interrelated:

> "The first rule, which is of a general nature, enounces the principle of peaceful enjoyment of property; it is set out in the first sentence of the first paragraph. The second rule covers the deprivation of possessions and subjects it to certain conditions; it appears in the second sentence of the same paragraph. The third rule recognises that the States are entitled, amongst other things, to control the use of property in accordance with the general interest, by enforcing such laws as they deem necessary for the purpose; it is contained in the second paragraph."[88]

8–48   The Article is the only one which is explicitly stated to apply to legal persons and it has been noted:

> "It may seem strange to include companies in the human rights arena, nevertheless the contracting states have chosen to confer on companies the protection of the human right which protects existing property rights. Presumably this relates to the fact that the property belonging to the company is ultimately owned by natural persons. This abstraction works to simplify the law by removing the need to identify which natural persons own the property concerned."[89]

8–49   Due to the text of Art.1, Protocol 1, there has been no need for the Strasbourg institutions to analyse the extent to which a company should be entitled to invoke the guarantee.[90] The case law of the institutions has, however,

---

[87] Rook, *Property Law & Human Rights* (Blackstone Press, 2001), at p.1.
[88] *Sporrong and Lonnroth v Sweden* (1982) 5 E.H.R.R. 35 [61].
[89] Rook, *op.cit.* at p.104.
[90] For an example of the straightforward application of Art.1, Protocol 1 to a company, see *SA Dangeville v France* App. No. 36677/97, April 16, 2002.

grappled with the issue of whether shareholders are entitled to claim that their rights under Art.1, Protocol 1 have been violated by virtue of interferences with the property of the company in which they have invested. In *X. v Austria*,[91] the Commission decided that where a shareholder owned a substantial proportion of the shares—here 91 per cent—he may be considered a victim with sufficient standing[92] to complain of an interference with the company's property. *Yarrow Plc and three shareholders v UK*[93] concerned the nationalisation of a subsidiary company, Yarrow Shipbuilders. Shareholders in the parent company claimed an infringement of their property rights as a result of the nationalisation. The Commission decided that one of the applicants, Yarrow Plc, could claim to be a victim because it held a majority interest in Yarrow Shipbuilders. The other applicants could not claim to have victim status as they did not have a majority of controlling interest in the nationalised company. In *Agrotexim v Greece*,[94] the court rejected the approach of the Commission in that case—it had found that a majority shareholder was a victim of measures affecting the property of the company. The Athens Council had taken measures with a view to expropriating land belonging to a brewery. The applicant companies were shareholders in the brewery holding just over 50 per cent of its shares. The applicants claimed victim status on the basis of the decline in the value of their shares. The court stated as follows:

> "[T]he piercing of the 'corporate veil' or the disregarding of the company's separate legal personality will be justified only in exceptional circumstances, in particular where it is established that it is impossible for the company to apply to the Convention institutions through the organs set up under its articles of incorporation or—in the event of liquidation— through its liquidator."[95]

8–50   This aggregate theory approach to the company can also be seen in the judgment of Keane J. in *Iarnród Éireann*. This aspect of his decision is criticised in the next section.

---

[91] Application No. 1706/62.
[92] Art.34 of the Convention provides that:
> "The Court may receive applications from any person, non-governmental Organisation or group of individuals claiming to be the victim of a violation by one of the High Contracting Parties of the rights set forth in the Convention or the protocols thereto. The High Contracting Parties undertake not to hinder in any way the effectiveness of this right."

The court has interpreted this provision to include companies. See Austin, "Commerce and the European Convention on Human Rights" (2004) C.L. Pract. 223. The *Agrotexim* case concerned the more complicated issue of a shareholder having standing to bring a case where the company's property was affected.
[93] (1983) 5 E.H.R.R. 498.
[94] (1996) 21 E.H.R.R. 250.
[95] *ibid.* at [66].

SHAREHOLDERS, PROPERTY AND THE COMPANY—THE PITFALLS OF THE
AGGREGATE APPROACH

8–51   Much theorising about property has been concerned with justifying
the very existence of a system of private property ownership. Metaphors such
as the "Tragedy of the Commons"[96] are not, however, of great assistance in
determining the extent to which particular property rights can be invoked under
the Constitution by a given person, whether that person is natural or legal. The
same may be said of attempts, such as Locke's,[97] to explain the way in which
property rights are acquired, as they clearly do not contemplate the corporate
owner. It is, perhaps, for this reason that attempts to fit the corporate owner
into theories of property ownership often involve the espousal of an aggregate
view of the company and base the property rights of the company on those of
the individual shareholders. Consider, for example, the Hegelian conception
of property rights discussed in the following extract:

> "The first transcendental feature means that property must, at some point,
> involve the intentions of entities that can cause physical changes in the
> world. The qualification 'at some point' is important. This transcendental
> feature does not require that *all* acquisitions of property involve intentions,
> as a corporation that purchases a factory demonstrates. Nevertheless,
> the first transcendental feature does imply that at least all initial
> acquisition—that is, acquiring a thing for the first time—is intentional.
> It also suggests that the standard case of other acquisition is intentional,
> and that corporate owners ultimately must be owned by entities capable
> of having intentions."[98]

8–52   Such an intuition in relation to property perhaps underlies Keane J.'s
decision in *Iarnród Éireann*. By basing the constitutional right of the company
on the interests of individual shareholders, he can be seen as taking an aggregate
approach to the company similar to that taken by the ECHR in *Agrotexim*—it
is the underlying property rights of the shareholder that are being protected.
Such an approach is particularly tempting when dealing with property rights
because of the intuitive identification of companies with shareholders' property
ownership and investment. The application of the aggregate theory of the
corporation in the context of property rights is, however, problematic in three
ways.

8–53   First, it arguably fails to capture the realities of the modern company:

> "When a corporation can no longer be identified with a relatively
> homogenous group of shareholders, when its behaviour can no longer

---

[96] Hardin, "The Tragedy of the Commons" in *Science*, Vol.62 (1968), at pp.1243, 1244–
1245.
[97] Locke, *Two Treatises of Government* [1698] (Peter Laslett ed., 2nd edn, Cambridge
University Press, 1994), at II.33, II.31.
[98] Munzer, *A Theory of Property* (Cambridge University Press, 1990), at p.71.

be portrayed as the inert mechanical execution of an owner's will, and as our attention is drawn to its distinctive organizational properties and processes, the posture of simply equating the corporation via personification or aggregation to a natural person loses whatever surface plausibility it might once have had."[99]

8–54 This criticism applies to only some companies. The "surface plausibility" of the aggregate approach retains its appeal as far as small, private companies are concerned. Indeed, as many companies in this jurisdiction are small private limited companies, the temptation to identify the property of the company with that of the directors and shareholders may prove tempting. It has already been argued[100] that reliance on corporate theory, while unobjectionable as a method of description, is an inadequate method of determining corporate constitutional protection. Where the aggregate theory is concerned, two further criticisms can be made.

8–55 The second problem with using an aggregate conception of the company to justify constitutional protection is that it is inconsistent with the separate legal personality of the company. The potential of this approach to destroy that doctrine was identified by Taney J. of the United States Supreme Court as long ago as 1839. In a decision[101] refusing to recognise the application of the Privileges and Immunities Clause of the Fourteenth Amendment to the United States Constitution to companies, he stated that if:

"the members of a corporation were to be regarded as individuals carrying on business in their corporate name, and therefore entitled to the privileges of citizens in matters of contract, it is very clear that they must at the same time take upon themselves the liabilities of the citizen and be bound by their contracts in like manner. The result of this would be to make a corporation a mere partnership in business, in which each stockholder would be liable to the whole extent of his property for the debts of the corporation; and he might be sued for them in any state in which he might happen to be found."[102]

8–56 Taney J.'s prophecy that the extension of protection to the company on the basis of the interests of its shareholders would destroy the doctrine of separate legal personality has not come to pass in the context of the United States Constitution.[103] Instead, shareholders have been able to have it both

---

[99] Dan-Cohen, *Rights, Persons, and Organisations: A Legal Theory for Bureaucratic Society* (University of California Press, 1986), at p.21. See also Blumberg, "The Corporate Entity in an Era of Multinational Corporations" (1990) 15 Del.J.Corp.L. 283. See *Yarrow Plc and three shareholders v UK* (1983) 5 E.H.R.R. 498, above at para.8–49.

[100] Above at paras 1–48 to 1–56.

[101] *Bank of Augusta v Earle* 38 U.S.(13 Pet.) 519 (1839).

[102] 38 U.S.(13 Pet.) 519 at 586 (1839).

[103] "[N]otwithstanding any philosophical inconsistency, the doctrine has not led to any abandonment of entity law or lack of full recognition of the corporation as a separate

ways—to merge their interests with those of the company where this is advantageous, while maintaining the shield of separate legal personality in less advantageous situations.[104]

8–57   Such an outcome has serious implications for the regulation of companies.[105] Furthermore, it led to the subversion of the equality guarantee from one concerned with autonomy values to a tool for the protection of corporate property. This development is discussed further in Chapter 14.[106]

8–58   Perhaps more fundamentally, the third difficulty with taking an approach which allows the company to rely on the Constitution in order to vindicate the putative property rights of shareholders is that this ignores the preliminary step of ascertaining what those property rights consist of. In his judgment in *Iarnród Éireann*, Keane J. recognises that the property rights of the company are distinct in law from those of the shareholders. The constitutional protection of property rights in Art.40.3 vindicates those rights already ascertained. It does not concern the creation of new property rights:

> "The right to property, understood in this way, does not provide any sort of argument for the existence of private property. It assumes and builds on independent arguments about the basis and distribution of property: it adds a particular immunity to what is otherwise a pre-existing bundle of property rights."[107]

8–59   The interests at stake when a shareholder argues that a company's property is being unconstitutionally interfered with consist of the right of participation in the company according to the terms set out in the articles of association.[108] It is well established that this right of participation does not include an entitlement to the underlying assets of the company,[109] neither does it entitle the shareholder to bring an action based on the property rights of the company.[110] This being the case, it is simply illogical to base the constitutional protection of a company's property rights on those enjoyed by its shareholders. The two interests are not the same. Indeed, returning to the case of *Chestvale*

---

juridical unit." Blumberg, "The Corporate Entity in an Era of Multinational Corporations" (1990) 15 Del.J.Corp.L. 283 at 297.

[104] See Blumberg, *op.cit.*

[105] See Allan, "Why Business Learns to Love Bills of Rights" [2001] J. Civ. Lib. 214.

[106] Below at paras 14–16 to 14–38.

[107] Waldron, *The Right to Private Property* (Clarendon Press, 1988), at p.18. He is discussing the Takings Clause of the Fifth Amendment but the same comments are appropriate in the context of Art.40.3.2.

[108] On the subject of property rights that fall short of "full" ownerhip, see Honore, "Ownership" in *Oxford Essays in Jurisprudence* (A.G. Guest ed., Clarendon Press, 1961), at pp.107–147. *Cf.* McConvill, "Do shares constitute property? Reconsidering a fundamental, yet unresolved, question" (2005) 79 ALJ 251.

[109] *Macaura v Northern Assurance* [1925] A.C. 619.

[110] See *Kerry Co-Operative Creameries Ltd v An Bord Bainne* [1990] I.L.R.M. 664; *O'Neill v Ryan* [1993] I.L.R.M. 557; discussed above at paras 8–28 to 8–29.

Properties Ltd v Glackin,[111] it is questionable whether the joining of a shareholder as a party to litigation should have any bearing on the question of a company's constitutional protection. The only way in which corporate constitutional protection can be justified is on a utilitarian basis. Whether any such basis can be identified in the context of Arts 43 and 40.3 is considered in the next section.

The Nature of the Constitutional Protection of Property and its Applicability to Companies

8–60   Having dealt with the above, the question remains whether the property guarantees in the Irish Constitution are susceptible to the dichotomised analysis proposed in Pt I of this book. Can they be said to have a rationale based on utility as well as autonomy? What values does the protection of property rights serve?

8–61   While Arts 43.2 and 40.3 mutually inform each other,[112] it is still the case that Art.43.1 appears to establish a general principle that all individuals are entitled to be potential property holders. It has been commented in relation to Art.43.1 that

> "it maintains ... that there is something about human nature (the nature we all share) which makes it wrong to exclude any (or all) of us from the class of potential proprietors."[113]

8–62   In *Article 26 of The Constitution and the Health (Amendment) (No.2) Bill 2004, Re*,[114] Murray C.J. considered the nature of the constitutional guarantee of property rights:

> "According to the text of Article 43, the private ownership of external goods is a 'natural right'. For that reason, it is 'antecedent to positive law'. It inheres in man, 'by virtue of his rational being'. The former Supreme Court, in *Buckley -v- Attorney General* [1950] IR 67 recalled that these rights had 'been the subject of philosophical discussion for many centuries'. But it did say that the constitutional guarantee meant that 'man by virtue, and as an attribute of, his human personality is so entitled to such a right that no positive law is competent to deprive him of it ...' The right to the ownership of property has a moral quality which is intimately related to the humanity of each individual. It is also one of the pillars of the free and democratic society established under the Constitution."[115]

---

[111] Discussed above at para.8–17.
[112] Above at paras 8–04 to 8–09.
[113] Waldron, *op.cit.* at p.21.
[114] [2005] I.E.S.C. 7.
[115] *ibid.*

8–63   The system of private property ownership was strongly linked to the idea of personal liberty in the minds of early commentators on the common law, such as Locke. This idea in turn caught the imagination of the framers of the United States Constitution:

> "The rationale of the judicial Solomons who cleaved personal rights from property rights would have confounded the pragmatic theorists of the founding era. For James Madison, the intellectual force behind the Constitution, property was synonymous with the very concept of rights ... Madison shared the Lockean philosophy that the purpose of government is to secure the private property of the individual. Property was primary not for its own sake, but because it was the central invention by which a liberal regime recognized the freedom of the individual ... Property defined a sphere of autonomy that made the individual distinct from the state."[116]

8–64   This idea of the "sphere of autonomy" explains the role of Art.40.3.2. The property rights enjoyed by the citizen must be vindicated because they are inherently linked to the liberty of the individual. Thus, it has been said that "property, in the scale of human well-being, ranks below life, but alongside liberty".[117]

8–65   There is, however, another line of thought which sees the institution of private property and the vindication of property rights in a utilitarian light. Such an approach to property can be traced back to Aristotle's *Politics* where he discusses private ownership and communal virtue. Aristotle espouses the idea that people will care more for what they own.[118] This nascent utilitarian defence of property was taken up by Demsetz who argued that the "primary function of property rights is that of guiding incentives to achieve a greater internalization of externalities".[119] According to this theory, if property is held in common, people will fail to realise the full impact of costs and benefits and will have no incentive to arrange their activities so as to maximise the benefits for all.[120] From this perspective, therefore, the institution of private property is justified on the utilitarian ground that it maximises benefits for all.

---

[116] Coyle, "Takings Jurisprudence and the Political Cultures of American Politics" (1993) 42 Cath.U.L.Rev. 817 at 829, references omitted. This approach can also be seen in the work of Rawls, who posits the right to own property as one of the basic liberties protected according to his first principles of justice. Rawls, *A Theory of Justice* (Oxford University Press, 1971), at pp.258 and 271–274.

[117] Harris, "Is Property a Human Right?" in *Property and the Constitution* (McClean ed., Hart Publishing, 1999), at p.87.

[118] "Property should be in a certain sense common, but, as a general rule, private; for, when everyone has a distinct interest, men will not complain of one another, and they will make more progress, because everyone will be attending to his own business." Aristotle, *Politics* 2.3, 5, cited in Hogan and Whyte, *op.cit.* at 37.

[119] Demsetz, "Toward a Theory of Property Rights" in *American Economic Review: Proceedings and Papers* 57 (1967), at p.348.

[120] "[P]roperty rights develop to internalise externalities when the gains of internalization become larger than the costs of internalisation". Demsetz, *op.cit.* at p.350. See also Hardin, *op.cit.*

8–66   The specific use of natural law language in the text of Art.43 appears to exclude this justification for the institution of private property. That may not, however, be of great significance, as Art.43.1 is concerned primarily with the inclusion of all individuals within the category of potential property owners. As far as Art.40.3.2 is concerned, however, it might be that allowing companies to assert the property rights they already have could be justified on the utilitarian basis that it creates greater security in relation to the system of private property ownership envisaged in Art.43. It is in this way that Art.40.3.2 could be seen as promoting utility as well as autonomy based values.[121]

8–67   From this perspective, claims by individuals to the vindication of their property rights implicates both autonomy and utility values. Claims by companies, on the other hand, implicates only the latter. This may mean that there is a dual standard of protection with companies receiving a lower measure of constitutional protection than individuals.[122]

CONCLUSION

8–68   Unlike some of the constitutional guarantees considered in this book, there have been a number of cases in which the Irish courts have considered the application of Arts 43 and 40.3 to the company. The approach taken in *Iarnród Éireann*, bases the protection of the company on the constitutional rights of the shareholders. This approach, similar to that taken in the cases under the European Convention on Human Rights discussed in paras 8–46 to 8–50, has been criticised. Instead, an approach which explores the values underlying the constitutional guarantees in relation to property has been put forward. Such an approach would differ from that taken by the United States Supreme Court in that it would recognise that an individual claim to vindication is stronger than that of a company as the latter is justified only by its utility. One possible impact of such an approach would be to alter the way in which the balance reached by the legislature is subject to review. In *Article 26 and the Planning and Development Bill, 1999, Re*,[123] Keane C.J. referred to the need to apply a proportionality test when assessing an alleged "unjust attack" on property rights in the light of the provisions of Art.43. As the company's property rights are protected only on a utilitarian basis, their regulation or even deprivation on such a basis might justify a lower level of scrutiny than that which would be appropriate where an individual's property rights were at stake. In this context, it should be noted that, unlike the United States

---

[121] Although see Waldron, *op.cit.* at pp.21–22.
[122] That property means something different to the individual is perhaps supported by the observation that individuals are arguably "irrational" economic actors in a way that companies rarely are, placing a personal value on ownership arrangements that are inefficient from a strictly economic perspective. See Buchanan, "Property as a Guarantor of Liberty" in *Property Rights and the Limits of Democracy*, The Shaftesbury Papers, 1 (Rowley ed., Edward Elgar Publishing Ltd, 1993), at pp.33–34.
[123] [2000] 2 I.R. 321, [2001] 1 I.L.R.M. 81.

Constitution, Bunreacht na hÉireann does not contain a takings clause similar to that of the Fifth Amendment, so that the calibration of what constitutes adequate compensation is left more flexible and a differentiation between companies and individuals in this context is a plausible approach.[124]

---

[124] The extent to which compensation is required under the Irish Constitution has been somewhat unclear. See *Dreher v Irish Land Commission and Att.-Gen.* [1984] I.L.R.M. 94; *O'Callaghan v Commissioners of Public Works* [1985] I.L.R.M. 364; *Electricity Supply Board v Gormley* [1985] I.R. 129; and *Article 26 and the Planning and Development Bill, 1999, Re* [2000] 2 I.R. 321, [2001] 1 I.L.R.M. 81. The position is now that compensation is a material factor in determining constitutionality and that an uncompensated deprivation will rarely be upheld. See *Article 26 of The Constitution and the Health (Amendment) (No.2) Bill 2004, Re* [2005] I.E.S.C. 7.

CHAPTER 9

FREEDOM OF EXPRESSION AND THE COMPANY

INTRODUCTION

9–01 This chapter assesses the extent to which companies can be said to enjoy freedom of expression under the Irish Constitution.[1] Article 40.6.1(i) of the Constitution provides as follows:

> "40.6.1 The State guarantees liberty for the exercise, subject to public order and morality, of
> (i) The right of the citizens to express freely their convictions and opinions.
>   The education of public opinion being, however, a matter of such grave import to the common good, the State shall endeavour to ensure that organs of public opinion, such as the radio, the press, the cinema, while preserving their rightful liberty of expression, including criticism of Government policy, shall not be used to undermine public order or morality or the authority of the State.
>   The publication or utterance of blasphemous, seditious, or indecent matter is an offence which shall be punishable in accordance with law."

9–02 As the Irish Constitution itself appears to recognise the special position of "organs of public opinion", media companies will be treated separately to non-media companies.[2]

9–03 Paragraphs 9–05 to 9–17 will examine freedom of expression of the media under the Irish Constitution. It will be noted that the particular protection given to media companies is primarily due to the interest of the public in hearing expression rather than the interests of the companies in speaking.

9–04 While it is beyond dispute that the media has some constitutional

---

[1] The phrases "freedom of expression" and "freedom of speech" will be used interchangeably throughout this chapter.
[2] For an interesting analysis of the position of the Australian media company in this context, see Anderson, "Corporations, Democracy and the Implied Freedom of Political Communication: Towards a Pluralistic Analysis of Constitutional Law" (1998) 22 MULR 1.

protection under the Irish Constitution due to its explicit constitutionally recognised role in the "education of public opinion", it is not entirely clear whether companies which do not have such a clear role are covered by Art.40.6.1(i). There has been a dearth of Irish judicial consideration of this matter. Paragraphs 9–18 to 9–158 will consider the extent to which the speech of non-media corporations is protected. This issue has arisen in other jurisdictions, most commonly in relation to commercial expression and corporate political expression and comparative material from the United States Supreme Court, the Canadian Supreme Court and the European Court of Human Rights ("ECHR") is referred to. Paragraphs 9–18 to 9–82 will focus on corporate political expression and paras 9–83 to 9–158 on commercial expression. It will be noted that the case law in this area also tends to base the protection of such expression on the rights of the audience as opposed to the speaker. In the political expression cases, however, the identity of the speaker has been deemed significant. The reasons for this difference and the implications for the putative free speech rights of the company will be explored. Paragraphs 9–159 to 9–168 will consider the most appropriate solution under the Irish Constitution in the light of the material discussed in the first three sections.

FREEDOM OF EXPRESSION AND THE MEDIA UNDER THE IRISH CONSTITUTION

9–05   In *Cullen v Toibin*,[3] O'Higgins C.J. stated that "the freedom of the press ... which is guaranteed by the Constitution ... cannot be lightly curtailed".[4] The Supreme Court has confirmed that Art.40.6.1(i) guarantees freedom of the press in a number of decisions,[5] including *Irish Times Ltd v Ireland*.[6] This section considers the position of media companies under the Irish Constitution, which appears to make specific provision for the media in Art.40.6.1(i). The reference in the first line to "citizens" is followed by the term "organs of public opinion" in the second paragraph. This could be compared to the reference to the press in the First Amendment to the United States Constitution,[7] although the right is more qualified in the text of the Irish Constitution. It acknowledges that these organs have a "rightful liberty of expression", but is somewhat unclear whether this is to be protected to the same extent as that of the citizen.[8]

---

[3]   [1984] I.L.R.M. 577.
[4]   *ibid.* at 582. Cited by O'Flaherty J. in *Irish Times Ltd v Ireland* [1998] 1 I.R. 359 at 396. See also Barrington J. at 405.
[5]   Examples of recent cases confirming this include *Irish Times v Ireland* [1998] 1 I.R. 359; *Kelly v O'Neill* [2000] 1 I.R. 354; *O'Brien v Mirror Group Newspapers* [2001] 1 I.R. 1; and *Jonathan v Ireland*, unreported, Supreme Court, May 31, 2002.
[6]   [1998] 1 I.R. 359. See O'Flaherty J. at 395, Denham J. at 399 and Barrington J. at 405.
[7]   The First Amendment to the US Constitution states: "Congress shall make no law ... abridging the freedom of speech, or of the press."
[8]   Hogan and Whyte, *Kelly: The Irish Constitution* (4th edn, Lexis-Nexis Butterworths, 2003) at p.1729; Law Reform Commission, *Report on the Civil Law of Defamation* (Law Reform Commission, 1991), at pp.116–120.

9–06 It is perhaps indisputable that the scope of Art.40.6.1(i) extends the protections therein to the media, but the extent of that protection is not so clear. One possibility is that the word "citizen" in the first paragraph does not include corporations so that the second paragraph merely confirms constitutional protection for media companies.[9] If, on the other hand, the first paragraph does refer to artificial as well as natural persons, then it would appear that the bodies mentioned in the second paragraph receive less protection, in that they are subject to the added limitation that they shall not "undermine the authority of the State". It may be that the limitation just referred to is implicit in the reference, at the beginning of Art.40.6.1 to "public order and morality". Such an interpretation would, however, render the subsequent reference to the "authority of the State" superfluous. The reference to the constitutional offence of sedition in the second clause appears to apply to all expression contemplated by Art.40.6.1(i) so that the limitation referring to the authority of the State arguably catches expression which falls short of sedition, yet undermines the authority of the State. In this respect, therefore, the text could be interpreted as providing a lower level of protection for the media than for individuals. Furthermore, it could be noted that the media right exists only in relation to the "education of public opinion" which is considered by the Constitution to be "a matter of ... grave import to the common good". It has also been argued that the media deserves extra protection because media speech is always public and that the specific mention of the "rightful liberty of expression" of the "organs of public opinion" is intended to reflect this.[10] The Law Reform Commission considered the issue in its *Report on the Civil Law of Defamation* and rejected the idea that the media should enjoy greater protection than the citizenry without much discussion.[11]

9–07 As far as identifying the "organs of public opinion" goes, the text itself refers to the radio, the press and the cinema. This is an illustrative rather than an exhaustive list,[12] and television has been included as an organ of public opinion.[13] Indeed, the media in general is probably covered by the guarantee.[14] The fact that an organ of public opinion is controlled by a company will not exclude it from the second paragraph of Art.40.6.1(i). In *Irish Times Ltd v Ireland*,[15] Barrington J. stated:

> "Article 40.6.1°(i) is unique in conferring rights and liberties upon the 'organs of public opinion'. 'Organs' are not capable of having rights so this reference must be taken to mean a reference to those persons whether natural or artificial (such as the applicants in the present action) who control the organs of public opinion."[16]

---

[9] O'Dell, "Reflections on a Revolution in Libel" (1991) 9 I.L.T. 214.

[10] McDonald, "Defamation Report—a Response to the LRC Report" (1992) 10 I.L.T. 70.

[11] Law Reform Commission, *op.cit.* at pp.118–120. See also Casey, *Constitutional Law in Ireland* (3rd edn, Round Hall Sweet and Maxwell, 2000), at p.545.

[12] This is indicated by the words "such as" which precede the list.

[13] *Lynch v Cooney* [1982] I.R. 337.

[14] *Carrigaline Co. Ltd v Minister for Transport* [1997] 1 I.L.R.M. 241.

[15] [1998] 1 I.R. 359.

[16] *ibid.* at 404–405, [1998] 2 I.L.R.M. 161 at 192.

9–08   Clearly, Barrington J. was unperturbed by the idea that a company could be viewed as having constitutional protection in this context. What must be explored, however, is the rationale for according such a guarantee to the corporate person.

9–09   In cases where the media have raised the guarantee of freedom of expression, the public nature of their function has been emphasised. An example of this is *Irish Times Ltd v Ireland*.[17] The applicants in this case were several newspapers and a television station. They sought judicial review of an order made by a Circuit Court judge in the course of criminal proceedings which restricted the right of the applicants to report the proceedings contemporaneously. This order was made by the Circuit Court judge on the basis of an apprehension that media reports of the trial would endanger its fairness and possibly result in its collapse.

9–10   In the High Court, it was argued that the order was in breach of Art.34.1 of the Constitution, which requires the public administration of justice.[18] In his judgment in favour of the respondents, Morris J. found that the trial judge, in making his order, had balanced the right of the accused persons to a fair trial under Art.38.1 with the "media right and the citizen's right of freedom of expression".[19] He found that in so doing, the trial judge had correctly ranked the former right above the latter.[20] The applicants appealed and the Supreme Court upheld their appeal. In his judgment, Hamilton C.J. referred to s.18(i) of the Defamation Act 1961 which recognises the media's right to contemporaneously report court proceedings.[21] Later, he stated that: "The public administration of justice and the right of the wider public to be informed by the media of what is taking place are matters of the greatest importance."[22] He noted that the right was not absolute and could be limited by law. In the case at hand, however, he found that there had been no "real risk" of an unfair trial and that the orders should thus be quashed. His approach was to focus on the right of the audience rather than that of the speaker.

---

[17] [1998] 1 I.R. 359.

[18] Art.34.1 states as follows:

> "Justice shall be administered in courts established by law by judges appointed in the manner provided by this Constitution, and, save in such special and limited cases as may be prescribed by law, shall be administered in public."

[19] [1998] 1 I.R. 359 at 370.

[20] He referred to the notion of a hierarchy of constitutional rights as set out in *The People v Shaw* [1982] I.R. 1 and *D. v DPP* [1994] 2 I.R. 476; *Irish Times Ltd v Ireland* [1998] 1 I.R. 359 at 370 and 373–374 respectively. For a criticism of this approach in this context, see O'Dell, "When Two Tribes Go To War" in *Law and The Media: Views of Journalists and Lawyers* (McGonagle ed., Round Hall, 1997), at p.250.

[21] Section 18(i) provides that:

> "A fair and accurate report published in any newspaper or broadcast by means of wireless telegraphy as part of any programme or service provided by means of a broadcasting station within the State or in Northern Ireland of proceedings publicly heard before any court established by law and exercising judicial authority within the State or Northern Ireland shall, if published or broadcast contemporaneously with such proceedings, be privileged."

[22] [1998] 1 I.R. 359 at 383.

9–11 O'Flaherty J., on the other hand, identified a number of different expression based interests in this case:

"... the freedom of the press to report court proceedings allied to which is the public's right to know what goes on in the courts of law, as well as the rights of the parties, on occasion certainly, to require that proceedings in which they are involved are eligible for publication".[23]

9–12 He gave each of these interests further consideration later in his judgment. With regard to the public's right to know what goes on in courts of law, he noted that as a result of the order,

"the public was destined never to learn anything about the course of the trial of those who pleaded not guilty because the media declined, for whatever reason, to publish any details of evidence afterwards".[24]

9–13 In considering the rights of the applicants he noted that "freedom of the press" was guaranteed under Art.40.6.1.[25] He held, allowing the appeal, that "the press are entitled to report, and the public to know, that the administration of justice is being conducted fairly and properly".[26]

9–14 Denham J.'s judgment emphasised the role of the press in exposing publicly the administration of justice. From her perspective "any curtailment of the press must be viewed as a curtailment of the access of the people to the administration of justice".[27] Describing the various constitutional rights which required balancing in this case, she stated:

"[A]lso in the balance was the freedom of expression of the community, a freedom of expression central to democratic government, to enable democracy to function. There was also the freedom of expression of the press."[28]

9–15 It also appears from her judgment that she views the role of the press as central to Art.40.6.1(i), at least in the context of reporting on criminal trials.[29]

---

[23] *ibid.* at 390.

[24] *ibid.* at 394.

[25] He pointed out that it was not confined to opinions and convictions and approved of Carroll J.'s finding to the same effect in *Att.-Gen. for England and Wales v Brandon Book Publishers Ltd* [1986] I.R. 597, [1998] 1 I.R. 359 at 395. See also the decision of Barrington J., [1998] 1 I.R. 359 at 405.

[26] [1998] 1 I.R. 359 at 396.

[27] *ibid.* at 398.

[28] *ibid.* at 399.

[29] Keane J. took a different view to the rest of the Supreme Court. He found that the freedom of the press to report on court proceedings was guaranteed by Art.34.1 and thus found it unnecessary to consider arguments based on Art.40.6.1(i). [1998] 1 I.R. 359 at 409–410.

9–16   What do these judgments tell us about the rationale for protecting the free speech of the media and the companies that often control them under the Irish Constitution? Barrington J. makes no reference to the audience, simply noting that the persons—corporate or otherwise—who control the organs of public opinion fall within the protection of Art.40.6.1. Denham and Morris JJ. similarly fail to explore the justifications for constitutionally protecting the media. Hamilton C.J., however, explicitly bases the protection of the media under Art.40.6.1 on the interests of its audience. Similarly, O'Flaherty J. recognises that the two are "allied". The approach of the latter two judges appears to enjoy textual support in Art.40.6.1 which refers to the role of the media in the "education of public opinion".

9–17   The media can thus be accurately described as having a right to free speech, but it must be noted that such a right is arguably guaranteed for its instrumental value in disseminating information to the public. The idea that free speech rights are guaranteed for the benefit of the audience as well as, or rather than, the speaker is one which will recur when we consider non-media corporate expression in the form of commercial speech and corporate political speech.

Corporate Political Expression

Introduction

9–18   That political expression is protected under the Irish Constitution seems clear from the text of Art.40.6.1(i). The connection between freedom of expression and the functioning of democracy is a recurring theme in Irish case law.[30] The quotation from the judgment of Denham J. in *Irish Times Ltd v Ireland*[31] reproduced above,[32] indicates the importance of speech to the functioning of the democratic state. In *Murphy v IRTC*,[33] Barrington J. stated of Art.40.6.1 that:

> "[It] is concerned with the public activities of the citizen in a democratic society. That is why ... the framers of the Constitution grouped the right to freedom of expression, the right to free assembly and the right to form associations and unions in the one sub-section. All three rights relate to the practical running of a democratic society."[34]

---

[30] *e.g.* see *Murphy v IRTC* [1997] 2 I.L.R.M. 467. See also *McKenna v An Taoiseach (No.2)* [1995] 2 I.R. 10; *Irish Times v Ireland* [1998] 1 I.R. 359; *Kelly v O'Neill* [2000] 1 I.R. 354; *O'Brien v Mirror Group Newspapers* [2001] 1 I.R. 1; *Jonathan v Ireland*, unreported, Supreme Court, May 31, 2002; *Desmond v Moriarty*, unreported, Supreme Court, January 20, 2004.
[31] [1998] 1 I.R. 359 at 399.
[32] At para.9–14.
[33] [1999] 1 I.R. 13.
[34] *ibid.* at 24.

9–19 No Irish decision appears to have determined whether the political expression of non-media companies is protected under Art.40.6.1(i). The free speech provisions of the European Convention on Human Rights, the United States Constitution and the Canadian Charter of Fundamental Rights and Freedoms have all been interpreted as giving particular protection to political expression. This section will examine the extent to which the political expression of the company has been recognised in these jurisdictions in order to gain a clearer understanding of the issues that arise when a company claims the right to free speech.

The European Convention on Human Rights

9–20 The European Convention on Human Rights protects freedom of expression in Art.10, which states as follows:

> "1. Everyone has the right to freedom of expression. This right shall include freedom to hold opinions and to receive and impart information and ideas without interference by public authority and regardless of frontiers. This Article shall not prevent States from requiring the licensing of broadcasting, television or cinema enterprises.
> 2. The exercise of these freedoms, since it carries with it duties and responsibilities, may be subject to such formalities, conditions, restrictions or penalties as are prescribed by law and are necessary in a democratic society, in the interests of national security, territorial integrity or public safety, for the prevention of disorder or crime, for the protection of health or morals, for the protection of the reputation or rights of others, for preventing the disclosure of information received in confidence, or for maintaining the authority and impartiality of the judiciary."

9–21 In *Autronic AG v Switzerland*,[35] the court referred to a number of earlier decisions[36] to confirm that Art.10 of the Convention applies to legal persons as well as natural persons:

> "In the Court's view, neither Autronic AG's legal status as a limited company nor the fact that its activities were commercial nor the intrinsic nature of freedom of expression can deprive Autronic AG of the protection of Article 10 (art. 10). The Article (art. 10) applies to "everyone", whether natural or legal persons. The Court has, moreover, already held on three occasions that it is applicable to profit-making corporate bodies."[37]

---

[35] (1990) 12 E.H.R.R. 485. Hereafter referred to as *Autronic*.
[36] *Sunday Times v UK* (1979) 2 E.H.R.R. 245; *Markt Intern Verlag GmbH v Germany* (1989) 12 E.H.R.R. 161; *Groppera Radio AG v Switzerland* (1990) 12 E.H.R.R. 321.
[37] *Autronic AG v Switzerland* (1990) 12 E.H.R.R. 485.

9–22 The court has never elaborated on its finding that Art.10 applies to legal persons. Of the three authorities cited in *Autronic*, one concerned a newspaper company,[38] which can perhaps be seen as a separate category.[39] In none of the cases was there any discussion of the extension of Art.10 to the corporate person.

9–23 In *Muller v Switzerland*,[40] the ECHR held that Art.10 did not "distinguish between the various forms of expression".[41] Notwithstanding this interpretation of the scope of Art.10, the court has still accorded political expression a privileged position when determining whether a particular violation was "necessary in a democratic society", finding that "freedom of political debate is at the very core of the concept of a democratic society which prevails throughout the Convention."[42] In *Bowman v UK*,[43] for instance, it was held that "free elections and freedom of expression, particularly freedom of political debate, together form the bedrock of any democratic system."[44] The court takes an expansive view of what constitutes such expression and debate concerning matters related to the public interest will generally be included.[45]

9–24 Thus, the position under the Convention appears to be that corporate political expression is protected, although the basis for this protection is not explicit.

Canada

9–25 Freedom of expression is protected under s.2(b) of the Canadian Charter of Fundamental Rights and Freedoms, which states as follows:

> "2. Everyone has the following fundamental freedoms:
>
> ...
>
>   (b) freedom of thought, belief, opinion and expression, including freedom of the press and other media of communication".

9–26 The Canadian Supreme Court has been loath to adopt a categorical approach to freedom of expression. Instead, the court has insisted that it engages in a case-by-case balancing. Thus, in *Committee for the Commonwealth v Canada*,[46] it noted that there was no separate category of "political expression":

---

[38] *Sunday Times v UK* (1979) 2 E.H.R.R. 245.
[39] Above, Introduction.
[40] Series A No. 133, judgment of May 24, 1988.
[41] *ibid.* at [27].
[42] *Lingens v Austria* Series A No. 103 (1986) at [42].
[43] *Reports* 1998-I.
[44] *ibid.* at [42].
[45] See *Thorgeir Thorgeirson v Iceland* Series A, No. 239 (1992); *Bladet Tromso & Stensaas v Norway, Reports* 1999-III; *Nilsen & Johnsen v Norway, Reports* 1999-VIII; *Fressoz & Roire v France, Reports* 1999-I; *Bergens Tidende v Norway, Reports* 2000-IV.
[46] [1991] 1 S.C.R. 139.

"Rather, the political nature of the speech at issue merely focuses on the competing interests that must be balanced on the constitutional scales. The characterization of the particular speech at issue, as political, commercial or otherwise, will merely be among the many factors to be taken into account."[47]

9–27 Nevertheless, in a number of decisions, the Supreme Court has made it clear that:

"The connection between freedom of expression and the political process is perhaps the linchpin of the s. 2(b) guarantee, and the nature of this connection is largely derived from the Canadian commitment to democracy. Freedom of expression is a crucial aspect of the democratic commitment, not merely because it permits the best policies to be chosen from among a wide array of proffered options, but additionally because it helps to ensure that participation in the political process is open to all persons."[48]

9–28 Despite its rhetoric to the contrary, therefore, the Canadian Supreme Court has effectively privileged political expression. Insofar as corporate political expression is concerned, the court has not made any explicit pronouncements on the issue. It has, however, recognised that expression can be protected for its informational value to the audience.[49]

The United States and corporate political speech

9–29 The United States Supreme Court has given the most comprehensive consideration to corporate political expression. The First Amendment to the United States Constitution protects free speech in the following terms: "Congress shall make no law … abridging the freedom of speech, or of the press …".[50]

9–30 The wording of this provision suggests that it ought to apply to all speech, regardless of the identity of the speaker. It appears to be a restraint on legislative competence, rather than a statement of rights. Indeed, in *First National Bank of Boston v Bellotti*,[51] the United States Supreme Court held that where a company sought the protection of the First Amendment, the relevant issue was not whether the company had a right to speak, but whether

---

[47] *ibid.* at 177.
[48] *Thomson Newspapers Ltd v Canada* [1998] 1 S.C.R. 877 at [92]. See also *R. v Guignard* [2001] 4 S.C.R. 472 at [20]; *Edmonton Journal v Alberta* [1989] 2 S.C.R. 1326 at 1336; *Irwin Toy Ltd v Quebec* [1989] 1 S.C.R. 927 at 928.
[49] *Rocket v Royal College of Dental Surgeons of Ontario* [1990] 2 S.C.R. 232.
[50] The following concerns only the former guarantee, as media companies are arguably a separate category under the Irish Constitution. Above, Section 1.
[51] 435 U.S. 765 (1978). Hereafter referred to as *Bellotti.* For a critical analysis of this case, see Raskin, "The Campaign Finance Crucible: Is Laissez Fair?" (2003) 101 Mich.L.Rev. 1532 at 1543–1548.

the speech at issue was deserving of constitutional protection.[52] Interestingly, the court did not maintain this position and the constitutional protection for corporate political expression has been considerably eroded. The following account will examine this case law before returning to the Irish Constitution to examine the possible position of corporate political expression thereunder.

Introduction—Buckley v Valeo: The stage is set

9–31   In contrast to the jurisdictions discussed above, political expression by companies has been given extensive consideration by the United States Supreme Court. Much of the relevant material derives from its case law on campaign finance. Before exploring the cases which concern corporate political speech, it is thus necessary to examine the landmark decision on campaign finance, *Buckley v Valeo*.[53]

9–32   In this case, the United States Supreme Court considered the constitutionality of legislation[54] which, *inter alia*, limited contributions an individual or group could make to an individual's campaign for political office as well as the amount of independent expenditures permissible on such a campaign. The Supreme Court found that the First Amendment was applicable because the electorate is dependant on the mass media for information. As using those channels of communication is expensive, the reduction of available funds impacts on the quantity of political expression.[55]

9–33   At the outset, the court emphasised the central importance of expression relating to the election of candidates to political office.[56] It then drew a distinction between contributions and expenditure. The former were held to be deserving of lower protection than the latter. This was because contributions were held to involve a symbolic expression of support that varied little with size. Also, "the transformation of contributions into political debate involves speech by someone other than the contributor."[57] Restrictions on contributions required that candidates find other ways of raising funds, but they did not reduce the overall funding available for political expression. In any event, restrictions on contributions could be justified by the need to avoid corruption, or the appearance thereof in the electoral system.

9–34   Expenditure limitations, on the other hand, were found to "impose direct and substantial restraints on the quantity of political speech".[58] These were

---

[52] 435 U.S. 765 (1978) at 776.
[53] 424 U.S. 1 (1976). Hereafter referred to as *Buckley*. For a brief account of the case law that follows, see Levine, "The (Un)Informed Electorate: Insights into the Supreme Court's Electoral Speech Cases" (2003) 54 Case W.Res.L.Rev. 225 at 262–276.
[54] Federal Election Campaign Act 1971.
[55] 424 U.S. 1 (1976) at 16–17.
[56] *ibid.* at 14–15.
[57] *ibid.* at 21.
[58] *ibid.* at 39.

not justified by concerns about corruption.[59] In this section of the judgment, the court focuses on the right of the speaker, referring to "the First Amendment right to speak one's mind ... on all public institutions".[60] As regards the argument that the expenditure limits were intended to ensure that wealthy parties did not drown out the voices of those with less resources, the court was adamant that:

> "[T]he concept that government may restrict the speech of some elements of our society in order to enhance the relative voice of others is wholly foreign to the First Amendment."[61]

9–35 The court thus found that the aspects of the legislation relating to expenditures were unconstitutional.[62]

9–36 The idea that money constitutes protected speech in this context has stood firm in the subsequent case law of the court.[63] Whatever the merits of this feature of *Buckley*,[64] its continued acceptance by the court has meant that a considerable body of jurisprudence exploring the rights of companies to provide campaign finance has evolved. Some of this case law is among the material discussed below. The Irish courts have never been faced with a freedom of expression based challenge to the Electoral Acts 1997–2002 and it may be that the money as speech analysis would be rejected. The campaign finance case law below is, however, of general application to corporate political expression[65] and the approach taken by the United States Supreme Court is, thus, a useful source of comparative material.

Bellotti *and the identity of the speaker*

9–37 The United States Supreme Court addressed the issue of corporate political speech in *First National Bank of Boston v Bellotti*.[66] The case concerned a challenge by the appellants[67] to a Massachusetts criminal statute

---

[59] *ibid.* at 46–47.

[60] *ibid.* at 48, references omitted.

[61] *ibid.* at 48–49.

[62] Blackmun J. and Burger C.J. dissented from the decision insofar as it related to contributions. Other limitations, on personal expenditure by a candidate and on the total expenditure on a campaign, were also found unconstitutional.

[63] The Supreme Court of Canada has also taken this view. See *Harper v Canada* [2004] 1 S.C.R. 827.

[64] See the dissenting opinion of White J., 424 U.S. 1 (1976) at 259–263. See also his dissent in *FEC v National Conservative Political Action Committee* 470 U.S. 480 (1985) at 508.

[65] See *Consolidated Edison Co. v Public Service Comm'n* 447 U.S. 530 (1980), below, at paras 9–50 to 9–51; *Pacific Gas & Electric Co. v Public Util. Comm'n* 475 U.S. 1 (1986), below at paras 9–52 to 9–55.

[66] 435 U.S. 765 (1978). Hereafter referred to as *Bellotti*. For a critical analysis of this case, see Raskin, *op.cit.* at 1543–1548.

[67] Two banks and three companies.

that prohibited them from making contributions or expenditures "for the purpose of … influencing or affecting the vote on any question submitted to the voters, other than one materially affecting any of the property, business or assets of the corporation". The statute also provided that where a question was submitted to voters which affected taxation of income, property or transactions of individuals, such a question would not qualify as one materially affecting the corporation in the ways described above. The corporation in this case wished to expend money to publicise its opposition to a referendum to amend the Massachusetts Constitution to allow for graduated personal income tax.

9–38   The Supreme Judicial Court of Massachusetts found that the case posed the question whether corporations had First Amendment rights and, if so, to what extent.[68] It referred to the right of corporations as persons under the Fourteenth Amendment not to be deprived of property without due process of law. The Massachusetts court found that corporations enjoyed First Amendment rights as an incident of their Fourteenth Amendment rights.[69] These rights only arose where expression related to the business assets or property of the corporation. Thus, it found that the impugned statute did not violate the First Amendment rights of corporations as it permitted expression on those matters.[70]

9–39   Powell J. delivered the majority opinion and found that the lower court had posed the wrong question. He noted that the First Amendment serves societal interests. From this perspective:

> "The proper question therefore is not whether corporations 'have' First Amendment rights and, if so, whether they are coextensive with those of natural persons. Instead, the question must be whether [the statute] abridges expression that the First Amendment was meant to protect."[71]

9–40   He pointed out that the type of speech at issue in the case was "at the heart of the First Amendment's protection"[72] as it was:

> "the type of speech indispensable to decisionmaking in a democracy, and this is no less true because the speech comes from a corporation rather than an individual. The inherent worth of the speech in terms of its capacity for informing the public does not depend upon the identity of its source, whether corporation, association, union, or individual."[73]

---

[68] *First National Bank v Att.-Gen.* 371 Mass. 773, 359 N.E.2d 1262 (1976).
[69] *ibid.*
[70] *ibid.*
[71] 435 U.S. 765 (1978) at 776.
[72] *ibid.*
[73] *ibid.* at 777, footnotes omitted. He also stated, at 778:
> "The question in this case, simply put, is whether the corporate identity of the speaker deprives this proposed speech of what otherwise would be its clear entitlement to protection."

9–41   The Massachusetts court had taken the view that a corporation's First Amendment rights were inextricably linked to its property rights under the Fourteenth Amendment. Powell J. disagreed with this, referring to *Grosjean v American Press Co.*[74] and pointing out that the First Amendment bound the states by virtue of the due process clause of the Fourteenth Amendment, which had long been held to apply to corporations.[75]

9–42   He stated that self-expression was not the only interest protected by the First Amendment and highlighted the commercial speech cases of the court,[76] noting that:

> "[they] illustrate that the First Amendment goes beyond protection of the press and the self-expression of individuals to prohibit government from limiting the stock of information from which members of the public may draw."[77]

9–43   The appellee put forward two justifications for the challenged restrictions on speech in the case. The first of these was that they were necessary to sustain the active role of citizens in the electoral process, thereby avoiding a loss of confidence in government. Powell J. rejected this argument because there was no evidence to suggest that corporate political speech "threatened imminently" to undermine the democratic process and threatened the confidence of the citizenry therein.[78] The court noted that there was less of a risk of corruption in a referendum than in the election of an individual. It was unmoved by the argument that corporate advertising could alter the outcome of the vote, recognising that that would be its purpose. As Powell J. pointed out, however, the weighing of competing arguments is something that is entrusted to the citizenry who may take the source of such arguments into account.[79]

9–44   The second justification put forward was that the restrictions protected corporate shareholders by preventing the use of corporate funds to put forward

---

[74] 297 U.S. 233 (1936). The reference is at 435 U.S. 765 (1978) at 780.

[75] 435 U.S. 765 (1978) at 780. See *Santa Clara County v Southern Pacific Railroad Co.* 118 U.S. 394 (1886) discussed below at paras 14–19 to 14–22.

[76] See below, at paras 9–90 to 9–117.

[77] 435 U.S. 765 (1978) at 783.

[78] *ibid.* at 789–790.

[79] *ibid.* at 790–792. This aspect of his opinion has been subject to the criticism that it is inconsistent:
> "This reasoning is, of course, incoherent. The Court says at once that corporate speech might lose protection if it were to become at some point too effective and overwhelming, and then in the next breath, that its effectiveness could not be the basis for regulating it. Which is it?"

Raskin, *op.cit.* at 1544, footnote omitted. For the argument that the court was wrong to ignore the "anti-democratic impact" of the decision, see Lansing and Sherman, "The 'Evolution' of the Supreme Court's Political Spending Doctrine: Restricting Corporate Contributions to Ballot Measure Campaigns after Citizens Against Rent Control v City of Berkeley" (1982) 8 J.Corp.L. 79.

views with which some shareholders might not agree.[80] Powell J. dismissed this justification, pointing out that minority shareholders had the derivative suit at their disposal should they wish to challenge such expenditure.

9–45   White J. delivered a strong dissenting opinion.[81] He emphasised that while corporate communications were within the scope of the First Amendment, they were subject to restrictions to which individual expression was not. He stated that:

> "Indeed, what some have considered to be the principal function of the First Amendment, the use of communication as a means of self-expression, self-realization, and self-fulfilment, is not at all furthered by corporate speech."[82]

9–46   White J. also recognised that the First Amendment protected the "interchange of ideas".[83] The restriction of corporate speech, however, had less of an impact on the amount of speech available to the public because there was nothing to prevent individuals concerned in the company from expressing them outside of the corporate form.[84]

9–47   He pointed out that:

> "It has long been recognized … that the special status of corporations has placed them in a position to control vast amounts of economic power which may, if not regulated, dominate not only the economy but also the very heart of democracy, the electoral process."[85]

9–48   In his view, corporate political expression, due to economic advantages enjoyed by corporations, bore no relation to the conviction with which the ideas expressed were held.[86] Furthermore, unlike the majority in the case, White J. was convinced by the argument that shareholders should not be coerced into supporting political expression with which they may not agree.[87]

9–49   Rehnquist J.'s dissent reflected his espousal of the concession theory of the corporation. He argued that:

> "A State grants to a business corporation the blessings of potentially perpetual life and limited liability to enhance its efficiency as an economic

---

[80] See *United States v CIO* 335 U.S. 106 at 113. For the view that shareholder protection was the key factor motivating campaign reform legislation since the Tillman Act 1907, see Raskin, *op.cit.* at 1547–1548.
[81] He was joined by Brennan and Marshall JJ.
[82] 435 U.S. 765 (1978) at 804–805.
[83] *ibid*. at 806.
[84] *ibid*. at 807–810.
[85] *ibid*. at 809.
[86] *ibid*. at 810.
[87] *ibid*. at 812–821.

entity. It might reasonably be concluded that these properties, so beneficial in the economic sphere, pose special dangers in the political sphere. Furthermore, it might be argued that liberties of political expression are not at all necessary to effectuate the purposes for which States permit corporations to exist."[88]

9–50   The decision in *Bellotti* was succeeded by the case of *Consolidated Edison Co. v Public Service Comm'n*.[89] The appellant utility company had been including inserts in its monthly electric bills which discussed issues concerning the use of nuclear power. The appellee had prohibited this practice. Powell J.[90] referred to *Bellotti* and pointed out that that case had held that a state could not confine corporate speech to certain topics. Speech was protected due to its potential to inform the public and this was not related to the identity of the speaker.[91] Rejecting the argument that billpayers were a captive audience,[92] the court held that the prohibition was unconstitutional.

9–51   Blackmun J., joined by Rehnquist J., dissented. The joint dissent focused on the monopoly status of the company. This, combined with its rate structure, meant that the utility's customers were being forced to subsidise speech with which they might not necessarily agree.[93]

9–52   The next case to consider the political expression rights of corporations was *Pacific Gas & Electric Co. v Public Util. Comm'n*.[94] The appellant corporation in this case had distributed a newsletter together with its monthly bills for a number of years. The appellee organisation, Toward Utility Rate Normalisation ("TURN"), had requested that the appellee Commission prohibit this practice on the basis that the appellant's customers should not be paying for the dissemination of its political speech. The Commission found that the envelopes were partially the property of the customers and decided to apportion the space therein so that TURN could use it to disseminate its own political materials four times a year.

9–53   Powell J. delivered the majority opinion of the court.[95] Referring back to *Bellotti* and *Consolidated Edison*, he reiterated that the protection of speech was not dependant on the identity of the speaker.[96] He pointed out that

---

[88] *ibid*. at 825–826. Like White J., Rehnquist J. pointed out that the denial of rights of political expression to corporations did not affect the free flow of information as long as individual speakers remained free to contribute their speech. 435 U.S. 765 (1978) at 828.

[89] 447 U.S. 530 (1980). Hereafter referred to as *Consolidated Edison*.

[90] Joined by Burger C.J. and Brennan, Marshall, Stewart and White JJ.

[91] 447 U.S. 530 (1980) at 533.

[92] *ibid*. at 541–542. This argument was accepted by both Rehnquist and Blackmun JJ. who dissented from this aspect of the court's decision.

[93] 447 U.S. 530 (1980) at 553.

[94] 475 U.S. 1 (1986). Hereafter referred to as *Pacific Gas*.

[95] He was joined by Burger C.J. and O'Connor and Brennan JJ.

[96] 475 U.S. 1 (1986) at 8.

compelled access such as that ordered by the Commission in this case penalises the expression of a particular point of view and forces speakers to alter speech to an agenda they do not set.[97] As the identity of the speaker is not germane, "[f]or corporations as for individuals, the choice to speak includes within it the choice of what not to say".[98] His decision appears to espouse a real entity conception of the company—an approach implicitly rejected by Rehnquist J. in his dissenting opinion.

9–54   Rehnquist J.'s dissent stated that he did not "believe that negative free speech rights, applicable to individuals and perhaps the print media, should be extended to corporations generally". In his view, negative free speech rights were enjoyed by natural persons because of their interest in self-expression and were part of the broader constitutional interest of the natural person in freedom of conscience.[99]

> "Extension of the individual freedom of conscience decisions to business corporations strains the rationale of those cases beyond breaking point. To ascribe to such artificial entities an 'intellect' or 'mind' for freedom of conscience purposes is to confuse metaphor with reality. Corporations generally have not played the historic role of newspapers as conveyers of individual ideas and opinion."[100]

9–55   He went on to note that *Bellotti* and *Consolidated Edison* both recognised that free speech rights of corporations do not arise from the value of self-expression, rather they arise as an instrumental way of furthering the First Amendment purpose of a free flow of information in order to foster self-government. The interest in remaining silent in this case was divorced from the latter rationale. Indeed, in allowing access, public debate would be enlarged. Rehnquist J. noted that the two most closely related constitutional liberties to that at stake in this case—the right to privacy and the right to silence—had not been granted to the corporation.[101]

The dangers posed by the corporate speech of non-profit companies

9–56   A number of the United States Supreme Court's decisions on campaign finance have concerned non-profit corporations. These cases illustrate the decline of the principle in *Bellotti, Consolidated Edison* and *Pacific Gas* that the identity of the speaker was irrelevant to the First Amendment protection of political expression.

---

[97]   See *Miami Herald Publishing Co. v Tornillo* 418 U.S. 241 (1980).
[98]   475 U.S. 1 (1986) at 16.
[99]   *ibid*. at 32–34.
[100]   *ibid*. at 33.
[101]   On the right to silence and the company, see Chap.5 above. In a concurring opinion, Marshall J. emphasised that he was not holding that the First Amendment rights of corporations were co-extensive with those of individuals, 475 U.S. 1 (1986) at 25–26.

9–57 The first of these cases was *FEC v National Right to Work Committee*.[102] It concerned a legislative prohibition on non-stock corporations soliciting contributions from persons other than their members. Only monies solicited from members could legally be used for political expenditures and contributions. The court identified a twofold rationale for the restrictions. First:

> "[T]o ensure that substantial aggregations of wealth amassed by the special advantages which go with the corporate form of organization should not be converted into political 'war chests' which could be used to incur political debts from legislators who are aided by the contributions."[103]

9–58 Secondly:

> "[T]o protect the individuals who have paid money into a corporation or union for purposes other than the support of candidates from having that money used to support political candidates to whom they may be opposed."[104]

9–59 Rehnquist J. delivered the unanimous opinion of the court, and stated:

> "In order to prevent both actual and apparent corruption, Congress aimed a part of its regulatory scheme at corporations. The statute reflects a legislative judgment that the special characteristics of the corporate structure require particularly careful regulation ... While 441b restricts the solicitation of corporations and labor unions without great financial resources, as well as those more fortunately situated, we accept Congress' judgment that it is the potential for such influence that demands regulation."[105]

9–60 In *FEC v National Conservative Political Action Committee*,[106] the court considered the constitutionality of legislation[107] which made it a criminal offence for a political action committee ("PAC")[108] to make expenditures over a certain limit to a presidential election campaign where the candidate had opted for public funding. In considering the level of constitutional protection accorded to political expenditure by such organisations, the court found that, while they were incorporated, the case was not a "corporations" case so that the expenditures were entitled to "full First Amendment protection".[109] This

---

[102] 459 U.S. 197 (1982). Hereafter referred to as *NRTWC*.
[103] *ibid*. at 207.
[104] *ibid*. at 208.
[105] *ibid*. at 209–210.
[106] 470 U.S. 480 (1985). Hereafter referred to as *NCPAC*.
[107] s.9021(f) of The Presidential Election Campaign Fund Act.
[108] PACs are a concept introduced by the Federal Election Campaign Fund Act. They are separate bodies with the explicit function of fundraising for election campaigns and their resources are separate from the corporate treasury.
[109] 470 U.S. 480 (1985) at 496.

was because the organisations in this case were "designed expressly to participate in political debate" and "quite different from the traditional corporations organized for economic gain".[110]

9–61   *FEC v Massachusetts Citizens For Life Inc*[111] concerned the constitutionality of s.316 of the Federal Election Campaign Act as applied to a non-stock, non-profit corporation set up to promote the right to life of the unborn. Section 316 prohibited corporations from using treasury funds to make any expenditure in connection with a federal election. Any expenditure for such purposes was to be made from a segregated fund consisting of voluntary contributions. The judgment of the court indicates that restrictions on corporate political expression are constitutional insofar as they prevent distortion of the free market in ideas. Thus, Brennan J. stated:

> "Direct corporate spending on political activity raises the prospect that resources amassed in the economic marketplace may be used to provide an unfair advantage in the political marketplace. Political 'free trade' does not necessarily require that all who participate in the political marketplace do so with exactly equal resources ... Relative availability of funds is after all a rough barometer of public support. The resources in the treasury of a business corporation, however, are not an indication of popular support for the corporation's political ideas. They reflect instead the economically motivated decisions of investors and customers. The availability of these resources may make a corporation a formidable political presence, even though the power of the corporation may be no reflection of the power of its ideas."[112]

9–62   The court held also that such restrictions could constitutionally be applied to a business corporation on the basis of the need to protect the dissenting stockholder, but that argument was inapplicable to an organisation whose members contributed to it for the express purpose of furthering its political expression.[113] The organisation in this case, however, had "features more akin to voluntary political associations than business firms, and therefore should not have to bear burdens on independent spending solely because of [its] incorporated status".[114] The court went on to identify three particular features of the MCFL which obviated the need for regulation. First, it was formed expressly to promote political activities and was restricted from engaging in business activities. Secondly, it had no shareholders or persons with a claim to its assets, which meant that there was no economic disincentive for its contributors to desist in supporting it. Thirdly, the organisation was independent of business influences and did not accept contributions from business organisations.[115]

---

[110]   *ibid.* at 500.
[111]   479 U.S. 238 (1986). Hereafter referred to as *MCFL*.
[112]   *ibid.* at 257–258.
[113]   *ibid.* at 260–261.
[114]   *ibid.* at 263.
[115]   *ibid.* at 264.

9–63 In *Austin v Michigan Chamber of Commerce*,[116] the court considered the constitutionality of s.54(1) of the Michigan Campaign Finance Act insofar as it prohibited corporations from using general treasury funds to make expenditures in connection with state candidate elections. The court referred to the:

> "corrosive and distorting effects of immense aggregations of wealth that are accumulated with the help of the corporate form and that have little or no correlation to the public's support for the corporation's political ideas".[117]

9–64 The Chamber of Commerce argued that the statute was overbroad in that it caught closely held corporations which might not have significant amounts of capital. This argument was rejected by the court:

> "Although some closely held corporations, just as some publicly held ones, may not have accumulated significant amounts of wealth, they receive from the State the special benefits conferred by the corporate structure and present the potential for distorting the political process. This potential for distortion justifies 54(1)'s general applicability to all corporations."[118]

9–65 The court distinguished *MCFL* by focusing on the three features of the organisation in that case which it found to be absent in the Chamber of Commerce. The latter was able to and did engage in economic activity. This meant that its contributors had a disincentive to disassociate themselves from it. The biggest point of distinction, however, was that it received the majority of its contributions from business corporations.[119]

The identity of the speaker revisited

9–66 More recently, the court revisited this area in *FEC v Beaumont*,[120] where it held that a limit on direct contributions to candidates for federal office by non-profit advocacy corporations was constitutional. The court pointed out that the rationale for regulating campaign funding by corporations was threefold. First, it protected dissenting shareholders. Secondly, it prevented

---

[116] 494 U.S. 652 (1990). Hereafter referred to as *Austin*. For a critical analysis of this case, see Fisch, "Frankenstein's Monster Hits the Campaign Trail: An Approach to the Regulation of Corporate Political Expenditure" (1991) 32 Wm.& Mary L.Rev. 587.

[117] 494 U.S. 652 (1990) at 260.

[118] *ibid.* at 661. The court had also stated at 660:
> "We emphasize that the mere fact that corporations may accumulate large amounts of wealth is not the justification for 54; rather, the unique state-conferred corporate structure that facilitates the amassing of large treasuries warrants the limit on independent expenditures."

Scalia J.'s dissent attacked this aspect of the court's decision at 687–690.

[119] 494 U.S. 652 (1990) at 661–665.

[120] 539 U.S. 146 (2003).

corruption or the appearance thereof. Thirdly, it obviated the danger of corporations being used as conduits for illegal donations.[121] Interestingly, the court appeared in this case to take a step back from its earlier assertion that the identity of the speaker was irrelevant to First Amendment analysis, stating in a footnote that:

> "Within the realm of contributions generally, corporate contributions are furthest from the core of political expression, since corporations' First Amendment speech and association interests are derived largely from those of their members ... and of the public in receiving information ... A ban on direct corporate contributions leaves individual members of corporations free to make their own contributions, and deprives the public of little or no material information."[122]

9–67   *FEC v McConnell*[123] concerned challenges to various provisions of the Bipartisan Campaign Reform Act of 2002. Title II of the Act reiterated the separate fund and disclosure requirement for corporations, trade unions and non-profit corporations. Under Title II, these requirements were also to be applicable to "electioneering communications" defined as any broadcast, satellite or cable communication identifying a candidate made within 60 days of a federal election, or within 30 days of a primary. The court found that these legislative provisions passed constitutional scrutiny. In so finding, the court reiterated its narrow exception for those non-profit corporations which met the *MCFL* criteria.[124]

9–68   In his dissenting opinion, Scalia J. suggested that the underlying assumption of the majority's position on Title II was that the speech of corporations could be abridged under the First Amendment. Referring back to *Bellotti* and *Pacific Gas*, Scalia J. stated that:

> "In the modern world, giving the government power to exclude corporations from the political debate enables it effectively to muffle the voices that best represent the most significant segments of the economy and the most passionately held social and political views. People who associate—who pool their financial resources—for purposes of economic enterprise overwhelmingly do so in the corporate form; and with increasing frequency, incorporation is chosen by those who associate to defend and promote particular ideas—such as the American Civil Liberties Union and the National Rifle Association, parties to these cases.

---

[121] *ibid.* at 154–156. See also *FEC v Colorado Republican Federal Campaign Comm.* 533 U.S. 431; *Cedric Kushner Promotions Ltd v King* 533 U.S. 158 (2001).

[122] 539 U.S. 146 (2003) at n.8, references omitted.

[123] 540 U.S. 93 (2003). Hereafter referred to as *McConnell*. For a general discussion of this decision in the context of campaign finance reform, see Issacharoff, "Throwing in the Towel: The Constitutional Morass of Campaign Finance" in *Election Law Journal*, Vol.3 (2004), at p.259.

[124] These criteria are set out above at para.9–62.

Imagine, then, a government that wished to suppress nuclear power—or oil and gas exploration, or automobile manufacturing, or gun ownership, or civil liberties—and that had the power to prohibit corporate advertising against its proposals. To be sure, the individuals involved in, or benefited by, those industries, or interested in those causes, could (given enough time) form political action committees or other associations to make their case. But the organizational form in which those enterprises already *exist*, and in which they can most quickly and most effectively get their message across, is the corporate form. The First Amendment does not in my view permit the restriction of that political speech.”[125]

9–69 With regard to the danger that corporate wealth could distort elections, he pointed out that as long as disclosure requirements were in place, no threat was posed. He made a similar point with regard to the issue of corruption, real or apparent.[126]

9–70 In his dissenting opinion, Thomas J. was critical of the argument that the aim of the legislation was to prevent corruption or the appearance thereof. Referring to *Austin*, he stated:

> “[T]he ‘corrosive and distorting effects’ described in *Austin* are that corporations, on behalf of their shareholders, will be able to convince voters of the correctness of their ideas. Apparently, winning in the marketplace of ideas is no longer a sign that ‘the ultimate good’ has been ‘reached by free trade in ideas,’ or that the speaker has survived ‘the best test of truth’ by having ‘the thought … get itself accepted in the competition of the market’ … It is now evidence of ‘corruption’. This conclusion is antithetical to everything for which the First Amendment stands.”[127]

9–71 Kennedy J. also dissented from the decision of the majority in relation to Title II. Like Thomas J., he too felt that *Austin* was incompatible with *Bellotti* and the First Amendment.[128] He also stated:

> “[T]he majority’s ready willingness to equate corruption with all organizations adopting the corporate form is a grave insult to nonprofit and for-profit corporations alike, entities that have long enriched our civic dialogue.”[129]

9–72 Kennedy J. was unimpressed with the idea that the possibility of establishing PACs was an answer to the corporation’s free speech rights. Apart

---

[125] 540 U.S. 93 (2003) at 258.
[126] *ibid*. at 259.
[127] *ibid*. at 274. The quotations are from *Abrams v United States*, 250 U.S. 616 (1919) at 630, Holmes J. dissenting.
[128] 540 U.S. 93 (2003) at 324–327.
[129] *ibid*. at 325–326.

from highlighting the burdens associated with such committees,[130] he stated that they required corporations to adopt "a false identity"[131] and referred to the scheme as one of "compulsory ventriloquism"[132]:

> "The hostility toward corporations and unions that infuses the majority opinion is inconsistent with the viewpoint neutrality the First Amendment demands of all Government actors, including the members of this Court. Corporations, after all, are the engines of our modern economy. They facilitate complex operations on which the Nation's prosperity depends. To say these entities cannot alert the public to pending political issues that may threaten the country's economic interests is unprecedented ... The costs of the majority's misplaced concerns about the 'corrosive and distorting effects of immense aggregations of wealth,' ... moreover, will weigh most heavily on budget-strapped nonprofit entities upon which many of our citizens rely for political commentary and advocacy. These groups must now choose between staying on the sidelines in the next election or establishing a PAC against their institutional identities. PACs are a legal construct sanctioned by Congress. They are not necessarily the means of communication chosen and preferred by the citizenry."[133]

Some conclusions from the case law

9–73   A number of interesting points arise from the foregoing. In *Bellotti*, *Consolidated Edison* and *Pacific Gas*, the court strongly denied that the identity of the speaker was of relevance under the First Amendment,[134] only to state the converse in *Beaumont*.[135] In the intervening period, the cases on campaign finance indicate that the court altered its conception of the danger of corruption generally and of that posed by the corporate form in particular.[136]

9–74   In *Buckley*, *Bellotti*, and *NRTWC*, the court had taken the view that the particular risk posed was that of a quid pro quo of political favours in return for campaign finance. In *NCPAC* and *MCFL*, however, the emphasis shifted away from the focus on corruption to the quality of the speech at issue. When dealing with a PAC and a non-profit corporation with the specific features identified in *MCFL*, it appears that campaign finance regulation is deemed less necessary, as speech by such entities is a true reflection of the political ideals of their individual members. This was contrasted with the situation where

---

[130] *ibid.* at 330–333.

[131] *ibid.* at 332.

[132] *ibid.* at 333.

[133] *ibid.* at 340. See also the dissenting judgment of Douglas J. in *United States v Auto Workers* 352 U.S. 567 (1957).

[134] See above, at paras 9–37 to 9–40. *Cf.* "Speech Exceptions" (2005) 118 Harv.L.Rev. 1709 at 1720–1724.

[135] See above, at para.9–66.

[136] For an interesting free speech argument in favour of corporate participation in political campaigning, see Bolodeoku, "Corporate Speech in a Democracy: What can Nigeria Learn from Abroad?" (2005) 13 Cardozo J.Int'l & Comp.L. 61.

a company uses treasury funds as, in that situation, there is no such direct nexus. Furthermore, the court at this point appears to have accepted the related argument, rejected by the majority in *Bellotti*, that corporate political expression could be curtailed in the interests of shareholders who disagreed with the content of that expression.

9–75 In *Austin*, the court altered its view of corruption to make it more applicable to non-profit corporations. According to *Austin*, it is legitimate to curtail First Amendment rights under the banner of the "corrosive and distorting effect" of corporate wealth which is unrelated to "true" political support. Furthermore, the fact that the corporate form has the potential to aggregate wealth is sufficient to justify regulation—that is the price paid for the "special benefits" that accompany incorporation.[137]

9–76 In *Beaumont*, a third justification for regulating non-stock companies is stated—to prevent corporations being used as conduits for illegal donations. The court also specifically accepted the argument that to allow corporate contributions to be made from treasury funds would be unfair to shareholders. This argument was rejected in *Bellotti* and the court's reasoning for choosing to accept it in this case is not explained. *McConnell* reiterated the approach taken in *Beaumont* and confirmed that only *MCFL* corporations were constitutionally protected from the requirement to set up PACs in order to raise campaign finance.

9–77 The case law discussed above reveals the complex interaction between corporate theory and the rationale underlying the First Amendment guarantee. In *Bellotti*, the majority Supreme Court opinion refuses to engage with any theoretical conception of the company. It also ignores the part of its decision in *Buckley* where expenditures were stated to be entitled to greater constitutional protection because of the interest of the speaker. Instead, the court espouses a theory of the First Amendment which echoes that of Alexander Meiklejohn.[138] Political speech is protected under the First Amendment because it adds to the pool of information from which the citizenry can draw when making decisions key to the functioning of democracy.

9–78 Rehnquist J.'s dissent in *Bellotti*, with his adoption of a concession theory of the company,[139] followed the expected pattern[140] in that it was against recognising the First Amendment rights of the company. In *Pacific Gas*, he married his concession theory conception of the company with an emphasis on the self-expression interests, which he identified as being the basis for the First Amendment protection of the right to refrain from speech. On this basis,

---

[137] *Austin v Michigan Chamber of Commerce* 494 U.S. 652 (1990) at 661—quotation reproduced above at para.9–64.
[138] Meiklejohn, *Free Speech and its Relation to Self-Government* (Harper and Brothers, 1948).
[139] See also *Consolidated Edison* 447 U.S. 530 (1980).
[140] Above at para.1–22.

he was against First Amendment protection of corporate silence. In *NCPAC*, he delivered a majority opinion in which he advocated full First Amendment protection for a non-profit incorporated body. In so doing, he explicitly stated that the case was not a corporations case because the impugned legislation applied to unincorporated bodies also.[141] Consistent with this approach, he reiterated in *MCFL* that the legislature was entitled to distinguish "between political activity by corporate actors and that by organizations not benefiting from 'the corporate shield which the State [has] granted to corporations as a form of quid pro quo' for various regulations".[142]

9–79   White J.'s decision in *Bellotti* emphasised the function of freedom of speech in promoting self-fulfilment. In his view, corporate speech was unrelated to that function because individuals could always express themselves outside the company. As far as his conception of the company was concerned, he took an aggregate view. It has been noted earlier that an aggregate conception of the company may lead to constitutional protection.[143] When an aggregate conception of the corporation is married with a primary focus on the individual self-fulfilment justification for freedom of expression, however, one logical result is to find that the individuals can express themselves elsewhere. White J. also found that the possibility of expression elsewhere meant that the pool of ideas available to the electorate would not necessarily be smaller if corporate speech was restricted.

9–80   The approach of these two judges can be contrasted with that of their colleagues on the Supreme Court bench who focused on the importance of an uninhibited flow of ideas rather than the source of those ideas. The most striking example of this are the majority opinions delivered by Powell J. in *Bellotti*, *Consolidated Edison*, and *Pacific Gas*. In each of these cases, the identity of the speaker is stated to be irrelevant as it is the speech that is protected. While no theory of the corporation is explicitly adopted, the decision in *Bellotti* arguably implicitly approves a natural entity conception of the company. In *Buckley*, the particular protection given to expenditures as opposed to contributions was predicated partly on the idea that the latter directly concerned "the First Amendment right to speak one's mind ... on all public institutions".[144] By maintaining that distinction in *Bellotti*—as well as the other campaign finance cases considered above—the court was implicitly accepting that the source of the communication was of some significance, rhetoric to the contrary notwithstanding. The identity of the speaker reared its head again in *Pacific Gas* where the court stated in one breath that the identity of the speaker was not relevant and in the next that for both companies and natural persons "the

---

[141]   See 470 U.S. 480 (1985) at 496.
[142]   479 U.S. 238 (1986) at 270, references omitted.
[143]   Above at para.1–27. See also Chap.5.
[144]   *Buckley v Valeo* 424 U.S. 1 (1976) at 48, references omitted. See discussion above at paras 9–31 to 9–36.

choice to speak includes within it the choice of what not to say".[145] As Rehnquist J. has pointed out, such an approach is arguably inconsistent with the instrumental rationale for protecting freedom of expression which the court has used to ignore the corporate identity of the speaker.[146]

9–81 It is in the campaign finance cases after *Bellotti* that the tension inherent in the approach of Powell J. comes to the fore. Thus, in *NCPAC*, for example, the court was at pains to emphasise that the speakers affected by the impugned regulation were not "traditional corporations organized for economic gain".[147] A similar approach was taken in *MCFL* and *Austin*. In *Beaumont*, the court finally stated explicitly that where a company was speaking, that speech was deserving of lower constitutional protection. The justification for this was partially predicated on an aggregate conception of the company. Companies' First Amendment rights "derived largely from those of their members ... and of the public in receiving information".[148] Souter J.'s majority opinion can thus be compared to White J.'s dissent in *Bellotti*.[149]

9–82 The dissenting opinions of Thomas and Scalia JJ. in *McConnell* demonstrate their slightly different understanding of the First Amendment. Both judges, like their aforementioned brethren, emphasised the interests of the audience. The dissent by Thomas J. contains a strong emphasis on the free marketplace of ideas in which the identity of the speaker is simply irrelevant. Scalia J.'s approach, while similar in its support for a free marketplace of ideas, is more attuned to the concerns of the majority in the case. He emphasised the importance of allowing corporations to participate in political debate. From his perspective, the possibility of speaking without using the corporate identity was not sufficient to satisfy the First Amendment interest in a free marketplace of ideas. The corporation, be it profit or non-profit in nature, had to be allowed to speak *qua* corporation precisely because its different identity meant that it had a different message. Insofar as the speech reaching that audience might be qualitatively different where its source is corporate in nature, the existence of disclosure requirements meant that the audience was equipped to evaluate it. As far as Scalia J. was concerned, provided that all products released into the free market in ideas are adequately labelled, the consumer is best left to select those she prefers. Kennedy J. took a similar approach, emphasising the importance of the contribution companies could make to political debate.

---

[145] *Pacific Gas & Electric Co v Public Util. Comm'n* 475 U.S. 1 (1986) at 16. See discussion above at paras 9–52 to 9–55.

[146] *Pacific Gas & Electric Co. v Public Util. Comm'n* 475 U.S. 1 (1986) at 32–34. See discussion above at paras 9–54 to 9–55.

[147] 470 U.S. 480 (1985) at 500.

[148] 539 U.S. 146 (2003) at n.8, references omitted.

[149] White J.'s dissent is considered above at paras 9–45 to 9–48.

NON-MEDIA COMPANIES—COMMERCIAL SPEECH

Introduction

9–83   One other category of expression that companies have a strong interest in protecting is commercial speech. Companies have successfully invoked freedom of expression guarantees in relation to commercial speech under the United States Constitution, the European Convention on Human Rights and the Canadian Charter of Fundamental Rights and Freedoms, but have yet to put forward such a claim in the context of the Irish Constitution. As with the preceding section, therefore, this section contains a comparative survey and analysis of the approach taken to this category of expression in a number of jurisdictions.

9–84   It will be seen that the United States Supreme Court has taken a categorical approach to commercial speech, which results in treating that category of speech differently, both in terms of its inclusion within the constitutional guarantee and also with regard to the standard of review applied by the court where a restriction is found to violate the guarantee. The ECHR[150] takes a similar, albeit less doctrinally distinct, approach. The Supreme Court of Canada, on the other hand, initially stated that it rejected a categorical approach, only to resile from that position in a later case. One of the striking aspects of the case law on commercial expression is its tendency to ignore the identity of the speaker and to treat corporate and individual expression alike. The focus is on the nature of the expression and the interests of the audience. This feature of commercial speech jurisprudence will be explored further in paras 9–159 to 9–168 when considering the extent to which companies may enjoy free speech rights under the Irish Constitution.

9–85   There is no Irish case law on the extent to which the commercial expression of the company is constitutionally protected. Indeed, there is no clear indication whether commercial expression by individuals is protected under the Irish Constitution. This section will consider that matter first.

Commercial expression under the Irish Constitution

9–86   It is unclear whether commercial expression by non-media companies is protected under Art.40.6.1(i). Indeed, it is unclear whether commercial expression by individual citizens is covered by the provision.[151] Even assuming that companies are considered "citizens"[152] within the meaning of the first

---

[150] Some decisions of the European Commission of Human Rights are also briefly referred to.

[151] For the argument that such protection "makes sense", see Quinn, "Comparative Commercial Speech" in *Human Rights: A European Perspective* (Heffernan and Kingston eds, Round Hall, 1994).

[152] See the *Report of the Constitutional Review Group*, 1996, which refers to this possibility at p.293.

paragraph, only the right to express "convictions and opinions" is specifically mentioned.[153] Much commercial expression is unlikely to fall within this category.[154] There was a body of case law which suggested that Art.40.6.1(i) protected the dissemination of non-factual matter only, factual matter falling under Art.40.3.1 in the form of a constitutional right to communicate.[155] If this was the case, then the protection of corporate commercial expression would depend on whether companies could be said to enjoy that personal right under Art.40.3.1. In *Att.-Gen. v Paperlink*,[156] it was accepted by the parties that corporate bodies did not enjoy the right to communicate.[157]

9–87 The decisions of the Supreme Court in *Irish Times Ltd v Murphy*[158] and *Murphy v IRTC*[159] suggest that there is an overlap between the two constitutional provisions such that some of the expression protected by the right to communicate is also protected in the context of Art.40.6.1(i). This is not particularly helpful in this context as the particular area of overlap contemplated in those cases is unlikely to arise in the context of commercial expression.[160]

9–88 A more fruitful line of enquiry for those concerned with finding a constitutional niche for commercial expression is provided by cases such as *Cullen v Toibin*,[161] *Att.-Gen. for England and Wales v Brandon Books Publishers Ltd*[162] and *Irish Times Ltd v Ireland*,[163] which found that both factual and non-factual expression is protected by Art.40.6.1(i). As was noted

---

[153] The full text of Art.40.6.1(i) is reproduced above at para.9–01.

[154] The imminent tobacco company litigation challenging the constitutionality of the Public Health (Tobacco) Amendment Act 2004 will require the Supreme Court to determine the free speech rights of tobacco companies in the context of advertising. At the time of writing, the litigation is still at an early stage. See *PJ Carroll & Co. Ltd v Minister for Health and Children* [2005] 1 I.R. 294, [2006] I.E.S.C. 36.

[155] *Att.-Gen. v Paperlink* [1984] I.L.R.M. 373; *Kearney v Minister for Justice* [1986] I.R. 116, [1987] I.L.R.M. 52; *McKenna v An Taoiseach*, unreported, High Court, June 8, 1992; *Oblique Financial Services Ltd v The Promise Production Co. Ltd* [1994] 1 I.L.R.M. 74; *O'Laoire v The Medical Council*, unreported, High Court, January 27, 1995; *Carrigaline Community Television Broadcasting Co. Ltd v Minister for Transport, Energy and Communications (No.2)* [1997] 1 I.L.R.M. 241; *Society for the Protection of the Unborn Child (Ireland) Ltd v Grogan (No.5)* [1998] 4 I.R. 343; *O'Brien v Mirror Group Newspapers*, unreported, Supreme Court, October 25, 2000, Denham J. dissenting.

[156] [1984] I.L.R.M. 373.

[157] *Att.-Gen. v Paperlink* [1984] I.L.R.M. 373. See Law Reform Commission, *op.cit.* at p.121.

[158] [1998] 2 I.L.R.M. 161.

[159] [1998] 2 I.L.R.M. 360.

[160] The type of expression caught by both constitutional provisions is described by Barrington J. as the "right to convey one's needs and emotions by words or gestures as well as by rational discourse". [1998] 2 I.L.R.M. 360 at 369. See Hogan and Whyte, *op.cit.* at p.1476. See also *Murphy v IRTC* [1997] 2 I.L.R.M. 467.

[161] [1984] I.L.R.M. 577.

[162] [1986] I.R. 597, [1987] I.L.R.M. 135.

[163] [1998] 1 I.R. 359 at 404–405.

in *Murphy v IRTC*, that provision is concerned with speech that has a public aspect to it. That being so, it is perhaps the more appropriate constitutional locus for any protection of commercial expression whether purely or partially factual in nature.

9–89 The United States Supreme Court has developed an extensive body of case law in relation to the constitutional protection of commercial expression. What can be seen from this case law, explored below,[164] is that the identity of the speaker is never referred to in commercial speech cases. This can be contrasted with the case law on political expression, considered in paras 9–29 to 9–82. This is because the identity of the speaker is deemed relevant in one context and not in another. The implications of this for corporate free speech rights generally will be considered in paras 9–159 to 9–168.

The United States

9–90 In its commercial expression jurisprudence, the court has taken a categorical approach, which applies to both the question of the applicability of the First Amendment and the standard of review thereunder. In the discussion of corporate political expression, it was seen that the court initially denied the relevance of the identity of the speaker, only to alter its position in later decisions. By placing commercial expression in a separate category and focusing on the value of such speech to the audience, the court side-stepped the issue of the propriety of granting companies constitutional protection.

Introduction—from Valentine *to* Virginia Pharmacy

9–91 The notion that commercial expression, such as advertising, could be protected speech under the First Amendment to the United States Constitution was rejected in 1942, in *Valentine v Chrestensen*.[165] In this decision, described later by Douglas J. as a "casual, almost offhand" ruling,[166] the court held that "purely commercial advertising"[167] fell outside the scope of free speech protection. The case remained good authority[168] for over 30 years, although some inroads were made into the principle that the First Amendment did not protect commercial expression in cases where the commercial element was held to be insufficient to oust First Amendment protection.[169]

9–92 The Supreme Court departed from *Valentine* in *Virginia State Board of*

---

[164] See below, at paras 9–90 to 9–117.
[165] 316 U.S. 52 (1942). Hereafter referred to as *Valentine*.
[166] Douglas J. in *Cammarano v United States* 358 U.S. 498 (1959) at 514.
[167] 316 U.S. 52 (1942) at 54.
[168] In several cases, the Supreme Court emphasised that expression benefiting from First Amendment protection was not purely commercial speech: *Murdock v Pennsylvania* 319 U.S. 105 (1943); *Jamison v Texas* 318 U.S. 413 (1943).
[169] See *Breard v Alexandria* 341 U.S. 622 (1951); *New York Times Co. v Sullivan* 376 U.S. 254 (1964); *Pittsburgh Press Co. v Pittsburgh Comm'n on Human Relations* 413 U.S. 376 (1973); *Bigelow v Virginia* 421 U.S. 809 (1975).

Pharmacy v Virginia Citizens Consumer Council, Inc,[170] where it struck down a ban on advertising the prices of prescription drugs. The case was taken, not by those who wished to advertise the drugs, but rather by an individual prescription drug consumer and two non-profit organisations.[171] Thus, the case focuses on the extent to which the First Amendment protects freedom to receive information rather than freedom to impart it, an approach which has dominated the commercial speech case law from the court ever since. Blackmun J., delivering the opinion of the court, stated that:

> "Freedom of speech presupposes a willing speaker. But where a speaker exists, as is the case here, the protection is afforded to the communication, to its source and to its recipients both."[172]

9–93 In considering the merits of departing from the approach taken in *Valentine,*[173] Blackmun J. expressed the issue raised by the appeal as follows:

> "Our question is whether speech which does 'no more than propose a commercial transaction,' is so removed from any 'exposition of ideas,' and from 'truth, science, morality, and arts in general, in its diffusion of liberal sentiments on the administration of Government,' that it lacks all protection. Our answer is that it is not."[174]

9–94 He stated that the fact that an advertiser may have a purely economic interest in the expression concerned did not exclude the advertisement from First Amendment protection, noting that

> "the particular consumer's interest in the free flow of commercial information ... may be as keen, if not keener by far, than his interest in the day's most urgent political debate."[175]

9–95 He went on to make the point that advertisements may be of general public interest, stating that:

> "Obviously not all commercial messages contain the same or even a

---

[170] 425 U.S. 748 (1976). Hereafter referred to as *Virginia Pharmacy*.

[171] *ibid.* at 753. These were the Virginia Citizens Consumer Council, Inc, and the Virginia State AFL-CIO.

[172] 425 U.S. 748 (1976) at 756. Later in his decision, however, he stated that where "there is a right to advertise, there is a reciprocal right to receive the advertising, and it may be asserted by the appellees." 425 U.S. 748 (1976) at 757. This statement does not fit well with the rest of the opinion as nowhere is it argued that the right to receive information is derived from the right of the advertiser. Indeed, the opinion takes precisely the reverse approach.

[173] 316 U.S. 52 (1942).

[174] Footnotes omitted. The quotations in the judgment are from the following cases, respectively: *Pittsburgh Press v Pittsburgh Comm'n on Human Relations* 413 U.S. 376 (1973) at 385; *Chaplinsky v New Hampshire* 315 U.S. 568 (1942) at 572; *Roth v United States* 354 U.S. 476 (1957) at 484.

[175] 425 U.S. 748 (1976) at 763.

very great public interest. There are few to which such an element, however, could not be added. Our pharmacist, for example, could cast himself as a commentator on store-to-store disparities in drug prices, giving his own and those of a competitor as proof. We see little point in requiring him to do so, and little difference if he does not."[176]

9–96 The court insisted that "no line between publicly 'interesting' or 'important' commercial advertising and the opposite kind could ever be drawn."[177] The court refused to draw such a line because advertising provides information which is relevant to the allocation of resources in a free enterprise economy, noting that:

> "[I]f it is indispensable to the proper allocation of resources in a free enterprise system, it is also indispensable to the formation of intelligent opinions as to how that system ought to be regulated or altered. Therefore, even if the First Amendment were thought to be primarily an instrument to enlighten public decisionmaking in a democracy, we could not say that the free flow of information does not serve that goal."[178]

9–97 The court rejected the argument that unrestrained advertising could adversely affect the pharmacist profession and consumers,[179] as it found those fears to be premised on the "advantages of [citizens] being kept in ignorance",[180] a "highly paternalistic approach"[181] unsupported by the First Amendment. In a decision reminiscent of Holmes's call for a "free trade in ideas"[182] and Brandeis's warning against succumbing to fear in stifling expression,[183] the court stated that the First Amendment perspective is that "the dangers of suppressing information" outweigh "the dangers of its misuse if it is freely available".[184]

9–98 This approach highlights the interest of the audience and Blackmun J. referred to the democratic theory of free speech, usually associated with Alexander Meiklejohn,[185] in order to justify extending First Amendment protection to advertising. This model focuses on the effect of speech on the audience, and, in particular, the role of expression in a democracy. According to this conception of free speech:

> "The primary purpose of the First Amendment is, then, that all the citizens

---

[176] *ibid.* at 764–765. This is in direct contrast to the approach taken by Powell J. in *Pittsburgh Press.*
[177] 425 U.S. 748 (1976) at 765.
[178] *ibid.*
[179] *ibid.* at 768.
[180] *ibid.* at 769.
[181] *ibid.* at 770.
[182] *Abrams v United States* 250 U.S. 616 (1919) at 630, Holmes J. dissenting.
[183] *Whitney v California* 274 U.S. 357 (1927) at 376–377, Brandeis J. concurring.
[184] 425 U.S. 748 (1976) at 770.
[185] Blackmun J. refers to Meiklejohn, *op.cit.*, 425 U.S. 748 (1976) at n.19.

shall, so far as possible, understand the issues which bear upon our common life. That is why no idea, no opinion, no doubt, no belief, no counterbelief, no relevant information, may be kept from them."[186]

9–99   It is not clear, however, whether Meiklejohn's conception of the First Amendment would encompass commercial expression. While he would probably agree with the court that the economy and government are closely related so that speech about the former should be protected,[187] bare advertising without more would be unlikely to come within his conception of expression which contributes to public debate on matters of importance:

> "The First Amendment does not intend to guarantee men freedom to say what some private interest pays them to say for its own advantage. It intends only to make men free to say what, as citizens, they think, what they believe, about the general welfare."[188]

9–100   This is similar to the approach which Rehnquist J. took in his dissent in *Virginia Pharmacy*, where he classified the majority decision as one

> "which elevates commercial intercourse between a seller hawking his wares and a buyer seeking to strike a bargain to the same plane as has been previously reserved for the free marketplace of ideas".[189]

Central Hudson—*the modern doctrine*

9–101   The next landmark decision, and the one which established the modern commercial speech doctrine of the United States Supreme Court, was *Central Hudson Gas & Electric Corp v Public Service Commission*.[190] The respondent in the case had ordered a ban on all promotional advertising by the appellant electric utility company. The ban was originally ordered due to low stocks and supplies of electricity, but after the shortage had ended the Commission had consulted with the public and decided to extend the ban. The New York Court of Appeals had rejected the company's appeal. It found that there was little value to advertising in the non-competitive electricity market and that the governmental interest in reducing energy consumption outweighed the weak constitutional value of the commercial speech at issue in the case.

---

[186] Meiklejohn, *op.cit.* at pp.88–89.
[187] In the work cited by Blackmun J., Meiklejohn wrote:
> "We are left free, as any self-governing people must leave itself free, to determine by specific decisions what our economy shall be. It would be ludicrous to say that we are committed by the Constitution to the economic cooperations of socialism. But equally ludicrous are those appeals by which, in current debate, we are called upon to defend the practices of capitalism, of 'free enterprise,' so-called, as essential to the American Way of Life. The American Way of Life is free because it is what we Americans freely choose—from time to time—that it shall be."

Meiklejohn, *op.cit.* at p.98.
[188] Meiklejohn, *op.cit.* at p.104.
[189] 425 U.S. 748 (1976) at 781.
[190] 447 U.S. 557 (1980).

9–102   Delivering the majority opinion of the Supreme Court, Powell J. took a different view. He held:

> "Commercial expression not only serves the economic interest of the speaker, but also assists consumers and furthers the societal interest in the fullest possible dissemination of information. In applying the First Amendment to this area, we have rejected the 'highly paternalistic' view that government has complete power to suppress or regulate commercial speech."[191]

9–103   He went on to state that the Constitution gives less protection to commercial expression than to other forms of expression. The reason the First Amendment protects commercial speech is "the informational function of advertising".[192] For this reason, only advertising which concerns lawful activity and which is not misleading is protected.[193]

9–104   Rehnquist J. dissented, emphasising that the corporation at issue here was a state-created monopoly and was thus in a different position to other corporations. Essentially, he argued that the concession theory of the corporation applied with even greater force to such a company and this justified withholding First Amendment protection.[194]

9–105   *Central Hudson* introduced a four-step analysis to be applied in commercial speech cases. The speech must concern a lawful activity and must be neither fraudulent nor misleading. Once this is established, the speech can only be restricted where the government's interest in doing so is substantial, the restrictions directly advance that interest and are no greater than necessary to advance that interest.[195]

9–106   Ever since *Central Hudson*, case law in relation to the regulation of commercial speech has applied this four-step test.[196] Much of the case law

---

[191] *ibid.* at 561–562.

[192] *ibid.* at 563.

[193] This qualification was foreshadowed in *Virginia Pharmacy*, where the court held that commercial expression, being profit motivated, could be subject to a requirement of verifiability without any chilling effect. 425 U.S. 748 (1976) at 772, n.24. For criticism of this aspect of *Virginia Pharmacy*, see Gollin, "Improving the Odds of the Central Hudson Balancing Test: Restricting Commercial Speech as a Last Resort" (1998) 81 Marq.L.Rev. 873 and Konrad, "Eliminating Distinctions Between Commercial and Political Speech: Replacing Regulation with Government Counterspeech" (1990) 47 Wash.& Lee L.Rev. 1129 at 1136–1139.

[194] 447 U.S. 557 (1980) at 576–588.

[195] *ibid.* at 566. For a straightforward application of the test, see *RMJ, Re* 455 U.S. 191 (1982)—lawyer advertising.

[196] *cf. APLA Ltd v Legal Services Commission (NSW)* 219 ALR 403 (2005)—High Court of Australia takes a different approach. Note that the US Supreme Court has held that the *Central Hudson* test does not apply to compelled speech: *Glickman v Wileman Brothers & Elliott, Inc*, 521 U.S. 457 (1997) and *United States v United Foods, Inc*, 533 U.S. 405 (2001).

has turned on the interpretation of the third and fourth steps of the test.[197] The way in which these steps are applied is critical in shaping the standard of review that is applied to government regulation of commercial speech. The third step, the "direct advancement" requirement, focuses on the relationship between the asserted state interest and the challenged regulation. The court has required varying amounts of evidence when applying this part of the *Central Hudson* test, with the current position being that the court takes a relatively strict view of the record.[198] The fourth step of the *Central Hudson* test requires that regulation be no more extensive than necessary to advance the governmental interest. In *Posadas de Puerto Rico Assoc v Tourism Co.*[199] the court recharacterised this aspect of the test as requiring a "fit" between the aims and means of the legislature.[200] This watering down of the *Central Hudson* test was criticised by Brennan J. in his dissenting opinion[201] but the "reasonable fit" approach was nevertheless approved of in *Board of Trustees, State University of New York v Fox.*[202] While there have been variations in the formulation of the third and fourth steps of the *Central Hudson* test, the court has consistently applied them in such a way as to grant reduced First

---

[197] For the view that the *Central Hudson* test favours regulation in comparison with the approach taken in *Virginia Pharmacy*, see Simpson, "The Commercial Speech Doctrine: An Analysis of the Consequences of Basing First Amendment Protection on the 'Public Interest'" (1994) 39 N.Y.L.Sch.L.Rev. 575.

[198] *e.g.* a stringent approach was applied in *Edenfield v Fane* 507 U.S. 761 (1993)—in-person solicitation by certified public accountants; *Rubins v Coors Brewing Co.* 514 U.S. 476 (1995)—ban on alcohol content labelling of beer and *44 Liquormart, Inc v Rhode Island* 517 U.S. 484 (1996)—ban on retail price advertising of liquor. A lower standard of review was applied, however, in *Greater New Orleans Broadcasting Association v United States* 527 U.S. 173 (1999)—ban on broadcast advertising for casino gambling. The case of *Lorillard Tobacco Co. v Reilly* 533 U.S. 525 (2001)—tobacco advertising restrictions—suggests a return to a stricter application of the third step of *Central Hudson*. This case is hereafter referred to as *Lorillard Tobacco*.

[199] 478 U.S. 328 (1986).

[200] *ibid.* at 341–343. The decision is also notable for its determination that "the greater power to completely ban casino gambling necessarily includes the lesser power to ban advertising of casino gambling," at 345–346, Rehnquist J. distinguishing *Bigelow* and *Carey v Population Services International* 431 U.S. 678 (1977). That aspect of the decision has been subject to heavy criticism, *e.g.* Cahill, "City of Cincinnati v Discovery Network, Inc: Towards Heightened Scrutiny for Truthful Commercial Speech?" (1994) 28 U.Rich.L.Rev. 225 at 233–234. That approach was subsequently rejected by the court in *Lakewood v Plain Dealer Publishing* 486 U.S. 750 (1988) at 762–769.

[201] 478 U.S. 328 (1986) at 348–359. Brennan J. was joined by Blackmun and Marshall JJ. Stevens J. also delivered a dissenting opinion in which Blackmun and Marshall JJ. joined, at 359–364.

[202] 492 U.S. 469 (1989). Hereafter referred to as *Fox*. See also *City of Cincinnati v Discovery Network Inc* 507 U.S. 410 (1993). For criticism of the reasonable fit test, see Locher, "Board of Trustees of the State University of New York v Fox: Cutting Back on Commercial Speech Standards" (1990) 75 Iowa L.Rev. 1335. More recent cases appear to have returned to the least restrictive means test: see *Rubins v Coors Brewing Co.* 514 U.S. 476 (1995)—ban on labelling beer alcohol content; *44 Liquormart, Inc v Rhode Island* 517 U.S. 484 (1996)—price-advertising ban for alcoholic beverages; and *Greater New Orleans Broadcasting* 527 U.S. 173 (1999)—ban on broadcasting casino gambling advertising.

Amendment protection for commercial expression.[203]

The United States commercial speech doctrine—some critical observations

9–107   The United States Supreme Court has taken an approach that places commercial speech in a separate category to other speech and accords that category a lower level of protection than that accorded to non-commercial speech under the First Amendment. This approach applies equally to individual and corporate speakers. The commercial speech doctrine has been subject to criticism for a number of reasons.

9–108   First, there are those who are of the view that commercial speech should not be protected at all. Rehnquist J. dissented from the decisions in both *Virginia Pharmacy* and *Central Hudson*. His dissent from the former evidences distaste for the constitutional protection of "commercial intercourse".[204] In *Central Hudson*, he suggested that *Virginia Pharmacy* was inconsistent with the intentions of the framers.[205] Indeed, it has been pointed out that, although the framers of the United States Constitution were aware of commercial advertising, no mention of it was made in their deliberations on the First Amendment or their discussions of freedom of expression.[206]

9–109   Secondly, it could be argued that the third and fourth steps of the *Central Hudson* test have not been consistently applied. The court has vacillated between various standards of review in a manner that creates legal uncertainty, both for the government and for the commercial speaker. That matter, however, could be remedied by a consistent application of those aspects of the *Central Hudson* test.

9–110   Thirdly, there are others who agree that the approach in *Valentine* was correctly departed from, but point out that there is a serious definitional problem.[207] It has been argued that the court has not been able to define accurately what distinguishes commercial from non-commercial speech.[208] Thus, the commercial speech doctrine risks lowering protection for speech that should receive First Amendment immunity.[209] In *Lorillard Tobacco*, for

---

[203] For criticism of the court's application of the fourth prong of the test, see Gollin, *op.cit.* For the view that the *Central Hudson* test has been strictly applied in modern case law, see Murphy, *op.cit.* at 1198–1201.

[204] See extract from his dissent, reproduced above, at para.9–100. See also Jackson and Jeffries, "Commercial Speech: Economic Due Process and the First Amendment" (1979) 65 Va.L.Rev. 1.

[205] See description of his dissent, above at para.9–100.

[206] Simpson, *op.cit.* at 577.

[207] Kozinski and Banner, "Who's Afraid of Commercial Speech?" (1990) 76 Va.L.Rev. 627. Redish "The First Amendment in the Marketplace: Commercial Speech and the Value of Free Expression" (1971) 39 Geo.Wash.L.Rev. 429.

[208] Simpson, *op.cit.* at 578; Konrad, *op.cit.* at 1139–1145; McIntyre, "Nike v Kasky: Leaving Corporate America Speechless" (2004) 30 Wm.Mitchell L.Rev. 1531.

[209] See Keller, "Lorillard Tobacco Co. v Reilly" (2002) 36 Akron L.Rev. 133, arguing that

example, Thomas J. dissented strongly from the application of the *Central Hudson* test, stating:

> "I have observed previously that there is no philosophical or historical basis for asserting that 'commercial' speech is of 'lower value' than 'noncommercial speech.' Indeed, I doubt whether it is even possible to draw a coherent distinction between commercial and noncommercial speech."[210]

9–111 This criticism has some merit. In *Virginia Pharmacy*, the public importance of commercial information was the basis for its First Amendment protection. Blackmun J. specifically pointed out that there were few commercial messages to which no public element could be added.[211] The failure to phrase the commercial message so as to render it more evidently political in nature was not fatal to the appellees in that case. The difficulty with this is that if most commercial messages are contributing, albeit indirectly, to public discourse, then it is unclear why they are given only partial constitutional immunity.

9–112 This point can be made about the speech in *Central Hudson* itself. It could be said that "promotional advertising of electricity coveys an implicit political and social message on the relative desirability of energy forms and the appropriate level of energy consumption".[212] This problem has arisen in a number of cases[213] and the court has yet to settle on a consistent approach to measuring the public element of commercial speech.

9–113 Indeed, the court has altered its definition on a number of occasions. In *Pittsburgh Press*, the court stated that commercial speech was speech that "does no more than propose a commercial transaction".[214] In *Central Hudson*, the test was whether the speech was "expression related solely to the economic

---

strict scrutiny should apply to commercial speech. For the interesting idea that the commercial speech doctrine could develop so as to denigrate protection for all speech, see Alstyne, "Remembering Melville Nimmer: Some Cautionary Notes on Commercial Speech" (1996) 43 UCLA L.Rev. 1653. There is also the danger, from another perspective, that too much protection will be given to unworthy speech—see Nienow, "In Re R.J.R. Reynolds Tobacco Co, Inc: The 'Common Sense' Distinction Between Commerical and Noncommercial Speech" (1986) 14 Hastings Const.L.Q. 869.

[210] 533 U.S. 525 (2001) at 575. Thomas J. referred to his opinion in *44 Liquormart, Inc v Rhode Island* 517 U.S. 484 (1996) at 520–522 and Kozinski and Banner, *op.cit.*, in this part of his judgment. 533 U.S. 525 (2001) at 574–575.

[211] See quote reproduced above at para.9–95.

[212] Note "Scope of Protection for Commercial Speech: Central Hudson Gas & Electric Corp v Public Service Commission" (1980) 94 Harv.L.Rev. 159 at 167.

[213] For other cases which arguably fall on the non-commercial side of the line, see *Bolger v Young Drugs Products Corp* 463 U.S. 60 (1983); and *Linmark Associates, Inc v Township of Willingboro* 431 U.S. 85 (1977). For the problem of cases where the speech can be seen as a mixture of commercial and non-commercial speech, see *Fox*, *Valentine* and *Riley v National Federation of the Blind, Inc* 487 U.S. 781 (1988).

[214] 413 U.S. 376 (1973) at 385.

interests of the speaker and its audience".[215] Then, in *Bolger v Young Drugs Products Corp*,[216] the court stated that, in order to be classified as commercial speech, speech must conform to at least two of the following criteria: first, that it be in the form of an advertisement, secondly, that it refer to a specific product and thirdly, that its speaker has an economic motivation.[217]

Corporate political and corporate commercial speech compared

9–114 As was noted in the section on corporate political expression, the court initially stated in those cases that the identity of the speaker was irrelevant. This holding was predicated on the idea that political expression constituted the core of the First Amendment. The case law demonstrates that the protection of such speech was based on its value to public discourse. Thus, the court, at least initially, focused on the audience's interest rather than the speaker's. As has been documented above, however, the court began to take the identity of the speaker into account when evaluating the constitutionality of restrictions on political speech. This is because the court began to take the view that the identity of the speaker in some way affected the quality of the speech and made it less deserving of protection.

9–115 In the commercial speech case law, a slightly different approach can be seen. Commercial expression is protected for its informational value, and it is unprotected when it is untrue or misleading. Bare commercial expression is motivated by financial gain. This is the case whether the source is an individual or a company. Thus, the source of the speech does not affect its quality so there is no difficulty in upholding corporate commercial expression under the First Amendment on the same basis as individual commercial expression. *Valentine* denied First Amendment protection to an individual advertiser. *Virginia Pharmacy* was an application by the potential audience. In *Bellotti*, the Supreme Court had held that the identity of the speaker was irrelevant to the matter of First Amendment protection.[218] Interestingly, in *Central Hudson*, Rehnquist J. alone referred to the corporate status of the speaker and the *Bellotti* decision. *Rubins*, *Discovery Network*, *44 Liquormart* and *Lorillard Tobacco* all concerned constitutional challenges by corporate persons, but in none of these cases was this adverted to. An examination of the application of the *Central Hudson* test indicates that the varying degrees of exactness with which it was applied were not linked to the corporate status of the litigant.

9–116 Such an analysis, while applicable to classic examples of commercial speech, such as straightforward advertising,[219] breaks down when borderline cases are considered. The problems created by the lack of a clear definition

---

[215] 447 U.S. 557 (1980) at 561.
[216] 463 U.S. 60 (1983).
[217] *ibid*. at 66–68.
[218] See discussion of *Bellotti* above at paras 9–37 to 9–49.
[219] It is, of course, arguable that at least some advertising is of artistic value.

came into sharp relief in 2003 in *Nike v Kasky*.[220] The case arose out of a public relations campaign by Nike in the late 1990s in which it sought to counter allegations in the media that it mistreated its employees in China, Indonesia and Vietnam. Nike issued advertisements, press releases, letters to newspaper editors and university athletics directors contradicting the allegations. Marc Kasky, a resident of California, took an action against Nike in the state court alleging that the statements issued by Nike were false and therefore illegal under California's Unfair Competition and Advertising Laws. Nike responded by maintaining that its statements about working conditions in the developing world were non-commercial in nature and thus deserved the full protection of the First Amendment. The trial judge and the California Court of Appeals[221] held in Nike's favour, dismissing the suit on the basis that the expression at issue formed "part of a public dialogue on a matter of public concern within the core area of expression protected by the First Amendment".[222] The California Supreme Court overturned this decision, finding that the speech was commercial in nature and thus the suit was not barred by the First Amendment.[223] Nike filed a motion for a writ of certiorari with the Supreme Court. The court initially granted it and then dismissed it as having been improvidently granted.[224]

9–117 The case highlights the difficulty with defining what is and is not commercial speech.[225] The court's decision to save a determination on the issue for another day was not unanimous and one dissenting opinion indicated that at least two of the judges would have been in favour of upholding Nike's case.[226] It also met with academic criticism of the potential chilling effect of the lack of clear guidelines.[227] It is arguable that if the case had been decided before *Virginia Pharmacy*, the court would have defined the speech as non-commercial as it would not have been likely to accord speech of this type no constitutional protection whatsoever.[228] There are alternative views to the effect

---

[220] 123 S.Ct. 2554.

[221] For a discussion of the decision in the Court of Appeals, see McGovern, "Kasky v Nike, Inc: A reconsideration of the Commercial Speech Doctrine" (2002) 12 DePaul LCA J.Art & Ent.L. 333.

[222] *Kasky v Nike, Inc* 93 Cal.Rptr.2d 854.

[223] *Kasky v Nike* 45 P.3d 243.

[224] *Nike, Inc v Kasky* 123 S.Ct. 2555.

[225] For the view that the Supreme Court of California was correct in deciding that the speech at issue was commercial, see Chemerinsky and Fisk, "What is Commercial Speech? The Issue Not Decided in Nike v Kasky" (2004) 54 Case W.Res.L.Rev. 1143.

[226] Dissenting judgment of Breyer J. joined by O'Connor J.

[227] McIntyre, *op.cit.*; Earnhardt, "Nike, Inc v Kasky: A Golden Opportunity to Define Commercial Speech—Why Wouldn't the Supreme Court Finally 'Just Do It'?" (2004) 82 N.C.L.Rev. 797; Pantaenius, "To Speak or not to Speak: The Interplay Between Unfair Trade Practice and Securities Laws Poses Challenges for Corporate Speech" (2003) 72 UMKC L.Rev. 257; Paladino, "Just [Can't] Do It: The Supreme Court of California Overly Restricted Nike's First Amendment Rights in Holding that its Public Statements were Commercial Speech" (2003) 33 U.Balt.L.Rev. 283.

[228] O'Neil, "Nike v Kasky—What Might Have Been" (2004) 54 Case W.Res.L.Rev. 1259.

that the speech was "safely on the commercial side of the line"[229] and that it "was more like the noncommercial speech ... and thus should receive utmost First Amendment protection".[230] Such comments highlight one problem with the categorical approach—it is "difficult to separate the wheat of political expression from the chaff of commercial law".[231]

The European Convention on Human Rights

9–118   The European Commission on Human Rights[232] took the view from an early stage that commercial expression was not excluded from Art.10.[233] The ECHR[234] was faced with a case which had a commercial expression dimension in *Barthold v Germany*,[235] but avoided deciding whether commercial advertising was protected by Art.10.[236] In *Groppera Radio AG v Switzerland*,[237] a majority of the Court implicitly determined that Art.10 did cover commercial expression.[238]

9–119   In *Markt Intern Verlag GmbH v Germany*,[239] the issue came before the Court again. The applicants were a publishing company concerned in promoting and defending the interests of small- to medium-sized retailers against large distributors and one of its journalists. One of its activities was to circulate newssheets aimed at various retail sectors providing information on the commercial practices of large-scale distribution undertakings. One such article appeared stating that a customer complaint had been ignored by a particular mail order firm and calling for reports of any similar behaviour by that firm. The firm succeeded in obtaining an injunction against Markt Intern under a German unfair competition law prohibiting it from repeating the account of the ignored complaint.

---

[229] Chemerinsky and Fisk, *op.cit.* at 1145.

[230] Teremenko, "Corporate Speech Under Fire: Has Nike Finally Done It?" (2003) 2 DePaul Bus. Comm. L.J. 207 at 236.

[231] Collins and Skover, "The Landmark Free Speech Case That Wasn't: The Nike v Kasky Story" (2004) 54 Case W.Res.L.Rev. 965 at 1039.

[232] Hereafter, the "Commission".

[233] See the decision of May 5, 1979 on the admissibility of application No. 7805/77, *X. and Church of Scientology v Sweden. Cf. Thoburn v Sunderland City Council and other appeals* [2003] Q.B. 151, [2002] 4 All E.R. 156, [2002] 3 W.L.R. 247.

[234] Hereafter, the "Court".

[235] (1985) 7 E.H.R.R. 383.

[236] The Court found that the material at issue imparted information and opinions which could not be divorced from its alleged publicity seeking aspects, so that is was not necessary to decide the point. (1985) 7 E.H.R.R. 383 at 397–398. See dissenting opinion of Judge Pettiti, which is critical of this failure to decide the issue, (1985) 7 E.H.R.R. 383 at 407.

[237] (1990) 12 E.H.R.R. 321.

[238] *ibid.* at 337. Judge Valticos expressed the opinion that Art.10 did not protect commercial expression in his concurring judgment, at 354.

[239] (1989) 12 E.H.R.R. 161.

9–120 The Court cited its decision in *Muller v Switzerland*[240] and found that expression of commercial information was covered by Art.10 because it was not limited to "certain types of information or ideas or forms of expression".[241] The Court went on to state that the margin of appreciation accorded to states was essential in matters concerning unfair competition[242] and that in this case, as the injunction had been upheld on reasonable grounds, the state was within that margin.[243] Essentially, the Court espoused a lower standard of review for restrictions on commercial expression, stating that: "The Court must confine its review to the question whether the measures taken at national level are justifiable in principle and proportionate."[244]

9–121 The dissenting judgments emphasised the importance of freedom of commercial expression and argued that the Court ought to have applied a stricter standard of review. For example, one joint dissent expressed the view that:

> "It is just as important to guarantee the freedom of expression in relation to the practices of a commercial undertaking as it is in relation to the conduct of a head of government ...".[245]

9–122 Another dissent stated that the "socio-economic press is just as important as the political and cultural press for the progress of our modern societies and for the development of every man".[246]

9–123 The matter arose again in *Autronic AG v Switzerland*,[247] where the respondent argued that Art.10 was inapplicable to the applicant company because its expression was motivated only by pecuniary gain.[248] The case concerned a refusal by the Swiss government to permit the applicant to retransmit broadcasts from another jurisdiction at trade fairs in order to promote

---

[240] Judgment of May 24, 1988, Series A, No. 133.

[241] (1989) 12 E.H.R.R. 161 at 171.

[242] *ibid.* at 174. The margin of appreciation is essentially the amount of discretion accorded to states. It has been described as follows:
"[B]y reason of their direct and continuous contact with the vital forces of their countries, State authorities are in principle in a better position than the international judge to give an opinion on the exact content of these requirements with regard to the rights of others as well as on the 'necessity' of a 'restriction' ...".
Murphy v Ireland App. No. 44179/98, judgment of July 10, 2003 at [67]. Importantly, however, the ECHR is the final arbiter on whether an impugned restriction meets the standards set out by the Convention. *ibid.* at [68].

[243] (1989) 12 E.H.R.R. 161 at 175–176.

[244] *ibid.* at 174. See also *Jacubowski v Germany* (1994) 19 E.H.R.R. 64.

[245] Joint dissenting opinion of Judges Gölcüklü, Pettiti, Russo, Spielmann, De Meyer, Carrillo Salcedo and Valticos, (1989) 12 E.H.R.R. 161 at 177.

[246] Individual dissenting opinion of Judge Martens, approved by Judge MacDonald, (1989) 12 E.H.R.R. 161 at 179. In his individual dissenting opinion, Judge Pettiti went even further, arguing that the margin of appreciation in commercial expression cases was slim because consumers have conflicting interests so that restraining speech cannot be seen as a defence of the general interest. (1989) 12 E.H.R.R. 161 at 178.

[247] (1990) 12 E.H.R.R. 485.

[248] *ibid.* at 498.

its cable aerial. The Court referred to its decisions in *Sunday Times v UK*,[249] *Groppera* and *Markt Intern* and stated that the fact that the applicant was a limited company engaged in commercial activity did not exclude the application of Art.10.[250] Judges Bindschdler-Robert and Matscher dissented. They did not dispute that a commercial entity could rely on Art.10 in connection with its commercial activities, but pointed out that in the cases cited by the majority, the content of the information being communicated was of interest to either the applicant or the intended audience. They argued that Art.10 was inapplicable here on the basis that the company did not identify with the expressed material— the purpose of the expression was merely to demonstrate the technical features of their product.[251]

9–124   In *Casado Coca v Spain*,[252] a case concerning restrictions on professional advertising,[253] the Court finally ruled definitively that commercial advertising was protected by Art.10. The Court, referring to its decision in *Autronic*, pointed out that Art.10 applied to everyone and drew no distinction between expression which aims to make a profit and that which does not.[254] It recognised that it had reserved its opinion on the applicability of Art.10 to advertising in *Barthold*, but stated that guidance as to its position was discernable from its decisions in *Markt Intern* and *Groppera*.[255]

9–125   In considering whether the restrictions complained of were necessary in a democratic society, the Court referred back to *Markt Intern* and pointed out that the margin of appreciation enjoyed by states was particularly essential in the area of advertising as well as that of fair competition.[256] The Court pointed out that advertising functioned so as to allow citizens to find out about the characteristics of goods and services offered to them. Advertising which was untruthful or misleading or which involved unfair competition could, however, be restricted. It also stated that in some situations even truthful, objective advertising could be restricted to ensure respect for the rights of others or due to the special circumstances of certain business activities or professions.[257]

9–126   That a different margin of appreciation was applicable in respect of restrictions on commercial expression is also indicated by the case of *Hertel v Switzerland*,[258] where the Court held that:

---

[249] (1979) 2 E.H.R.R. 245.
[250] (1990) 12 E.H.R.R. 485 at 499.
[251] *ibid*. at 505.
[252] (1994) 18 E.H.R.R. 1.
[253] *cf. R. v General Medical Council, Colman Ex p.* [1990] 1 All E.R. 489.
[254] Indeed, the Court went so far as to suggest that the drawing of such a distinction could be contrary to Art.14, (1994) 18 E.H.R.R. 1 at [35].
[255] (1994) 18 E.H.R.R. 1 at [35].
[256] *ibid*. at [50].
[257] *ibid*. at [51]. The Court went on to find that, due to the special features of the legal profession, the ban on advertising passed scrutiny, (1994) 18 E.H.R.R. 1 at [54]–[57].
[258] *Reports* 1998-VI, pp. 2325–2326, judgment of August 25, 1998.

"It is however necessary to reduce the extent of the margin of appreciation when what is at stake is not a given individual's purely 'commercial' statements, but his participation in a debate affecting the general interest, for example, over public health ...".[259]

9–127 *VgT Verein gegen Tierfabriken v Switzerland*[260] reiterated the lower level of protection for commercial expression under Art.10. The applicant was an animal rights association which had made an advertisement showing pigs being kept in bad conditions, contrasting this with the conditions enjoyed by pigs not in captivity, and exhorting the public to eat less meat for the sake of health, animals and the environment. They failed to have the advertisement aired because of a ban on political advertising. The Court found that the advertisement was indeed political and stated that:

"[I]n the present case the extent of the margin of appreciation is reduced, since what is at stake is not a given individual's purely 'commercial' interests, but his participation in a debate affecting the general interest."[261]

9–128 Applying this standard of review, the Court found that there had been a violation of Art.10.

9–129 *Demuth v Switzerland*[262] arose from the refusal of the applicant's application for a broadcasting licence for a specialist television channel concerning cars. The Court, in considering whether the refusal was necessary in a democratic society, noted that the proposed channel may have contributed to the ongoing debate about motorised society, but found that its purpose would be primarily commercial.[263] Referring to *Markt Intern* and *VgT Verein*, the Court reiterated the importance of the margin of appreciation in commercial broadcasting and stated that "where commercial speech is concerned, the standards of scrutiny may be less severe."[264]

---

[259] *ibid*. at [47]. The Court in this case found that the restriction of freedom of expression in this case was not necessary in a democratic society. Interestingly, the dissenting judgments all focus on the commercial context of the case.

[260] (2002) 34 E.H.R.R. 4. Hereafter referred to as *VgT Verein*.

[261] *ibid*. at [71].

[262] App. No. 38743/97, judgment of November 5, 2002.

[263] *ibid*. at [41]. See the dissenting opinion of Judge Gaukur who stated that the margin of appreciation should be reduced in this case because the expression was not merely commercial in nature but referred to matters of public interest.

[264] App. No. 38743/97, judgment of November 5, 2002 at [42]. See also [43]:
"In exercising its power of review, the Court must confine itself to the question whether the measures taken on the national level were justifiable in principle and proportionate in respect of the case as a whole."
See also *Krone Verlag GmbH (No.3) v Austria* App. No. 39069/97, judgment of December 11, 2003. The court does not view all paid advertisements as commercial expression—see *Murphy v Ireland* App. No. 44179/98, judgment of July 10, 2003.

The significance of the speech and the relevance of the speaker

9–130   The ECHR emphasised early on in its case law that Art.10 applied to both natural and artificial persons without distinction.[265] In any case, commercial expression is protected under Art.10 on the basis of its informational value to consumers rather than the right of the speaker. While the court does not take a rigid categorical approach to the classification of speech like that taken by the United States Supreme Court, it does treat commercial expression differently by according states a greater margin of appreciation in these cases. Interestingly, in cases such as *Hertel* and *VgT Verein*, where the expression is seen as being more than merely commercial in nature and the margin of appreciation is thus smaller, the Court will refer to the right of the speaker as well as the right of the audience.[266]

Canada

9–131   Sections 1 and 2(b) of the Canadian Charter of Rights and Freedoms 1982[267] provide as follows:

> "Section 1   The *Canadian Charter of Rights and Freedoms* guarantees the rights and freedoms set out in it subject only to such reasonable limits prescribed by law as can be demonstrably justified in a free and democratic society.
>
> Section 2   Everyone has the following fundamental freedoms:
>
> ...
>
> (b) freedom of thought, belief, opinion and expression, including freedom of the press and other media of communication;".

9–132   The Canadian Supreme Court has emphasised that it does not take a categorical approach to commercial expression when considering the compatibility of restrictions thereon under the Charter. At the same time, however, it has applied a lower standard of review in a number of commercial expression cases.

9–133   In the 1980s, three lower courts issued conflicting judgments on commercial expression. In *Klein and Law Society of Upper Canada, Re*,[268] the High Court of Ontario held that commercial expression was not protected under s.2(b), Callaghan J. stating:

> "The Charter reflects a concern with the political rights of the individual and does not ... reflect a similar concern with the economic sphere nor with its incidents such as commercial speech."[269]

---

[265] *Autronic AG v Switzerland* (1990)12 E.H.R.R. 485.
[266] See quotations reproduced above at paras 9–126 to 9–127.
[267] Hereafter referred to as "the Charter".
[268] (1985) 16 D.L.R. (4th) 489.
[269] *ibid*. at 532.

9–134   Later in the judgment, he stated:

> "Commercial speech contributes nothing to democratic government
> because it says nothing about how people are governed or how they
> should govern themselves. It does not relate to government policies or
> matters of public concern essential to a democratic process. It pertains to
> the economic realm and is a matter appropriate to regulation by the
> Legislature."[270]

9–135   The dissenting judge, Henry J., echoed the majority opinion in *Virginia
Pharmacy*,[271] emphasising the indispensable role played by commercial
advertising in the functioning of the market economy whose performance is of
concern to the body politic.[272]

9–136   *Irwin Toy Ltd v Procureur général du Québec*[273] concerned a challenge
to the regulation of advertising aimed at children. Jacques J.A., in the Court of
Appeal of Quebec, held that there was no basis for distinguishing between
different types of expression under the Charter and that commercial expression
was as deserving of protection as other types of expression because of the
important role it played in assisting people to make informed economic choices.
He went on to state, however, that commercial expression might be subject to
reasonable limits under s.1 of the Charter of a nature that would not be
reasonable in the case of political expression.[274] This case was appealed to
the Supreme Court of Canada.[275]

9–137   Before hearing the *Irwin Toy* appeal, the Canadian Supreme Court
delivered its judgment in *Ford v Quebec*.[276] In this case, the court was faced
with a challenge to Quebec legislation[277] which required, *inter alia*, that all
commercial advertising in Quebec must be in the French language. The court
noted that:

> "While the words 'commercial expression' are a convenient reference
> to the kind of expression contemplated by the provisions in issue, they
> do not have any particular meaning or significance in Canadian

---

[270] *ibid.* at 539.

[271] He quoted from that case in his dissent, (1985) 16 D.L.R. (4th) 489 at 510.

[272] (1985) 16 D.L.R. (4th) 489 at 509–511.

[273] [1986] R.J.Q. 2441.

[274] *ibid.*

[275] Below at paras 9–145 to 9–149. Before *Irwin Toy* came before the Supreme Court, the
Alberta Court of Appeal handed down its decision in *Grier v Alberta Optometric
Association* (1987) 42 D.L.R. (4th) 327 in which it followed the decision of the Quebec
Court of Appeal in the former case.

[276] [1988] 2 S.C.R. 712. See also *Devine v Quebec* [1988] 2 S.C.R. 790.

[277] The impugned statutory provisions were ss.58 and 69, and ss.205 and 208 to the extent
they applied thereto, of the Charter of the French Language, R.S.Q., c.C-11. The
challenge concerned both the Charter and the Quebec Charter. The arguments relating
to the latter are not discussed.

constitutional law, unlike the corresponding expression 'commercial speech', which in the United States has been recognized as a particular category of speech entitled to First Amendment protection of a more limited character than that enjoyed by other kinds of speech."[278]

9–138   The court considered the case law from Canadian courts and the United States discussed above. As regards the latter, the court took the view that the *Central Hudson* approach was problematic in that it involved the courts in evaluating regulatory policy in the area of consumer protection. The court referred to academic criticism of the *Central Hudson* doctrine and indicated that it would not follow that approach.[279]

9–139   The Attorney-General of Quebec argued that the Charter did not cover commercial expression. He pointed out, *inter alia*, that to protect the expression at issue in this case would be tantamount to protecting an economic right. This was not contemplated by the Charter, according to his submissions, because in contrast to the United States Constitution, it specifically omitted the protection of property rights from its ambit.[280]

9–140   The court rejected these submissions and went on to consider the values underlying the constitutional protection of freedom of expression. Referring to academic commentary,[281] it identified three main values:

> "The first is that freedom of expression is essential to intelligent and democratic self-government ... The second theory is that freedom of expression protects an open exchange of views, thereby creating a competitive market-place of ideas which will enhance the search for the truth ... The third theory values expression for its own sake. On this view, expression is seen as an aspect of individual autonomy. Expression is to be protected because it is essential to personal growth and self-realization."[282]

9–141   The court held that the case before it did not require it to delineate the boundaries of what did and did not come within the ambit of s.2(b) of the Charter. It noted that the facts required it to decide only the narrower question of whether

> "the respondents have a constitutionally protected right to use the English language in the signs they display, or more precisely, whether the fact

---

[278] [1988] 2 S.C.R. 712 at 754.
[279] *ibid*. at 759.
[280] See the court's summary of the Attorney-General's submissions, [1988] 2 S.C.R. 712 at 762–763.
[281] Emerson, "Towards a General Theory of the First Amendment" (1963) 72 Yale L.J. 877; Sharpe, "Commercial Expression and the Charter" (1987) 37 U.T.L.J. 229.
[282] [1988] 2 S.C.R. 712 at 765, quoting Sharpe, *op.cit.* at 232.

that such signs have a commercial purpose removes the expression contained therein from the scope of protected freedom".[283]

9–142   It answered the latter formulation in the negative, stating as follows:

"Over and above its intrinsic value as expression, commercial expression which, as has been pointed out, protects listeners as well as speakers plays a significant role in enabling individual self-fulfilment and personal autonomy. The Court accordingly rejects the view that commercial expression serves no individual or societal value in a free and democratic society …".[284]

9–143   Earlier in the judgment, the court had pointed out that cases raising freedom of expression issues involved two distinct questions. First, whether the restricted expression was within the ambit of s.2(b) of the Charter, and secondly, whether the impugned restriction was justified under s.1.[285] As regards the latter matter, the court noted that its decision was not concerned with the issue of the permissible scope of regulation of advertising where different governmental interests could come into play when assessing the reasonableness of limits on commercial expression.[286]

9–144   The Canadian Supreme Court rejected the *Central Hudson* doctrine in *Ford*, but its approach indicated that future cases might apply a different standard of review to restrictions on commercial expression.

9–145   After the Supreme Court judgment in *Ford* was handed down, *Irwin Toy* came before it.[287] The court pointed out that the commercial element to the speech in *Ford* had raised only an ancillary question, one that fell to be determined in this case.[288] It found that the advertising at issue in the case before it came within the scope of freedom of expression because it aimed to

---

[283]   [1988] 2 S.C.R. 712 at 766.

[284]   *ibid.* at 767.

[285]   *ibid.* at 766. The Canadian Supreme Court applies a proportionality test in cases of alleged Charter infringement. This test was set out in *R. v Oakes* [1986] 1 S.C.R. 103 and was described by McLachlin J. in *RJR-MacDonald Inc v Canada* [1995] 3 S.C.R. 199 at [130] as follows:
"The first requirement is that the objective of the law limiting the Charter right or freedom must be of sufficient importance to warrant overriding it. The second is that the means chosen to achieve the objective must be proportional to the objective and the effect of the law—proportionate, in short, to the good which it may produce. Three matters are considered in determining proportionality: the measures chosen must be rationally connected to the objective; they must impair the guaranteed right or freedom as little as reasonably possible (minimal impairment); and there must be overall proportionality between the deleterious effects of the measures and the salutary effects of the law."

[286]   [1988] 2 S.C.R. 712 at 767. *Cf. Montréal (City) v 2952–1366 Québec Inc* [2005] 3 S.C.R. 141, where the Supreme Court seemed to apply its usual standard of review under the Charter to what was arguably a form of advertising.

[287]   *Irwin Toy Ltd v Quebec* [1989] 1 S.C.R. 927.

[288]   [1989] 1 S.C.R. 927 at 966–967.

convey a meaning and could not be excluded for lacking expressive content. Reiterating the approach taken in *Ford*, the court pointed out that there was no sound basis for excluding commercial expression from the ambit of s.2(b).[289] The court then went on to decide that the regulation at issue here was intended to control attempts to convey meaning.[290] This added up to a finding that the impugned provisions constituted limitations to s.2(b) of the Charter which had to be justified under s.1 to withstand review.[291] The court went on to take its usual approach to this test, examining the evidence on which the measures were introduced and ultimately concluding that they were justified. In so finding, the court emphasised the vulnerability of children to advertising.[292]

9–146   In exploring the impugned measures as against s.1 of the Charter, the court did not appear to apply a weaker standard of review, notwithstanding its comments in *Ford*.[293] These comments resurfaced, however, in *Rocket v College of Dental Surgeons of Ontario*,[294] a case which concerned restrictions on advertising imposed on members of the dental profession. After reiterating that commercial speech was encompassed by s.2(b), the court added a *caveat*:

> "Although it has been clearly held that commercial expression does not fall outside the ambit of s.2(b), the fact that expression is commercial is not necessarily without constitutional significance."[295]

9–147   It stated that, in considering the position under s.1, the fact the expression was wholly in the commercial sphere was part of the context to be taken into account.[296] It found that professional advertising had expressive content and, as the restriction had as its purpose the restriction of the content of expression, it infringed s.2(b).[297]

9–148   In considering whether the restriction was justified under s.1, the court stated that the Canadian approach "did not apply special tests to restrictions on commercial expression" but took a "case sensitive" approach.[298] The court noted that the expression restricted here was economically motivated and the loss occasioned by its restriction would constitute

> "merely loss of profit, and not loss of opportunity to participate in the political process or the 'marketplace of ideas', or to realize one's spiritual or artistic self-fulfilment … This suggests that restrictions on expression

---

[289] *ibid.* at 971.

[290] *ibid.* at 977.

[291] *ibid.* at 979.

[292] *ibid.* at 979–1000.

[293] Above at paras 9–137 to 9–144.

[294] [1990] 2 S.C.R. 232.

[295] *ibid.* at 241.

[296] *ibid.* at 242.

[297] *ibid.* at 244–246.

[298] *ibid.* at 246–247. See also McLachlin J. in *RJR-MacDonald Inc v Canada* [1995] 3 S.C.R. 199.

of this kind might be easier to justify than other infringements of s.2(b)."[299]

9–149 The court also found, however, that the expression did serve an important public interest by enhancing the potential for patients to make informed choices about a relatively important consumer decision—choice of dentist.[300] It made the point that in most commercial speech cases there were "two opposing factors—that the expression is designed only to increase profit, and that the expression plays an important role in consumer choice". The reason the court was loath to adopt a categorical approach such as the *Central Hudson* doctrine was that the "precise mix" of these two elements could vary from case to case.[301]

9–150 In *RJR-MacDonald Inc v Canada*,[302] the court considered a constitutional challenge by two tobacco companies[303] to legislative provisions[304] which imposed restrictions on tobacco advertising and promotion. While the court unanimously agreed that there had been a violation of s.2(b), there were differing views in relation to the s.1 analysis, with a majority finding that the impugned legislation was in violation of the Charter.[305]

9–151 McLachlin J. referred to the dissenting judgment of La Forest J. in which he emphasised the fact that the appellants were motivated by profit in order to justify a lower standard of review.[306] McLahlin J. disagreed with that approach, stating that:

> "[T]he same may be said for many business persons or corporations that challenge a law as contrary to freedom of expression. While this Court has stated that restrictions on commercial speech may be easier to justify than other infringements, no link between the claimant's motivation and the degree of protection has been recognized. Book sellers, newspaper owners, toy sellers—all are linked by their shareholders' desire to profit

---

[299] [1990] 2 S.C.R. 232 at 247.

[300] *ibid.*

[301] *ibid.*

[302] [1995] 3 S.C.R. 199.

[303] RJR-MacDonald Inc and Imperial Tobacco Ltd.

[304] ss.4, 5, 6, 8 and 9 of the Tobacco Products Control Act 1988 S.C. 1988, c.20.

[305] Lamer C.J. and Sopinka, McLachlin, Iacobucci and Major JJ. found that the impugned sections were not justified under s.1 of the Charter. La Forest, L'Heureux-Dubé, Gonthier and Cory JJ., dissenting, would have found the impugned sections justified and therefore saved under s.1.

[306] He stated that:
"It must be kept in mind that tobacco advertising serves no political, scientific or artistic ends; nor does it promote participation in the political process. Rather, its sole purpose is to inform consumers about, and promote the use of, a product that is harmful, and often fatal, to the consumers who use it. The main, if not sole, motivation for this advertising is, of course, profit."
[1995] 3 S.C.R. 199 at [75]. Thus, at [77], "an attenuated level of s.1 justification" was appropriate in this case.

from the corporation's business activity, whether the expression sought to be protected is closely linked to the core values of freedom of expression or not. In my view, motivation to profit is irrelevant to the determination of whether the government has established that the law is reasonable or justified as an infringement of freedom of expression."[307]

9–152   In his dissenting judgment, La Forest J. referred to the point made by Dickson C.J in *R. v Keegstra*[308] that:

"While we must guard carefully against judging expression according to its popularity, it is equally destructive of free expression values, as well as the other values which underlie a free and democratic society, to treat all expression as equally crucial to those principles at the core of s.2(b)."[309]

9–153   La Forest J. appeared to deem the identity of the speakers to be significant in this case, stating that:

"The *Charter* was essentially enacted to protect individuals, not corporations. It may, at times it is true, be necessary to protect the rights of corporations so as to protect the rights of the individual. But I do not think this is such a case … the courts must ensure that the *Charter* not become simply an instrument 'of better situated individuals to roll back legislation which has as its object the improvement of the condition of less advantaged persons'."[310]

9–154   He took the view that a lower standard of review was appropriate in this case and said that:

"it cannot seriously be argued that the 'dignity' of the three large corporations whose rights are infringed in these cases is in any way comparable to that of minority group members dealt with in *Ford*."[311]

9–155   One provision[312] of the challenged legislation required tobacco companies to place unattributed health warnings on their products. Interestingly, McLachlin J. found that this violated the Charter because the right to freedom of expression includes "the right to say nothing or the right not to say certain things".[313] In this respect, her judgment can be compared to that of the United

---

[307] [1995] 3 S.C.R. 199 at [171].

[308] [1990] 3 S.C.R. 697.

[309] *ibid.* at 760, referred to [1995] 3 S.C.R. 199 at [72].

[310] [1990] 3 S.C.R. 697 at [118], references omitted. The internal quotation is from the judgment of Dickson C.J. in *R. v Edwards Books and Art Ltd* [1986] 2 S.C.R. 713 at 779. *Cf. Shell Canada Products Ltd Appellant v City of Vancouver* [1994] 1 S.C.R. 231.

[311] [1990] 3 S.C.R. 697 at [110].

[312] s.9.

[313] [1990] 3 S.C.R. 697 at [124]. This quotation is from the judgment of Lamer J. in *Slaight Communications Inc v Davidson* [1989] 1 S.C.R. 1038 at 1080.

States Supreme Court in *Pacific Gas*.[314] La Forest J., on the other hand, while agreeing with the quotation she referred to,[315] found that the fact that the health warnings were not attributed to the appellants was fatal to their s.2(b) argument because is was "common knowledge amongst the public at large that such statements emanate from the government, not the tobacco manufacturers".[316] Thus, there was no danger that the public would attribute the statements to the appellants. It appears, therefore, that he too was willing to entertain the idea that the companies enjoyed a right to silence.

WHOSE SPEECH?

9–156   Before exploring the comparative material in the context of the Irish Constitution, the question of who speaks when the company speaks must be addressed. It has been suggested that:

> "Corporate political expression is simply shareholder speech or the product of shareholder associational activity. First amendment guarantees of individual freedom must afford protection for this expression."[317]

9–157   This approach to corporate freedom of expression espouses the aggregate theory of the company. Another way of approaching corporate expression is to see it as a corporate product—it is the company as a real entity that is speaking:

> "Like other organizational activities, speech may also be a global, nondistributive phenomenon, emanating from the corporation without being traceable or reducible to individual utterances."[318]

9–158   As far as the first approach is concerned, it can be countered by the argument, rejected by the United States Supreme Court in *Bellotti* only to be accepted in *Beaumont*,[319] that even if such expression is "the product of shareholder associational activity", protecting the speech of the company does not protect the dissenting shareholder.[320] As far as the second approach is concerned, it undermines corporate claims to constitutional protection insofar as the guarantee is concerned with autonomy, as it disassociates the speech of the company from that of individuals. The idea that corporate expression is

---

[314] Discussed above at paras 9–52 to 9–55.
[315] It is reproduced in his judgment also. [1990] 3 S.C.R. 697 at [113].
[316] [1990] 3 S.C.R. 697 at [115].
[317] Note (1978) 92 Harv.L.Rev. 163 at 165–166.
[318] Dan-Cohen, *Rights, Persons and Organizations: A Legal Theory for Bureaucratic Society* (University of California Press, 1986), at p.107.
[319] 000 U.S. 02-403 (2003).
[320] It has been suggested that a requirement of shareholder unanimity would obviate this difficulty. Brudney, "Business Corporations and Shareholder Rights under the First Amendment" (1981) 91 Yale L.J. 235.

uttered in a different voice may, however, favour constitutional protection depending on the theory of freedom of expression adhered to.

THE NATURE OF THE GUARANTEE UNDER THE IRISH CONSTITUTION AND ITS APPLICABILITY TO THE COMPANY

9–159   Freedom of expression is a complex guarantee which has a number of underlying values. Writing in the context of the First Amendment to the United States Constitution, Schauer stated that:

> "To view the first amendment as being grounded in one and only one theoretical justification is a mistake. Instead, there may be several theoretical foundations for the first amendment, occasionally mutually exclusive, but more often just compatibly different."[321]

9–160   While Schauer was writing in the context of the United States Constitution, the point made is applicable to Art.40.6.1(i) of the Irish Constitution also. This guarantee of freedom of expression can be seen as one which is concerned with the self-fulfilment of the individual[322]—an autonomy-based value—as well as the preservation of a free flow of ideas[323]—a utility-based value. The former value justifies the protection of the speaker as well as the audience. Where the latter is emphasised, the emphasis is usually on the interests of the audience and the contribution of the speech to society as a whole.[324] The notion of a "marketplace of ideas" was idealised by Holmes in his famous dissent in *Abrams v United States*,[325] where he stated:

> "[W]hen men have realized that time has upset many fighting faiths, they may come to believe even more than they believe the very foundations of their own conduct that the ultimate good desired is better reached by free trade in ideas—that the best test of truth is the power of the thought to get itself accepted in the competition of the market ..."[326]

---

[321]   Schauer, "Public Figures" (1984) 25 Wm.& Mary L.Rev. 905 at 930. See also Shiffrin, "The First Amendment and Economic Regulation: Away from a General Theory of the First Amendment" (1984) 78 Northwest.U.L.Rev. 1212.

[322]   That individual self-fulfilment is an aspect of the Irish constitutional guarantee has been confirmed in *Murphy v IRTC* [1998] 2 I.L.R.M. 360. See also *Holland v Governor of Portlaoise Prison*, unreported, High Court, June 11, 2004.

[323]   See *Irish Times Ltd v Ireland* [1998] 1 I.R. 359; *Murphy v IRTC* [1998] 2 I.L.R.M. 360; *Kelly v O'Neill* [2000] 1 I.R. 354.

[324]   In the context of the Irish Constitution, it may be that there is a "right to information" under Art.40.3 which serves to protect this autonomy-based interest. See Denham J., dissenting, in *De Rossa v Independent Newspapers Ltd* [1999] 4 I.R. 432 at 437. *C.f. Independent Newspapers v Ireland* (Application No.55120/00) judgment of the European Court of Human Rights, June 16, 2005.

[325]   250 U.S. 616 (1919).

[326]   *ibid*. at 630.

9–161 The idea that freedom of expression is essential to the pursuit of truth bases protection primarily on the interests of the audience rather than those of the speaker. To this extent it can be seen as a utility-based guarantee—the speaker enjoys the right because of the contribution of the speech to the greater good. Another way of looking at the protection of expression in terms of its contribution is to see it as being based on "listener autonomy". A listener autonomy approach "insists that listeners must be given information so they can exercise their autonomy and develop their individual capacities as they direct that development".[327]

9–162 A more refined version of Holmes's approach is to emphasise the importance of freedom of expression to the democratic system.[328] This latter approach, which appears to be espoused by the ECHR,[329] has some support in this jurisdiction.[330] It has been stated that the free speech guarantee in the Irish Constitution is "concerned with the public activities of the citizen in a democratic society" and relates to "the practical running of a democratic society".[331]

9–163 This approach to freedom of expression values political expression highly for its function in promoting participative democracy. In all of the comparative case law considered in this chapter, expression that is deemed "political" is highly valued for this function. When it comes to the political expression of the corporate speaker, no cases have yet dealt with this matter under the Irish Constitution. Given judicial pronouncements on the democratic function of Art.40.6.1(i),[332] it seems likely that such expression is protected regardless of the speaker. The question is whether a distinction should be drawn in terms of the level of protection for the political expression of the company as opposed to that of the individual.

9–164 The United States Supreme Court has found that such a distinction is merited. The reasoning is that political expression is valued for its contribution to the pool of ideas that make up political debate. As was pointed out in paras 9–66 to 9–76, the approach of the majority in *Beaumont* is based on the idea that corporate political speech pollutes that pool due to the economic motivation of the speaker. Cases such as *McConnell* emphasise the self-serving economic motivation of corporate political expression, which the United States Supreme Court believes renders it less "authentic" than individual expression. Furthermore, a majority of the United States Supreme Court does not believe that disclosure of the source of the speech is adequate to offset this.[333] The

---

[327] Carpenter, "The Anti-Paternalism Principle in the First Amendment" (2004) 37 Creighton L.Rev. 579 at 641.

[328] Meiklejohn, *op.cit.*

[329] See case law discussed above at para.9–23.

[330] See Denham J. in *Irish Times Ltd v Ireland* [1998] 1 I.R. 359 at 399.

[331] Barrington J. in *Murphy v IRTC* [1998] 2 I.L.R.M. 360 at 369.

[332] See discussion above at paras 9–18 to 9–19.

[333] Contrast the approach of the majority opinion in *McConnell* 000 U.S. 02-1674 (2003) with that of the dissenting opinion of Scalia J., above at paras 9–68 to 9–69 and 9–82.

approach of the dissenting judges in *McConnell*,[334] on the other hand, suggests that the uniqueness of the corporate voice means that it adds something extra to the pool of ideas and ought to be protected.

9–165 This idea that the economic motivation behind corporate speech renders it less worthy of constitutional protection presumably does not apply to speech by individuals. This distinction was justified by the United States Supreme Court on the basis of a concession theory approach to the company.[335] Another approach, one which would explain more about freedom of expression, is to recognise that speech by an individual, while contributing to political debate, also furthers an autonomy-based value which is not implicated when the company speaks—that of self-fulfilment. The dissenting judgment of La Forest J. in *RJR-MacDonald Inc*, with its reference to the "dignity"—or lack thereof—appears to grasp this distinction.[336] It is submitted that this approach indicates a more coherent reason for reduced protection for corporate political expression under Art.40.6.1(i).

9–166 As far as commercial expression is concerned, its protection under the Irish Constitution has yet to be confirmed or denied. It has been argued that such speech is not of sufficient value to merit constitutional protection at all: "[T]he domination of profit … breaks the intrinsic connection between speech and any vision, or attitude, or value of the individual or group engaged in advocacy."[337] This approach, which has been judicially endorsed on a number of occasions,[338] perhaps overlooks the value of such expression to the audience. Certainly, in the jurisdictions considered in paras 9–90 to 9–155, commercial speech has been deemed worthy of constitutional protection on the basis of that value. Whether such an approach would be appropriate under the Irish Constitution would depend on whether the free market was seen as being inherently linked with the political system favoured by the Constitution. It is submitted that such an interpretation is certainly possible, particularly in the light of the protection of private property under Arts 43 and 40.3.1 and the recognition of the unenumerated right to earn a livelihood.

9–167 The case law discussed in paras 9–90 to 9–155 indicates that commercial speech receives a lower level of protection in a number of jurisdictions and this appears to be the case whether the speech emanates from

---

[334] Discussed above at paras 9–68 to 9–72 and 9–82.

[335] This theory is described above at paras 1–14 to 1–22.

[336] See quotation above at para.9–154.

[337] Baker, *Human Liberty and Freedom of Speech* (Oxford University Press, 1989), at p.202—original emphasis not reproduced. That approach indicates a lower level of protection for individual as well as corporate expression, an approach which may unduly restrict the notion of self-fulfilment.

[338] See O'Callaghan J. in *Klein and Law Society of Upper Canada, Re* (1985) 16 D.L.R. (4th) 489; the submissions by the Attorney-General of Quebec in *Ford v Quebec* [1988] 2 S.C.R. 712; and Rehnquist J. in *Virginia Pharmacy* and *Central Hudson*.

an individual or a company.[339] As far as the United States Supreme Court is concerned, this appears to be due to the fact that all such speech is economically motivated and thus deserving of a lower level of protection. The economic motivation of the speaker also appears to reduce the protection available for the speech under the European Convention on Human Rights.[340] The rationale behind such an approach is difficult to ascertain.[341] When applied to the individual speaker, it apparently assumes that there is no self-fulfilment element to the speech. In this regard, the lower value attached to commercial expression can be seen as part of a philosophy according to which the economic activities of individuals are not considered crucial to their personal development. Whatever the merits of that conception of the citizen,[342] it has rarely been made explicit in the case law because the protection of commercial speech is generally based on the interests of the audience.

9–168 The weaker protection of commercial expression also assumes that the profit motive behind such speech renders it of less value to the audience. The reasons for taking such a motive into account appear to be based on the protection of the audience and the presumed inability of the audience to effectively evaluate commercial speech. Even theorists who are in favour of protecting commercial expression see it as a less-favoured type of speech:

> "[I]t is wrong to concentrate on the author's profit motive, and ignore the recipients' interests in the acquisition of information ... Although the existence of profit (or some other ulterior) motive does not necessarily exclude a publication from constitutional protection, it should be taken into account in borderline areas."[343]

CONCLUSION

9–169 This chapter has explored the extent to which the company enjoys freedom of expression under the Irish Constitution. Speech emanating from media companies is definitely within the rubric of Art.40.6.1(i) due to its role in educating public opinion.[344] Where speech by non-media companies is

---

[339] Interestingly, in interpreting the free speech provisions contained in Art.19 of the International Covenant on Civil and Political Rights, the United Nations Human Rights Committee has taken the view that commercial expression should be protected to the same extent as other types of expression. *Ballantyne, Davidson & McIntyre v Canada*, Communications Nos 359/1989 and 385/1989, Views of the United Nations Human Rights Committee of March 31, 1993.

[340] See cases discussed above at paras 9–118 to 9–130.

[341] For the view that commercial expression should receive full First amendment protection, see Smolla, "Information, Imagery, and the First Amendment: A Case for Expansive Protection of Commercial Speech" (1993) 71 Tex.L.Rev. 777.

[342] It has been criticised in the context of the interpretation of Art.40.1 in this jurisdiction. See reference below at para.14–48.

[343] Barendt, *Freedom of Speech* (Oxford University Press, 1987), at p.57.

[344] In the case of the press, of course, individual journalists may also claim rights as citizens to freedom of expression.

concerned, the matter is less clear. This chapter has focused on two particular types of speech which companies may engage in—commercial expression and political expression. The peculiar problems with recognising constitutional protection for commercial expression under the Irish Constitution have been considered. It is submitted that commercial expression, whether by a company or an individual, is best protected under Art.40.6.1(i). This is because the primary rationale for protecting commercial expression is its value to the audience. Political expression by companies should also be protected under that Article on the same basis.

9–170 The experience of the United States Supreme Court and the ECHR suggest that all commercial expression and some political expression—that of the company—should receive a lower level of protection.[345] To the extent that a differentiated level of constitutional protection is appropriate, it could perhaps be realised in this jurisdiction within the proportionality test approved in *Murphy v IRTC*.[346] Indeed, in the context of commercial expression, the use of a proportionality test would obviate the need for the classification approach of *Central Hudson* which has been criticised for its rigidity.[347] In the context of corporate political expression, the consistent application of a proportionality doctrine could also be beneficial.[348]

---

[345] *cf.* "Free Speech Protections for Corporations: Competing in the Markets for Commerce and Ideas" (Note) (2004) 117 Harv.L.Rev. 2272.

[346] [1998] 2 I.L.R.M. 360.

[347] The wisdom of too rigid a classification in this context is questionable. See *Nike v Kasky* 123 S.Ct. 2554 and the academic commentary thereon: Chemerinsky and Fisk, *op.cit.*; Earnhardt, *op.cit.*; Pantaenius, *op.cit.*; Paladino, *op.cit.*; O'Neil, *op.cit.*; Collins and Skover, *op.cit.*; Teremenko, *op.cit.*

[348] *cf.* Hogan, "The Constitution, Property Rights and Proportionality" (1997) 32 Ir. Jur. (New Series) 373.

CHAPTER 10

THE RIGHT TO A GOOD NAME

INTRODUCTION

10–01 This chapter considers the extent to which companies may be able to rely on the right to a good name under Art.40.3 of the Constitution. Article 40.3 reads as follows:

> "1 The State guarantees in its laws to respect, and, as far as practicable, by its laws to defend and vindicate the personal rights of the citizen.
> 2 The State shall, in particular, by its laws protect as best it may from unjust attack and, in the case of injustice done, vindicate the life, person, good name, and property rights of every citizen."

10–02 The inclusion of the right to a good name in Art.40.3.2 is a somewhat unusual feature of the Irish Constitution. In *Maguire v Ardagh*,[1] McGuinness J. pointed out that:

> "This constitutional right to protection of one's good name is not one which is found in by any means all statements of basic human rights. The rights to protection of one's life, person and property are much more universal in constitutional statements of rights or bills of rights throughout the world. The right to protection of one's good name is not specifically found, for instance, in the European Convention on Human Rights. It is not included as a right in the United States Constitution; nor is it included in the Canadian Charter of Rights and Freedoms contained in the Constitution Act, 1982, nor in the Commonwealth of Australia Constitution Act, 1900."[2]

10–03 The precise interests protected by this guarantee appear to be connected to the idea of "character". Thus, in *Vozza v O'Floinn*,[3] Kingsmill Moore J. held this right to be violated where the continued existence of a defective order operated "as a blot on character"[4] in the context of a defective criminal conviction.

---

[1] [2002] 1 I.R. 385.
[2] *ibid.* at 619.
[3] [1957] I.R. 227.
[4] *ibid.* at 250.

10–04 There are relatively few cases which refer to the right to a good name although a number of cases have arisen in the context of the right to defend one's good name. In *Haughey, Re,*[5] the Supreme Court held that the right to one's good name necessarily implied that the citizen enjoyed the right to defend that good name when it was impugned. The case arose in the context of proceedings before the Dáil Public Accounts Committee which was enquiring into the state of public funds. In the course of the proceedings, the applicant had not been permitted to cross-examine witnesses who had tendered evidence which was prejudicial to him, nor had he been allowed to address that committee in his own defence.[6]

10–05 The right to defend one's good name has since arisen in a number of cases[7] which were essentially concerned with the fairness of procedures.[8] To enjoy the right to defend one's good name under Art.40.3.1, one must have the right to a good name in the first place. The Irish courts have not yet decided whether the company can rely on the right to a good name. As has already been pointed out, this is a right which does not receive positive protection under the European Convention on Human Rights or the United States Constitution and there is, thus, a dearth of comparative material with respect to the nature of such a right, as well as its application to the company.

10–06 Defamation case law may, however, prove useful in this context. In *Hynes-O'Sullivan v O'Driscoll,*[9] two Supreme Court judges[10] indicated that the law of defamation implicated this constitutional right, a connection that has since been reiterated in numerous defamation cases.[11] The courts have taken the view that the right to a good name is adequately protected by the common law tort of defamation and that there is no need to augment the common law rules in order to protect this right under the Constitution.[12] Thus, to the

---

[5] [1971] I.R. 217.

[6] *cf. K Security v Ireland*, unreported, High Court, Gannon J., July 15, 1977.

[7] *ibid.; Condon v CIÉ*, unreported, High Court, November 16, 1984; *O'Rourke and White v Martin* [1984] I.L.R.M. 333; *M v Medical Council* [1984] I.R. 485; *Goodman International Ltd v Hamilton (No.1)* [1992] 2 I.R. 542, [1992] I.L.R.M. 145; *Goodman International Ltd v Hamilton (No.2)* [1993] I.L.R.M. 81; *Maguire v Ardagh* [2002] 1 I.R. 385; *Ansbacher (Cayman) Ltd, Re* [2002] 2 I.R. 517, [2002] 2 I.L.R.M. 366; *Commission to Inquire into Child Abuse, Re* [2002] 3 I.R. 459.

[8] See *Haughey, Re* [1971] I.R. 217 at 264. The constitutional right to fair procedures in non-criminal proceedings is guaranteed under Art.40.3.1 and the availability of that constitutional guarantee to the company is considered below in Chap.12.

[9] [1988] I.R. 436, [1989] I.L.R.M. 349.

[10] Henchy and McCarthy JJ. [1988] I.R. 436 at 450 and 454, respectively; [1989] I.L.R.M. 349 at 360 and 365 respectively.

[11] *Hynes-O'Sullivan v O'Driscoll* [1988] I.R. 436, [1989] I.L.R.M. 349; *Kennedy v Hearne* [1988] I.R. 481; *Burke v Central Independent Television Plc* [1994] 2 I.R. 61, [1994] 2 I.L.R.M. 161; *Foley v Independent Newspapers (Ireland) Ltd* [1994] 2 I.L.R.M. 61; *Hunter v Gerald Duckworth & Co. Ltd* [2000] 1 I.R. 510; *McDonnell v Brady* [2001] 3 I.R. 588. For an article discussing the relationship between the right to a good name and freedom of expression in this context, see O'Dell, "Does Defamation Value Free Expression?" (1990) 12 D.U.L.J. 50.

[12] *Hunter v Gerald Duckworth & Co. Ltd* [2000] 1 I.R. 510 at 513. See also McMahon and Binchy, *Law of Torts* (3rd edn, Butterworths, 2004), at paras 34.05–06.

extent that defamation protects the same interest as that protected under Art.40.3.2, the case law on this common law tort may shed some light on the constitutional guarantee.

COMPANIES AND THE TORT OF DEFAMATION AT COMMON LAW

10–07 When examining the way in which the law of defamation protects the company, there are two important matters which arise as their resolution helps to illuminate the concept of the putative corporate right to a good name. The first is whether a company's reputation is affected only in relation to its trading activities. If this was the case, companies could recover for defamatory statements relating to fraud, insolvency etc., but not for those related to, for example, social corporate responsibility. The second issue is the extent to which the company must prove loss. The existing position under English law is that companies can recover for defamatory comments relating to their general reputation and there is no requirement to prove special damage,[13] provided that loss of goodwill is likely on the facts. Interestingly, as we shall see in the discussion below, the European Court of Human Rights ("ECHR") has endorsed this approach despite its potential to chill speech critical of unethical corporate practices.[14]

10–08 Companies have long been held entitled to recover for injury to reputation at common law. In *Metropolitan Saloon Omnibus Co. v Hawkins*,[15] Pollock C.B. held:

> "That a corporation at common law can sue in respect of a libel, there is no doubt. It would be monstrous if a corporation could maintain no action for slander of title through which they lost a great deal of money ... it appears to me clear that a corporation at common law may maintain an action for libel by which its property is injured."[16]

10–09 This early pronouncement suggests strongly that the corporate

---

[13] At common law, there is no need to prove damage in relation to libel—defamatory statements in physical form—or in relation to slander *per se*. Damage is presumed in these cases. A false defamatory oral statement will constitute slander *per se* where it alleges any of the following about the plaintiff: commission of a serious crime; affliction with a loathsome disease; participation in serious sexual misconduct; or professional incompetence, professional misconduct, or other matters tending to harm the plaintiff in his business, occupation, or trade. Langvardt, "A Principled Approach to Damages in Corporate Defamation Cases" (1990) 27 Am.Bus.L.J. 491 at 498.

[14] For a discussion of how such an approach can chill such speech, see discussion of the US Supreme Court case of *Nike v Kasky* 123 S.Ct. 2554—*Kasky v Nike, Inc* 93 Cal.Rptr.2d 854 (California Court of Appeals); *Kasky v Nike* 45 P.3d 243 (California Supreme Court)—above at paras 9–116 to 9–117.

[15] (1859) 4 H. & N. 87.

[16] *ibid*. at 90. See also the decision of the Irish Court of Exchequer in *Praeger & Co. v Shaw* (1885) 4 I.C.L.R. 660, and *Eglantine Inn Ltd v Smith* [1948] N.I.L.R. 29, both cited in McDonald, *The Irish Law of Defamation* (2nd edn, Round Hall, 1989), at p.274.

defamation victim must prove special damage in order to recover. However, later cases soon established that this was not necessary, and furthermore, that a company could recover for defamation in relation to more than its trading reputation.[17]

10–10   In *South Hetton Coal Co. v North-Eastern News Assoc.*,[18] the Court of Appeal of England and Wales considered the extent to which a company could rely on the law of libel. Lord Esher M.R. stated as follows:

> "I have considered the case, and I have come to the conclusion that the law of libel is one and the same as to all plaintiffs; and that, in every action of libel, whether the statement complained of is, or is not, a libel, depends on the same question—*viz.*, whether the jury are of opinion that what has been published with regard to the plaintiff would tend in the minds of people of ordinary sense to bring the plaintiff into contempt, hatred, or ridicule, or to injure his character. The question is really the same by whomsoever the action is brought—whether by a person, a firm, or a company. But though the law is the same, the application of it is, no doubt, different with regard to different types of plaintiffs. There are statements which, with regard to some plaintiffs, would undoubtedly constitute a libel, but which, if published of another kind of plaintiffs, would not have the same effect. For instance, it might be stated of a person that his manners were contrary to all sense of decency or comity, and such that, if the statement were true, they would render him deserving in the minds of persons of ordinary sense of contempt, ridicule, or hatred; but, if the same thing were said with regard to a firm, or company, it would be impossible that it should have the same effect, because a firm or company as such cannot have indecent or vulgar manners … There are other statements which would have the same effect, whether they were made with regard to a person, or a firm, or a company; as, for instance, statements with regard to conduct of business."[19]

10–11   In the same case, Lopes L.J. also considered the extent to which a company could sue for libel. He stated:

> "I am of the opinion that, although a corporation cannot maintain an action for libel in respect of anything reflecting upon them personally, yet they can maintain an action for a libel reflecting on the management of their trade or business, and this without alleging or proving special damage. The words complained of, in order to entitle a corporation or company to sue for libel or slander, must injuriously affect the corporation or company as distinct from the individuals who compose it. A corporation

---

[17] It has been held that a company may maintain an action in defamation where an imputation to its sole director where one is the alter ego of the other. *Wiggins v Rigby*, Supreme Court of Victoria, August 10, 2000.

[18] [1894] 1 Q.B. 133.

[19] *ibid.* at 138–139.

or company could not sue in respect of a charge of murder, or incest, or adultery, because it could not commit these crimes. Nor could it sue in respect of a charge of corruption or of an assault, because a corporation cannot be guilty of corruption or of an assault, although the individuals composing it may be. The words complained of must attack the corporation or company in the method of conducting its affairs, must accuse it of fraud or mismanagement, or must attack its financial position."[20]

10–12 Kay L.J. pointed out that a company "has a trading character, the defamation of which may ruin it".[21]

10–13 While the above quotations could be construed as limiting a company's recovery to cases where the defamatory material relates to its trading reputation, that case concerned the publication of statements about the unsanitary living conditions in housing provided by the plaintiff to its employees.[22] It, thus, appears that the common law position goes beyond recompensing the company in relation to defamation of trading character. In *Eglantine Inn v Smith*,[23] the defamation complained of concerned a company's policy on employees joining trade unions. These cases appear to deal with the general reputation of the company, rather than any trading reputation as such.[24]

10–14 The corporate defamation plaintiff was considered recently by the English Court of Appeal in the case of *McDonalds v Steel and Morris*.[25] The case arose out of a libel action taken by McDonalds Plc against the applicants for the dissemination of a leaflet highly critical of the company's practices in the realm of the environment, animal welfare, treatment of employees, unethical advertising and a number of other areas. The applicants had defended this libel action and lost in the High Court. In their appeal to the Court of Appeal, they had argued, *inter alia*, that as a large multinational public corporation McDonalds Plc should not have a right to maintain an action for defamation at common law and that the High Court judge had erred in his ruling that there was no need to prove special damage provided that loss of good will was likely.[26]

---

[20] *ibid*. at 140.

[21] *ibid*. at 145.

[22] See also *D. and L. Caterers, Ltd and Jackson v D'Ajou* [1945] K.B. 210, where it was held that a company could recover for injury to its reputation without the need to prove special damage where the slander affected its trading reputation or where the words spoken impute a crime punishable by imprisonment. See also *Lewis v Daily Telegraph* [1964] A.C. 234—a company which has been libelled in relation to its trading reputation need not prove special damage.

[23] [1948] N.I.L.R. 29.

[24] See also *D. and L. Caterers, Ltd and Jackson v D'Ajou* [1945] K.B. 210 where a company recovered in relation to an allegation that it was operating contrary to wartime regulations issued by the Ministry of Food.

[25] *McDonald's Corp v Steel*, unreported, CA of England and Wales Civ Div, March 31, 1999.

[26] The appellants had argued in the Court of Appeal that the trial judge ought to have taken

10–15   The appeal was dismissed by the Court of Appeal. It held that it was clear that corporations were entitled to take defamation proceedings at common law and that it would not be possible to draw a distinction between large multinational companies, which the appellants argued should be unable to take such actions, and other companies. In relation to the argument that a corporate defamation plaintiff should be required to prove actual damage, the court found that damage to trading reputation could be just as difficult to quantify as damage to individual reputation and that it might not cause immediate quantifiable loss.

Reputation under the European Convention on Human Rights

10–16   The right to a good name is not specifically protected under the European Convention on Human Rights. It does, however, receive some recognition in Art.10 of the Convention, which guarantees freedom of expression in the first paragraph before going on to state in the second that:

> "The exercise of these freedoms, since it carries with it duties and responsibilities, may be subject to such formalities, conditions, restrictions or penalties as are prescribed by law and are necessary in a democratic society … for the protection of the reputation or rights of others …".

10–17   Thus, while there is no right to reputation as such, the Convention recognises that freedom of expression may be restricted where reputation is at issue, provided that any restrictions on freedom of expression are "necessary in a democratic society".[27]

10–18   The defendants in *McDonalds v Steel and Morris*, having failed to obtain leave to appeal to the House of Lords, took their case to Strasbourg where they argued that the failure to restrict damages, the complex procedures and the absence of legal aid meant the defamation proceedings in the British courts had violated their rights to freedom of expression under Art.10 of the Convention. The European Commission on Human Rights[28] found that their rights had not been interfered with and that the defamation proceedings were justified under Art.10(2) to protect the reputation of others.

10–19   Before this case reached the ECHR, the Court of Appeal of England and Wales heard the case of *Jameel (Mohammed) v Wall Street Journal Europe*

---

into account the provisions of Art.10 of the Convention. At the time of the trial, the Convention was not incorporated into English Law so that the judge was under no obligation, at least as a matter of English Law, to apply its provisions.

[27] Ireland's strongly pro-plaintiff defamation regime has been found by the ECHR to swing the balance too far in favour of reputation due to the large quantum of damages available in defamation cases. See *Independent News and Media Plc v Ireland* App. No. 55120/00.

[28] *S and M v UK* (1993) 18 E.H.R.R. CD 172.

Sprl,[29] in which it was argued that Art.10 of the Convention required a change in the law of defamation to the effect that a corporation should be required to prove special damage in order to succeed in an action for defamation. Lord Phillips M.R. delivered the decision of the court. He noted that the Faulk's Committee had held that no such requirement should be imposed. [30] The defendant also made the more specific point that the fact that the company concerned was a foreign corporation which did not trade within the jurisdiction should mean that it ought to be required to prove special damage. Referring to the decision of the Commission in the *Steel and Morris* litigation, Lord Phillips noted that that case had concerned a foreign corporation. He concluded that, provided such a company could prove it had a trading reputation within the jurisdiction, the same rules ought to apply to it in relation to defamation law.[31]

10–20 When the *Steel and Morris* case came before the ECHR,[32] it held that:

> "The Court further does not consider that the fact that the plaintiff in the present case was a large multinational company should in principle deprive it of a right to defend itself against defamatory allegations or entail that the applicants should not have been required to prove the truth of the statements made. It is true that large public companies inevitably and knowingly lay themselves open to close scrutiny of their acts and, as in the case of the businessmen and women who manage them, the limits of acceptable criticism are wider in the case of such companies … However, in addition to the public interest in open debate about business practices, there is a competing interest in protecting the commercial success and viability of companies, for the benefit of shareholders and employees, but also for the wider economic good. The State therefore enjoys a margin of appreciation as to the means it provides under domestic law to enable a company to challenge the truth, and limit the damage, of allegations which risk harming its reputation …".[33]

10–21 The House of Lords in *Jameel*[34] was thus able to rely on the margin of appreciation left to it by the Strasbourg court in considering the issue of special damage. The Law Lords were divided on this issue and there is an interesting divergence of viewpoints on the appropriate calibration of the

---

[29] [2005] 2 W.L.R. 1577.
[30] *ibid.* at 1611. The reference is to *The Report of the Faulks Committee on Defamation 1975* Cmnd.5909 at [336].
[31] [2005] 2 W.L.R. 1577 at 1611–1613. He made the point that failure to treat foreign corporations on a par with British ones "would be likely to constitute discrimination in the accordance of article 6 rights, contrary to the prohibition imposed by article 14". At 1613.
[32] *Steel and Morris v UK* [2005] ECHR 68416/01, judgment of February 15, 2005. For a discussion of the litigation see Hudson, "Free Speech and Equality of Arms—the Decision in *Steel and Morris v UK*" [2005] E.H.R.L.R. 301.
[33] App. No. 68416/01, judgment of February 15, 2005 at [94], references omitted.
[34] *Jameel v Wall Street Journal Europe Sprl* [2006] U.K.H.L. 44.

balance between the values of protecting reputation and freedom of expression where the reputational interest is claimed by a corporate plaintiff.

10–22   Lord Bingham first assessed the position under English law before going on to consider whether this position was compatible with the Convention. He turned first to the Court of Appeal decision in *South Hetton Coal Co v North-Eastern News Assoc.*,[35] as interpreted by Lord Keith *Derbyshire County Council v Times Newspapers Ltd*[36] and concluded that English law had no requirement of proof of special damage by a corporate defamation plaintiff.

10–23   After establishing that English law did not require proof of special damage, Lord Bingham considered whether Art.10 of the Convention required a revision of this position. Correctly taking the view that *Steel and Morris* did not require such revision, Lord Bingham went on to consider the merits of *South Hutton* from first principles. Ultimately, he rejected the need to prove special damage on the basis that "the good name of a company, as that of an individual, is a thing of value."[37] He also rejected the argument that a publication, if truly damaging to a corporation's commercial reputation, will result in provable financial loss, pointing out that a prompt libel action might prevent such a loss accruing.[38]

10–24   Lord Hope agreed with Lord Bingham but made a number of additional comments. In particular, he was opposed to singling out trading corporations for special treatment, holding that they should be treated the same way as trade unions and charities.[39]

10–25   Lord Scott considered first the function of defamation law in protecting reputation, noting that "[r]eputation is valued by individuals for it affects their self-esteem and their standing in the community" and considering the argument that:

> "[c]orporations, it is said, have no feelings to be hurt and cannot feel shame. If they are to sue for libel they should be required to show that the libel has caused them actual damage."[40]

10–26   Referring to the importance of image to the corporation—advertising and sponsorship activities etc.—Lord Scott emphasised the importance and value of its general reputation to the trading corporation:[41]

> "If reputation suffers, sponsorship invitations may be reduced, advertising

---

[35] [1894] 1 Q.B. 133.
[36] [1993] A.C. 534.
[37] *Jameel v Wall Street Journal Europe Sprl* [2006] U.K.H.L. 44 at [26].
[38] *ibid.*
[39] *ibid.* at [100].
[40] *ibid.* at [119].
[41] *ibid.* at [120].

opportunities may become difficult, customers may take their custom elsewhere. If trade suffers, profits suffer."[42]

10–27   He also adverted to the practical difficulty a corporation might face in proving special damage.[43]

10–28   One of the interesting aspects of his decision is its focus on the different types of corporation. While this was mentioned in passing by the other Lords, Lord Scott alone considered its possible significance. He seemed to take the view that the question of whether a statement was actionable might depend on the objects clause of the company. Comparing the varying purposes for which entities such as trading, charitable and holding companies were incorporated, he was of the view that:

> "Whether publications containing disparaging or derogatory remarks about a company can be complained of by the company as being defamatory will depend upon the nature of the remarks and the nature of the corporation's objects and reputation."[44]

10–29   Both Lord Hoffman and Baroness Hale dissented on the question of special damage. Baroness Hale's dissent placed the focus on freedom of expression. Lord Hoffman's judgment—which concurred with the free speech aspects of Baroness Hale's—also emphasised the function of defamation in protecting reputation.

10–30   Lord Hoffman took a particular view of the nature of the reputational interests protected by freedom of expression. He pointed out that:

> "In the case of an individual, his reputation is a part of his personality, the 'immortal part' of himself and it is right that he should be entitled to vindicate his reputation and receive compensation for a slur upon it without proof of financial loss. But a commercial company has no soul and its reputation is no more than a commercial asset, something attached to its trading name which brings in customers. I see no reason why the rule which requires proof of special damage to commercial assets in other torts, such as malicious falsehood, should not also apply to defamation."[45]

10–31   Lord Hoffman's judgment captures the intuition that companies have different interests to individuals and these differences matter in some way. He does not make explicit any principled or philosophical basis for the distinction but it is possible to discern one from the quotation above by focusing on the interests he identifies therein.

---

[42] *ibid.*
[43] *ibid.* at [121].
[44] *ibid.* at [125].
[45] *ibid.* at [91].

10–32   It appears that the rationale for his approach relates to his view that the only interests companies have in this context are interests in property. Implicit in this approach is the idea that the company's only purpose is profit maximisation, thus the only function of defamation law as regards a company is to protect property. This property interest is, according to Lord Hoffmann, less deserving of protection than the reputational interest of an individual because reputation, to the individual, is an aspect of the "immortal part" of himself.[46]

10–33   Underpinning Lord Hoffman's approach is an implicit assumption about the rationale for protecting interests and the prioritising of some interests over others. One way to articulate the distinction is to dichotomise interests into two categories: those concerned with the values of autonomy and those which are valued for some instrumental purpose. From such a perspective, the former category of interests is protected for its own sake, whereas the latter is protected only where this furthers some other purpose. The latter category of interests are thus protected on a utilitarian basis.[47]

10–34   This approach to corporate reputation can be applied in a variety of contexts to justify differing levels of protection for corporate, as opposed to individual, interests.[48] It is particularly appropriate in the context of defamation because of the freedom of expression dimension. Where corporate reputational interest clashes with the value of freedom of expression, the balance between the two may be adjusted in favour of the latter. On the other hand, the reputational interest individuals have is connected to their status as autonomous beings. That interest, even when pitted against freedom of expression,[49] is deserving of a greater degree of protection because of a philosophical commitment to autonomy as a prioritised value, protected for its own sake.

10–35   Baroness Hale's judgment focuses on freedom of expression. In fact, hers is the only judgment to approach the case from this perspective. Favouring the overruling of *South Hetton* and the imposition of a requirement that a corporate defendant prove special damage, she thought that this

> "would achieve a proper balance between the right of a company to protect its reputation and the right of the press and public to be critical of it. These days, the dividing line between governmental and non-governmental organisations is increasingly difficult to draw. The power wielded by the major multi-national corporations is enormous and

---

[46] The ECHR in *Steel and Morris*, on the other hand, saw the balance as lying in favour of the utilitarian purpose of the pursuit of corporate profit.

[47] See Dan-Cohen, *Rights, Persons and Organizations: A Legal Theory for Bureaucratic Society* (University of California Press, 1986), at pp.55–118.

[48] See O'Neill, "The Right to Silence and the Company" (2004) Ir. Jur. (New Series) 111.

[49] Freedom of expression itself may be protected on the basis of autonomy values—self-realisation of the individual—or on some instrumental basis—the free marketplace of ideas.

growing. The freedom to criticise them may be at least as important in a democratic society as the freedom to criticise the government."[50]

10–36 The concern that corporations are powerful and need to be curtailed is a commonplace in popular discourse and has spawned a range of responses including a burgeoning scholarship in respect of corporate social responsibility. One powerful mechanism for the achievement of the "proper balance" referred to by Baroness Hale is to recognise that corporate interests may be less deserving of protection than individual interests because they rest on fundamentally different philosophical foundations. Thus, one might accept a legal rule which subtracts from the marketplace of ideas where that is necessary to protect the dignity of the individual. Where the profit maximising rights of a company are concerned, that balance could be readjusted on a principled and rational basis.

10–37 The approach of the majority of the Law Lords in *Jameel* to the issue of special damages protects corporate reputation at the inevitable expense of freedom of expression. It is true to say that a different balance was not required by the ECHR and that the House of Lords was within its margin of appreciation in reaching the conclusion it did. Lord Bingham's judgment recognises that the fact that Strasbourg case law provides a particular level of protection in the context of Art.10 does not preclude the UK courts from providing a higher degree of protection, but nonetheless finds that the appropriate balance lies in favour of corporate reputation as opposed to freedom of expression. The approach of the majority in *Jameel* has the undeniable advantage of clarity and avoids, among other nuisances, the need to distinguish between different types of corporation.[51] While it offers clarity and simplicity, however, it does so at the expense of a more philosophically principled approach which rationalises the intuitive distinction between individual and corporate reputation in a manner more favourable to expression in the context of the reputation/ free speech balance.

UNITED STATES CONSTITUTION

10–38 The United States Constitution contains no explicit protection of the right to a good name and its defamation law case law, with its fault-based liability,[52] has been criticised for over-emphasising freedom of expression and under-protecting reputation.[53] In *Dun and Bradstreet v Greenmoss Builders*

---

[50] At [128].

[51] Although Lord Scott's approach arguably still leaves some room for this.

[52] *New York Times v Sullivan* 376 U.S. 254 (1964); *Curtis Publishing Co. v Butts* and *Associated Press v Walker* (consolidated cases) 388 U.S. 130 (1967); *Rosenbloom v Metromedia, Inc* 403 U.S. 29 (1971); *Gertz v Welch* 418 U.S. 323 (1974). For an analysis of the appropriate degree of fault in the context of defamation of a corporate plaintiff, see Fetzer, "The Corporate Defamation Plaintiff as First Amendment 'Public Figure': Nailing the Jellyfish" (1982) 68 Iowa L.Rev. 35; Dotseth, "Redefining the Corporate 'Jellyfish': Corporate Plaintiffs in Defamation Actions" (1989) 14 J.Corp.L. 907.

[53] *Hill v Church of Scientology of Toronto* [1995] 2 S.C.R. 1130; *Reynolds v Times*

Ltd,[54] the United States Supreme Court was presented with a case involving a corporate defamation plaintiff. An employee of the defendant had made an error in reading bankruptcy records and a false statement had thus been included in a credit report relating to the plaintiff which was circulated to five subscribers. The majority opinion simply ignores this, an omission criticised in the dissenting opinion of Brennan J.:

> "Though the individual's interest in reputation is certainly at the core of notions of human dignity ... the reputational interest at stake here is that of a corporation ... The commercial context does not increase the need for presumed damages, but if anything reduces the need to presume harm. At worst the commercial damages caused by such action should be no more difficult to ascertain than many other traditional elements of tort."[55]

THE NATURE OF THE CORPORATE REPUTATION

10–39   The nature of the corporate reputation has been considered in the following terms:

> "When it is said that in an action for defamation damages are given for an injury to the plaintiff's reputation, what is meant? A man's reputation, his good name, the estimation in which he is held in the opinion of others, is not a possession of his as a chattel is. Damage to it cannot be measured. Apart from special damages strictly so called and damages for a loss of clients or customers, money and reputation are not commensurables. It seems to me that, properly speaking, a man defamed does not get compensation for his damaged reputation. He gets damages because he was injured in his reputation, that is simply because he was publicly defamed. For this reason, compensation by damages operates in two ways—as a vindication of the plaintiff to the public and as consolation to him for a wrong done. Compensation is here a solatium rather than a monetary recompense for harm measurable in money."[56]

10–40   The quotation above, from a judgment of the High Court of Australia, takes a bifurcated view of the tort of defamation. Where reputation alone is at stake, there is no need to prove damage. Where pecuniary loss is at issue, on the other hand, damages are not presumed. The issues of reputation and proof

---

Newspapers [1999] 4 All E.R. 609; [1999] 3 W.L.R. 1010. For the view that US case law achieves the appropriate balance between freedom of expression and protection of reputation as regards the corporate defamation plaintiff, see Yannucci, "Debunking 'The Big Chill': Why Defamation Suits by Corporations are Consistent with the First Amendment" (1995) 39 St.Louis U.L.J. 1187. For an opposing view, see Jackson, "The Corporate Defamation Plaintiff in the Era of SLAPPS: Revisiting *New York Times v Sullivan*" (2001) 9 Wm.& Mary Bill Rts.J. 491.

[54] 472 U.S. 749 (1985).
[55] *ibid*. at 790, references omitted.
[56] Windeyer J. in *Uren v John Fairfax* (1966) 117 CLR 118 at 150.

of damage are inextricably entwined when the plaintiff is a company. Arguing against the proposition that a company should only be able to sue for defamation relating to its trading reputation, McDonald stated:

> "[S]ome companies do clearly have a reputation in addition to their trading reputations, because they are involved in other activities as well, such as subscribing to charities and political parties, or sponsoring sporting, cultural or civic activities. Of course, it can be said that these may, indirectly, affect a trading reputation. But, if indirect effect is to be given such a meaning, then the question becomes one of semantics only since the imputations would then be actionable."[57]

10–41 This reducing of all statements to their impact on the trading reputation of a company surely indicates that what is really at issue in all corporate defamation suits is injury to a valuable asset—goodwill. It has been argued that it is this asset which is at issue when one speaks of a company's reputation:

> "What a company does have is a reputation as being, for example, one which is concerned for the environment or as a fair trader. Indeed the image of the company in the eyes of the public is regarded as a valuable asset and one on which large sums of advertising and public relations money are spent. But is this anything more than part of the goodwill of the company, that is something which may be measured in money terms and which, for example, would account for a substantial part of the purchase price of a company? This raises the question whether there can be damage to the reputation of a company which is separable from damage to its goodwill. If reputation can only be measured in terms of goodwill, then it would follow that a company should in theory only be able to sue for special damage."[58]

10–42 It has been pointed out that the presumed damages rule is justified only in relation to defamation of natural persons:

> "The principal aim of the common law's presumed damages doctrine is to protect the reputational interests and dignity of natural persons. By relieving plaintiffs of the burden of proving actual reputational harm, the doctrine reflects a philosophical bias that reputational interests are so important as to justify an irrebuttable presumption of such harm, a presumption arising upon proof of falsehood that ordinarily would seem likely to harm reputation. In other words, the presumed damages doctrine holds that reputation is so valuable, and so often not amenable to ready proof of harm even though harm has occurred, that the legal system should not take chances with a rule requiring reputational injury to be proved. The effect of such a rule, the argument continues, could be to deny

---

[57] McDonald, *op. cit.* at p.275.
[58] Kidner, "Defaming a Company by Disparaging its Products" [1992] J.B.L. 570 at 573.

recovery to a deserving plaintiff who simply was unable to prove reputational injury."[59]

THE NATURE OF THE RIGHT TO A GOOD NAME UNDER ART.40.3.2

10–43   It is not entirely clear what is meant by the term "good name" under Art.40.3.2. In *Hynes-O'Sullivan v O'Driscoll*, Henchy J. referred to the "constitutional right to one's reputation"[60] and the cases tend to use the words "reputation" and "good name" interchangeably.[61] The scope of the term reputation is unclear. In particular, it is not clear whether it would include goodwill of the type enjoyed by a company. Some of the cases in relation to the right to a good name have arisen in the context of possible injury to professional or business reputation.[62] As all of these cases concerned individuals, however, it is possible that reputation in this context is narrower than the concept in defamation law. Some hint at this possible narrower meaning can be derived from the juxtaposition of the right to a good name with the idea of "character".[63] It has been noted that defamation law itself has "strong personal dignity overtones"[64] and it is possible that these overtones are more prevalent in the context of the constitutional right to a good name. From this perspective, the constitutional guarantee would be concerned with the dignity of the individual rather than any pecuniary loss. Some support for this can be garnered from the judgment of McGuinness J. in *Maguire v Ardagh*, where she stated:

> "The inclusion of this specific right in the Irish Constitution marks a recognition by the framers of the Constitution of the damage that can be done to a citizen even in a situation where he or she is not subjected to legal penalties, to loss of liberty or property, or to physical injury. In considering the balance which must be held between the rights of the Oireachtas as such and those of the individual citizen and the priorities which must be given to each, the right to protection of the individual's good name has to be given due weight."[65]

---

[59] Langvardt, *op.cit.* at 516, references omitted.

[60] [1988] I.R. 436 at 449, [1989] I.L.R.M. 349 at 360.

[61] *Vozza v O'Floinn* [1957] I.R. 227 at 245; *M v Medical Council* [1984] I.R. 485 at 501; *Hunter v Gerald Duckworth & Co. Ltd* [2000] 1 I.R. 510 at 513; *McDonnell v Brady* [2001] 3 I.R. 588 at 599; *Maguire v Ardagh* [2002] 1 I.R. 385 at 411, 412, 433, 483, 484, 493, 499 and 501; *Commission to Inquire into Child Abuse, Re* [2002] 3 I.R. 459 at 475.

[62] *M v Medical Council* [1984] I.R. 485; *Goodman International Ltd v Hamilton (No.1)* [1992] 2 I.R. 542, [1992] I.L.R.M. 145; *Goodman International Ltd v Hamilton (No.2)* [1993] I.L.R.M. 81.

[63] *Vozza v O'Floinn* [1957] I.R. 227 at 250; *Haughey, Re* [1971] I.R. 217 at 262.

[64] Langvardt, *op.cit.* at 496.

[65] [2002] 1 I.R. 419 at 619–620.

10–44 The distinction in this extract between property rights and the right to a good name is one portended in the first case concerning the right to a good name, *Vozza v O'Floinn*.[66] In this case, it was held that, "if the conviction stands on the records, the prosecutor will suffer serious hurt in his reputation and good name and perhaps in his property."[67]

10–45 The application of the narrower concept of the right to a good name would arguably sit better with the provisions of Art.40.3.2 as a whole. The references to the "person" and "life" import the irresistible inference that the dignity and autonomy of natural persons is what is at issue in this Article. On the other hand, the reference to "property" may not be so readily restricted to the individual citizen.[68]

10–46 In the context of defamation proceedings, it may well be that the company is protected only under common law, and not constitutional law. For a company asserting its reputation—trading or otherwise—the unavailability of constitutional buttressing for its submissions may not be of much practical relevance. On the other hand, in proceedings concerning the right to defend one's good name, the company may seek to rely on the constitutional guarantee. Insofar as such arguments might relate to the good name of the company itself, it is submitted that there is no constitutional basis for them.

---

[66] [1957] I.R. 227.
[67] *ibid*. at 245.
[68] In relation to the right to property and the company, see above, Chap.8.

CHAPTER 11

THE RIGHT TO LITIGATE AND THE RIGHT OF ACCESS TO THE COURTS

INTRODUCTION

11–01 This chapter considers the extent to which companies may invoke the right to litigate and the right of access to the courts, both of which are guaranteed under Art.40.3 of the Irish Constitution.[1] In this context, particular attention is paid to the case law concerning security for costs under s.390 of the Companies Act 1963.

11–02 The distinction between the right to litigate and the right of access to the courts was established by the Supreme Court in *Tuohy v Courtney*,[2] where it considered the constitutionality of s.11 of the Statute of Limitations 1957 which provided for a six-year limitation period for the initiation of actions in tort or contract. The section made no provision for litigants who only realised that they had suffered loss after the expiry of the period. The plaintiff was such a litigant. The court found that the right to litigate and not the right of access to the courts was at issue here. This was because the Statute of Limitations did not prevent the plaintiff from initiating litigation, but gave the defendant the right to elect to defeat the claim by invoking the limitation period. The right to litigate was described as "the right to achieve by action in the courts the appropriate remedy upon proof of an actionable wrong causing damage or loss as recognised by the law".[3]

THE CONTEXTUAL APPLICATIONS OF THE TWO RIGHTS

11–03 The right to litigate has been invoked to challenge statutory limitation periods[4] and it has been held to give a plaintiff the right to an adequate

---

[1] *Tuohy v Courtney* [1994] 3 I.R. 1, [1994] 2 I.L.R.M. 503.
[2] *ibid*. No such distinction had been made in the earlier case of *Quinn v Ryan* [1965] I.R. 70, (1966) 100 I.L.T.R. 105.
[3] [1994] 3 I.R. 1 at 45, [1994] 2 I.L.R.M. 503 at 513. It has been argued that the right to litigate is "a facet of the right of access to the courts, rather than ... a separate and free-standing right". Casey, *Constitutional Law in Ireland* (3rd edn, Round Hall, Sweet & Maxwell, 2000), at p.414.
[4] *O'Brien v Keogh* [1972] I.R. 144; *Brady v Donegal County Council* [1989] I.L.R.M. 282; *O'Brien v Manufacturing Engineering Co.* [1973] I.R. 334, (1974) 108 I.L.T.R. 105; *Tuohy v Courtney* [1994] 3 I.R. 1, [1994] 2 I.L.R.M. 503; *Article 26 and ss 5 and*

opportunity to establish her case.[5] The right of access to the courts has been recognised in a case challenging the requirement to obtain the *fiat* of the Attorney-General before suing a Minister,[6] and in *Byrne v Ireland*[7] it was referred to in the context of the citizen's right to sue the State in tort. It has also been invoked to allow what has been described as an *actio popularis* to proceed.[8] It does not necessarily, however, require the State to provide civil legal aid.[9]

11–04 In *Article 26 and ss. 5 and 10 of the Illegal Immigrants (Trafficking) Bill 1999, Re*,[10] the Supreme Court held that:

> "It would be contrary to the very notion of a state founded on the rule of law, as this State is, and one in which, pursuant to Article 34 justice is administered in courts established by law, if all persons within this jurisdiction, including non-nationals, did not, in principle, have a constitutionally protected right of access to the courts to enforce their legal rights ...
>
> It may be that in certain circumstances a right of access to the courts of non-nationals may be subject to conditions or limitations which would not apply to citizens. However, where the State, or State authorities, make decisions which are legally binding on, and addressed directly to, a particular individual, within the jurisdiction, whether a citizen or non-national, such decisions must be taken in accordance with the law and the Constitution. It follows that an individual legally bound by such a decision must have access to the courts to challenge its validity. Otherwise, the obligation on the State to act lawfully and constitutionally would be ineffective."[11]

11–05 The above extract appears to hold out some hope that the company may be able to rely on this constitutional guarantee in that it is not necessary to be a "citizen" to rely on this aspect of Art.40.3. It should be noted, however, that the judgment concerned the position of natural persons only and the general

---

10 *of the Illegal Immigrants (Trafficking) Bill 1999, Re* [2002] 2 I.R. 360; *White v Dublin Corporation*, unreported, High Court, June 21, 2002.
5 *Bula Ltd v Tara Mines Ltd (No.1)* [1987] I.R. 85, [1988] I.L.R.M. 149.
6 *Macauley v Minister for Posts and Telegraphs* [1966] I.R. 345.
7 [1972] I.R. 241.
8 *Society for the Protection of the Unborn Child (Ireland) Ltd v Coogan* [1989] I.R. 734, [1990] I.L.R.M. 70. See Hogan and Whyte, *Kelly: The Irish Constitution* (4th edn, Lexis-Nexis Butterworths, 2003), at p.1454.
9 *O'Shaughnessy v Att.-Gen.*, unreported, High Court, February 16, 1971; *Application of J.C.*, unreported, High Court, July 25, 1985; *MacGairbhith v Att.-Gen.*, unreported, Supreme Court, March 29, 1995; *M.C. v The Legal Aid Board* [1991] 2 I.R. 43; *Stevenson v Landy*, unreported, High Court, February 10, 1993; *Kirwan v Minister for Justice* [1994] 2 I.R. 417, [1994] 1 I.L.R.M. 444; *McBrearty v Morris*, unreported, High Court, May 13, 2003. See also *Airey v Ireland* (1980) 2 E.H.R.R. 305 and Cousins, "Access to the Courts" (1992) 14 D.U.L.J. 51.
10 [2002] 2 I.R. 360.
11 *ibid.* at 385.

tenor of it indicates that companies were not within its contemplation.[12] The court did, however, emphasise the "obligation on the State to act lawfully and constitutionally", rather than any right as such on the part of the litigant and that emphasis might be thought to avail the company. Indeed, the case has been relied upon to allow foreign registered companies to rely on the constitutional protection of property rights.[13]

Security for costs

11–06   One context in which the right of access to the courts often arises is that of security for costs. Order 29, r.6 of the Rules of the Superior Courts 1986 empowers the High Court to make an order requiring a potential litigant to provide security for costs. In *Malone v Brown Thomas & Co. Ltd*,[14] the Supreme Court refused to grant such an order in the circumstances of the instant case, holding that no unnecessary obstacle should be placed in the way of those seeking to go to court. Whether or not security for costs is required will depend on the particular circumstances of the case. An order granting security will not be a breach of the litigant's constitutional right of access in every case,[15] but that right is a factor to be taken into account when setting the amount.[16]

11–07   Where the company is the litigant, the provisions of s.390 of the Companies Act 1963 must be taken into account. This provides that:

> "Where a limited company is plaintiff in any action or other legal proceeding, any judge having jurisdiction in the matter, may, if it appears by credible testimony that there is reason to believe that the company will be unable to pay the costs of the defendant if successful in his defence, require sufficient security to be given for those costs and may stay all proceedings until the security is given."

11–08   In *Peppard v Bogoff*,[17] the Supreme Court rejected the argument that s.278 of the Companies Act 1908[18]—which was phrased identically to s.390 of the Companies Act 1963—*required* the making of orders for security for costs. The discretionary nature of the provision was reiterated by the Supreme Court in *SEE Company Ltd v Public Lighting Services Ltd and Petit Jean*

---

[12] See also *Murphy v Greene* [1990] 2 I.R. 566, where Griffin J. stated, at 578, that "it is beyond question that every individual, be he a citizen or not, has a constitutional right of access to the courts".

[13] *Shirley v O'Gorman & Co. Ltd* [2006] I.E.H.C. 27. Cf. *Texuna International Ltd v Cairn Energy Plc* [2005] 1 B.C.L.C. 579.

[14] [1995] 1 I.L.R.M. 369.

[15] *Salih v General Accident* [1987] I.R. 628.

[16] *Fallon v An Bord Pleanála* [1992] 2 I.R. 380, [1991] I.L.R.M. 799.

[17] [1962] I.R. 180.

[18] The UK rule is now contained in s.726(1) of the Companies Act 1985—to be replaced by the UK Companies Act 2006—supplemented by Pt 25 of the UK Civil Procedure Rules. See *Classic Catering Ltd v Donnington Park Leisure Ltd* [2001] 1 B.C.L.C. 537.

(UK) Ltd.[19] In that case, the Supreme Court took into account the delay on the part of the applicant under s.390 and the fact that there was evidence which tended to show that the inability of the company to provide security derived largely from the events the subject matter of the action. McCarthy J. held that:

> "The argument that the section of the Companies Act was mandatory was rejected in *Peppard v Bogoff* [1962] IR 180. The consequent discretionary nature of the order is emphasised when read in the light of the constitutional right of access to the courts, a right not limited to the High Court, and the nature of the right of appeal to this court as provided by Article 34.4.3 of the Constitution."[20]

11–09 One aspect of the case law in respect of s.390 is that an order may be refused where the plaintiff company can demonstrate that the defendant's conduct has put it in the precarious financial position of which the defendant is complaining. The plaintiff in such a case must adduce some evidence to support that assertion.[21]

11–10 The requirement to provide security for costs clearly places an obstacle in the way of a plaintiff's access to the courts, but the constitutionality of that obstacle has been defended in the Irish courts. Thus, in *Salih v General Accident*,[22] O'Hanlon J. stated:

> "With regard to the constitutional argument, it appears to me that any right of access to the courts to prosecute civil claims cannot be an unfettered right and I consider that the right to apply for security for costs in the very limited category of cases where this is recognised by our law to intend to do justice between the parties, is reasonable, and is not in breach of any constitutional rights that the plaintiff may be able to assert in the circumstances of the present case."[23]

11–11 The general rule for natural persons is that: "It is always a matter to be taken into account that any plaintiff should not be driven from the judgment seat unless the justice of the case makes it imperative."[24] The application of this general rule to companies was rejected by Keane J. in *Lismore Homes Ltd (in receivership) v Bank of Ireland Finance Ltd*[25] who went on to hold:

---

[19] [1987] I.L.R.M. 255.

[20] *ibid.* at 258. This case was followed in *Campbell Seafoods Ltd v Brodrene Gram A/S*, unreported, High Court, Costello J., July 21, 1994.

[21] *SEE Company Ltd v Public Lighting Services Ltd and Petit Jean (UK) Ltd* [1987] I.L.R.M. 255; *Campbell Seafoods Ltd v Brodrene Gram A/S*, unreported, High Court, Costello J., July 21, 1994; *Rayan Restaurant Ltd v Julies Company Restaurant Ltd* [2005] I.E.H.C. 137, unreported, High Court, Budd J., April 18, 2005.

[22] [1987] I.R. 628.

[23] *ibid.* at 631.

[24] Browne-Wilkinson V.C. in *Porzelack K.G. v Porzelack (UK)* [1987] 1 W.L.R. 420.

[25] [1992] 2 I.R. 57.

"Section 390 of the Act of 1963 expressly envisages that an impecunious plaintiff company may be required to give security for costs and it may well be that in many cases this will mean the end of the action, unless someone other than the company itself is prepared to put up the security. To refrain from granting an order for security, save in the exceptional circumstances already referred to, simply because it might have the effect of stifling the plaintiff companies' actions would be to render the section nugatory."[26]

11–12   The justification for s.390 is that it avoids abuse of the corporate form to avoid costs orders. Thus, in *Harrington v JVC*,[27] O'Hanlon J. referred approvingly to the judgment of Megarry V.C. in *Pearson v Naydler*[28] where he noted that:

"A man may bring into being as many limited companies as he wishes, with the privilege of limited liability; and s 447 provides some protection for the community against litigious abuses by artificial persons manipulated by natural persons. One should be slow to whittle away this protection as one should be to whittle away a natural person's right to litigate despite poverty."[29]

11–13   In *Lismore Homes*,[30] Murphy J., in the Supreme Court, emphasised that the section applies only to limited liability companies which have various rights and privileges associated with that limited liability and must accept some of the consequential burdens.[31] The existence or otherwise of a potential injustice under the section is a matter which is considered by the court when deciding as to whether or not to make an order for security for costs in the first place.

11–14   One interesting aspect of the Irish case law is that there appears to be no discretion in relation to the amount that must be fixed as security for costs under s.390. This is in contrast to the interpretation of s.447 of the Companies Act 1948 in the United Kingdom, which was disapproved of by Murphy J. in *Lismore Homes*:

"I find myself in disagreement with the line of authorities which has grown up in the neighbouring jurisdiction in relation to the proper interpretation and application of what is a statutory provision identical to our own. No matter what argument is made in relation to justice or fairness in the United Kingdom or the constitutional right of access to the courts in this jurisdiction, I think that the plain meaning of the words is clear. If the court is satisfied that a limited company, which is a plaintiff

---

[26] *ibid.* at 63.
[27] Unreported, High Court, O'Hanlon J., March 16, 1995.
[28] [1977] 1 W.L.R. 899.
[29] *ibid.* at 904.
[30] [2001] 3 I.R. 536.
[31] *ibid.* at 546–547.

in an action, will be unable to pay the costs of the defendant if successful in his defence, the court may in its discretion require security to be given. If it so decides, then the security to be given is defined in the Act of 1963, as 'sufficient security to be given for those costs'."[32]

11–15 In *Framus Ltd v CRH Ltd*,[33] Herbert J. considered whether to require the plaintiff company to provide security for costs in the context of an application for an order of discovery. He found that such an order would not seriously impede the plaintiff's case, adding that it was thus "unnecessary to consider whether the Constitutional guarantee of access to the Courts applies to a body incorporated in the State".[34]

11–16 Earlier in his judgment, he considered whether a lack of means or assets alone could justify making an order for security for costs in the context of an application for discovery. He held that such a finding:

"would amount to a discrimination on the basis of means alone as regards access to a valuable interlocutory remedy. Such a discrimination would be invidious and unjust and in the case of a natural person at least might be unconstitutional as an infringement of such person's right of access to the Courts as guaranteed by the Constitution of Ireland."[35]

11–17 In *Irish Press Plc v EM Warburg Pincus & Co. International Ltd*,[36] McGuinness J., referring to *SEE Co. Ltd v Public Lighting Services*, stated:

"While I accept, as was submitted by Counsel for the defendants in this case, that the constitutional right of access to the courts is primarily available to natural persons and that the courts must be careful not to render s.390 nugatory, it seems to me that in his judgment the learned McCarthy J is expressing the general tenor of judgments in this Court and in the Supreme Court in regard to security for costs under s.390 of the Companies Act, 1963."[37]

11–18 The foregoing cases do not make it entirely clear whether companies enjoy a constitutionally protected right of access to the courts. In the context of the European Convention on Human Rights, it has been argued that s.390 constitutes an unjustified interference with corporate property rights. In *Superwood Holdings Plc v Ireland*,[38] Murphy J., in the High Court, considered the compatibility of s.390 with the European Convention on Human Rights. Noting that the State was entitled to regulate the right to private property under

---

[32] *ibid.* at 546.
[33] [2004] 2 I.R. 20.
[34] [2002] I.E.H.C. 113 at [27]. The plaintiff had not in fact sought to argue that it had such a right.
[35] [2002] I.E.H.C. 113 at [14].
[36] [1997] 2 I.L.R.M. 263.
[37] *ibid.* at 274.
[38] [2005] I.E.H.C. 232, unreported, High Court, Murphy J., July 5, 2005.

Art.1 of Protocol 1, he stated that:

> "Given the balance between the rights of plaintiffs and of defendants
> and the rights of limited liability companies and their responsibility in
> providing security for costs as identified by Murphy J. in Lismore Homes
> v. Bank of Ireland [2001] 3 I.R. 536, the State is entitled to distinguish
> between corporate bodies and individual persons and, in exceptional
> cases, to impose an obligation to give security for costs in circumstances
> of, inter alia, protracted, unsuccessful litigation."

11–19   As far as Art.14 was concerned, he seemed to take the view that the
discrimination on the ground that a party was a company was not a forbidden
ground under Art.14.[39] He noted:

> "The argument in Lismore is clear: companies enjoy privileges not
> available to individual persons. It is logical that the principle of limited
> liability demands that companies, as distinct from individual persons,
> who sue, may be required to give security for the reasonable costs of
> potentially successful defendants."

11–20   He went on to refer to the decision of the European Court of Human
Rights ("ECHR") in *Tolstoy v UK*,[40] where it was held that:

> "Like the Government and the Commission, the court is unable to share
> the applicant's view that the security for costs order impaired the very
> essence of his right of access to court and was disproportionate for the
> purposes of article 6 …".[41]

11–21   As indicated in *Tolstoy*, the right of access to the courts is protected
under Art.6 of the Convention. This general right has been relied upon by
corporate applicants.[42] The impact of the European Convention on Human
Rights on the more specific question of security for costs has been considered
in the English courts.[43] In *Classic Catering Ltd v Donnington Park Leisure
Ltd*,[44] Judge Weeks noted as follows:

> "Assuming without deciding that art 6 of the convention extends to

---

[39] *ibid.*:
> "Article 14 of the Convention, relied on by Superwood, prohibits 'discrimination
> on any ground such as sex, race, colour, language, religion, political or other opinion,
> national or social origin, association with a national minority, property, birth or
> other status.' On the ejusdem generis rule 'other status' cannot include any general
> grounds other than those referred to."

[40] [1995] 20 E.H.R.R. 442.

[41] *ibid.* at [62].

[42] *National & Provincial, Leeds & Yorkshire Building Societies v UK* App. No. 21319/93
(1995).

[43] *Nasser v United Bank of Kuwait* [2002] 1 All E.R. 401, [2002] 1 W.L.R. 1868.

[44] [2001] 1 B.C.L.C. 537—decided prior to the CA ruling in *Nasser v United Bank of
Kuwait* [2002] 1 All E.R. 401, [2002] 1 W.L.R. 1868.

companies as well as individuals, it does not seem to me to follow from the right to a fair trial that the possibility, or even the probability, of stifling is in itself a decisive factor in considering whether or not to order security. In my judgment, it is one of the factors to be taken into consideration."[45]

11–22   Subsequent cases have tended to assume that companies may rely on the Convention in this context.[46]

THE NATURE OF THE RIGHTS AND THEIR APPLICATION TO THE COMPANY

11–23   Both the right to litigate and the right of access to the courts can be seen as aspects of the system for the administration of justice envisaged in Art.34. In *Macauley v Minister for Posts and Telegraphs*,[47] Kenny J. held that there was a right, under Art.40.3, to have recourse to the High Court to defend and vindicate a legal right. He found that this right existed at common law and derived from the breadth of the High Court's jurisdiction under Art.34.3.1.[48] Similarly, in *Byrne v Ireland*,[49] Budd J. based the right of the citizen to sue the State in tort on both Arts 40.3 and 34. In a number of other cases,[50] however, the right to litigate has been described as an aspect of the property rights of the citizen.

11–24   In *Tuohy v Courtney*, the Supreme Court held that in that case, which concerned a constitutional challenge to s.11 of the Statute of Limitations 1957, the classification of the right to litigate as a personal or property right—or both—would make no material difference to the constitutional protection that would apply to it—the distinction may, however, make a difference to the application of the right to the company. If the right to litigate is seen as a corollary of Art.34, then there is no reason why it should not apply to the company. This is because, thus conceived, the right to litigate can be seen as an aspect of the institutional arrangements envisaged by the Constitution. Its vindication, as with the right of access to the courts, can be seen as promoting the utility-based value of maintaining the rule of law regardless of the individual beneficiary in a given case.

---

[45] *cf. Plus Group Ltd v Pyke* [2002] EWCA Civ 147.
[46] *Vedatech Corporation v Crystal Decisions (UK) Ltd* [2002] EWCA Civ 356; *Vadetech Corporation v Seagate Software Group Ltd* [2001] EWCA Civ 1924, although see the judgment of Ward L.J. at [34], where he reserved his opinion as to the application of the *Nasser* case—which set out the appropriate test post-incorporation of the Convention—to corporate plaintiffs.
[47] [1966] I.R. 345.
[48] *cf. Leopardstown Club Ltd v Templeville Developments Ltd* [2006] I.E.H.C. 133.
[49] [1972] I.R. 241.
[50] *O'Brien v Keogh* [1972] I.R. 144; *O'Brien v Manufacturing Engineering Co.* [1973] I.R. 334, (1974) 108 I.L.T.R. 105; *Brady v Donegal County Council* [1989] I.L.R.M. 282; *Campbell v Ward* [1981] I.L.R.M. 60. Although see *Moynihan v Greensmyth* [1977] I.R. 55. See discussion in Hogan and Whyte, *op.cit.* at pp.1448–1449. See also Osborough, (1979–1980) D.U.L.J. 101.

CHAPTER 12

THE RIGHT TO JUSTICE AND FAIR PROCEDURES

INTRODUCTION

12–01 This chapter considers the extent to which a company may rely on the constitutional right to justice and fair procedures in the context of civil proceedings.[1] That the Constitution embodies a general requirement of justice and fair procedures was first indicated by the judgment of Walsh J. in *McDonald v Bord na gCon*,[2] where he stated that:

> "[I]n the context of the Constitution natural justice might be more appropriately termed constitutional justice and must be understood to import more than the two well-established principles that no man shall be judge in his own cause and *audi alteram partem*."[3]

12–02 The same judge stated in *East Donegal Cooperative Ltd v Att.-Gen.*,[4] in the context of the presumption of constitutionality, that procedures provided for by legislation were intended by the Oireachtas to be conducted "in accordance with the principles of constitutional justice".[5]

12–03 In *Glover v BLN Ltd*,[6] Walsh J. explained what was meant by the idea of constitutional justice in more detail:

> "[T]he dictates of constitutional justice require that statutes, regulations or agreements setting up machinery for taking decisions which may affect rights or impose liabilities should be construed as providing for fair procedures."[7]

12–04 No catalogue of the "dictates" of constitutional justice is available in

---

[1] The right to justice and fair procedures in the context of criminal proceedings is explored in Part II, above.
[2] [1965] I.R. 217, (1965) 100 I.L.T.R. 89. See Casey, "Natural Justice and Constitutional Justice—the Policeman's Lot Improved" (1970–1980) 2 D.U.L.J. 95 and Hogan, "Natural and Constitutional Justice: *Adieu* to *Laissez-Faire*" (1984) 19 Ir. Jur. (New Series) 309.
[3] [1965] I.R. 217 at 242, (1965) 100 I.L.T.R. 89 at 102.
[4] [1970] I.R. 317, (1970) 104 I.L.T.R. 81.
[5] [1970] I.R. 317 at 341, (1970) 104 I.L.T.R. 81 at 92.
[6] [1973] I.R. 388.
[7] *ibid.* at 425.

the Irish cases, although in *S. v S.*,[8] O'Hanlon J. referred to Arts 34.1, 34.3.1, 38.1 and 40.3 and stated that:

> "[T]he combined effect of [these] constitutional provisions appears ... to guarantee ... something equivalent to the concept of 'due process' under the American Constitution in relation to causes and controversies litigated before the Court."[9]

12–05   In *McDonald*, Walsh J. had stated that constitutional justice entailed more than the rules *audi alteram partem* and *nemo iudex in causa sua* and it has been applied to a number of cases in a manner broader than the limits of those two maxims.[10]

12–06   The requirements of constitutional justice, insofar as they are implicated by the various grounds for judicial review, have been applied in cases involving companies without any reference being made to the corporate nature of the applicant.[11]

United States

12–07   The requirement of fair procedures under the Due Process Clause of the Fourteenth Amendment to the United States Constitution has also been held to be applicable to corporations. In *Honda Motor Co. Ltd v Oberg*,[12] a corporation was successful in arguing that the Court of Appeals of Oregon had violated the due process clause by refusing to judicially review an award of punitive damages.[13] Generally speaking, however, the due process clause has been relied upon to protect corporate property rights.[14]

European Convention on Human Rights

12–08   Under the European Convention on Human Rights, the requirements of fair procedures in the context of civil proceedings are set out in Art.6(1) which provides in relevant part:

---

[8]   [1983] I.R. 68.

[9]   *ibid.* at 79.

[10]   See *Haughey v Moriarty* [1999] 3 I.R. 1, where the Supreme Court overturned a High Court decision refusing to quash orders for discovery that had been made by the Moriarty Tribunal. See also *S. v S.* [1983] I.R. 68, where a common law rule of evidence was deemed contrary to the precepts of constitutional justice and *Maguire v Ardagh* [2002] 2 I.R. 385, which elevated the right of cross-examination to a constitutional requirement.

[11]   *International Fishing Vessels Ltd v Minister for the Marine (No.1)* [1989] I.R. 149; *Eircell Ltd v Leitrim County Council* [2000] 1 I.R. 479, [2000] 2 I.L.R.M. 81; *Spin Communications Ltd v IRTC* [2001] I.E.S.C. 12; *Manning v Benson and Hedges Ltd* [2004] 3 I.R. 556.

[12]   512 U.S. 415 (1994).

[13]   *cf. TXO Production Corporation v Alliance Resources Corporation* 509 U.S. 443 (1993), where an award of punitive damages was held not to violate the due process clause.

[14]   See discussion above, in Chap.8 at paras 8–38 to 8–45.

"In the determination of his civil rights and obligations ... everyone is entitled to a fair and public hearing within a reasonable time by an independent and impartial tribunal established by law. Judgment shall be pronounced publicly ...".

12–09   The right to an impartial and independent tribunal was relied upon by corporate applicants in *Sovtransavto Holding v Ukraine*[15] and *Immobiliare Saffi v Italy*.[16] The latter case implicitly accepted that the applicant was entitled to a hearing "within a reasonable time".

THE NATURE OF THE RIGHT AND ITS APPLICATION TO THE COMPANY

12–10   The status of the concept of constitutional justice appears to be twofold. It is implied by Art.34.1 and as such, is a constitutional requirement inherently connected to the judicial function and the administrative law doctrine of *ultra vires*. Thus, echoing the extract from *East Donegal Cooperative Ltd* reproduced in the introduction to this chapter, Costello P. held, in *McCormack v Garda Síochána Complaints Board*,[17] that:

> "It is now established as part of our constitutional and administrative law that the constitutional presumption that a statute enacted by the Oireachtas intended that proceedings, procedures, discretions and adjudications permitted, provided for, or prescribed by Acts of the Oireachtas are to be conducted in accordance with the principles of constitutional justice. It follows therefore that an administrative decision taken in breach of the principles of constitutional justice will be an ultra vires one and may be the subject of an order of *certiorari*. Constitutional justice imposes a constitutional duty on a decision-making authority to apply fair procedures in the exercise of its statutory powers and functions."[18]

12–11   This duty, it appears, is a correlative of an unenumerated right to justice and fair procedures under Art.40.3. Thus, in *Garvey v Ireland*,[19] O'Higgins C.J.[20] held that:

> "[B]y Article 40, s.3, there is guaranteed to every citizen whose rights may be affected by decisions taken by others the right to fair and just procedures. This means that under the Constitution powers cannot be exercised unjustly or unfairly."[21]

---

[15] (2004) 38 E.H.R.R. 44. See also *APB Ltd, APP and EAB v UK* (1998) 25 E.H.R.R. CD 141.
[16] (2000) 30 E.H.R.R. 756.
[17] [1997] 2 I.R. 489.
[18] *ibid*. at 499–500.
[19] [1980] I.R. 75.
[20] He was joined by Parke J.
[21] [1980] I.R. 75 at 97.

12–12 Griffin J., in the same case, said that "Article 40.3 of the Constitution ... has been held by this Court to be a guarantee of fair procedures".[22]

12–13 The right appears to perform a dual function. On the one hand, it can be instrumental in the vindication of the substantive rights of the citizen—such as their good name,[23] or right to earn a livelihood.[24] This function of the right is illustrated by the following extract from the judgement of O'Dálaigh C.J. in *Haughey, Re*[25]:

> "The provisions of Article 38.1 of the Constitution apply only to trials of criminal charges in accordance with Article 38; but in proceedings before any tribunal where a party to the proceedings is on risk of having his good name, or his person or property, or any of his personal rights jeopardised, the proceedings may be correctly classed as proceedings which may affect his rights, and in compliance with the Constitution, the State, either by its enactments or through the Courts must outlaw any procedures which will restrict or prevent the party concerned from vindicating these rights."[26]

12–14 In this respect, it could only be relied upon by a company which had such an underlying constitutional right.

12–15 In any case, the close connection of the right with the judicial function and the *ultra vires* doctrine in administrative law, suggests that it performs an important institutional function by ensuring that the organs of the State act within competence. In this regard, it can be seen as a right which is based on utility and is, thus, appropriate for application to the company in all cases, regardless of any other substantive entitlements the company might enjoy under the Constitution.

12–16 That this is the correct approach is supported by the decision of the Supreme Court in *Eurofood IFSC Ltd, Re.*[27] In that case, Fennelly J. referred to the principles of fair procedures enunciated by Gannon J. in *Healy v Donoghue*,[28] as follows:

> "Among the natural rights of an individual whose conduct is impugned and whose freedom is put in jeopardy are the rights to be adequately informed of the nature and substance of the accusation, to have the matter tried in his presence by an impartial and independent court or arbitrator,

---

[22] *ibid*. at 108.
[23] *Haughey, Re* [1971] I.R. 217.
[24] *Glover v BLN Ltd* [1973] I.R. 388.
[25] [1971] I.R. 217.
[26] *ibid*. at 264. This was approved by Hamilton C.J. in *Haughey v Moriarty* [1999] 3 I.R. 1 at 76.
[27] [2004] 4 I.R. 370.
[28] [1976] I.R. 325.

to hear and test by examination the evidence offered by or on behalf of his accuser, to be allowed to give or call evidence in his defence, and to be heard in argument or submission before judgment be given. By mentioning these I am not to be taken as giving a complete summary, or as excluding other rights such as the right to reasonable expedition and the right to have an opportunity for preparation of the defence."[29]

12–17   Fennelly J., delivering the unanimous decision of the court in *Eurofood*, stated of the above principles that: "In an appropriate case, they may be invoked both by bodies corporate and by non-citizens."[30]

12–18   Indeed, in many cases, companies have successfully relied on the right to fair procedures without any objection being taken to their entitlement to that constitutional guarantee. For example, in *Manning v Benson and Hedges Ltd*,[31] Finlay-Geoghegan J. allowed an application by a number of corporate defendants to dismiss a claim for want of prosecution. The defendants sought to rely on their right to fair procedures under the Constitution and invoked both Arts 34 and 40.3 of the Constitution. Finlay-Geoghegan J. referred to the jurisdiction to dismiss for want of prosecution as having two constitutional bases, noting that:

> "Whilst in some of the cases the judgments have referred to matters under both these headings, they appear to be potentially separate grounds upon which the inherent jurisdiction to dismiss may be exercised."[32]

12–19   In *Ryanair v Labour Court*,[33] Hanna J. considered an application for judicial review brought by a company against a decision of the Labour Court. He posed the question:

> "[W]ere the procedures of the Labour Court so flawed or inadequate and the proceedings conducted before and by it so defective as to amount to an injustice and a breach of the applicant's legal and constitutional rights?"

12–20   He went on to find that: "The applicant has not satisfied me that there has been any injustice or want of fairness or compromise of the applicant's legal and constitutional rights."

12–21   That the right to fair procedures and justice is applicable to the company in civil proceedings is perhaps unsurprising given the similar conclusion reached in respect of criminal proceedings in Part II. An additional feature of the right in civil proceedings, however, is in respect of the duties it might impose on a company.

---

[29] [1976] I.R. 325 at 335; approved by Fennelly J. in *Eurofood IFSC Ltd, Re* [2004] 4 I.R. 370 at 419.
[30] [2004] 4 I.R. 370 at 419.
[31] [2004] 3 I.R. 556.
[32] *ibid*. at 569.
[33] [2005] I.E.H.C. 330.

The Horizontal Application of the Right— Constitutional Duties of the Company

12–22   In *Glover v BLN Ltd*,[34] the defendant company had failed to give the plaintiff—their employee—the opportunity to answer complaints against him. Walsh J., in the Supreme Court, found that this was a breach of the constitutional requirements of fair procedures.[35] That this constitutional duty was applicable horizontally was reiterated in *Tierney v An Post*.[36] In that case, which concerned disciplinary proceedings leading to the dismissal of the plaintiff from the position of postmaster, Keane J. stated that:

> "The statement of the law [in *Glover*] is not confined to contracts of service. It is in accordance with the general principle laid down in *Meskell v Coras Iompair Éireann* [1973] IR 121 that constitutional rights may be protected or enforced in proceedings between private citizens and not merely in proceedings against the State."[37]

12–23   The above employment cases[38] demonstrate that the company has a constitutional duty to observe fair procedures when dealing with individuals. The general idea of imposing constitutional duties on the company as a means of regulation was canvassed by Adolf Berle as long ago as 1952.[39] Berle was writing in the context of the United States Constitution which is vertically applicable[40] and his concern was thus to justify imposing constitutional duties on companies.[41] He did this by emphasising the state-like nature of the company, focusing on its economic power and the fact that it existed by virtue of state concession.

12–24   The United States Supreme Court moved slightly away from the strictly vertical application of constitutional rights in *Bivens v Six Unknown Named Agents of Federal Bureau of Narcotics*[42] where it recognised a limited tort of abuse of constitutional authority. In a subsequent case, *Correctional Services*

---

[34] [1973] I.R. 388.

[35] For the view that the case does not involve the horizontal application of the Constitution, see Forde, *Company Law* (3rd edn, Round Hall Sweet & Maxwell, 1999), at p.89.

[36] [2000] 1 I.R. 536, [2000] 2 I.L.R.M. 214.

[37] [2000] 1 I.R. 536 at 547, [2000] 2 I.L.R.M. 214 at 225.

[38] See also *Maher v Irish Permanent Plc* [1998] 4 I.R. 302; *Carroll v Bus Atha Cliath* [2005] 4 I.R. 184.

[39] Berle, "Constitutional Limitations on Corporate Activity—Protection of Personal Rights from Invasion through Economic Power" (1952) 100 U.Pa.L.Rev. 933.

[40] *i.e.* it applies only between the State and private parties, not between private parties. See *Civil Rights Cases* (1833) 109 U.S. 3. *Cf. Bivens v Six Unknown Named Agents of Federal Bureau of Narcotics* 403 U.S. 388 (1971), which provides for a limited tort of abuse of constitutional authority. But see *Correctional Services Corporation v Malesko* 534 U.S. 61 (2001), where the US Supreme Court refused to apply *Bivens* to a private corporation.

[41] For a modern approach to companies, human rights duties, see Wood and Scharffs, "The Applicability of Human Rights Standards to Private Corporations: An American Perspective" (2002) 50 Am.J.Comp.L. 531.

[42] 403 U.S. 388 (1971).

Corp v Malesko,[43] however, the court refused to apply *Bivens* to a private corporation acting on behalf of the federal government and there seems to be no scope for imposing constitutional duties on business corporations even in that limited context.

12–25   The Irish Constitution is already horizontally applicable,[44] and it is well established that:

> "[I]f one citizen has a right under the Constitution there exists a correlative duty on the part of other citizens to respect that right and not to interfere with it."[45]

12–26   Thus, there is no question but that companies owe constitutional rights to individuals.[46] The converse, however, has never been tested—*i.e.* whether individuals owe constitutional duties to companies.

12–27   There is a good argument to the effect that the horizontal application of the right to fair procedures should remain a one-sided arrangement. Allowing a company to rely on the right as against the State furthers the utility value of institutional integrity. Such an approach is politically aligned to the liberal tenet that "exercises of state power require special justification".[47] Allowing a company to rely on the right as against an individual, however, performs no such function.

12–28   This Part has focused on the position of the company under Art.40.3 of the Irish Constitution. It has demonstrated the utility values underlying rights such as freedom of expression, property and the unenumerated rights of access to the courts and fair procedures. An analysis of these constitutional guarantees using the autonomy/utility dichotomy introduced in Chapter 3 indicates that, save for the right to a good name, their application to the company is appropriate.

12–29   Chapter 8 of this Part assessed the extent to which companies enjoy constitutionally guaranteed property rights under the Irish Constitution. It was seen that the Irish case law on this point is conflicting. The approaches taken under the United States Constitution and the European Convention on Human Rights were analysed before returning to consider in detail the way in which this matter was dealt with in the most recent Irish authority. It was concluded

---

[43] 534 U.S. 61 (2001).

[44] *i.e.* it applies between private parties as well as being vertically applicable. *Murtagh Properties Ltd v Cleary* [1972] I.R. 330; *Murphy v Stewart* [1973] I.R. 97; *McGrath v Maynooth College* [1979] I.L.R.M. 166; *Parsons v Kavanagh* [1990] I.L.R.M. 560.

[45] Budd J. in *Educational Co. of Ireland Ltd v Fitzpatrick (No.2)* [1961] I.R. 345 at 368.

[46] See *Pierce v The Dublin Cemeteries Committee* [2006] I.E.H.C. 182, where the plaintiff was held to have *locus standi* to rely upon his constitutional right to earn a livelihood as against the defendant statutory corporation.

[47] Bamforth, "The Public Law–Private Law Distinction: A Comparative and Philosophical Approach" in *Administrative Law Facing the Future: Old Constraints and New Horizons* (Leyland and Woods eds, Blackstone Press, 1997), at p.139.

that the latter approach, which relies on an aggregate theory of the company, is inappropriate and a number of criticisms were made in relation to it. The chapter concluded by applying the utility/autonomy analysis to Arts 43 and 40.3.

12–30 Chapter 9 concerned freedom of expression and it revealed the way in which a dichotomised analysis of the Constitution can explain differing levels of protection for the company as opposed to the individual. As corporate constitutional protection is premised on the value of utility, it is generally weaker than that accorded to the individual. The exception to this is those rare cases where individual constitutional protection is also premised on utility. This equality of constitutional protection has been accorded to companies in a number of jurisdictions in the context of commercial expression. Generally, however, the fact that an individual, rather than a company, is asserting freedom of expression will implicate the autonomy values underlying the guarantee as well as the utility values that apply where a company makes such a claim. It is for this reason that a company's constitutional claim to freedom of expression is generally weaker than that of an individual.

12–31 Chapter 10 considered the application of the right to a good name to the company. It found that, while the company is arguably capable of enjoying a "good name", the value underlying this constitutional guarantee appears to be solely autonomy based. It concludes that the company is thus restricted to private law remedies to vindicate its "good name".

12–32 Chapters 11 and 12 assessed the applicability of the unenumerated rights of access to the courts and fair procedures to the company. It found that the right of access to the courts was appropriate for corporate application as it can be seen as a right which is bound up with the institutional arrangements envisaged in the Constitution. The same was found to be true of the right to fair procedures. While this right originated in natural law, its current constitutional status appears to be due to its importance to the rule of law. Thus, as was the case with many of the guarantees under Art.38.1, the right to fair procedures is prima facie applicable to the company. As the right can also be instrumental in the vindication of substantive autonomy-based rights, however, its application to the company is neither as broad nor as strong as that in relation to the individual.

12–33 A further matter which arose in Chapter 12 was the horizontal application of the company. As private parties owe each other constitutional duties, the question of how the company fits into this arises. It has already been held that the company owes constitutional duties to individuals. This chapter concluded that individuals should not be held to owe constitutional duties to the company and explained this finding in terms of the utility/autonomy framework.

PART IV

GUARANTEES NOT APPLICABLE TO THE COMPANY UNDER BUNREACHT NA HÉIREANN

CHAPTER 13

GUARANTEES OF NO RELEVANCE TO THE COMPANY

13–01 The Irish Constitution contains a number of guarantees which no corporate litigant could rely on.[1] Some of these are contained in, or implied by, Art.40.3 which reads as follows:

> "1   The State guarantees in its laws to respect, and, as far as practicable, by its laws to defend and vindicate the personal rights of the citizen.
>
> 2   The State shall, in particular, by its laws protect as best it may from unjust attack and, in the case of injustice done, vindicate the life, person, good name, and property rights of every citizen."

13–02 Dealing first with the rights specified in Art.40.3.2, it appears that only two of the four rights mentioned have any potential application to the company—the right to a good name and property rights. These have been dealt with in other chapters.[2] The right to life as envisaged under the Irish Constitution clearly has no relevance to the company. While it might be possible to imagine a definition of "life" susceptible to "death" which would include the company,[3] the right to life enshrined in Art.40.3 has clearly been interpreted as applying to human life only.[4] The company is not capable of "living" in the sense envisaged by the Constitution and so this protection is simply irrelevant to it.

13–03 As for the reference to the protection and vindication of "the person", this has not received much attention in the case law. It appears that it may have some connection with the moral character of individuals.[5] In any event, it is

---

[1]   At least, not on its own behalf. The position of companies litigating to vindicate the constitutional rights of individuals is outside the scope of this book. See Introduction, above at n.4.

[2]   Chaps 10 and 8, respectively.

[3]   *e.g.* the forced removal from the Companies Register or the revocation of a corporate charter could be considered interferences with a putative corporate "right to life". *Cf* Brewer J., dissenting, in *Hale v Henkel* 201 U.S. 43 at 83–84. The quotation is reproduced above at para.5–31.

[4]   *Ryan v Att.-Gen.* [1965] I.R. 294; *McGee v Att.-Gen.* [1974] I.R. 284, (1975) 109 I.L.T.R. 29; *Burke v Central Independent Television Plc* [1994] 2 I.R. 61, [1994] 2 I.L.R.M. 161; *DPP v Delaney* [1997] 3 I.R. 453, [1998] 1 I.L.R.M. 507.

[5]   *JG v Governor of Mountjoy Prison* [1991] 1 I.R. 373. See Hogan and Whyte, *Kelly: The Irish Constitution* (4th edn, Lexis-Nexis Butterworths, 2003), at pp.1403–1404.

difficult to imagine an interpretation of this guarantee that could be relied upon by a company.

13–04 The courts have interpreted Art.40.3.1 as guaranteeing certain unenumerated rights.[6] While some of these may be applicable to the company,[7] a number of them are clearly irrelevant to the corporate person. These rights include those such as the right to bodily integrity,[8] the right to marital privacy,[9] the right to individual privacy,[10] the right of autonomy,[11] the right to travel within and outside the state,[12] rights relating to the family,[13] the right to marry,[14] the right to procreate[15] and the right to dignity.[16]

13–05 Article 40.4 contains a number of guarantees which are also clearly inapplicable to the company as they can only ever concern a natural person. These include the right to personal liberty in Art.40.4.1 and the habeas corpus procedures set out in Art.40.4.2–40.4.4.

---

[6] *Ryan v Att.-Gen.* [1965] I.R. 294. See Hogan and Whyte, *op.cit.* at pp.1415–1485.

[7] See Chaps 11 and 12.

[8] *Ryan v Att.-Gen.* [1965] I.R. 294.

[9] *McGee v Att.-Gen.* [1974] I.R. 284, (1975) 109 I.L.T.R. 29.

[10] *Kennedy v Ireland* [1987] I.R. 587, [1988] I.L.R.M. 472. *Cf. Caldwell v Mahon* [2006] I.E.H.C. 86, Hanna J. approving the discussion of privacy in the decision of Ackerman J. in *Bernstein v Bester* (1996) 4 BCLR (South Africa) 449. Although see the discussion of Art.40.5, below, Chap 15.

[11] *A Ward of Court (No.2), Re* [1996] 2 I.R. 79, [1995] 2 I.L.R.M. 401.

[12] *M v Att.-Gen.* [1979] I.R. 73.

[13] Arts 41 and 40.3 guarantee certain rights relating to the family.

[14] This appears to be guaranteed under Arts 41 and 40.3. See *Ryan v Att.-Gen.* [1965] I.R. 294; *McGee v Att.-Gen.* [1974] I.R. 284, (1975) 109 I.L.T.R. 29. See also Hogan and Whyte, *op.cit.* at pp.1468–1469.

[15] *Murray v Ireland* [1985] I.R. 532, [1985] I.L.R.M. 542.

[16] *A Ward of Court (No.2), Re* [1996] 2 I.R. 79, [1995] 2 I.L.R.M. 401.

CHAPTER 14

COMPANIES AND EQUALITY
BEFORE THE LAW

INTRODUCTION

14–01 This chapter focuses on the guarantee of equality before the law under Art.40.1 of the Irish Constitution and assesses how this fits into the utility/autonomy structure for analysing corporate constitutional protection. It considers whether the extension of a constitutional guarantee of equality to the company could serve any utilitarian purpose. Jurisprudence interpreting the equivalent guarantees[1] under the United States Constitution, the EC Treaty and the European Convention on Human Rights is used as a point of comparison. Paragraphs 14–02 to 14–09 consider the Irish constitutional guarantee and the case law which indicates that companies may not rely on it. Paragraphs 14–12 to 14–15 explore the extent to which companies enjoy specific equality rights at a supra-constitutional level under the EC Treaty. Paragraphs 14–16 to 14–38 examine the position of the company under the equal protection clause of the Fourteenth Amendment of the United States Constitution and paras 14–39 to 14–42 examine the company under Art.14 of the European Convention on Human Rights. Paragraphs 14–43 to 14–61 return again to the Irish equality guarantee and analyse the values that underlie it and why it is inapplicable to the company.

IRELAND

14–02 Article 40.1 of the Constitution reads as follows:

"All citizens shall, as human persons, be held equal before the law.
This shall not be held to mean that the State shall not in its enactments have due regard to differences of capacity, physical and moral, and of social function."

14–03 It must be stated frankly from the outset that the text of the guarantee does not bode well for the corporate litigant. The reference to "citizens" may

---

[1] This is not to say that the guarantees are directly equivalent. In fact, their substantive content is quite different.

not, in and of itself, exclude the company from protection.[2] It is the phrase "as human persons" and its interpretation in the case law that presents the greater difficulty. The emphasis by the courts on this phrase has restricted the application of Art.40.1 greatly and the jurisprudence in relation to this equality guarantee has been described as "remarkably underdeveloped".[3]

Can the guarantee ever be invoked by a company?

14–04 There have been a number of cases in which it has been indicated that corporate persons cannot rely on Art.40.1. In *Macauley v Minister for Posts and Telegraphs*,[4] the plaintiff challenged s.2 of the Ministers and Secretaries Act 1924 which required the *fiat* of the Attorney-General to sue a Minister. The plaintiff argued that, as the Minister would not require such a *fiat* in order to sue an ordinary citizen, the legislation breached the guarantee of equality before the law. Kenny J. rejected this argument, stating that:

> "The guarantee in the Constitution of equality before the law relates to the position of the citizen as a human person. The fiat is required only when a Minister is being sued as a Minister, not when he is being sued as a human person. The Act of 1924 deals with actions taken against a Minister as a corporation sole ... It follows, I think, that the necessity ... to get the fiat is not an infringement of the guarantee."[5]

14–05 This case indicates that the guarantee of equality applies only as between human persons and that it applies only to those persons acting in that capacity.

14–06 A case which further supports the view that the corporate litigant cannot rely on Art.40.1 is *East Donegal Cooperative v Att.-Gen.*[6] In this case, a provision of the Livestock Marts Act 1967 was under challenge. This provision enabled the Minister for Agriculture to exempt from the Act's application "any particular business". The Supreme Court found that this was unconstitutional as it potentially discriminated between individuals. Another provision, which permitted a similar exemption for "businesses of any particular class or kind" was upheld. Walsh J. stated:

> "[T]his primarily does not involve the making of a distinction between citizens but rather permits the making of a distinction which would benefit or otherwise affect all businesses of the particular class or kind involved."[7]

---

[2] See discussion above at paras 2–12 to 2–22. See also *Iarnród Éireann v Ireland* [1996] 3 I.R. 321, [1995] 2 I.L.R.M. 161, discussed above at paras 8–19 to 8–26.
[3] Hogan and Whyte, *Kelly: The Irish Constitution* (4th edn, Lexis-Nexis Butterworths, 2003) at p.1324.
[4] [1966] I.R. 345.
[5] *ibid.* at 355.
[6] [1970] I.R. 317, (1970) 104 I.L.T.R. 81.
[7] [1970] I.R. 317 at 350, (1970) 104 I.L.T.R. 81 at 96.

14–07 While the above cases take a restrictive view of the class of persons to whom the constitutional guarantee applies, it was *Quinn's Supermarket v Att.-Gen.*[8] that explicitly sounded the death knell for the corporate litigant's entitlement to invoke Art.40.1. In this case, the Supreme Court was presented with a constitutional challenge to a ministerial order[9] which made it an offence to trade during certain hours while exempting shops selling kosher meat. The plaintiffs relied mainly on Art.44.2.3, which prohibits religious discrimination. In relation to their submissions on Art.40.1, Walsh J. stated:

> "It need scarcely be pointed out that under no possible construction of the constitutional guarantee could a body corporate or any entity but a human being be considered to be a human person for the purpose of this provision. In my view this provision has no bearing whatsoever upon the point to be considered in the present case, as no question of human equality or inequality arises. It is also quite clear that the provision cannot be invoked to support the terms of the Order of 1948 by reference to differences of capacity, physical or moral, and of social function."[10]

14–08 Similarly discouraging is the judgment by Kenny J. in *Abbey Films Ltd v Att.-Gen.*[11] The case raised the question of whether it was contrary to Art.40.1 to provide that a company could appear in court only by a solicitor, whereas a citizen could appear in person. Kenny J. stated:

> "Even if Article 40.1 were held to be applicable to a company (which the Court refrains from deciding), the nature of a company and its difference of capacity from that of an individual are such as would justify [the differing treatment]."[12]

14–09 In *Kerry Co-Operative Creameries Ltd v An Bord Bainne*,[13] Costello J. reserved his position on the question of a company relying on Art.40.1.[14]

Theorising a doctrine of corporate equality—some possibilities

14–10 Leaving aside the text of the Irish equality clause, there is a more fundamental difficulty with applying an equality guarantee to corporate persons. That difficulty is a conceptual one. How can we posit a theory of corporate equality?

---

[8] [1972] I.R. 1.

[9] Victuallers' Shops (Hours of Trading on Weekdays) (Dublin, Dun Laoghaire and Bray) Order 1948 (S.I. No. 175 of 1948).

[10] [1971] I.R. 1 at 14. See also *Cityview Press v An Chomhairle Oiliúna* [1980] I.R. 381, where McMahon J. doubted whether Art.40.1 had any bearing on a challenge to the imposition of different levies on different businesses [1980] I.R. 381 at 392. The matter was not brought up again in the Supreme Court.

[11] [1981] I.R. 158.

[12] *ibid.* at 172.

[13] [1990] I.L.R.M. 664.

[14] *ibid.* at 717.

14–11   Before considering the nature of the constitutional guarantee under Art.40.1, therefore, the prior question of the possibility of applying *any* equality guarantee to a company will be addressed. A brief examination of case law relating to the equality guarantees under the EC Treaty, the Fourteenth Amendment to the United States Constitution and the European Convention on Human Rights may shed some light on what a concept of corporate equality could mean. What follows explores two possibilities. First, it is possible to conceive of an equality guarantee which simply requires that all companies be treated equally in relation to other companies. Secondly, it is possible to conceive of a guarantee which requires that companies be treated equally to individuals.

CORPORATE EQUALITY UNDER THE EC TREATY—THE EUROPEAN COURT
OF JUSTICE AND FREEDOM OF ESTABLISHMENT

14–12   Title III of the EC Treaty is devoted to the fundamental freedoms of movement of persons, services and capital. It makes specific provision for the right of establishment in Chapter 2, which includes Arts 43 to 48. Article 43 provides as follows:

> "Within the framework of the provisions set out below, restrictions on the freedom of establishment of nationals of a Member State in the territory of another Member State shall be prohibited. Such prohibition shall also apply to restrictions on the setting-up of agencies, branches or subsidiaries by nationals of any Member State established in the territory of any Member State.
>
> Freedom of establishment shall include the right to take up and pursue activities as self-employed persons and to set up and manage undertakings, in particular companies or firms within the meaning of the second paragraph of Article 48, under the conditions laid down for its own nationals by the law of the country where such establishment is effected, subject to the provisions of the Chapter relating to capital."

14–13   Article 48 EC "places legal persons on the same footing as natural persons for the purpose of exercising that freedom"[15]:

> "Companies or firms formed in accordance with the law of a Member State and having their registered office, central administration or principal place of business within the Community shall, for the purposes of this Chapter, be treated in the same way as natural persons who are nationals of Member States.
>
> 'Companies or firms' means companies or firms constituted under civil or commercial law, including cooperative societies, and other legal

---

[15] Case C-140/03, *Commission v Hellenic Republic*, Opinion of Advocate General Ruiz-Jarabo Colomer at [5].

persons governed by public or private law, save for those which are non-profit-making."

14–14 Thus, companies which are "nationals" of other Member States enjoy some form of equality guarantee in this jurisdiction in that they cannot be discriminated against, in the context of freedom of establishment, under Art.43. The only forbidden basis for discrimination under this provision is the nationality of the company. This guarantee is enforceable in the Irish courts and as a rule of European community law, it is a guarantee with a supra-constitutional pedigree.[16]

14–15 These provisions of the EC Treaty perform a similar function to the equal protection clause of the Fourteenth Amendment to the United States Constitution considered in the next section, in that they promote inter-state commerce. As Articles of the EC Treaty, they are amenable to a utilitarian interpretation. As with all of the Articles promoting market integration, they are concerned with discrimination insofar as it prevents the attainment of this goal, rather than any impact such discrimination might have on the autonomy of the individual. Such an approach is appropriate in the context of the EC Treaty, which is essentially an economic constitution. Whether the same interpretation is appropriate in the context of a traditional national Constitution is questionable.

THE UNITED STATES

Introduction

14–16 The second paragraph of the Fourteenth Amendment[17] provides that:

> "No State shall make or enforce any law which shall abridge the privileges or immunities of citizens of the United States, nor shall any State deprive any person of life, liberty, or property, without due process of law, nor deny to any person within its jurisdiction the equal protection of the laws."[18]

---

[16] See Art.29.4.10 of the Irish Constitution.

[17] The full text of the Fourteenth Amendment reads as follows:

"All persons born or naturalized in the United States, and subject to the jurisdiction thereof, are citizens of the United States and of the State wherein they reside.

No State shall make or enforce any law which shall abridge the privileges or immunities of citizens of the United States, nor shall any State deprive any person of life, liberty, or property, without due process of law, nor deny to any person within its jurisdiction the equal protection of the laws."

The first paragraph reverses the Supreme Court's decision in *Scott v Sandford* 60 U.S. 393 (1857) to the effect that black people were not citizens of the states and could not sue in federal courts.

[18] For a general analysis of the case law relating to the equal protection clause, see Lundin, "Making Equal Protection Analysis Make Sense" (1999) 49 Syracuse L.Rev. 1191.

14–17 The Supreme Court held in *Bolling v Sharpe*[19] that the guarantee of equal protection of the laws is also applicable to the federal government by means of its incorporation into the due process clause of the Fifth Amendment.[20]

14–18 The Fourteenth Amendment, together with the Thirteenth[21] and Fifteenth[22] Amendments, was adopted to facilitate the abolition of slavery at the end of the American Civil War. In the *Slaughterhouse Cases*,[23] decided just four years after the adoption of the Fourteenth Amendment, Miller J. commented that the equal protection clause was enacted to protect former slaves.[24] He thus refused to accept that the clause had any application in the commercial context of the cases before him. This limitation on the contextual application of the clause was, however, shortlived.

Santa Clara and the equal protection clause

14–19 While the United States Supreme Court soon abandoned Miller J.'s approach and eschewed the contextual restrictions on the equal protection clause,[25] the fact that the clause refers to "persons" might have been thought to have presented a problem. This, however, was simply ignored. *Santa Clara County v Southern Pacific Railroad Co.*[26] presented the issue of whether California was barred by the equal protection clause from taxing corporate property differently from individual property. In a decision described as "puzzling and controversial",[27] Waite C.J. stated:

> "The court does not wish to hear argument on the question whether the provision in the Fourteenth Amendment to the Constitution, which forbids

---

[19] 347 U.S. 497 (1954).

[20] "The Fifth Amendment ... does not contain an equal protection clause as does the Fourteenth Amendment which applies only to the states. But the concepts of equal protection and due process, both stemming from our American ideal of fairness, are not mutually exclusive. The 'equal protection of the laws' is a more explicit safeguard of prohibited unfairness than 'due process of law,' and, therefore, we do not imply that the two are always interchangeable phrases. But, as this Court has recognized, discrimination may be so unjustifiable as to be violative of due process ...".
347 U.S. 497 (1954) at 499.

[21] This Amendment was adopted in 1865. It abolishes slavery.

[22] This Amendment was adopted in 1870. It provides for the right to vote regardless of "race, color, or previous condition of servitude".

[23] 83 U.S. (16 Wall.) 36 (1872) at 77–78. He also held that the privileges and immunities clause had not fundamentally altered the relationship between the federal government and the states, and his holding in relation to the equal protection clause must be seen in this light.

[24] 83 U.S. (16 Wall.) 36 (1872) at 81.

[25] See below at paras 14–24 to 14–38.

[26] 118 U.S. 394 (1886).

[27] Horowitz, "*Santa Clara* Revisited: The Development of Corporate Theory" in *Corporations and Society: Power and Responsibility* (Samuels and Miller eds, Greenwood Press, 1987), at p.13.

a State to deny to any person within its jurisdiction the equal protection of the laws, applies to the corporation. We are all of the opinion that it does."[28]

14–20 It should be noted that the Supreme Court never actually reached the constitutional issue in that case as the measures under attack were found to be in violation of California law. Thus, the statement that the equal protection clause applied to the company was *obiter*.[29] Later cases, however, cited the case as authority for that proposition and within a short period of time, the statement that the company could claim this constitutional protection became axiomatic.[30]

14–21 The decision failed to address the question of the intended beneficiaries of the clause and its availability to corporate persons appears to have been determined without any reflection. The court refused to hear oral argument on the matter and, thus, the report offers no insight into the thinking behind the decision. The written brief on behalf of the corporation, however, may shed some light on the reasoning behind Waite C.J.'s terse direction:

"Whatever may be the legal nature of a corporation as an artificial, metaphysical being, separate and distinct from the individual members, and whatever distinctions the common law makes, in carrying out the technical legal conception, between property of the corporation and that of the individual members, still in applying the fundamental guaranties of the constitution, and in thus protecting rights of property, *these metaphysical and technical notions must give way to the reality*. The truth cannot be evaded that, *for the purpose of protecting rights, the property of all business and trading corporations* IS *the property of the individual corporators*. A State depriving a business corporation of its property without due process of law, *does in fact deprive the individual corporators of their property*. In this sense, and within the scope of these grand safeguards of private rights, there is no real distinction between artificial persons or corporations, and natural persons."[31]

14–22 The dissenting judgment by Field J.[32] in the *Slaughterhouse Cases*

---

[28] 118 U.S. 394 (1886) at 396. There were a number of companion cases to *Santa Clara*: *San Mateo* 13 F 745; *Sacramento v Central Pacific Ry* 18 F 385; *California v Northern Ry* 18 F 385.

[29] It has been pointed out that the statement by Waite J. was *obiter*. Furthermore, the later citation of *Santa Clara* as authority for the application of the due process clause of the Fourteenth Amendment ignores the actual finding in that case. See Sherry, "States are People Too" (2000) 75 Notre Dame L.Rev. 1121 at 1124, where the author highlights this "sleight of hand".

[30] *Pembina Consolidated Mining Co. v Pennsylvania* 125 U.S. 181; *Ry v Mackey* 127 U.S. 205; *Ry v Herrick* 127 U.S. 210; *Ry v Beckwith* 129 U.S. 29; *Railroad Co. v Gibbes* 142 U.S. 386; *Road Co. v Sandford* 164 U.S. 578.

[31] Reproduced in Horowitz, *op.cit.* Emphasis in the original text.

[32] Joined by Chase C.J. and Bradley and Swayne JJ.

had foreshadowed this expansion of the equal protection clause to apply to the corporation. In his dissent, he espoused a much broader attitude towards the Fourteenth Amendment, reiterating his interpretation of the clause in an earlier case, *San Mateo*,[33] where, sitting on circuit, he had stated as follows:

> "Private corporations are, it is true, artificial persons, but ... they consist of aggregations of individuals united for some legitimate business ... It would be a most singular result if a constitutional provision intended for the protection of every person against partial and discriminating legislation by the states, should cease to exert such protection the moment the person becomes a member of a corporation ... On the contrary, we think that it is well established by numerous adjudications of the Supreme Court of the United States ... that whenever a provision of the constitution, or of a law, guarantees to persons the enjoyment of property ... the benefits of the provision extend to corporations, and that the court will always look beyond the name of the artificial being to the individuals whom it represents."[34]

14–23   This aggregate theory approach to corporate constitutional protection has already been criticised in Chapter 8.[35] One further point which arises in this chapter, however, is the way in which the early reliance on that theory led to the distortion of the equal protection clause. Before examining the way in which the United States Supreme Court has applied the equality guarantee to companies, a brief exploration of the historical and political context of the United States case law just discussed is apposite.

The historical context and the federalism debate

14–24   Any analysis of the early Supreme Court case law on the equal protection clause must be placed in the context of the court's nascent jurisprudence on the Fourteenth Amendment[36] at that time. In particular, *Santa Clara*, together with its companion cases, must be read as a significant departure from the court's holding in the *Slaughterhouse Cases*. At stake in that case was the extent to which the Fourteenth Amendment had changed the constitutional relationship between the federal government and the states. As has been pointed out:

> "Justice Miller's 'race theory' interpretation of the Fourteenth Amendment reinforced traditional fears of centralized power and was meant to produce as little change in the federal balance of power as possible."[37]

---

[33] 13 F 745.
[34] Extract from *San Mateo* 13F reproduced in Horowitz, *op.cit.* at p.17.
[35] Above at paras 8–51 to 8–59.
[36] Added to the Bill of Rights in 1868.
[37] Horowitz, *op.cit.* at p.16.

14–25 Indeed, the major legacy of the *Slaughterhouse Cases* was to render the privileges and immunities clause a "dead letter". Unlike the equal protection clause, it never recovered from this judicial emasculation and remains moribund to this day.[38] In any case, any potential that clause might have held for the corporate litigant was dashed by the Supreme Court in *Paul v Virginia*,[39] where it found that the company was not a "citizen" for the purposes of the privileges and immunities clause.[40]

14–26 One aspect of the case law relating to the application of the equal protection clause to the company which has no Irish analogue is its development to cover foreign corporations. Again, this jurisprudence must be analysed in the context of the balance between state sovereignty and federalism. In *Trustees of Dartmouth College v Woodward*,[41] almost 50 years before the adoption of the Fourteenth Amendment, the Supreme Court had held that:

> "A corporation is an artificial being, invisible, intangible, and existing only in contemplation of law. Being the mere creature of law, it possesses only those properties which the charter of its creation confers upon it, either expressly or as incidental to its very existence."[42]

14–27 This concession theory of the company reflected the reluctance of the United States Supreme Court to extend constitutional protection to corporate litigants in its earliest cases following the adoption of the Bill of Rights. By the 1870s, general incorporation laws were introduced and these undermined the rationale of the concession theory. Nonetheless, the Supreme Court continued to confine the company by means of the *ultra vires* doctrine up until the 1920s.[43] *Santa Clara* disrupted this pattern but the concession theory held fast for a longer time in the context of the equal protection clause when relied upon by foreign corporations.[44] In this regard, the case law can be seen as

---

[38] The clause has only been successfully invoked to strike down legislation on two occasions since the *Slaughterhouse Cases*. In *Colgate v Harvey* 296 U.S. 404 (1935) the clause was used to strike down state legislation, but that decision was overruled in *Madden v Kentucky* 309 U.S. 83 (1940). In 1999, the clause was briefly resuscitated in *Saenz v Roe* 526 U.S. 489 (1999), where the Supreme Court relied on it to invalidate a Californian law, but the case has not been cited in any subsequent decisions of the court. For a general overview of the current debate on the balance between federalism and state sovereignty in the US Supreme Court, see Westover, "Structural Interpretation and the New Federalism: Finding the Proper Balance Between State Sovereignty and Federal Supremacy" (2005) 88 Marq.L.Rev. 693.

[39] 75 U.S. (8 Wall.) 168 (1868).

[40] The court gave no reasons for that finding. For the argument that the privileges and immunities clause should be applied to foreign corporations, see Carpinello, "State Protective Legislation and Nonresident Corporations: the Privileges and Immunities Clause as a Treaty of Nondiscrimination" (1988) 73 Iowa L.Rev. 351.

[41] 17 U.S. (4 Wheat.) 518 (1819).

[42] *ibid.* at 636.

[43] Horowitz, *op.cit.* at p.26.

[44] The term "foreign" in this context refers to companies which are not resident in the state in which proceedings are brought. The term "alien" is used to refer to companies that are nonresident in the US. See Bungert, "Equal Protection for Foreign and Foreign

reaching a precarious compromise between federalism and state sovereignty. For as long as the legal recognition of companies was seen as being based solely on the concession of the state in which they were incorporated, the Supreme Court would not require the states to recognise corporations incorporated outside of their jurisdiction. Thus, despite the success of the corporate litigant in *Santa Clara*, the Supreme Court held later that term, in *Fire Association of Philadelphia v New York*,[45] that the equal protection clause did not apply in a situation where the laws of one state discriminated against a corporation from another state.

14–28   In *Pembina Consolidated Mining Co. v Pennsylvania*,[46] two years later, the Supreme Court significantly altered the balance of state/federal government relations by holding that the equal protection clause applied to foreign corporations.[47] The court held that:

> "Under the designation of person there is no doubt that a private corporation is included. Such corporations are merely associations of individuals united for a special purpose, and permitted to do business under a particular name, and have a succession of members without dissolution."[48]

14–29   In *Gulf C & SFR Co. v Ellis*,[49] Brewer J. considered the constitutionality of legislation which required railroad companies to pay the fees of those successfully suing them while preventing them from recovering attorney fees when unsuccessfully sued. He held that:

> "It is well settled that corporations are persons within the meaning of the fourteenth amendment ... The rights and securities guarantied to persons by that instrument cannot be disregarded in respect to these artificial entities called 'corporations' anymore than they can be in respect to the individuals who are the equitable owners of the property belonging to such corporations. A state has no more power to deny to corporations the equal protection of the law than it has to individual citizens."[50]

14–30   These cases made explicit the aggregate theory of the company that arguably motivated the *Santa Clara* and *San Mateo* decisions. The legacy of

---

Corporations: Towards Intermediate Scrutiny for a Quasi-Suspect Classification" (1994) 59 Mo.L.Rev. 569 at 575–576.

[45]   119 U.S. 110 (1886).

[46]   125 U.S. 181 (1888).

[47]   The Fourteenth Amendment requires that the beneficiaries of the guarantee be within the jurisdiction of the state in question, a requirement that raises particular difficulties for the corporate litigant. See Bungert, *op.cit.* at 602–606.

[48]   125 U.S. 181 (1888) at 189.

[49]   165 U.S. 150 (1897).

[50]   *ibid.* at 155. See also *Minneapolis & St Louis Ry v Beckwith* 129 U.S. 26 (1889); *Southern Ry v Greene* 216 U.S. 400 (1910).

these decisions was to open the door for the corporate annexation of the equal protection guarantee.

Applying the equal protection clause to foreign corporations—treating all companies alike

14–31 As noted above, the United States Supreme Court held that the Fourteenth Amendment required states to extend the equal protection of their laws to foreign companies. Many of the cases in this area concern the unequal taxation of foreign corporations under state law. In *Air-Way Electric Appliance Corp v Day*,[51] for example, the court invalidated a state law which taxed foreign corporations based on the number of no-par shares outstanding. Butler J. held that the classification in that case was unconstitutional:

> "It is clear that the mere number of authorized nonpar value shares is not a reasonable basis for the classification of foreign corporations for the purpose of determining the amount of such annual fees. Such a classification is not based on anything having relation to the purpose for which it is made ... The act has no tendency to produce equality; and it is of such a character that there is no reasonable presumption that substantial equality will result from its application."[52]

14–32 In *Metropolitan Life Insurance Co. v Ward*,[53] the court considered a challenge to an Alabama statute which taxed out-of-state insurance companies at a higher rate than domestic ones. Alabama attempted to justify this difference of treatment on the basis that its purpose was to protect domestic insurers from competition. The court held that that purpose was "purely and completely discriminatory, designed only to favour domestic industry within the State, no matter what the cost to foreign corporations also seeking to do business there".[54]

14–33 Taxation measures are not the only way in which states attempt to discriminate between companies. *Northeastern Banking Corp v Board of Governors of the Federal Reserve System*[55] concerned the constitutionality of regional banking laws which allowed for the acquisition by out-of-state banking holding companies of banks in Connecticut and Massachusetts, provided that the home state of the acquiring company permitted a similar arrangement with holding companies in the same state as the target company. The Supreme Court found that legitimate concern for the independence of local banking institutions was the motivation behind the statutes and that they were, therefore, not contrary to the equal protection clause.[56] It also pointed out that:

---

[51] 266 U.S. 71 (1924).
[52] *ibid*. at 85.
[53] 470 U.S. 869 (1985).
[54] *ibid*. at 878.
[55] 472 U.S. 159 (1985).
[56] For criticism of this approach, see Crockett, "The Constitutionality of Regional Banking Laws: Northeast Bankcorp. Inc. v. Board of Governors of the Federal Reserve System"

"The States in question … are not favoring local corporations at the expense of out-of-state corporations. They are favoring out-of-state corporations domiciled within the New England region over out-of-state corporations from other parts of the country, and to this extent their laws may be said to 'discriminate against the latter'."[57]

Equality between individuals and companies in the United States Supreme Court

14–34   *Santa Clara* itself concerned the differing treatment of corporations as against individuals for taxation purposes and *Gulf C & SFR Co. v Ellis* indicates that the equal protection clause has been interpreted so as to guarantee equality of treatment between companies and individuals. Even if companies were held to be able to rely on Art.40.1, however, it is unlikely that they could argue unequal treatment in relation to individuals. The second paragraph of Art.40.1 of the Irish Constitution permits different treatment of the beneficiaries of the first paragraph where this is justified by virtue of a difference in social function or physical or moral capacity. It is now well-settled that Art.40.1 of the Irish Constitution "imports the Aristotelian concept that justice demands that we treat equals equally and unequals unequally".[58] In this regard, it is submitted that even if a company was held to fall within the scope of the first paragraph, its claim would most likely be defeated by the second.[59] Thus, any equality claim under the Irish Constitution could never be framed in the same terms as *Gulf C & SFR Co. v Ellis*.

Equality and fundamental rights—the inequality in the United States Supreme Court's equality doctrine

14–35   When analysing the case law in relation to the equal protection clause, it should be noted that the United States Supreme Court has not applied a uniform standard of review in all cases before it. The early approach of the Supreme Court required that the criteria for differentiating were reasonable in relation to the goal of that differentiation.[60] This approach, which is referred

---

(1986) 27 B.C.L.Rev. 821. For a brief discussion of regional banking legislation in this context, see Zak, "Regional Banking Statutes and the Equal Protection Clause" (1984) 84 Colum.L.Rev. 2025.

[57]   472 U.S. 159 (1985) at 177.

[58]   Walsh J. in *de Búrca v Att.-Gen.* [1976] I.R. 38 at 68, (1977) 111 I.L.T.R. 37 at 52. See also *Nicolaou v An Bord Uchtála* [1966] I.R. 567, (1968) 102 I.L.T.R. 1; *Hartley v Governor of Mountjoy Prison*, unreported, Supreme Court, December 21, 1967; *O'Brien v Keogh* [1972] I.R. 144; *Somjee v Minister for Justice* [1981] I.L.R.M. 324; *Article 26 Part V of the Planning and Development Bill 1999, Re* [2000] 2 I.R. 321, [2001] 1 I.L.R.M. 81.

[59]   See judgment of Kenny J. in *Abbey Films Ltd v Att.-Gen.* [1981] I.R. 158 at 172. Quotation reproduced above, at para.14–08.

[60]   *McLaughlin v Florida* 379 U.S. 184 (1964). See Dowdle, "The Descent of Antidiscrimination: On the Intellectual Origins of the Current Equal Protection Jurisprudence" (1991) 66 N.Y.U.L.Rev. 1165.

to in the literature[61] as "rational basis" or "low level" review, gives a large amount of discretion to the legislature which is free to discriminate as long as it does not do so in an arbitrary fashion. A similar approach can be discerned in a number of Irish cases.[62]

14–36 In n.4 of *United States v Carolene Products Co*,[63] Story J. observed that "more exacting scrutiny" might be applicable under the Fourteenth Amendment in certain contexts:

> "It is unnecessary to consider now whether legislation which restricts those political processes which can ordinarily be expected to bring about repeal of undesirable legislation, is to be subjected to more exacting judicial scrutiny under the general prohibitions of the Fourteenth Amendment than are most other types of legislation ...
>
> Nor need we inquire whether similar considerations enter into review of statutes directed at particular religions ... or national ... or racial minorities ... [or] whether prejudice against discrete and insular minorities may be a special condition, which tends seriously to curtail the operation of those political processes ordinarily to be relied upon to protect minorities, and which may call for a correspondingly more searching judicial inquiry."[64]

---

[61] See Tribe, *American Constitutional Law* (2nd edn, The Foundation Press, 1988), at pp.1439–45; Tussman & Broeck, "The Equal Protection of the Laws" (1949) 37 Cal.L.Rev. 344 at 344.

[62] See *Dillane v Att.-Gen.* [1980] I.L.R.M. 167; *Murphy v Att.-Gen.* [1982] I.R. 241; *Brennan v Att.-Gen.* [1983] I.L.R.M. 449; *Article 26 Part V of the Planning and Development Bill 1999, Re* [2000] 2 I.R. 321, [2001] 1 I.L.R.M. 81. But see also *Hunt v O'Donovan* [1975] I.R. 139, (1973) 107 I.L.T.R. 53; *O'Brien v Manufacturing Engineering Co* [1973] I.R. 334, (1974) 108 I.L.T.R. 105. *Cf. Lowth v Minister for Social Welfare* [1998] 4 I.R. 321 at 340–341, [1999] 1 I.L.R.M. 5 at 13.

[63] 304 U.S. 144 (1938).

[64] *ibid.* at 155. This footnote heralded the debut of "strict scrutiny" applied by the Warren Court. Essentially, what this means is that a government classification will only be constitutional where it is necessary for the realisation of a compelling government interest. A classification will only be considered necessary where there are no other less intrusive means of achieving the government interest. See *Regents of the University of California v Bakke* 438 U.S. 265 (1978). The strict scrutiny test is applied in cases where the legislature uses a suspect classification, *i.e.* one which suggests discriminatory intent. The following will render a criterion for classification suspect: prejudice against discrete and insular minorities, use of irrational group stereotypes, stigmatisation of a politically powerless segment of society and reference to an unalterable personal trait. Bungert, *op.cit.* at 581. It is also applied where a legislative act impairs fundamental rights or interests and it is in this context that it is relevant to the idea that shareholders' rights might form the basis for a corporate claim to protection under Art.40.1. A similar two-tier approach to equality can be discerned in two recent decisions of the Irish Supreme Court. In *Article 26 of the Constitution and the Employment Equality Bill, Re*,[95] the court held that some bases for discrimination[95] are "presumptively, at least, proscribed by Article 40.1".[95] It has been noted that the language used by the court in *An Blascaod Mór Teoranta v Commissioners of Public Works* [2000] 1 I.R. 1, [2000] 1 I.L.R.M. 401 contains "clear echoes of US constitutional equality doctrine".[65] The willingness of the Irish courts to overlook the restrictions of the contextual approach to Art.40.1 in the

14–37 When dealing with an equal protection challenge put forward by a company, the rational basis or lower standard of review applies.[65] Thus, while the company can be said to enjoy the equal protection of the laws under the Fourteenth Amendment, it is a weaker guarantee than that enjoyed by individual members of a minority and this diluted standard applies also to individuals operating in a commercial context.

14–38 The "more exacting scrutiny" referred to in *Carolene Products* is also applied where a legislative act impairs fundamental rights or interests.[66] In the context of the United States Constitution, these fundamental rights or interests are limited by the aim of minority protection illustrated by the quotation from *Carolene Products*.[67] Only rights which are in some way connected with the minority protection will be considered fundamental.

THE EUROPEAN CONVENTION ON HUMAN RIGHTS

14–39 Article 14 of the Convention states as follows:

> "The enjoyment of the rights and freedoms set forth in this Convention shall be secured without discrimination on any ground such as sex, race, colour, language, religion, political or other opinion, national or social origin, association with a national minority, property, birth or other status."

14–40 Article 14 of the European Convention on Human Rights contains an equality guarantee which has been described as "parasitic"[68] in that it is only applied by reference to the other Convention guarantees. The court has reiterated in a number of cases that this provision

> "complements the other substantive provisions of the Convention and the Protocols. It may be applied in an autonomous manner as breach of Article 14 does not presuppose breach of those other provisions. On the other hand, it has no independent existence since it has effect solely in

---

context of the political cases may also be indicative of an approach akin to that of *Carolene Products*. While these cases provide an interesting point of comparison, what is of more interest in the context of this book is the extent to which the US Supreme Court has applied a stricter test in the context of interferences with constitutional rights.

[65] For the argument that an intermediate level of scrutiny is appropriate to the foreign company cases, see Bungert, *op.cit.*

[66] *Skinner v Oklahoma ex. rel. Williamson* 316 U.S. 535 (1942). For a discussion of a so-called "intermediate scrutiny" approach, see Bungert, *op.cit.* at 583.

[67] Such rights include access to the courts—*Griffin v Illinois* 351 U.S. 12 (1956); voting rights—*Reynolds v Sims* 377 U.S. 533 (1964); travel—*Shapiro v Thompson* 394 U.S. 618 (1969); privacy and sexual autonomy—*Skinner v Oklahoma ex. rel. Williamson* 316 U.S. 535 (1942).

[68] Harris, O'Boyle and Warbrick, *Law of the European Convention on Human Rights* (Butterworths, 1995), at p.463.

relation to 'the enjoyment of the rights and freedoms' safeguarded by the other substantive provisions."[69]

14–41 The test for a violation of Art.14 developed by the European Court of Human Rights ("ECHR") reflects this parasitic nature of the guarantee:

"[D]ifference in treatment in the exercise of a right laid down in the Convention must not only pursue a legitimate aim: Article 14 is likewise violated when it is clearly established that there is no reasonable relationship of proportionality between the means employed and the aim sought to be realised."[70]

14–42 The ECHR has allowed companies to rely on Art.14. For example, in *Pine Valley Developments Ltd v Ireland*,[71] the court held that there had been a violation of the applicants' rights under Art.14 in conjunction with Art.1 of Protocol 1. The court held that this violation was in respect of the rights of both the individual applicant in the case and the company of which he was the managing director and sole beneficial shareholder.[72] It should be noted that, in considering whether these applicants were entitled to claim that they were "victims" for the purposes of the Convention, the court looked behind the company and recognised that its interests were, in reality, the same as those of the individual applicant.[73] This approach is not always taken, however, and in *National & Provincial Building Society v UK*,[74] where there was no individual applicant, the court considered an argument that the respondent was guilty of a violation of Art.14 in conjunction with Art.1 of Protocol 1. While the court rejected the applicants' case, it did so on the merits.[75] Both of these cases involved interferences with property, however, and it may be significant that

---

[69] *Van der Mussele v Belgium*, judgment of November 23, 1983, Series A, No. 70 at [43]. See also *Marckx v Belgium* (1979) 2 E.H.R.R. 330; *Rasmussen v Denmark* (1984) 7 E.H.R.R. 371; *Abdulaziz, Cabales and Balkandali v UK* 7 E.H.R.R. 471 (1984).

[70] *Belgian Linguistics* (1979) 1 E.H.R.R. 252 at [7]. The court has also applied a differential standard of review in respect of some bases for discrimination. Thus, discrimination based on sex is treated as suspect and requires "weighty reasons" to pass muster under the Convention. See *Abdulaziz, Cabales and Balkandali v UK* (1984) 7 E.H.R.R. 471 at [78]; *Schuler-Zgraggen v Switzerland* (1993) 16 E.H.R.R. 405 at [67]; *Burghartz v Switzerland* (1994) 18 E.H.R.R. 101 at [27]. The same might be said of illegitimacy where it impacts adversely on the child. (see *Marckx, Inze v Austria* (1987) 10 E.H.R.R. 39); race (see *East African Asians v UK* (1973]) 3 E.H.R.R. 76); and religion (see *Hoffman v Austria* (1993) E.H.R.R. 293). For a general introduction to Art.14, see Livingstone, "Article 14 and the Prevention of Discrimination in the European Convention on Human Rights" (1997) 1 E.H.R.L.R. 25; Monaghan, "Limitations and Opportunities: A Review of the Likely Domestic Impact of Article 14 ECHR" (2001) 2 E.H.R.L.R. 167.

[71] (1992) 14 E.H.R.R. 319.

[72] *ibid.* at [64].

[73] *ibid.* at [42]. Note that the other corporate applicant, Pine Valley Developments Ltd, was in a different position due to the particular facts of the case. *ibid.* at [53].

[74] Judgment of October 23, 1997, *Reports* 1997-VII, 2353.

[75] *ibid.* at [84]–[92].

this Convention right is guaranteed to both legal and natural persons under Art.1 of Protocol 1.[76]

THE NATURE OF THE GUARANTEE AND ITS
APPLICABILITY TO THE COMPANY

14–43   There is little room for arguing that the Irish constitutional guarantee is intended to perform a utilitarian function comparable to that of the EC Treaty. The guarantee of equality in Art.40.1 is one which seems to be concerned with autonomy values and the protection of the individual. This seems clear from the phrase "as human persons" which, it has been pointed out,[77] was influenced by Catholic social teaching prevalent at the time of the enactment of the Constitution. Of course, similar natural law influences can be discerned in the guarantees considered in Part III of this book, yet some of these, it has been argued, can perform a utilitarian function as well as furthering the autonomy values underlying them.[78] The equality guarantee, however, is different because it appears to be concerned only with equality between human beings in relation to their human attributes. This feature is indicated in the text, but comes into clearer relief when the case law on the guarantee is examined. Two main limitations on the scope of Art.40.1 emerge. The first concerns the contextual restrictions on Art.40.1 and the second concerns the bases for discrimination that are forbidden thereunder.

The forbidden bases of discrimination

14–44   The first of these limitations on the scope of Art.40.1 can be discerned from the judgment of Walsh J. in *Quinn's Supermarket*,[79] where he held that the guarantee of equality for "human persons" was

> "related to their dignity as human beings and a guarantee against any inequalities grounded upon an assumption, or indeed a belief, that some individual or individuals or classes of individuals, by reason of their human attributes or their ethnic or racial, social or religious background, are to be treated as the inferior or superior of other individuals in the community. This list does not pretend to be complete; but it is merely intended to illustrate the view that this guarantee refers to human persons for what they are in themselves rather than to any lawful activities, trades or pursuits which they may engage in or follow."[80]

14–45   This quotation indicates that the guarantee applies only in relation to discrimination based on some aspect inherent in the idea of the "human person".

---

[76] For further discussion of Art.1 of Protocol 1, see below, Chap.8.
[77] Doyle, *Constitutional Equality Law* (Thomson Round Hall, 2004), at pp.56–58.
[78] *e.g.* see the discussion of property above, Chap.8.
[79] [1972] I.R. 1.
[80] *ibid.* at 13–14.

Discrimination which is not founded on an assumption or belief that falls into this category does not come within the ambit of Art.40.1. It also indicates that the guarantee may not apply in all contexts. This latter aspect of Walsh J.'s reasoning was made explicit in the judgment of Kenny J.

The contextual restrictions on Art.40.1

14–46　In his judgment in *Quinn's Supermarket*, Kenny J. stated:

> "This guarantee, however, is one of equality before the law in so far as the characteristics inherent in the idea of human personality are involved: it does not relate to trading activities or to the hours during which persons may carry on business for neither of these is connected with the essentials of the concept of human personality."[81]

14–47　This contextual approach to the equality guarantee meant that it was held to be inapplicable in cases where the discrimination complained of did not affect "the characteristics inherent in the idea of human personality".[82] Later that year, in *Murtagh Properties v Cleary*,[83] the same judge commented that the guarantee applied to persons' "essential attributes as persons, those features which make them human beings".[84] No real guidance was given in either decision as to the situations in which these elusive characteristics would be involved and the majority of cases in the two decades following *Quinn's Supermarket* provided only a checklist of a variety of contexts in which Art.40.1 would not apply.[85] Such an approach lends itself strongly to the conclusion that the principle of equality simply does not apply to commercial activities.

14–48　This approach has been criticised for "attributing to human personality an unrealistically small ambit".[86] It has been commented that:

> "If rights such as the right to work, to earn a livelihood, to choose and follow a profession or career, are natural personal rights, they are such because the ordinary conditions of the world, in which the human

---

[81] *ibid.* at 31. See also *Murtagh Properties v Cleary* [1972] I.R. 330; *de Búrca v Att.-Gen.* [1976] I.R. 38, (1977) 111 I.L.T.R. 37; *Murphy v Att.-Gen.* [1982] I.R. 241; *Condon v Minister for Labour* [1981] I.R. 62; *Brennan v Att.-Gen.* [1984] I.L.R.M. 290; *Greene v Minister for Agriculture* [1990] 2 I.R. 17, [1990] I.L.R.M. 364.

[82] [1972] I.R. 1 at 31, Kenny J.

[83] [1972] I.R. 330.

[84] *ibid.* at 335.

[85] See High Court judgment by Pringle J. in *de Búrca v Att.-Gen.* [1976] I.R. 38, (1977) 111 I.L.T.R. 37; *Murphy v Att.-Gen.* [1982] I.R. 241; *Brennan v Att.-Gen.* [1984] I.L.R.M. 290; *Madigan v Att.-Gen.* [1986] I.L.R.M. 136; *O'Reilly v Minister for the Environment* [1986] I.R. 143; *Browne v Att.-Gen.* [1991] 2 I.R. 58—taxation; *McMenamin v Ireland* [1996] 3 I.R. 100, [1997] 2 I.L.R.M. 177.

[86] Hogan and Whyte, *op.cit.* at 1343, *e.g.* this approach led to Walsh J. holding that Art.40.1 was inapplicable to a ministerial order on trading hours which distinguished between different shopkeepers on religious grounds.

personality has to exist, impose necessities on that personality to which working, earning a livelihood, following a career etc. are a response; the same can be said, with only a very slight expansion of these rights, of engaging in business, acquiring property (the 'external goods' which Article 43 recognises man has a natural right to own) and negotiating ancillary trading and working conditions. If all such matters are subtracted from the concept of the 'human person', not much remains; so that it seems more satisfactory to understand that expression in Article 40.1 as visualising the complex of activities which human existence for most people involves."[87]

14–49   Some support for a broader application of the equality guarantee can be garnered from the judgment of Barrington J. in *Brennan v Att.-Gen.*[88] where he held that:

"Article 40.1 is not dealing with human beings in the abstract but with human beings in society. There may be differences and distinctions made between individuals in the course of their trading activities or otherwise which are not based on an assumption that those individuals are superior or inferior to other people. With such distinctions Article 40.1 is not normally concerned. But a law can be based upon an assumption that some individuals are inferior to others as human persons and yet manifest itself, in the social or economic sphere, in some superficially trivial regulation, such as who may or may not sit on a park bench; who may or may not own a horse worth more than five pounds or who may or may not serve a drink in a public bar."[89]

14–50   This judicial endorsement of a broader ambit for Art.40.1, which still takes a restrictive view of the relevant bases of discrimination, was rejected on appeal. O'Higgins C.J. delivered the judgment of the Supreme Court and he endorsed the restrictive contextual approach of *Quinn's Supermarket*, holding that:

"[A] complaint that a system of taxation imposed on occupiers of land … has proved to be unfair, even arbitrary or unjust, is not cognisable under the provisions of Article 40.1. This section deals, and deals only, with the citizen as a human person; and requires for each citizen, as a human person, equality before the law … The inequality … in this case does not concern [the plaintiffs'] treatment as human persons. It concerns the manner in which as occupiers and owners of land their property is rated and taxed. Every person who owns or occupies the land in question will be treated in exactly the same way because the tax is related not to the person but to the land which, irrespective of who he may be, he occupies."[90]

---

[87]   Hogan and Whyte, *op.cit.*
[88]   [1983] I.L.R.M. 449.
[89]   *ibid.* at 481.
[90]   [1984] I.L.R.M. 355 at 364.

14–51 In *de Búrca v Att.-Gen.*,[91] however, O'Higgins C.J. took a marginally broader approach. Both he and Walsh J. held in that case that the Juries Act 1927 was contrary to Art.40.1 insofar as it treated citizens without certain property qualifications[92] differently to those who had the requisite qualifications for the purposes of jury service.

14–52 O'Higgins C.J. stated that:

> "If [jury] service be regarded as a right, then this means the exclusion of many thousands of citizens merely because they do not possess a particular type of property. On the other hand, if service be regarded as a duty, these provisions mean that the obligation to discharge this duty is confined to a particular section of citizens not because they are property owners but because they have a particular interest in a particular type of property. Without question, this is not holding all citizens as human persons to be equal before the law … I cannot see that this discrimination can be excused or condoned by the second sentence of s. 1 of Article 40. This is not a question of having due regard to the differences of capacity, physical or moral, or of social functions, because it is based on a particular type of property qualification."[93]

14–53 It has been suggested[94] that the Supreme Court implicitly abandoned the contextual restrictions on Art.40.1 in *Article 26 of the Constitution and the Employment Equality Bill, Re.*[95] In that case, the court referred to Walsh J. in *Quinn's Supermarket*, which only limits the guarantee insofar as the bases of discrimination are concerned. The court ignored the judgment of Kenny J. in *Murtagh Properties*, which limits the guarantee in respect of the context of any discrimination. The court went on to apply the test set out by Barrington J. in *Brennan* in order to ascertain whether the discrimination on the basis of age was justified. Had the court taken the narrower context approach of Kenny J. in *Murtagh Properties*, it might have held that Art.40.1 was inapplicable in the context of the statutory regulation of employment conditions.

14–54 The guarantee has been held to apply in a number of cases in the context of referenda and electoral politics.[96] It has been argued that these

---

[91] [1976] I.R. 38, (1977) 111 I.L.T.R. 37.

[92] The Act stipulated that only rated occupiers of land having a rateable valuation over a prescribed minimum qualified for jury service.

[93] [1976] I.R. 38 at 62, (1977) 111 I.L.T.R. 37 at 48. See also Walsh J. [1976] I.R. 38 at 68–69, (1977) 111 I.L.T.R. 37 at 52–53.

[94] Hogan and Whyte, *op.cit.* at 1346–1348.

[95] [1997] 2 I.R. 321.

[96] *O'Donovan v Att.-Gen.* [1961] I.R. 114; *Sherwin v Minister for the Environment*, unreported, High Court, Costello P., March 11, 1997; *McKenna v An Taoiseach (No.2)* [1995] 2 I.R. 10, [1996] 1 I.L.R.M. 81; *Coughlan v Broadcasting Complaints Commission* [2000] 3 I.R. 1; *Breathnach v Ireland* [2001] 3 I.R. 230; *Kelly v Minister for the Environment* [2002] 4 I.R. 191; *Redmond v Minister for the Environment* [2001] 4 I.R. 61; *The Green Party v RTÉ* [2003] 1 I.R. 558; *King and Stack v The Minister for the*

cases are *sui generis* and do not indicate a general pattern of broadening the contextual reach of Art.40.1.[97] It is certainly true to say that this body of case law is relatively self-contained.[98] In any event, it is difficult to envisage a case in which the type of company at issue in this book could stake a claim to equality in relation to the political process.[99]

14–55   In two cases from 2000,[100] the court noted that this restrictive approach had been subjected to criticism but, the point not being essential in either of these cases, it declined to give its view on the correct approach to Art.40.1, thus leaving the matter unresolved.[101] In a more recent decision, *Xnet Information Systems Ltd, Re, Higgins v Stafford*,[102] O'Neill J. referred to the equality guarantee in the context of the constitutional right to earn one's livelihood and there are a number of other High Court decisions which appear to be expanding the scope of the guarantee.[103]

Is the guarantee applicable to the company by virtue of the interests of the shareholders?

14–56   The restrictive interpretation of Art.40.1, together with the case law considered in paras 14–04 to 14–08, demonstrates that the extension of this constitutional guarantee to the company is extremely unlikely. One interesting point which emerges from the case law of the ECHR, considered in paras 14–39 to 14–42, is the possibility of extending protection to the company based on the interests of the shareholders. Similarly, some of the early case law from the United States Supreme Court discussed in paras 14–28 to 14–30 relied on an aggregate theory of the company.[104] As discussed in Chapter 8, such an approach may result in the extension of constitutional rights to a company where to do so would vindicate the constitutional rights of individual

---

Environment [2004] 3 I.R. 345; unreported, Supreme Court, November 13, 2006. This trend is also discernable in the context of the separation of powers—see *Howard v Commissioner of Public Works* [1994] 1 I.R. 101, [1993] I.L.R.M. 665.

[97] Doyle, *op.cit.* at pp.90–93.

[98] The application of a different, more exacting test to such legislation can be compared to the approach taken in the US Supreme Court. See the quotation from *United States v Carolene Products* 304 U.S. 144 (1938) at 155, reproduced above, para.14–36.

[99] Where a group of citizens form a non-profit company in order to further political processes, however, the situation may be different.

[100] *Riordan v An Taoiseach* [2000] 4 I.R. 537 and *Article 26 Part V of the Planning and Development Bill 1999, Re* [2000] 2 I.R. 321, [2001] 1 I.L.R.M. 81.

[101] See also *Ring v Att.-Gen.* [2004] 1 I.R. 185. *Cf. Devoy v Att.-Gen.* [2004] 4 I.R. 481.

[102] Unreported, High Court, O'Neill J., October 10, 2006. See discussion in O'Neill, "Relieving Directors—The Irish Approach" (2007) 28 *Co Law* 116.

[103] *Delargy v Minister for the Environment and Local Government* [2005] I.E.H.C. 94; *The Representatives of Terence Chadwick (deceased) v Fingal County Council*, unreported, High Court, O'Neill J., October 17, 2003; *Liddy v The Minister for Public Enterprise*, unreported, High Court, Finnegan P., February 4, 2003. Although see also *The Criminal Assets Bureau v P.S.* [2004] I.E.H.C. 351. *Cf. Enright v Ireland* [2003] 2 I.R. 321.

[104] *Pembina Consolidated Mining Co. v Pennsylvania* 125 U.S. 181 (1888); *Gulf C & SFR Co. v Ellis* 165 U.S. 150 (1897).

shareholders. While that approach to corporate constitutional protection has been criticised in Chapter 8, the case of *The Green Party v RTÉ*[105] raises the possibility of such an approach being taken under Art.40.1. This possible development thus merits further analysis. In this case, Carroll J. held that a political party could rely on the guarantee. Her judgment interprets *Quinn's Supermarket* broadly:

> "The first question to be dealt with is whether Article 40.1 of the Constitution applies to the applicant. I am satisfied that the applicant which is made up of individual human persons can rely on the equality provision in Article 40.1. If the guarantee against inequality can be relied on in relation to ethnic, racial, social or religious background (see *Quinn's Supermarket v Attorney General* [1972] I.R. 1) then, in my opinion, the political beliefs which people hold should also be factored into the equation."[106]

14–57 Carroll J.'s judgment, by extending constitutional protection to the party on the basis of the rights of its individual members, can be seen as holding out some hope for the company attempting to build on the aggregate theory approach taken by Keane J. in *Iarnród Éireann v Ireland*.[107] Such an approach would base the equality right of the company on the interests of its shareholders.

14–58 Any company trying to get around the textual restrictions of Art.40.1 by relying on *The Green Party v RTÉ* and *Iarnród Éireann* approach faces a number of significant obstacles. Even if the contextual restrictions described above were abandoned, there is still the problem of the basis of discrimination. This is really at the heart of Art.40.1 and is its main limiting feature.[108] It is submitted that the categories of forbidden bases of discrimination are limited to those which are inherently linked to the human person.[109] Thus, for example, discrimination based on the pedigree[110] of an individual falls foul of the guarantee. This means that it is unlikely that an argument based on the equality rights of the shareholders could be relied upon in order to extend the protection of Art.40.1 to a company.

---

[105] [2003] 1 I.R. 558.
[106] *ibid.* at 565.
[107] [1996] 3 I.R. 321, [1995] 2 I.L.R.M. 161.
[108] See Whyte, "A Comment on the Constitutional Review Group's Proposals on Equality" in *Discrimination Law in Ireland and Europe* (Duncan and Byrne eds, Irish Centre for European Law, Dublin, 1997); O'Dowd, "The Principle of Equality in Irish Constitutional and Administrative Law" (1999) 11 ERPL 769 at 808–823. See also Doyle, *op.cit.* at pp.125–147.
[109] Above at paras 14–44 to 14–45.
[110] *An Blascaod Mór Teoranta v Commissioners of Public Works* [2000] 1 I.R. 1, [2000] 1 I.L.R.M. 401.

Conclusion

14–59 An analysis of the case law interpreting Art.40.1 indicates that it is not susceptible to an interpretation which reads a utility-based rationale into the clause. In this respect, it can be contrasted with the type of equality guarantee contained in the EC Treaty. Similarly, the interpretation of the equal protection clause of the Fourteenth Amendment of the United States Constitution to protect companies is unlikely to be embraced in this jurisdiction. In the United States, that clause has performed the utilitarian function of promoting interstate commerce by prohibiting protectionism. The case law discussed in paras 14–16 to 14–38 can thus be seen as a crucial element in the balancing of federalism and state sovereignty and the attainment of economic integration.

14–60 It has been noted that the extension of this guarantee to companies is out of keeping with the purpose behind the clause. An examination of the context in which the Fourteenth Amendment was added to the Bill of Rights indicates that it was concerned with protecting the autonomy of recently emancipated slaves.[111] As was pointed out by Black J., this purpose of the clause was not realised as the equal protection clause was hi-jacked by corporate litigants.[112] Viewed in this way, the history of the equal protection clause can be interpreted as an account of the distortion of a constitutional guarantee intended to promote individual autonomy into a corporate tool to protect corporate property. Indeed, the doctrinal shift in *Carolene Products* arguably constitutes a decision to reclaim the equal protection clause and return it to its original autonomy related values of protecting vulnerable minorities from discrimination.

14–61 Given the textual limitations of Art.40.1, no similar distortion of the guarantee is likely to occur in this jurisdiction. Nevertheless, by applying the utility/autonomy analysis to this provision of the Constitution, the purpose of the provision is made more clear and its application to individuals alone is given a sound philosophical, as well as textual, basis.

---

[111] Black J., dissenting, in *Connecticut General Life Insurance Co. v Johnson* 303 U.S. 77 (1938) at 85–90.

[112] Black J. pointed out that in the first 50 years following its enactment, only 0.5 per cent of cases in which the clause was applied concerned racial equality. 303 U.S. 77 (1938) at 89–90.

CHAPTER 15

INVIOLABILITY OF THE DWELLING AND CORPORATE PRIVACY

INTRODUCTION

15–01   Article 40.5 of the Constitution provides that: "The dwelling of every citizen is inviolable and shall not be forcibly entered save in accordance with law." While the use of the term "citizen" may not be fatal to a company seeking the protection of this guarantee,[1] the reference to the "dwelling" may prove more of a stumbling block. This chapter shall examine the position of the company in respect of analogous guarantees under the Fourth Amendment to the United States Constitution and Art.8 of the European Convention on Human Rights. As well as exploring the application of Art.40.5, this chapter will also explore whether a company can be said to enjoy a more general right to privacy. It shall go on to consider the nature of the interests protected by such guarantees and whether they are appropriate for application to a company.

ARTICLE 40.5 AND THE MEANING OF "DWELLING"

15–02   It appears that the word "dwelling" is interpreted relatively strictly and does not extend to business premises. In *Abbey Films Ltd v Att.-Gen.*,[2] McWilliam J. considered the constitutionality of s.15 (1) of the Restrictive Practices Act 1972[3] under which the defendant had exercised his power to

---

[1]   See para.14–03, n.2.

[2]   [1981] I.R. 158.

[3]   This read as follows:

   "For the purpose of obtaining any information necessary for the exercise by the Examiner of any of his functions under this Act, an authorised officer may, on production of his authorisation if so required:

   (a)   at all reasonable times enter and inspect premises at which any activity in connection with the business of supplying or distributing goods or providing a service, or in connection with the organisation or assistance of persons engaged in any such business, is carried on,

   (b)   require the person who carries on such activity and any person employed in connection therewith to produce to the authorised officer any books, documents or records relating to such activity which are in that person's power or control, and to give to the authorised officer such information as he may reasonably require in regard to any entries in such books, documents and records,

search the business premises of the plaintiff company without a warrant or court order. McWilliam J. held that:

> "I am not satisfied that office premises are a dwelling or that a company is a citizen within the meaning of the Constitution. Nor am I satisfied that entry into premises cannot be authorised by the Oireachtas in any manner other than by an order of a court or a warrant. It also appears to me to be very doubtful whether, having regard to the expression 'human persons' in s. 1 of Article 40, personal rights can be attributed to a company for the purposes of the application of the Constitution."[4]

15–03 In *DPP v MacMahon*,[5] the Supreme Court considered whether evidence obtained by the Gardaí when they were trespassing on a licensed premises was admissible in criminal proceedings. In *Att.-Gen. v O'Brien*,[6] it had been held that where evidence was obtained by unlawful means, but without any conscious and deliberate violation of a constitutional right, it would be admissible unless the court excluded it in the exercise of its discretion. In *MacMahon*, therefore, the question arose whether the actions of the Gardaí violated the defendant's constitutional protection under Art.40.5. Finlay C.J. stated that:

> "The act of entering, as a trespasser, the public portion of a licensed premises which is open for trade does not, of course, constitute any invasion or infringement of any constitutional right of the owner of those premises."[7]

15–04 Thus, the case was treated by the court as one concerning the admissibility of illegally obtained evidence, rather than unconstitutionally obtained evidence.

15–05 The "dwelling" referred to in Art.40.5 appears to be limited to the home of the citizen—the guarantee cannot be invoked unless the citizen in question actually lives in the violated dwelling. That this is so is evident in *O'Brien*, where it was held that where a family live together in a family home

---

>   (c) inspect and copy or take extracts from any such books, documents and records,
>   (d) require a person mentioned in paragraph (*b*) to give to the authorised officer any information he may require in regard to the person carrying on such activity (including in particular, in the case of an unincorporated body of persons, information in regard to the membership thereof and its committee of management or other controlling authority) or employed in connection therewith,
>   (e) require a person mentioned in paragraph (*b*) to give to the authorised officer any information which the officer may reasonably require in regard to such activity."

[4] [1981] I.R. 158 at 165–166.
[5] [1986] I.R. 393, [1987] I.L.R.M. 87.
[6] [1965] I.R. 142.
[7] [1986] I.R. 393 at 398, [1987] I.L.R.M. 87 at 91.

the entire house constitutes the "dwelling" of each family member under Art.40.5. If, however, one family member was to occupy a portion of the house apart from the other family members, then the remainder would not be his or her dwelling.[8] In *DPP v Lawless*,[9] the Court of Criminal Appeal held that the guarantee could only be invoked by a person whose home was the dwelling that was entered and this approach has also been taken in the more recent case of *DPP v Delaney*.[10]

15–06 The above cases appear to exclude the company from the protection of Art.40.5. There is, however, some authority which interprets the reference to the "dwelling" more broadly. In *Hanahoe v Hussey*,[11] Kinlen J. considered the position of a law firm whose premises had been searched. He stated that:

> "This Court accepts without question that any such intrusion on the personal rights of a citizen, building, privacy, property and the inviolability of a dwelling-house must therefore be closely scrutinised and expressly justified."[12]

15–07 He also approved the judgment of Lord Diplock in *R v IRC Rossminster Ex p.*,[13] where he stated that:

> "The construing court ought ... to remind itself, if reminder should be necessary, that entering a man's house or office, searching it and seizing his goods against his will are tortious acts against which he is entitled to the protection of the court unless the acts can be justified either at common law or under some statutory authority."[14]

15–08 He also approved a decision of the European Court of Human Rights ("ECHR")[15] in which a broad approach was taken to Art.8 of the European Convention on Human Rights in the context of a lawyer's premises.

15–09 While *Hanahoe* may indicate that the courts are willing to interpret the word "dwelling" broadly, the case did not concern a search or seizure of corporate property but that of a partnership. In *Simple Imports Ltd v Revenue Commissioners*,[16] the Supreme Court considered the validity of a number of search warrants issued in respect of the applicant company's premises. Keane J. held that the courts must ensure that search warrants comply with legislative

---

[8] [1965] I.R. 142 at 169.
[9] 3 Frewen 30 (1985).
[10] [2003] 1 I.R. 263.
[11] [1998] 3 I.R. 69.
[12] *ibid.* at 92.
[13] [1980] A.C. 952. Approved by Kinlen J. [1998] 3 I.R. 69 at 92.
[14] [1980] A.C. 952 at 1008.
[15] *Niemitz v Germany* (1993) 16 E.H.R.R. 97, discussed below at paras 15–43 to 15–46.
[16] [2000] 2 I.R. 243.

requirements. He noted that this was a common law principle which dated back to the case of *Entick v Carrington*,[17] where it was held that:

> "[O]ur law holds the property of every man so sacred, that no man can set his foot upon his neighbour's close without his leave; if he does he is a trespasser, though he does no damage at all; if he will tread upon his neighbour's ground, he must justify it by law …".[18]

15–10   According to Keane J.:

> "Under the Constitution, this principle is expressly recognised, in Article 40.5, in the case of the dwelling of every citizen. Protection against unjustified searches and seizures is not, however, confined to the dwelling of the citizen: it extends to every person's private property."[19]

15–11   This opinion is open to a number of interpretations. It could be that the company enjoys protection from searches and seizures at common law but not under the Constitution. Alternatively, the judgment could be intended to indicate that companies can rely on Art.40.5. These possibilities will be returned to at the end of this chapter.

THE FOURTH AMENDMENT OF THE UNITED STATES CONSTITUTION

15–12   The Fourth Amendment applies to both the federal and state governments.[20] It provides as follows:

> "The right of the people to be secure in their persons, houses, papers, and effects, against unreasonable searches and seizures, shall not be violated, and no Warrants shall issue, but upon probable cause, supported by Oath or affirmation, and particularly describing the place to be searched, and the persons or things to be seized."

15–13   This provision was the first of the Bill of Rights guarantees to be applied to a company. In *Hale v Henkel*,[21] two corporations resisted criminal contempt charges arising out of their refusal to comply with subpoenas under anti-trust legislation. The companies based their argument on the Fifth Amendment privilege against self-incrimination. As has been discussed in an earlier chapter,[22] the United States Supreme Court held that the privilege was not applicable to the company. Of its own accord, however, the court went on

---

[17] [1765] 2 Wils. 275.
[18] *ibid.* at 291.Referred to by Keane J. [2000] 2 I.R. 243 at 250.
[19] [2000] 2 I.R. 243 at 250. See also *Creavan v Criminal Assets Bureau* [2004] I.E.S.C. 92 at [73].
[20] *Wolf v Colorado* 338 U.S. 25 (1949).
[21] 201 U.S. 43 (1906).
[22] Above, Chap.5, at paras 5–26 to 5–46.

to hold that the Fourth Amendment was applicable to the subpoena in the case. Brown J. held that:

> "[W]e do not wish to be understood as holding that a corporation is not entitled to immunity, under the 4th Amendment, against unreasonable searches and seizures. A corporation is, after all, but an association of individuals under an assumed name and with a distinct legal entity. In organizing itself as a collective body it waives no constitutional immunities appropriate to such body. Its property cannot be taken without compensation. It can only be proceeded against by due process of law, and is protected, under the 14th Amendment, against unlawful discrimination. Corporations are a necessary feature of modern business activity, and their aggregated capital has become the source of nearly all great enterprises."[23]

15–14 Harlan J. took the view that the Fourth Amendment was not applicable to the company:

> "In my opinion, a corporation—'an artificial being, invisible, intangible, and existing only in contemplation of law'—cannot claim the immunity given by the 4th Amendment; for it is not a part of the 'people,' within the meaning of that Amendment. Nor is it embraced by the word 'persons' in the Amendment. If a contrary view obtains, the power of the government, by its representatives, to look into the books, records, and papers of a corporation of its own creation, to ascertain whether that corporation has obeyed or is defying the law, will be greatly curtailed, if not destroyed."[24]

15–15 McKenna J. took the view that the Fifth and Fourth Amendments were linked, stating that:

> " [If] the purpose and effect of the 4th Amendment receives illumination from the 5th, or, to express the idea differently, if the amendments are the complements of each other, directed against the different ways by which a man's immunity from giving evidence against himself may be violated, it would seem a strong, if not an inevitable, conclusion, that, if corporations have not such immunity, they can no more claim the protection of the 4th Amendment than they can of the 5th."[25]

15–16 Brewer J., joined by the Chief Justice, dissented on the basis that both the Fifth and the Fourth Amendments were applicable to the company:

> "The immunities and protection of articles 4, 5, and 14 of the amendments

---

[23] 201 U.S. 43 (1906) at 76, references omitted.

[24] *ibid.* at 78.

[25] *ibid.* at 83. This view of the two amendments was based on the decision in *Boyd v United States* 116 U.S. 616 (1886).

to the Federal Constitution are available to a corporation so far as, in the nature of things, they are applicable. Its property may not be taken for public use without just compensation. It cannot be subjected to unreasonable searches and seizures. It cannot be deprived of life or property without due process of law."[26]

15–17   He set out the text of the three amendments and went on to consider *Santa Clara v Southern Pacific Ry*[27] and a number of other decisions applying the Fourteenth Amendment to the company. He emphasised the similarity in the textual provisions, stating that "if the word 'person' in that amendment includes corporations, it also includes corporations when used in the 4th and 5th Amendments."[28]

15–18   He went on to state of the company that:

"Indeed, it is essentially but an association of individuals, to which is given certain rights and privileges, and in which is vested the legal title. The beneficial ownership is in the individuals, the corporation being simply an instrumentality by which the powers granted to these associated individuals may be exercised."[29]

15–19   This passage endorses an aggregate theory of the corporation as does the portion of Brown J.'s opinion cited above. Harlan J.'s opinion to the effect that the Fourth Amendment is inapplicable to the company endorses a concession theory of the company. It has already been noted in Chapter 5 that Brown J.'s opinion espouses two theoretical perspectives of the company.[30] The concession theory is used to deny the company the protection of the Fifth Amendment's self-incrimination clause while an aggregate theory is used to justify extending the protection of the Fourth Amendment.

15–20   In later cases, the court reiterated the protection of the company under the Fourth Amendment. For example, in *Silverthorne Lumber Co. v United States*,[31] the government had engaged in an unauthorised search of a corporation's offices and was ordered in federal district court to return the seized records. The government then issued a subpoena for the same documents. The Supreme Court held that "the rights of a corporation against unlawful search and seizure are to be protected even if the same result might have been reached in a different way".[32] In *Federal Trade Commission v American Tobacco Co.*,[33] subpoenas calling for the production of all correspondence

---

[26] 201 U.S. 43 (1906) at 83–84.
[27] 118 U.S. 394 (1886).
[28] 201 U.S. 43 (1906) at 85.
[29] *ibid.*
[30] Above at paras 5–28 to 5–29.
[31] 251 U.S. 385 (1920).
[32] *ibid.* at 392.
[33] 264 U.S. 298 (1924).

sent and received by a group of companies over a whole year were not enforced by the Supreme Court. The court deemed the subpoenas a "fishing expedition" and held that it was "contrary to the first principles of justice to allow a search through all the respondents' records, relevant or irrelevant, in the hope that something will turn up".[34]

15–21 In *Go-Bart Importing Co. v United States*,[35] a government agent falsely claimed that he had a warrant and arrested two people and seized a number of corporate documents. The company sought to have these documents excluded from evidence and the court held in its favour. The court was critical of the "lawless invasion of the premises and ... general exploratory search in the hope that evidence of crime might be found".[36] While the Supreme Court did not make explicit the constitutional basis for the decision to exclude the evidence, the applicant had relied on the Fourth and Fifth Amendments. Given that the company has consistently been excluded from the protection of the self-incrimination clause of the Fifth Amendment,[37] it seems likely that the Fourth Amendment constituted the basis for the decision.

15–22 As has been pointed out:

"These early cases involving a corporation's assertion of its Fourth Amendment right were easy to decide because the government malfeasance was so blatant ... In each case the government overstepped the bounds of fairness in the investigation, causing the Court to apply the Fourth Amendment as a shield to prevent the misuse of the investigatory power. The corporate nature of the victims of governmental impropriety appeared to be immaterial to the Court's decisions, and indeed the Court never alluded to the complainant's status in excluding the evidence or rejecting the subpoena."[38]

15–23 In *Oklahoma Press Publishing Co. v Walling*,[39] the court took a more restrictive view of the company's Fourth Amendment rights, allowing the Department of Labor to have broad access to the documents of a newspaper corporation and stating that:

"Historically private corporations have been subject to broad visitorial power, both in England and in this country. And it long has been established that Congress may exercise wide investigative power over

---

[34] *ibid.* at 306.
[35] 282 U.S. 344 (1931).
[36] *ibid.* at 358.
[37] Above at paras 5–26 to 5–46.
[38] Henning, "The Conundrum of Corporate Criminal Liability: Seeking a Consistent Approach to the Constitutional Rights of Corporations in Criminal Prosecutions", (1996) 63 Tenn.L.Rev. 793 at 831.
[39] 327 U.S. 186 (1946).

them, analogous to the visitorial power of the incorporating state, when their activities take place within or affect interstate commerce."[40]

15–24   The court went on to find that corporations are not able to avail of all of the constitutional protections available to individuals "in these and related matters".[41]

15–25   In *United States v Morton Salt Co.*,[42] the court allowed the Federal Trade Commission broad authority to inspect a corporation's price lists, holding that:

> "Corporations can claim no equality with individuals in the enjoyment of a right to privacy … They are endowed with public attributes. They have a collective impact upon society, from which they derive the privilege of acting as artificial entities … The Federal Government allows them the privilege of engaging in interstate commerce. Favors from government often carry with them an enhanced measure of regulation."[43]

15–26   In *See v City of Seattle*,[44] a case concerning an individual's business premises, the court took a more expansive approach and held the Seattle fire inspection system unconstitutional. It referred to the Fourth Amendment protections to which commercial and business premises were entitled, stating that:

> "The businessman, like the occupant of a residence, has a constitutional right to go about his business free from unreasonable official entries upon his private commercial property. The businessman, too, has that right placed in jeopardy if the decision to enter and inspect for violation of regulatory laws can be made and enforced by the inspector in the field without official authority evidenced by a warrant."[45]

15–27   In *Colonnade Catering Corp v United States*,[46] the court examined the extent to which private commercial property was protected. Ignoring the corporate ownership of the premises, the court based its decision on the historically close regulation of the liquor industry. In *United States v Biswell*,[47] the court held that the firearms industry was exempt from a warrant requirement of the Fourth Amendment, the basis of a theory of implied consent. The court reasoned that anyone entering that kind of business "does so with the knowledge

---

[40] *ibid.* at 204.
[41] *ibid.* at 204–205.
[42] 338 U.S. 632 (1950).
[43] *ibid.* at 652.
[44] 387 U.S. 541 (1967).
[45] *ibid.* at 543.
[46] 397 U.S. 72 (1970).
[47] 406 U.S. 311 (1972).

that his business records, firearms, and ammunition will be subject to effective inspection".[48]

15–28 In *Marshall v Barlow*,[49] the court pointed out that both *Colonnade Catering* and *Biswell* were "exceptions" which

> "represent responses to relatively unique circumstances. Certain industries have such a history of government oversight that no reasonable expectation of privacy ... could exist for the proprietor over the stock of such an enterprise."[50]

15–29 In *Marshall*, the court invalidated surprise inspection systems under the Occupational Safety and Health Act 1970. This legislation permitted searches without warrants in order to investigate health and safety standards. The court held that the warrant clause of the Fourth Amendment applied to "commercial buildings" as well as private homes. White J., delivering the majority opinion in the case, noted that the history of the clause suggests that it protected merchants in the colonies immediately preceding the Revolution:

> "The Warrant Clause of the Fourth Amendment protects commercial buildings as well as private homes. To hold otherwise would belie the origin of that Amendment, and the American colonial experience ... The general warrant was a recurring point of contention in the Colonies immediately preceding the Revolution. The particular offensiveness it engendered was acutely felt by the merchants and businessmen whose premises and products were inspected for compliance with the several parliamentary revenue measures that most irritated the colonists ... Against this background, it is untenable that the ban on warrantless searches was not intended to shield places of business as well as of residence."[51]

15–30 The court rejected the Secretary of Labor's argument that the federal government can regulate any corporation involved in interstate commerce without regard to Fourth Amendment protections. The court thus moved away from its holding in *Morton Salt* and ignored the fact that the premises were owned by a company and not an individual.

15–31 In *Dow Chemical Corp v United States*,[52] however, the court returned to a restrictive view of the extent of corporate Fourth Amendment protection.[53] In that case, a challenge was mounted to the use of aerial surveillance

---

[48] *ibid.* at 316.
[49] 436 U.S. 307 (1978).
[50] *ibid.* at 313, references omitted.
[51] *ibid.* at 311–312, references omitted.
[52] 476 U.S. 227 (1986).
[53] Although it has been argued that the judgment leaves the door open for future corporate Fourth Amendment challenges, Mayer, "Personalizing the Impersonal: Corporations and the Bill of Rights" (1990) 41 Hastings L.J. 577 at 611.

photographs to monitor compliance with emission standards at a chemical plant. The court found that the industrial plant was "more comparable to an open field and as such ... open to the view and observation of persons in aircraft lawfully in public airspace".[54]

15–32   It has been noted that:

> "The Court adheres to its mantra that corporations are protected by the Fourth Amendment, yet that recitation is largely irrelevant. Instead, the corporation has only an abbreviated constitutional protection compared to the individual. While the Court uses the phrase 'reasonable expectation of privacy' in relation to the corporation, there is no realistic basis for concluding that a corporate entity has any privacy because that is a term applicable to individuals, not organizations. The Fourth Amendment protects the corporation from the government to the extent that the government may not abuse its power over the corporation, but it does not create an area protected from the scrutiny of the sovereign. Unlike the individual, there is no zone of privacy that a corporation a priori may lay claim to under the Fourth Amendment."[55]

15–33   From *See* on, the court abandoned theories of the company and focused instead on the historical origins of the Fourth Amendment. It has been argued that this shift in approach is partly due to the development of modern regulatory powers which involved more intrusive requests which implicated privacy rather than property.[56] The extent to which such a development might impact on the position of the company under the Irish Constitution will be considered at the end of this chapter.

ARTICLE 8 OF THE EUROPEAN CONVENTION ON HUMAN RIGHTS

15–34   Article 8 of the European Convention on Human Rights provides as follows:

> "1. Everyone has the right to respect for his private and family life, his home and his correspondence.
> 2. There shall be no interference by a public authority with the exercise of this right except such as is in accordance with the law and is necessary in a democratic society in the interests of national security, public safety or the economic well-being of the country, for the prevention of disorder and crime, for the protection of health or morals or for the protection of the rights and freedoms of others."

15–35   The right to respect for "family life" can safely be presumed to exclude

---

[54] 476 U.S. 227 at 239.
[55] Henning, *op.cit.* at 840–841.
[56] Mayer, *op.cit.* at 632.

the company as an applicant. As for respect for corporate "private life", that issue arose in the case of *B Company v Netherlands*.[57] The Commission did not reach the issue but the general tenor of this admissibility decision suggests that it might have been decided against the applicant companies.

15–36 In another admissibility decision, *Noviflora AB v Sweden*,[58] the government of the respondent State argued that the protection of private life and correspondence in Art.8 was not implicated by a search of a lawyer's premises leading to a seizure of company documents on the basis that there was "no indication that the seized documents did not exclusively relate to the applicant company's business premises".[59] The Commission expressed no view on this although it did rule that part of the case to be admissible, thus implicitly accepting that that company's arguments were not "manifestly ill-founded".

15–37 The guarantee in Art.8 of respect for one's "home" has generated case law in both that court and the European Court of Justice ("ECJ"). While it is not a direct source of Community law, the ECJ has drawn on the Convention in a number of cases in the development of its fundamental rights jurisprudence[60] and some of this case law is considered here.

15–38 The choice of the word "home" in the English text of the Convention seems to presuppose a link with the individual which is not necessarily implied by the use of the word "domicile" in the French text.[61]. At an early stage, the Commission suggested that the word "home" bore its usual meaning in the English text and that no expansive reading of the term was merited.[62] In a subsequent decision,[63] considered below, the court referred to the French text in a judgment which finally extended the term "home" to cover the business premises of a company.

15–39 In *Gillow v UK*,[64] the ECHR held that the term "home" presupposed the existence of occupied premises in which the applicant had "sufficient continuing"[65] connections. In *X v Belgium*,[66] the Commission held that the

---

[57] App. No. 20062/92—Ruling on admissibility.

[58] App. No. 14369/88—Ruling on admissibility.

[59] Para.2(a) of the section entitled "The Law".

[60] The European Convention on Human Rights has been drawn upon by the ECJ in cases concerning fundamental rights under Community law—see, *e.g. Rutuli v Minister for the Interior* Case 36/75 [1975] E.C.R. 1219, [1976] 1 C.M.L.R. 140; *Johnston v Chief Constable of the Royal Ulster Constabulary* Case 222/84 [1986] E.C.R. 1651; *P v S and Cornwall* Case C-13/94 [1996] E.C.R. I-2143; *Hauer v Land Rheinland-Pfalz* Case 44/79 [1979] E.C.R. 3727, [1980] 3 C.M.L.R. 42. See also the Joint Declaration of April 5, 1977 by the Parliament, Council and Commission on Fundamental Rights [1977] OJ C103/1.

[61] See the discussion in Emberland, *The Human Rights of Companies* (Oxford University Press, 2006), at pp.114–115.

[62] *X v Belgium* App. No. 5488/72.

[63] *Colas Est SA v France* App. No. 37971/97.

[64] (1989) 11 E.H.R.R. 335.

[65] *ibid.* at [46].

[66] App. No. 5488/72.

word "home" bore its usual meaning in the English language and that no more expansive an interpretation was required.

15–40   In *Hoechst AG v Commission*[67] and two companion cases,[68] the ECJ held that corporate privacy protection was a fundamental principle of Community law. These cases involved searches and seizures of company premises by Commission officials in the context of suspected violations of competition law. The court held that it was a general principle of Community law that:

> "[A]ny intervention by the public authorities in the sphere of private activities of any person, whether natural or legal, must have a legal basis and be justified on the grounds laid down by law and ... provide ... protection against arbitrary or disproportionate intervention."[69]

15–41   The court went on to hold, however, that this did not mean that there was a fundamental right to the inviolability of business premises belonging to legal persons. In distinguishing between individuals and companies, the court relied on Art.8 of the ECHR and held that it was "concerned with the development of man's personal freedom and may not therefore be extended to business premises".[70]

15–42   In *Chappell v UK*,[71] the ECHR accepted that the right to respect for one's home and private life applied to premises that were simultaneously used as an individual's residence and as an office for that same individual's limited liability company.[72] The claim in that case related to the intrusiveness of police searches in furtherance of a copyright infringement investigation.

15–43   In *Niemitz v Germany*,[73] the European Commission and the ECHR held that Art.8 applied to a search of a lawyer's office undertaken in the context of a criminal investigation. The decision of the Commission found that the search constituted an interference with the applicant's right to respect for his private life and home. The court rejected the argument that Art.8 applied only to the private life of an individual, holding that:

> "[I]t would be too restrictive to limit the notion [of private life] to an 'inner circle' in which the individual may live his own personal life as

---

[67] Cases 46/87, 227/88, [1989] E.C.R. 2859.
[68] *Dow Benelux NV v Commission* Case 85/87 [1989] E.C.R. 3137 and *Dow Chemical Iberica SA v Commission* Case 97-99/87 [1989] E.C.R. 3165.
[69] Cases 46/87, 227/88 [1989] E.C.R. 285 at [19].
[70] *ibid.* at [18].
[71] Series A, No. 152 (1989).
[72] *ibid.* at [51]. Note that the government accepted that there had been an interference with the applicant's rights under Art.8 and the court held that it saw no reason to differ on that point.
[73] (1993) 16 E.H.R.R. 97. See also *Cremieux v France* (1993) 16 E.H.R.R. 357; *Miaihle v France* (1993) 16 E.H.R.R. 332.

he chooses and to exclude therefrom entirely the outside world not encompassed within that circle. Respect for private life must also comprise to a certain degree the right to establish and develop relationships with other human beings."[74]

15–44 Such an interpretation of Art.8 appears at first reading to offer considerable scope for the extension of the guarantee to business premises. On a closer reading, however, the case appears to apply to lawyers' premises only. The Commission referred to privacy that is a "necessary basis for the lawyer-client relationship"[75] and stated that:

"[H]aving regard to these particular features of a lawyer's professional activities in his law office ... the search of his office amounts to an interference with his right to respect for his private life and home under Article 8(1) of the Convention."[76]

15–45 The contextual limitations of the holding are reiterated later in the decision where the Commission goes on to state:

"The interference complained of affected the applicant in his position as a lawyer, *i.e.* as an independent organ in the administration of justice and as independent counsel of his clients, with whom he must entertain a relationship of confidentiality, ensuring the secrecy of information received from his clients and documents relating thereto. Such are also the demands of the right to a fair trial and the effective use of the defence rights as envisaged by Article 6(1) and (3) of the Convention in cases of representation by counsel."[77]

15–46 The court took a similar approach, emphasising the context in which the case arose:

"More importantly, having regard to the materials that were in fact inspected, the search impinged on professional secrecy to an extent that appears disproportionate in the circumstances; it has, in this connection, to be recalled that, where a lawyer is involved, an encroachment on professional secrecy may have repercussions on the proper administration of justice and hence on the rights guaranteed by Article 6 of the Convention. In addition, the attendant publicity must have been capable of affecting adversely on the applicant's professional reputation, in the eyes both of his existing clients and of the public at large."[78]

---

[74] (1993) 16 E.H.R.R. 97 at [29].
[75] *ibid.* at [58].
[76] *ibid.* at [59].
[77] *ibid.* at [74].
[78] *ibid.* at [37].

15–47   In *Hanahoe v Hussey*,[79] discussed above, Kinlen J. approved of the *Niemitz* decision.

15–48   In *Colas Est SA v France*,[80] the ECHR was presented with a case in which there had been searches and seizures on the premises of three road construction companies. The searches and seizures had been conducted by the French Directorate General for Competition, Consumer Affairs and Repression of Fraud as part of an investigation into suspected unlawful contract practices among large public contractors. The searches did not require and were not accompanied by warrants. The court held that the right to protection of one's home extended to the business premises of the three companies. It reiterated a point it had made in *Niemitz*:

> "[T]he word '*domicile*'—in the French version of Article 8—has a broader connotation than the word 'home' and may extend, for example, to a professional person's office."[81]

15–49   As has been pointed out, the *Chappell* and *Niemitz* cases differed from the situation in *Colas Est*:

> "*Colas Est SA* and its companion applicants were not 'individuals' as the term is consistently applied by the court when referring to the objective of privacy protection. *Niemitz* and *Chappell* concerned, it is true, business premises, too, and that gives these judgments' rationale some influence ... in the present context. But the contested measures in those cases were carried out on the premises of individual human beings and where those human beings also had their homes. The concern for individuals in *Niemitz* and *Chappell* was crucial to the court's finding of extension of private life and home to the business context in these judgments. Indeed, in *Niemitz*, the court emphasized as a reason for its generous interpretation of 'private life' and 'home', the importance to the individual of the right to establish and develop relationships with other human beings, even in the business context."[82]

15–50   In *Colas Est*, the court nonetheless found that Art.8 was applicable to the company, stating in a crucial paragraph:

> "The Court reiterates that the Convention is a living instrument which must be interpreted in the light of present-day conditions ... As regards the rights secured to companies by the Convention, it should be pointed out that the Court has already recognised a company's right under Article

---

[79] [1998] 3 I.R. 69.
[80] App. No. 37971/97 April 16, 2002.
[81] *ibid*. at [41].
[82] Emberland, "Protection of Unwarranted Searches and Seizures of Corporate Premises under Article 8 of the European Convention on Human Rights: The *Colas Est SA v France* Approach", (2003) 25 Mich.J.Int'l L. 77 at 90.

41 to compensation for non-pecuniary damage sustained as a result of a violation of Article 6 § 1 of the Convention ... Building on its dynamic interpretation of the Convention, the Court considers that the time has come to hold that in certain circumstances the rights guaranteed by Article 8 of the Convention may be construed as including the right to respect for a company's registered office, branches or other business premises."[83]

15–51 It then went on to consider the application of Art.8(2) to the case. The court appeared to accept the argument that companies enjoyed a lower level of protection under Art.8,[84] but went on to find for the applicants. In finding that there had been a violation of the companies' rights, particular emphasis was placed on the fact that no warrant had been required.[85]

15–52 In *Limburgse Vinyl Maatschappij NV v Commission*,[86] the Court of First Instance of the European Communities reiterated the narrow approach to Art.8 in Community law. The ECJ reserved its position on the matter when the case came before it.[87] In *Rocquette Frères SA v Directeur general de la concurrence, de la consommation et de la répression des frauds*,[88] the ECJ received a request from the French Cour de Cassation to make a preliminary ruling on the extent to which the *Niemitz* judgment had overturned or amended the *Hoechst* rationale in requiring court orders for searches and seizures of corporate premises. The ECJ reiterated what it had held in *Hoechst*, affirming that:

> "[T]he need for protection against arbitrary or disproportionate intervention by public authorities in the sphere of private activities of any person, whether natural or legal, constitutes a general principle of Community law."[89]

15–53 It took into consideration the developments in ECHR case law since *Hoechst*, in particular the decision in *Colas Est*. The ECJ also held that there existed in theory under Community law a principle that required judicial review by national courts before the undertaking of searches and seizures of corporate premises. The court, however, adopted a lower level of protection for the corporate person:

> "For the purposes of determining the scope of [the general principle described above] in relation to the protection of business premises, regard must be had to the case-law of the European Court of Human Rights

---

[83] App. No. 37971/97 April 16, 2002 at [41]. Note, however, that the government appears to have conceded this point—[32].

[84] App. No. 37971/97 April 16, 2002 at [49].

[85] *ibid.* at [48] and [49].

[86] [1999] E.C.R. II-931, II-1056 at [420].

[87] Cases C-238/99 P, C-244/99 P, C-245/99 P, C-247/99 P, C-250/99 P, C-251/99 P, C-252/99 P and C-254/99 P [2002] E.C.R. I-08375 at [251].

[88] Case C-94/00 October 22, 2002.

[89] *ibid.* at [27].

subsequent to the judgment in *Hoechst*. According to that case law ...
the right of interference established by Article 8(2) of the ECHR 'might
well be more far-reaching where professional or business activities or
premises were involved than would otherwise be the case'."[90]

15–54   Thus, the position under Art.8 of the Convention, from the point of
view of both Convention and Community law, appears to be that the provision
may be relied upon by companies, but that companies may enjoy a reduced
level of protection under this provision.

CORPORATE PRIVACY?

15–55   The use of the word "dwelling" in Art.40.5 suggests that on a literal
reading of the provision, it cannot apply to corporate premises. The decision
of Kinlen J. in *Hanahoe v Hussey*, which places a broad interpretation on the
word, can be read as applying only in the particular context of searches of
lawyers' premises, particularly as his judgment expressly refers to *Niemitz*.[91]
The passage quoted above from the decision of Keane J. in *Simple Imports
Ltd* recognises that "protection from unjustified searches and seizures ...
extends to every person's private property".[92] He pointed out that: "Under the
Constitution, this principle is expressly recognised, in Article 40.5, in the case
of the dwelling of every citizen." While the guarantee was applied in the case
of the company in *Simple Imports Ltd*, Keane J.'s judgment appears to suggest
that the basis for the protection in this context was the common law rather
than the Constitution.[93]

15–56   One issue which arises in this context is the extent to which there can
be said to be a corporate right to privacy. The first step in establishing such a
right would be to identify business activity as falling within the scope of the
constitutional protection of privacy. Paragraphs 15–34 to 15–54, above, noted
that Art.8 of the European Convention on Human Rights appears to allow for
more interference with privacy in the context of business activity than might
be acceptable in other contexts. A similar approach has been taken in this
jurisdiction in the High Court decision of *Caldwell v Mahon*.[94] In that case,
Hanna J. considered the extent to which the business dealings of an individual
were within the scope of the constitutional guarantee of privacy. In respect of
the applicability of privacy in a business context, he doubted whether the case
law relied upon[95] brought him to the point of "identifying a right to privacy in

---

[90] *ibid.* at [29].
[91] See also *Caldwell v Mahon* [2006] I.E.H.C. 86.
[92] *Simple Imports Ltd v Revenue Commissioners* [2000] 2 I.R. 243 at 250.
[93] Although see the approach taken by McKechnie J. in *The Competition Authority v The
      Irish Dental Assoc* [2005] 3 I.R. 208 at 222, which suggests that a corporate right to
      privacy is protected under the Constitution.
[94] [2006] I.E.H.C. 86.
[95] *Kennedy v Ireland* [1987] I.R. 587; *Haughey v Moriarty* [1999] 3 I.R. 1.

the context of business transactions conducted through limited liability companies". In *Haughey v Moriarty*,[96] he noted Hamilton C.J. had said the following on the relevance of privacy to business affairs:

> "For the purpose of this case, and not so holding, the Court is prepared to accept that the constitutional right to privacy extends to the privacy and confidentiality of a citizen's banking records and transactions."[97]

15–57 Hanna J.'s interpretation of this was that it did "not appear to put even the more personalised right to privacy with which *Haughey* was concerned, beyond question". He went on to distinguish *Hanahoe v Hussey*,[98] noting that:

> "[N]ot only did the solicitors involved sue as a firm, but also they sued personally. There is no doubt as to the existence of a personal right. Therefore, insofar as the focus of the Court was turned upon the 'invasion' of the applicant's privacy, it was done so in the context of the solicitors carrying on their practice as solicitors in premises belonging to them."

15–58 Hanna J. went on to comment that:

> "An individual's business affairs, conducted through what the respondents describe as a 'maze of offshore companies', must fall well beyond the level of constitutional protection afforded to, *e.g.*, a solicitor/client relationship."

15–59 While he was unwilling to find that there was no right to privacy in respect of business affairs, he noted that "such right can only exist at the outer reaches of and the furthest remove from the core personal right to privacy".

15–60 In this part of his judgment, he adopted the approach taken by Ackerman J. in the South African case of *Bernstein v Bester*[99] where he noted:

> "A very high level of protection is given to the individual's intimate personal sphere of life and the maintenance of its basic preconditions and there is a final untouchable sphere of human freedom that is beyond interference from any public authority. So much so that, in regard to this most intimate core of privacy, no justifiable limitation thereof can take place. But this most intimate core is narrowly construed. This inviolable core is left behind once an individual enters into relationships with persons outside this closest intimate sphere; the individual's activities then acquire a social dimension and the right to privacy in this context becomes subject to limitation."

---

[96] [1999] 3 I.R. 1.
[97] *ibid.*
[98] [1998] 3 I.R. 69.
[99] [1996] (4) B.C.L.R. (South Africa) 449.

15–61   Hanna J. took the view that the context in which the case before him arose was at a remove from the "inviolable core" of the privacy guarantee and was thus more susceptible to interference in the common good.[100]

15–62   *Caldwell* thus does not hold out much hope of a general right to corporate privacy as it seems to exclude business activities from the contextual application of the guarantee even where claimed by an individual.

THE NATURE OF THE GUARANTEE UNDER ART.40.5 AND THE COMPANY

15–63   Returning to the provisions of Art.40.5 of the Constitution, the discussion of privacy in the preceding section helps to illustrate why a company may not rely on it. In this context, a comparison of the constitutional protection of the dwelling and the common law protection from unreasonable searches and seizures may be of assistance. Perhaps the key to Art.40.5 lies in its concern with the privacy interests of the individual rather than any concern with property or restraining government *per se*. The Irish case law considered above suggests that the guarantee is highly individualised—thus, it cannot be relied upon unless there is an intrusion into the dwelling in which one actually resides. The concern is to protect a particular zone of privacy traditionally associated with the autonomy of the individual.[101] That this is the case is supported by the location of Art.40.5 in the part of the Constitution headed "Liberty". Of course, property may also be seen as an inherent aspect of liberty[102] and it is possible to construe Art.40.5 as being concerned with property rather than privacy. It is submitted, however, that the limitation of the provision to the dwelling indicates that it concerns only the individual's zone of privacy. It is not intended, on a more general basis, to prevent governmental overreaching. That this is the correct interpretation is indicated by cases such as *O'Brien*, *Lawless* and *Delaney*, which demonstrate that only a narrow category of searches based on defective warrants are unconstitutional, as opposed to merely illegal.

15–64   The common law prohibition, on the other hand, is primarily concerned with protecting property and preventing governmental abuses, and its

---

[100]   Hanna J.'s interpretation of the privacy guarantee thus seems close to the concept of "substantive autonomy" discussed by Fenwick and Phillipson—"Breach of Confidence as a Privacy Remedy in the Human Rights Era" (2000) 63 M.L.R. 660 at 662–663. The authors discuss privacy as a derivative of individual autonomy. In respect of the horizontality of the privacy guarantee and Art.40.5 see *Atherton v DPP* [2006] 1 I.R. 245, discussed in Carolan, "Stars of Citizen TV: Video Surveillance and the Right to Privacy in Public Places" (2006) 28 D.U.L.J. 326.

[101]   In *Att.-Gen. v O'Brien* [1965] I.R. 142 at 168, Walsh J. stated:
      "'It must be the defendant's own privacy which is invaded by the officers. Evidence obtained in violation of the rights of only third persons is not excludable by the defendant' (Wigmore on Evidence, (revised) 1961, vol. 8, at s. 2184a (viii) and the cases noted thereunder)."

[102]   See discussion of property rights above at paras 8–62 to 8–64.

application to the company is thus more appropriate.[103] Thus, at common law, the protection serves the institutional value of ensuring searches and seizures are legal. Such an analysis might explain why companies are able to rely on the guarantee under the Fourth Amendment to the United States Constitution. While early cases under the Fourth Amendment referred to privacy as the rationale for the prohibition,[104] in its more recent case law, considered above, the United States Supreme Court has emphasised the historical concern of the framers of the Fourth Amendment to restrain governmental intrusion. The warrant clause appears to be a general prohibition on government rather than a personal guarantee. It has been noted that the United States Supreme Court has, in its more recent case law, begun to refer more and more to the common law origins of the Fourth Amendment when interpreting it.[105]

15–65 Furthermore, the phrasing of the Fourth Amendment is broader than that of Art.40.5 and the reference to papers and effects suggests a concern to protect property rather than privacy.[106] It has been argued that the true purpose of the Fourth Amendment is to protect property only insofar as that furthers the protection of specifically individual and personal privacy, but the United States Supreme Court has moved away from this approach towards a more general conflation of the privacy and property interests served by the Fourth Amendment.[107]

15–66 As far as the European Convention is concerned, the application of Art.8 to the company is perhaps more surprising as the general tenor of the provision appears to be concerned with privacy rather than property rights. The *Colas Est* decision, however, is arguably concerned more with the dynamism of the Convention than any philosophical consideration of the rationale behind Art.8. The approach of the ECJ mirrors that of the ECHR. Interestingly, throughout the *Rocquette* decision, however, reference is made to the invasion of "privacy" inherent in searches and seizures.[108] In any event, the ECJ's fundamental rights case law is concerned primarily with restraining the excesses of the Community institutions and the extension of protection to the company fits within this purpose.

---

[103] See Sklansky, "The Fourth Amendment and Common Law" (2000) 100 Colum.L.Rev. 1739.

[104] *e.g.* see *Katz v United States* 389 U.S. 347 (1967); *United States v Chadwick* 433 U.S. 1 (1977); *Arizona v Hicks* 480 U.S. 321 (1987).

[105] Sklansky, *op.cit.*

[106] Or it can be seen as protecting privacy through the medium of property rights. This would still entail a broader range of protection. "The Fourth Amendment ... protects some aspects of liberty and privacy—although neither word is mentioned in the text—but does so largely in terms of property, and a person's relationship to it." Cloud, "The Fourth Amendment During the Lochner Era: Privacy, Property and Liberty in Constitutional Theory" (1996) 48 Stan.L.Rev. 555 at 562.

[107] See Cloud, *op.cit.* at 581–597.

[108] Case C-94/00 at [59] and [79].

CONCLUSION

15–67   The particular function of Art.40.5 appears to be to protect individuals in their homes. This function is narrower than that performed by the search and seizure prohibitions at common law and under the Convention. It is concerned with the autonomy value of respecting a particular aspect of personal privacy—that pertaining to an individual's home. While other search and seizure guarantees perform the function of restraining government overreaching, this utility value does not appear to underlie the Irish guarantee and it is thus inapplicable to the company. As with the equality guarantee considered in the last chapter, the question of whether the company may rely on Art.40.5 leads to a consideration of the values that underlie that provision and a clarification of the nature of the guarantee.

15–68   This Part has explored those constitutional guarantees which the company may not rely on under the Irish Constitution. Chapter 13 described the constitutional guarantees which are *a priori* unavailable to the company because it is incapable of enjoying them.

15–69   Chapter 14 examined the guarantee of equality before the law under Art.40.1. While it found that it was possible to conceive of an equality guarantee that could apply to the company, it went on to analyse the Irish guarantee and found that it was not amenable to an interpretation which would ascribe to it some utilitarian purpose. The chapter also explored the possibility of relying on an aggregate theory to extend Art.40.1 to protect a company. It concluded that such an approach would not work in the context of Art.40.1. One point which emerges from the discussion of the United States Supreme Court's approach to equality is that the early cases relied on an aggregate theory of the company and the property rights of shareholders to justify applying the equal protection clause to the company. The subsequent conversion of that guarantee, from one protecting the autonomy of vulnerable individuals into a virtual charter of corporate property rights, adds another criticism of the use of this approach to those set out in Chapter 8.

15–70   Chapter 15, in its exposition of Art.40.5, found that it is concerned primarily with autonomy values. It, thus, contrasted the values underlying the common law guarantee—and the guarantee under EC Law—with those underlying the particular protection provided by Art.40.5. Consideration of the constitutional guarantee of privacy led to the conclusion that it was not available to the company, in part due to contextual limitations.

CONCLUSION

Existing Irish case law indicates that there is considerable confusion over the issue of corporate constitutional protection. In a number of cases, companies have put forward arguments based on the Constitution and these have been accepted—and rejected—on the merits in a manner which belies the controversial nature of the proposition that companies are entitled to claim the benefit of constitutional guarantees. Indeed, in general, little judicial attention has been given to this matter.

The task of developing a coherent approach to this issue is one which falls ultimately to judges. The matter is an important one because the extension of constitutional guarantees to companies can have far-reaching effects both on the regulation of companies and on the coherence of constitutional jurisprudence generally. As the United States experience demonstrates, allowing companies to rely on constitutional guarantees can lead to the distortion of those guarantees and the subversion of the values underlying them.

This is not an inevitable outcome of allowing companies to take advantage of the provisions of Bunreacht na hÉireann. The crucial point is to use a methodology which explains *why* a company is allowed to rely on a given guarantee. It has been argued throughout this book that the answer to that question should not be sought in corporate theory. Thus, the answer to the question "Can Y Ltd rely on X guarantee?" should not be answered merely with the statement—explicit or implied—"Yes because Y Ltd can be metaphorically compared to a human being"—relying on the real entity theory of the company; or "No because Y Ltd is a fictitious creation of the State"— relying on the concession theory of the company; or "Yes because Y Ltd has shareholders who have the right to participate in the company on the terms set out in its articles of association"—relying on the aggregate theory of the company.

The reliance on the last statement by Keane J. in *Iarnród Éireann v Ireland* was heavily criticised in Chapter 8. It was also pointed out that the temptations of this approach may be easily understood in a jurisdiction where small companies with few members abound. With regard to the criticism made of this approach, it should be noted that this book does not argue that shareholders waive their constitutional rights when they invest in a company. Rather, it demonstrates that those rights, insofar as they concern property, are not converted by some constitutional alchemy into rights to the underlying assets of the company.

The solution to the problem of corporate constitutional protection does not appear in the text or the generally accepted interpretive methods used in Irish constitutional jurisprudence. While each interpretive method may have some bearing on the issue, none provides a coherent response to the question "Do companies enjoy constitutional protection and in relation to which constitutional provisions?"

This book has thus attempted to address a *lacuna* in Irish constitutional jurisprudence by proposing a methodology to address the issue of corporate constitutional protection. In so doing, it has highlighted the deficiencies of an approach which relies on corporate theory alone to justify the extension, or denial, of protection to the corporate litigant. The methodology proposed in Chapter 3 of this book and applied to the provisions of Bunreacht na hÉireann in Parts II, III and IV is one which emphasises the differences between the company and the individual. It seeks to carve out a place for companies within the Irish Constitution without anthropomorphising the company or deconstructing it into its constituent shareholders. Instead, the focus is on the Constitution itself and the values served by the various guarantees therein.

This shift of focus from the metaphysics of the company to the philosophy behind the Irish Constitution means that the analysis of whether a company may rely on, for example, the right to silence involves reflection on the purpose of that guarantee. In this regard, the material contained in Parts II, III and IV is of general relevance to Irish constitutional scholarship.

The application of the utility/autonomy methodology to the various guarantees contained in the Constitution has led to a number of interesting conclusions. In some cases, the analysis has allowed a determination that a particular guarantee simply does not apply to the company. In others, the finding has been that the particular guarantee does apply, but in a different form than that applied in the case of individuals. Of course, there are also those guarantees which apply to both the company and the individual. In relation to those guarantees, the use of the utility/autonomy methodology may lead to the conclusion that constitutional protection is stronger in the case of the individual than in the case of the company. It has been suggested that this differing strength of constitutional protection may possibly be accommodated within the application of a proportionality doctrine. Essentially, this would involve a court in recognising that differing bases of protection may mean that what is, for example, a disproportionate interference with property rights may vary depending on whether a company or an individual is making that claim.

Another important outcome of the approach taken to corporate constitutional protection in this book is its impact on the horizontal application of constitutional guarantees. Hohfeld's jural correlatives illustrate clearly the way in which the extension of constitutional protection to one party necessarily impacts on the autonomy of others. If companies' rights under the Irish Constitution were to create duties on the part of individuals, this would degrade the autonomy interests of the latter. By recognising the utilitarian basis of corporate constitutional protection, the methodology proposed in Chapter 3 ensures that this does not occur. As was pointed out in Chapter 12, the utility basis of corporate constitutional protection indicates that only the State owes the company duties while, at the same time, the company owes duties to individuals.

Throughout this book, the question "Do companies have a right to Z?" has been transformed into the question "What values underpin Z?". Viewed from this perspective, those cases where a company relies on a constitutional guarantee provide ideal opportunities for philosophical reflection of a depth rarely experienced in the Irish courts since the halcyon days of natural law interpretation. If nothing else, the serious reflective engagement with the document which sets out the fundamental rights of individuals is a development which surely can only be welcomed by even the most vehement opponent of corporate constitutional protection.

INDEX